THE GANG THAT WOULDN'T WRITE STRAIGHT

THE GANG THAT WOULDN'T WRITE STRAIGHT

WOLFE, THOMPSON, DIDION, AND THE NEW JOURNALISM REVOLUTION

MARC WEINGARTEN

 Crown Publishers * **New York**

Published in the United States by Crown Publishers, an imprint of the Crown
Publishing Group, a division of Random House, Inc., New York.
www.crownpublishing.com

Crown is a trademark and the Crown colophon is a registered trademark of Random
House, Inc.

Library of Congress Cataloging-in-Publication Data
Weingarten, Marc.
  The gang that wouldn't write straight : Wolfe, Thompson, Didion, and the New
Journalism revolution / Marc Weingarten—1st ed.
  Includes bibliographical references and index.
  1. American prose literature—20th century—History and criticism.
2. Reportage literature, America—History and criticism.   3. Journalism—
United States—History—20th century.   4. Thompson, Hunter S.—Criticism and
interpretation.   5. Didion, Joan—Criticism and interpretation.   6. Wolfe, Tom—
Criticism and interpretation.   I. Title.
  PS366.R44W45 2005
  818'.540809—dc22   2005015378

ISBN 13: 987-1-4000-4914-1
ISBN 10: 1-4000-4914-8

Printed in the United States of America

Design by Lauren Dong

10 9 8 7 6 5 4 3 2 1

First Edition

For Lynn

Contents

THE GANG
THAT
WOULDN'T
WRITE
STRAIGHT

INTRODUCTION

"**M**aybe we should just blow up the *New Yorker* building."

That was Jimmy Breslin talking. It was a story meeting, an electrical brainstorm to generate some provocative ideas for *New York*, the Sunday supplement of the *New York Herald Tribune*. Clay Felker, the magazine's editor, had mentioned that the great literary magazine of his youth had gotten so dull lately, so deadly dull. "Look . . . we're coming out once a week, right?" Felker told his staff, which included general assignment reporter Tom Wolfe, columnist Breslin, assistant editor Walter Stovall, and art director Peter Palazzo. "And *The New Yorker* comes out once a week. And we start out the week the same way they do, with blank paper and a supply of ink. Is there any reason why we can't be as good as *The New Yorker*? Or better. They're so damned boring."

"Well, Clay," Tom Wolfe suggested, "maybe we can do that. How about blowing up *The New Yorker* in *New York*?"

Bingo. Felker loved the idea, and it was timed perfectly. This year, 1965, was the fortieth anniversary of *The New Yorker*, and the magazine was going to throw a big party for itself at the St. Regis Hotel. Besides, it was payback time. Lillian Ross had zinged Wolfe in a March 16 Talk of the Town piece called "Red Mittens!" "Zongggggggggggg! Innnnnnnnn! Swinging!" Ross's piece began. "They're hot! They're so far in that they're coming out the other side. And they're fed up to the gillies with teenagery." It went on like that. The thirty-four-year-old reporter had been flattered and amused by the piece, but turnabout was fair play, after all.

The culture of *The New Yorker* was shrouded in mystery, particularly its editor, William Shawn, who refused interviews and kept a profile so low that the witness protection program couldn't have provided deeper cover. Wolfe called Shawn for an interview anyway, and the editor strongly advised Wolfe to beg off the story: "If we tell someone we want to do a profile and that person doesn't want to cooperate, we don't do the profile. We would expect you to extend us the same courtesy."

One night, while dining with a number of writers and editors at a West Village restaurant, Wolfe happened to find himself sitting across the table from Renata Adler, a *New Yorker* staff writer. Might she help him suss out details of Shawn's life? But Adler acted quickly to close ranks around the magazine, and the *Tribune* reporter found himself hitting a lot of dead ends, promising leads that would just sputter out. But there were sources closer to home, as it turned out. Walt Stovall's wife, Charlayne Hunter, had been one of the first two black students to integrate the University of Georgia and was now working as a Talk of the Town reporter for *The New Yorker*. Wolfe didn't want to compromise her position at the magazine, so he delicately danced around the subject, prodding Hunter to solicit information without actually telling her what he was doing. She gave Wolfe a trove of great stories regarding *The New Yorker*'s byzantine, cumbersome editing process. From a freelancer he picked up a choice anecdote about Shawn's preference for using Coke bottles as ashtrays. He received a detailed description of Shawn's apartment from a social acquaintance who had attended a dinner party there, and so on.

The best material was to be found at the magazine's fortieth-anniversary party in the ballroom at the St. Regis Hotel. It was an invite-only affair, but no one stopped the *New York* reporter when he walked right in. Wolfe kept himself as inconspicuous as a man in a white suit can be, flitting around the edges of the party, keeping a close watch on Shawn.

By the time Wolfe sat down to write the article, he quickly realized that a straight-down-the-middle parody of *The New Yorker* would beget more of what the magazine offered: gray prose. "Something that's dull is funny for about a page," said Wolfe. "So I figured that I would treat them in a way that they would hate the most—like the *National Enquirer,* something that would be totally inappropriate."

Using what Wolfe called his "hyperbolic style," he wrote more than ten thousand words, far more than the originally proposed few thousand words. But Felker loved every word of it and showed it to the *Tribune*'s editor, Jim Bellows, for his approval. Bellows, a two-fisted newspaperman who loved nothing more than to stir up controversy, flipped out. He might not have personally cared about the relative merits of *The New Yorker*, but he recognized a hot story when he saw one. Four days before the first installment hit the streets, Bellows messengered two copies of Wolfe's piece to Shawn at *The New Yorker*'s offices with a card that read "With my compliments."

What the *Tribune* received in return for this gesture of good faith was a salvo. Shawn was incensed by this poisonous yellow journalism. He reeled off a letter to the *Tribune*'s owner, Jock Whitney, calling the piece "murderous" and "certainly libelous," and urged the *Trib*'s distinguished publisher to literally stop the presses and pull the piece from the Sunday supplement. If the paper's legal department did in fact have reason to believe that the story was legally actionable, Whitney would have to give serious thought to killing the story.

But Bellows would have none of it. He sent the letter in full to reporters at *Time* and *Newsweek*, then handed the story over to the copy-editing department. Let the boneyard at *The New Yorker* rattle; Wolfe's story was going to run on Sunday.

"Tiny Mummies! The True Story of the Ruler of 43rd Street's Land of the Walking Dead!" screamed the headline in the April 11 issue of *New York*. Peter Palazzo ran an illustration of *The New Yorker*'s monocled Victorian icon Eustace Tilley, but swathed him in a mummy's shroud. "They have a compulsion in the *New Yorker* offices, at 25 West Forty-Third Street, to put everything in writing," Wolfe wrote.

They have *boys* over there on the nineteenth and twentieth floors, the editorial offices, practically caroming off each other—bonk old bison heads!—at the blind turns in the hallways because of the fantastic traffic in memos. They just *call* them boys. "Boy, will you take this please . . ." Actually, a lot of them are old men with starched white collars with the points curling up a little, "big lunch" ties, button-up sweaters, and black basket-weave sack socks, and they are all over the place transporting these thousands of messages with their kindly old elder bison shuffles shoop-shooping along.

Wolfe explicated the magazine's complex memo distribution system:

> There are different colors for different "unit tasks." Manuscripts are typed on maize-yellow bond, bud-green is for blah-blah-blah, fuchsia demure is for blah-blah-blah, Newsboy blue is for blah-blah-blah, and this great *cerise,* a kind of mild cherry red, is for urgent messages, immediate attention and everything. So here are these old elder bison messengers batting off each other in the halls, hustling cerise memos around about some story somebody is doing.

Wolfe characterized Shawn as an absentminded, passive-aggressive manager, his office a "kind of horsehair-stuffing atmosphere of old carpeting . . . and happy-shabby, baked-apple gentility." He made up words like *prestigeful* and used sentence fragments such as "William Shawn—editor of one of the most powerful magazines in America. The Man. Nobody Knows."

The second story, "Lost in the Whichy Thickets," ran the following Sunday and was even more audacious. Here Wolfe had the temerity to question the value of the magazine's literary worth:

> *The New Yorker* comes out once a week, it has overwhelming cultural prestige, it pays top prices to writers—and for forty years it has maintained a strikingly low level of literary achievement. *Esquire* comes out only once a month, yet it has completely outclassed *The New Yorker* in literary contribution even during its cheesecake days . . .

In both form and content, the two stories were a frontal attack on the battlements of an august institution. Shawn was a funeral director, his writers the walking dead, his staffers "tiny mummies."

Felker's instincts were right on the money. The indignant letters poured in from the unknown and the famous alike—Muriel Spark, Richard Rovere, Ved Mehta, E. B. White, even the notoriously elusive J. D. Salinger.

"At first I found all the attention quite frightening," said Wolfe thirty-eight years later. "Here I was, this general assignment reporter making $130 a week, which even in those days was very sad, and all these big names were coming down on my head. Clay was rocked, too."

According to Wolfe, Shawn hired a lawyer to tail the *Tribune* reporter, hoping to catch him in some damning, libelous act. When Wolfe agreed to be interviewed about the controversy by radio personality Tex McCrary, he spotted a mysterious suited figure in the front row of McCrary's audience, writing everything down in a little black notebook.

Dwight Macdonald, one of America's most prominent postwar intellectuals and a staff writer for *The New Yorker* since 1951, wrote a thirteen-thousand-word counterattack that ran in two issues of the *New York Review of Books* and methodically refuted Wolfe's two stories. (Felker had originally offered to run Macdonald's pieces in the *Trib*, but Macdonald declined—"why print it in the *Trib* and keep their pot boiling?")

The first piece was called "Parajournalism, or Tom Wolfe and His Magic Writing Machine," in which Macdonald skewered Wolfe's style of writing as being "a bastard form, having it both ways, exploiting the factual authority of journalism and the atmospheric license of fiction. Entertainment rather than information is the aim of its producers, and the hope of its consumers." Macdonald went on:

> The genre originated in *Esquire* but it now appears most flamboyantly in the New York *Herald Tribune*, which used to be a staidly respectable newspaper but has been driven by chronic deficits—and by a competitive squeeze between the respectable, and profitable, *Times,* and the less substantial but also profitable *News*—into some very unstaid antics. Dick Schaap is one of the *Trib*'s parajournalists. "David Dubinsky began yelling, which means he was happy," he begins an account of a recent political meeting. Another is Jimmy Breslin, the tough-guy-with-heart-of-schmaltz bard of the little man and the big celeb. . . . But the king of the cats is, of course, Tom Wolfe, an *Esquire* alumnus who writes mostly for the *Trib*'s Sunday magazine, *New York*, which is edited by a former *Esquire* editor, Clay Felker, with whom his writer-editor relationship is practically symbiotic.

Macdonald went on to attack Wolfe's mannerist style, skewer his penchant for "elaboration rather than development," and speculate that "Wolfe will not be read with pleasure, or at all, years from now, and perhaps not even next year." In the second piece, Macdonald really laid into Wolfe. He dismissed the reporter's two *New Yorker* stories outright: "their ideas bogus, their information largely misinformation, their facts often non-facts and the style which they were communicated to the reader neither orderly nor meaningful."

"Well, I passed it off lightly," said Wolfe of Macdonald's criticism, "but I wasn't happy about it. Macdonald was a good writer and he understood the art of attack, but I tried to act as if I didn't care." Did Wolfe harbor ambitions to one day be published in *The New Yorker*? "I didn't think that way. It never occurred to me that *The New Yorker* would want anything of mine, because my approach was so different than theirs."

"Tiny Mummies" brought into the open what had been hiding in plain sight for a few years now, which was the widening rift between traditional reporters and the "parajournalists" of whom Macdonald had so witheringly and disparagingly written. As the de facto ringleader of this irreverent bunch, as well as the writer with the biggest cojones, Wolfe was most vulnerable to attack. But as it turned out, the decade's most exciting developments in reporting would bear Wolfe's imprint far more than *The New Yorker*'s.

Wolfe and many of his contemporaries recognized, some earlier than most, one salient fact of life in the sixties: the traditional tools of reporting would be inadequate to chronicle the tremendous cultural and social changes of the era. War, assassination, rock, drugs, hippies, Yippies, Nixon: how could a traditional just-the-facts reporter dare to provide a neat and symmetrical order to such chaos? Many of them couldn't and didn't. Witness *Time*'s and *Newsweek*'s clumsy mishandling of the hippie movement, or the embarrassing countercultural appropriations of broadcast journalism (Dan Rather reporting from Vietnam in a Nehru jacket, to name just one egregious example).

Within a seven-year period, a group of writers emerged, seemingly out of nowhere—Tom Wolfe, Jimmy Breslin, Gay Talese, Hunter S. Thompson, Joan Didion, John Sack, Michael Herr—to impose some order on all of this American mayhem, each in his or her own distinctive manner (a few old hands, like Truman Capote and Norman Mailer, chipped in as well). They came to tell us stories about ourselves in ways that we couldn't, stories about the way life was being lived in the sixties and seventies and what it all meant. The stakes were high; deep fissures were rending the social fabric, the world was out of order. So they became our master explainers, our town criers, even our moral conscience–the New Journalists.

Was it a movement? Not a movement in the Kerouac-Ginsberg-Corso sense or in the Abstract Expressionist sense. Many of these writers were cordial with each other, but they didn't share apartments or sex partners. But consider the fact that most of the books and articles discussed in this book were all written within seven years of each other. Not just any stories, either, but *The Electric Kool-Aid Acid Test, Fear and Loathing in Las Vegas, Slouching Towards Bethlehem, Dispatches*–some of the greatest journalism of the twentieth century, stories that changed the way their readers viewed the world. It was an unprecedented outpouring of creative nonfiction, the greatest literary movement since the American fiction renaissance of the 1920s.

The first rule of what came to be known as New Journalism was that the old rules didn't apply. The leaders of the movement had all been reared in the traditional methods of fact gathering, but they all realized that journalism could do more than merely provide an objective correlative of events. More important, they realized that *they* could do more. Convinced that American journalism's potential hadn't yet been explored to its fullest, they began to think like novelists.

As soon as Wolfe codified this new reporting tendency with the name "New Journalism" in the 1973 anthology that he co-edited with E. W. Johnson, critics emerged to strike it down, confusing Wolfe's theorizing with self-promotion. There's no fixed definition for New Journalism, granted, and its critics have often pointed to its maddeningly indeterminate meaning as a major shortcoming. How can you have a movement when no one knows what that movement represents? Is New Journalism the participatory gonzo journalism of Hunter S. Thompson? Jimmy Breslin's impressionistic rogue's tales? Tom Wolfe's jittery gyroscopic prose? The answer is that it's journalism that reads like fiction and rings with the truth of reported fact. It is, to borrow the title of a 1997 anthology of literary journalism, the art of fact.

The greatest New Journalists burned with a Promethean flame. Wildly ambitious and gifted, many of them either thwarted novelists or fiction writers who moonlighted as journalists, they applied their writerly skills to the tools of reporting and produced nonfiction that stood up with the best fiction. Working with empathetic editors such as Harold Hayes, Clay Felker, and Jann Wenner—the three greatest magazine editors of the postwar era—the New Journalists could write as long as they pleased: three thousand words or fifty thousand, whatever the subject warranted, for an audience that genuinely cared about what they had to say. Fans of the work came to regard the New Journalists' output as holy writ. They became literary rock stars, their bylines familiar to most, their lectures standing-room-only sellouts in universities across the country. The work of the New Journalists was distinctly of its time, but it hasn't lost its shock of the new; the collections of Wolfe, Thompson, Didion, and the others still shore up the backlists of their publishers quite nicely.

This was a great time for magazines and newspapers, after all, a pre-cable, pre-Internet era when the print media reigned supreme among educated and culturally savvy readers. *Esquire, Rolling Stone, New York*—the readers of these publications could barely afford to miss an issue, lest they miss out on something. And a new generation of writers was reading as well. The greatest work of New Journalism's golden era—the last, great good time of American journalism, which roughly spans the years 1962 to 1977—left a profound impression on what Robert Boynton has called the "New New Journalists," who learned the best lessons of their elders and carry on the tradition today.

This is how it all went down. . . .

1

RADICAL LIT: SOME ROOTS OF A REVOLUTION

"New Journalism" is a slippery phrase. When Tom Wolfe made it the title of a 1973 anthology featuring pieces from such writers as Gay Talese, Hunter Thompson, Joan Didion, Norman Mailer, and others, he meant it to be a declaration of independence from any journalism that had preceded it. But there were others—particularly the *New Yorker* crowd that had been stung by "Tiny Mummies"—who criticized Wolfe for trying to trademark a technique that had existed for over two hundred years. They contended that there was nothing new about New Journalism.

They were both right. New Journalism had been flitting around the edges of American and British journalism since the earliest newspaper days. It was also true that writers such as Wolfe, Thompson, and Mailer didn't emerge fully formed from the empyrean. But had anyone ever *really* written like Wolfe, Thompson, or Mailer? No literary movement emerges from a vacuum, however, and here are some of the writers and movements that paved the way.

In his introduction to the 1973 anthology, Tom Wolfe makes a strong, self-serving argument for the literary supremacy of creative nonfiction over the novel, which he felt had suffered a precipitous status slippage.

He has little use for fiction writers like Jorge Luis Borges and Gabriel García Márquez—too enamored of myth, too "neo-fabulist." Modish experimental writers Donald Barthelme, John Hawkes, and John Barth, with their abstruse word games and dense allusiveness, were too busy with literary trickery to bother looking out of their own windows.

"In New York in the early 1960s," he wrote, "what with all the talk of 'the death of the novel,' the man of letters seemed to be on the rise again. There was considerable talk of creating a 'cultural elite,' based on what the local literati believed existed in London. Such hopes were dashed, of course, by the sudden emergence of yet another horde of Visigoths, the New Journalists."

Wolfe compares his journalism contemporaries to eighteenth- and nineteenth-century giants Dickens, Balzac, and Fielding, writers who accurately portrayed their times in social realist fiction. The new fiction of the late sixties and seventies, with its inward turn away from the "hulking carnival" of contemporary American culture, left a huge void for New Journalists to fill.

Suffice it to say, Wolfe's theory had a few logic holes. There were novelists who were laying claim to the cultural landscape of America in some of the best postwar fiction—Joseph Heller's *Catch-22* and James Baldwin's *Another Country*, for example. But Wolfe's contention that contemporary journalists were for the first time working up the literary hierarchy was true. They had come from a very long way down to do so.

Wolfe's notion of New Journalists as the new "Visigoths," a threat to the established order, stretches back to the earliest days of print media. Beginning with the Tudor era in fifteenth-century England, the British monarchy maintained an iron grip on the dissemination of public information. The history of journalism is in many ways a history of oppression and censorship. Countless government decrees in Great Britain—the Privy Council's assumption of a censorship role, the suppression of the press by Oliver Cromwell in 1655—forced newspapers underground. A black market emerged in the middle of the seventeenth century, as broadsheets that reported on specific news events were distributed clandestinely.

All of this iron-fisted regulation on the free exchange of ideas in the press created a thriving market for satire. Satirists could get away with more pointed protest than straight journalists, because they were moving targets who attacked with playful misdirection—subversion as comic entertainment. Jonathan Swift, a Dubliner born to English parents, witnessed the corruption of English politics while apprenticing under Sir William Temple, an English diplomat and a retired member of the Irish parliament. In 1710, Swift became editor of the *Examiner,* which became the press organ of the Tory party. A fierce critic of the English government's dominion over Ireland, Swift wrote a series of impassioned broadsides condemning Great Britain's foreign policy. His 1729 essay "A Modest Proposal," which advocated eating Irish children as the best palliative for the country's overpopulation and food shortage, laid Ireland's abject poverty at the feet of the Brits, but disguised it as a mordantly funny satire:

> There is likewise . . . great advantage in my scheme, that it will prevent those voluntary abortions, and that horrid practice of women murdering their bastard children, alas! too frequent among us! sacrificing the poor innocent babes I doubt more to avoid the expense than the shame, which would move tears and pity in the most savage and inhuman breast.

Two hundred and forty years prior to Hunter S. Thompson's gonzo journalism, Swift was practicing a particularly virulent kind of savagery in print, despite his close ties to the Catholic Church.

In 1836, twenty-one-year-old Charles Dickens was a parliamentary reporter for the British newspaper the *Morning Chronicle* when his editor, John Black, suggested that he focus less on matters of state and more on the streets of London. So Dickens ventured out, recording the mores of daily life among the working and middle classes. The result was a series of five articles called "Street Sketches," which became so popular that Dickens wrote forty-eight more sketches for the *Chronicle* and the *Evening Chronicle.*

Writing under the pseudonym Boz, Dickens created a series of modest portraits that captured ordinary working men and women—bank clerks, shopkeepers, bakers, market men, laundresses—who went about their business with little ceremony or ambition, the silent majority of a society that adhered closely to a rigid class code and had little use for the human flywheels of the industrial economy. Dickens's writing existed in a shadow region between speculative fiction and reportage, which gave Dickens the license to speculate on the inner lives of his characters with great specificity. Here, Dickens trains his focus on one such man, one of the "passive creatures of habit and endurance:"

> We thought we almost saw the dingy little back office into which he walks every morning, hanging his hat on the same peg, and placing his legs beneath the same desk: first, taking off that black coat which lasts the year through, and putting on the one which did duty last year, and which he keeps in his desk to save the other. There he sits till five o'clock, working on, all day, as regularly as the dial over the mantel-piece, whose loud ticking is as monotonous as his whole existence: only raising his head when some one enters the counting-house, or when, in the midst of some difficult calculation, he looks up to the ceiling as if there were inspiration in the dusty skylight with a green knot in the centre of every pane of glass.

Here is a journalist filling in the blanks of his subject's life as he saw fit. The success of the Boz series would give creative license for other writers to do the same.

It's a stone fact that New Journalism emerged from the gutter, not only via reformist-minded writers with real concerns but also via exploiters who milked the class-based prejudices of the working class for every last drop of profit. The literary art of the scandal sheet can't be overlooked. Tom Wolfe has always regarded the best tabloid reporting as the apotheosis of New Journalism. It's where the high-beam writing style, the racy description and zippy dialogue, really ratcheted up to full throttle.

In the nineteenth century, the most clever and enterprising scandal monger was Joseph Pulitzer. A Hungarian immigrant who found work as a reporter for Carl Schurz's German-language weekly *Westliche Post* shortly after arriving in St. Louis in 1868, Pulitzer quickly insinuated himself into the civic fabric of St. Louis despite his foreign heritage, becoming a member of the Missouri State Assembly in 1872. The next few years found Pulitzer reporting for Charles Dana's *New York Sun* (he covered the disputed presidential election between Rutherford Hayes and Samuel Tilden in 1876), traveling across Europe, and buying and selling shares in various newspapers. In 1878 Pulitzer brought the St. Louis *Evening Dispatch* out of receivership for $2,500 and merged it with the *Post,* which he had bought previously.

Pulitzer cast himself as a champion of the disenfranchised, offering his readers long investigative pieces that exposed the chicanery of St. Louis's venal robber barons, corrupt politicians, and other such villains of the industrial age. The *Post-Dispatch* ran stories that dug deeper, with more factual accuracy, than any other newspaper in the country. But the *Post-Dispatch* also trafficked freely in sensationalism, the better to keep its working-class readership entertained. Under the stewardship of managing editor John A. Cockerill, the *Post-Dispatch* ran scurrilous gossip items on the city's prominent social families as well as breathless accounts of grisly murder, adulterous sex, and public hangings. Within four years, the *Post-Dispatch* was the leading paper in St. Louis.

Pulitzer brought his serious reporting and tawdry gossip to New York in 1883, when he bought the *New York World* from financier Jay Gould for $346,000. The competition was much stiffer in New York, where the *Sun*, the *Herald*, the *Tribune*, and the *Times* jostled for market share. But Pulitzer would be not deterred by the hothouse atmosphere of New York's Park Row press culture. Instead, he took the high road and the low road at the same time, espousing causes that benefited the workingman: a front-page story in the May 24, 1883, issue passionately argued for the newly constructed Brooklyn Bridge to be toll-free for all who used it.

The *New York World*'s funhouse brand of journalism made Pulitzer a wealthy mogul, but other papers were leaning toward a more responsible, less subjective approach by the turn of the century. Not everyone was enamored of Pulitzer's trickery; an expanding educated class was demanding a more substantive approach to news gathering. The *New York Times* under the stewardship of managing editor Carr Van Anda was creating the template for the modern newspaper, with its scrupulous and thorough reporting and its use of the "inverted pyramid" technique. The inverted pyramid, which was widely adapted by American newspapers at the turn of the century, organized a story with the lead stating the salient theme in the opening paragraph, the body of the story in the middle paragraphs, and the sharp, clever kicker at the end. The inverted pyramid, which organized the who, what, where, when, and why of a story into a compact format, legitimized a story's claims to factual accuracy. It was an airtight system, and newspapers regarded it as unassailable.

Reporting techniques became more refined. Writers were now placing stories in their proper historical context, instead of writing about events in a vacuum. The newspaper business was, in short, becoming downright respectable and honorable. If an audience existed for well-ordered news stories written in a measured style, there was no need for a reporter to get his or her hands dirty in the muck of idle gossip and circulation-boosting stunts. By 1921, the *New York Times,* with a circulation of three hundred thousand (five hundred thousand for the Sunday edition), had proven that serious journalism could engage readers as effectively as yellow journalism.

But the lure of the gutter is eternal. In the late nineteenth century, William Randolph Hearst's *New York Journal* had supplanted Pulitzer's *World* as the foremost purveyor of populist reporting, with a staff that had been poached largely from the *World* itself. Although the *Journal*'s overheated tone presaged the shrillness of supermarket tabloids, Hearst was not averse to hiring good writers who could leaven the junk with substance.

This impulse to mingle with the disenfranchised was strong among the more ambitious American journalists of the era. The rapid rise of modern capitalism at the turn of the century created a new class of protest writers, determined to record with documentary accuracy the indignities of those who dwelled on the margins. It also simply made for very good copy. Jack London put himself squarely at the center of his 1902 chronicle of lower-class London life, *The People of the Abyss.* Going undercover as a denizen of the East End of London, which at the time was the most depraved slum in the world, the San Francisco native experienced the stinging lash of social neglect. London's underworld is otherworldly; the notion of the abyss is used as a running metaphor throughout the book, the slum as an infernal black hole where no one escapes.

"I went down into the under-world of London with an attitude of mind which I may best liken to that of the explorer," London writes in the preface to *The People of the Abyss.* "Further, I took with me certain simple criteria with which to measure the life of the under-world. That which made for more life, for physical and spiritual health, was good; that which made for less life, which hurt, and dwarfed, and distorted life, was bad."

He found little that was good, and by the end of the book had no reason to think that conditions would improve, barring the complete abdication of the country's ruling class that had cruelly tamped down the East Enders. *The People of the Abyss* is advocacy journalism in the guise of a minutely observed chronicle of institutionalized despair.

Eric Blair developed his social consciousness from a relatively privileged perch. As the son of an agent in the Opium Department of the Indian Civil Service, Blair and his family (which he once described as being "lower-middle-upper class") were inextricably linked to the British Empire and comfortably insulated from the deprivations of imperial India—even though the country's contrasts of gilt-edged Raj opulence and squalor were plainly visible. Blair was inscripted into the usual educational career track—prep school at Sussex, then the prestigious Wellington and Eton secondary schools—and it stoked his desire to be a writer.

At Eton, he read the great social satirists Jonathan Swift and Laurence Sterne as well as Jack London's *The People of the Abyss,* which swung his political views against the very system that had nurtured him. Rather than follow the prescribed path of Britain's learned class (Oxford, Cambridge, etc.), Blair, who began using the pen name George Orwell in 1933 while writing criticism and essays for the *New Adelphi* journal, enrolled in the Imperial Police Force to gather experiences for his writing, serving in Burma for five years. The Empire's benign neglect of Burma and its exclusionary elitism repulsed him. Disgusted with being a functionary in the Empire's vast machine, he resigned in 1927. Orwell could not be a party to "every form of man's dominion over man," he wrote in his 1937 book *The Road to Wigan Pier.* "I was conscious of an immense weight of guilt that I had to expiate. I wanted to submerge myself, to get right down among the oppressed; to be one of them and on their side against the tyrants."

With this burning objective, Orwell moved to London with only one thing on his mind—to write about this oppressed class. Finding cheap lodging near the Portobello Road, Orwell set about submerging himself into the city's forsaken underworld just as Jack London had. "I knew nothing about working-class conditions," Orwell was to write nearly a decade later in *The Road to Wigan Pier.* "The frightful descent of a working man suddenly thrown onto the streets after a lifetime of steady work, his agonized struggles against economic laws which he does not understand . . . all this was outside the range of my experience."

Orwell abandoned the middle-class appurtenances of London life and booked himself into a common lodging house in the same East End slum where Jack London had done his research for *The People of the Abyss*. In frail health from his Burmese experience, and suffering from an infected foot, Orwell nonetheless plunged into the maelstrom with dedicated mind and spirit.

Orwell's experiences, which he was eventually to recount in his 1931 book *Down and Out in Paris and London*, transpired over a longer period of time than Jack London's (in all, Orwell's life as a member of the working poor spanned three years). Unlike London, who booked another room in comfortable lodgings in order to maintain a "port of refuge . . . into which I could run now and again to assure myself that good clothes and cleanliness still existed," Orwell allowed himself no such safe harbor. When his paltry savings ran out, he scrounged around for whatever work he could find, with fitful results. He fraternized with tramps and manual workers and joined up with them in the search for sustainable work. In Paris, he became a kitchen *plongeur*, scrubbing dirty dishes in a hotel restaurant short of hot water, electric light, and suitable pots and pans.

> There was . . . an atmosphere of muddle, petty spite and exasperation. Discomfort was at the bottom of it. It was unbearably cramped in the kitchen, and dishes had to be put on the floor, and one had to be thinking constantly about not stepping on them. The cook's vast buttocks banged against me as she moved to and fro. A ceaseless, nagging chorus of orders streamed from her:
>
> "Unspeakable idiot! How many times have I told you not to bleed the beetroots? Quick, let me get to the sink! Put those knives away; get on with the potatoes. What have you done with my strainer? Oh, leave those potatoes alone. Didn't I tell you to skim the bouillon? Take that can of water off the stove. Never mind the washing up, chop this celery. No, not like that, you fool, like this. There! Look at you letting those peas boil over!"

This is Orwell the incipient novelist using an insider's observations to gird a social critique, a reporter replicating the grinding, unrelenting nature of menial labor using a fiction writer's tools. Orwell's descriptive powers create a vividly grim tableau. He and his fellow beggars "defiled the scene, like sardine-tins and paper bags on the seashore." A septuage-narian tramp resembled "a herring-gutted starveling." Boredom "clogged our souls like cold mutton fat." More so than Jack London, Orwell wanted to transcend the stereotypes and fashion a more nuanced portrait of life lived on the margins. In *Down and Out,* poverty isn't monolithic; even the tramps themselves have their own subtle class snobbery, and self-loathing drips from their disparaging comments about their fellow beggars.

The irony of *Down and Out in Paris and London* is that its verisi-militude is in some respects fabricated. Orwell admitted in *The Road to Wigan Pier* that "nearly all the incidents described . . . actually hap-pened, though they have been rearranged," though what "nearly" means remains open to debate. In the introduction to the French edition of the book, published in 1935, Orwell wrote that "all the characters I have described in both parts of the book are intended more as representative types . . . than as individuals." As his biographer Bernard Crick has pointed out, Orwell admired Dickens's talent for "telling small lies in order to emphasize what he regards as a big truth." In Orwell's determi-nation to tell the big truth, he smooths over the messy road bumps of his narrative, conflating characters into composites, or creating them out of whole cloth if necessary.

This was to became a major tenet of New Journalism three decades later—blurring facts and characters like a watercolorist to arrive at some greater emotional or philosophical truth. To this day, journalists grapple with the notion of creating composites, and gifted writers such as Gail Sheehy have been harshly criticized for doing so. For traditional journal-ists and critics of New Journalism, it's the antithesis of the well-ordered inverted pyramid technique, but Orwell's story throws the pyramid's limitations into bold relief. Lazy journalists can abuse composites, dis-torting facts into fabulism. But Orwell isn't excluding or altering facts so much as he's reordering them, molding the raw material into something compact and cohesive, so that the archetypes can work as representative characters, and his story retains its narrative power.

With the advent of World War II and an epic litany of atrocities to report, journalists brought the global terror home by way of newspaper dispatches and the major newsweeklies, particularly *Time* and *Newsweek.*

A handful of journalists, most notably the Scripps-Howard syndicate's Ernie Pyle, managed to convey scenes of graphic horror with a painterly knack for the quotidian. But there were limitations to the ways in which correspondents could report on the horrors of war. In a global conflict that pitted the forces of good against evil, there was little room for nuance or ambiguity and lots of opportunities to beat the drum for American triumphalism.

The New Yorker, a magazine that found many of its male contributors conscripted into the war effort, published the most imaginative war correspondence. A. J. Liebling, a veteran of the *New York World-Telegram,* was a master of the low-life profile. A staff writer for the magazine's Talk of the Town section, where he was confined to a few hundred words, Liebling flexed his artistic muscle in the longer pieces he wrote for the magazine, where religious hucksters, bookies, boxers, tummlers, and other fast-buck hustlers were lovingly and humorously portrayed. Liebling, who had done some reporting in France for *The New Yorker* just prior to Pearl Harbor for the magazine's Letter from Paris section (he was on a Norwegian tanker headed back to New York on December 7, 1941), returned to Europe in 1942, this time to devote his energies to reporting on the war. His pieces from the front lines, such as "The Foamy Fields," his classic March 1943 story about the African campaign in Tunisia, are similar in spirit to Orwell's ground-level reportage. Liebling plunks himself squarely in the middle of his stories and then applies his sardonic yet clinical eye to the particulars of entrenched warfare life:

> The five-gallon can, known as a flimsy, is one of the two most protean articles in the Army. You can build houses of it, use it as furniture, or, with slight structural alterations, make a stove or locker out of it. Its only rival for versatility is the metal shell of the Army helmet, which can be used as an entrenching tool, a shaving bowl, a wash basin, or a cooking utensil, at the discretion of the owner.

One writer who straddled the disparate cultures of both *Time* and *The New Yorker,* and thus moved seamlessly from weekly deadline dispatches to in-depth reportage, was John Hersey, the whiz-kid Yale grad who covered more terrain during the war—in both the geographic and psychological senses—than perhaps any other journalist of his generation. The son of missionaries based in China, Hersey had a blinkered childhood, unaware of the larger cultural currents unfolding beyond the walls of his father's mission in Tientsin. When his parents moved to New York in 1924, Hersey attended the Briarcliff Manor public schools, then Yale, where he was a star football player and a contributor to the college newspaper.

Hersey was intent on becoming a journalist from an early age; as an adolescent, he self-published his own newsletter, the *Hersey News,* and was determined to get a job at Henry Luce's *Time,* which was the endgame for many aspiring reporters during the 1930s. For Hersey, *Time* was "the liveliest enterprise of its type" and he wanted, "more than anything, to be connected with it." After serving for a short time as novelist Sinclair Lewis's secretary, Hersey was hired as a *Time* copyboy, but he quickly nabbed a plum assignment when Japan invaded China in 1937. Shorthanded, and cognizant of Hersey's Chinese upbringing, *Time* pressed Hersey into service. He was only twenty-five years old.

From there, Hersey journeyed throughout Japan, China, and Europe for *Time, Life,* and *The New Yorker;* he witnessed German atrocities in Poland and the Baltic states, and reported on the conflict between Chinese Communists and Nationalists in Shanghai, Ichang, and Peiping. In 1943, Hersey wrote an important antecedent to the impressionistic school of reporting. "Joe Is Home Now" was a piece that drew from forty-three interviews Hersey conducted with returning soldiers.

"Joe Is Home Now" is a key precursor to the wartime New Journalism of John Sack and Michael Herr. Hersey makes no pretense about the story being factual. "I guess I'd been thinking from the beginning, and had been experimenting a little bit with the pieces I did for *Life,* the notion that journalism could be enlivened by using the devices of fiction," Hersey told *The Paris Review* in 1986. "My principal reading all along had been fiction, even though I was working for *Time* on fact pieces."

Two years before the war's end, at the apex of the country's veneration of "our boys" as stolid heroes, here was Hersey listening to stories of emotional dispossession and psychic fragmentation, of discharged soldiers struggling to readjust to civilian life. Two decades before the Vietnam War, Hersey's interview subjects were articulating a kind of post-traumatic stress disorder. Hersey combined his best anecdotes into a single composite character called Joe Souczak, and then stitched a single narrative out of his material.

"Joe Is Home Now," which ran in the July 3, 1943, issue of *Life,* is perhaps a little too melodramatic for a writer of Hersey's skill; it reads like a movie treatment for a Hollywood postwar weepie such as *The Best Years of Our Lives.* But its formal innovation is important. For one thing, the bleak, gray tones of the story made it an uncharacteristic *Life* feature (by contrast, the same issue contains a jubilant photo essay called "*Life* Goes to an Aircraft-Carrier Party"). The reporting is invisible, concealed by an omniscient voice that moves from scene to scene and unspools Souczak's anguished internal monologue. The discharged solider, who has lost an arm in the war, encounters indifference and hostility at every turn as he tries to get a job, attempts to reconnect with his girlfriend, and pull his life together.

> The father said: "How was it in this war, son?"
>
> Joe said: "I don't know but it's rougher than the last."
>
> Joe's younger brother Anthony said: "How many Germans you kill, Joe?"
>
> Joe said: "Nobody who is a soldier answers that, Tony. You don't like to talk about it, mostly you don't even know, the range is big."
>
> Anthony went over and touched Joe's empty left sleeve and said: "What happened, Joe?"

For all intents and purposes, "Joe Is Home Now" is a work of fiction derived from fact. In a 1985 interview, Hersey articulated why he felt fiction to be a more powerful tool than journalism for revealing the truth behind tumultuous historical events: "The journalist is always the mediator between the material and the reader, and the reader is always conscious of the journalist interpreting and reporting events. . . . So, to me, fiction is the more challenging and desirable medium for dealing with the real world than journalism. But there are always things that ask for a direct account while the material is still too hot for fiction. In those cases I resort to reportage."

"Survival," Hersey's stirring 1943 *New Yorker* piece that recounted Lieutenant John F. Kennedy's harrowing tale of survival after his PT boat was hit by a Japanese destroyer in the South Pacific, was reportage that became the springboard for Kennedy the politician; when Kennedy ran for the House of Representatives for the first time in 1946, his father, Joe, had a hundred thousand copies of the *Reader's Digest* reprint distributed to voters throughout Boston. It's a tale that's almost too good to be true—Kennedy, the stalwart and fearless naval officer, saving the lives of his comrades by virtue of sheer determination and fortitude, relying on keen survival instincts and a bit of good fortune. The story was turned into a best-selling book called *PT 109* and was adapted into a Hollywood film as well, transforming Hersey's profile in courage into American myth—an unintended and somewhat ironic turn of events for Hersey, whose war reportage tended to focus on the antiheroic.

In late 1945 Hersey traveled to postwar China and Japan in search of stories for both *Life* and *The New Yorker*. Before embarking, he sat down with *The New Yorker*'s managing editor, William Shawn, who suggested that Hersey might want to write about the lives of the survivors of the atomic bombs the United States had dropped on Hiroshima and Nagasaki on August 6 and 9. Shawn believed that a report on the aftereffects of the most cataclysmic event in the history of warfare might alter readers' perceptions of what had thus far been an abstraction: the mushroom clouds that had led to Japan's surrender and America's triumph. In all the thousands of words that had been written about the bomb, not one had actually considered the human factor, an oversight that Shawn couldn't fathom and wanted to rectify.

Hersey was drawn to the idea of documenting the impact of the bomb "on people rather than on buildings." But he was unsure how to approach it—how to telescope an enormous tragedy down to human scale. En route from North China to Shanghai on a destroyer, Hersey was bedridden with the flu and was given some reading material by some crew members from the ship's library. One of the books, Thornton Wilder's 1927 novel *The Bridge of San Luis Rey*, gave him the narrative template for his Hiroshima story. Hersey was struck by the way Wilder retold a tragedy—in his case, the collapse of a rope suspension bridge in Peru—by focusing on its five victims, tracing their lives backward in time up to the point where their fates are intertwined in a single horrific event.

Upon arriving in Hiroshima on May 25, Hersey cast about for any residents of the island who could speak English. Having read a report to the Holy See on the bombing, written by a German Jesuit priest, Hersey sought out and found Father Wilhelm Kleinsorge, who introduced Hersey to other potential interview subjects. All told, he met around fifty people, and then narrowed that group down to six—Kleinsorge, a clerk, a seamstress, a physician, a Methodist minister, and a surgeon. Hersey spent six weeks rigorously interviewing his subjects, then returned to New York on June 12.

Six weeks later, Hersey shaped his copious notes and interview transcripts into a 150-page, thirty-thousand-word story with the title "Some Events at Hiroshima." The original intention was to run the story in four consecutive issues of the magazine, but that presented a continuity problem; a reader who hadn't read the first installment would need a synopsis of it to understand the second section, while someone who had already read the first issue would feel bogged down by a recapitulation. Shawn suggested that the entire story take up a single issue—an unprecedented move for the magazine. *The New Yorker*'s editor in chief, Harold Ross, had misgivings about such a radical move; *New Yorker* readers, after all, had grown accustomed to the magazine's mixture of the serious and the lighthearted. Could readers do without their *New Yorker* cartoons in favor of a long, depressing analysis of unfathomable human tragedy? Ross stewed on the matter for a week, at one point pulling out the first issue of the magazine, which stated, "*The New Yorker* starts with a serious declaration of purpose." That sealed the deal for Ross—the magazine would run the story in a single issue, to the exclusion of everything else—but not without numerous emendations and changes that Ross believed were essential to delivering maximum emotional impact.

It was customary for *The New Yorker* to immediately set all rough drafts into galley form shortly after they were received, in order for Ross and Shawn to visualize the pieces as they would appear in the magazine. For "Some Events at Hiroshima," Ross, a meticulous line editor, scribbled hundreds of notes in the margins of the proof for Hersey to read. "It was the first experience I had had with editing as careful as that," said Hersey, who frequently published stories in *Life* without a single editorial change.

For ten twenty-hour days, Ross and Shawn tabled less pressing magazine matters and holed themselves up in Ross's office, furiously making changes for Hersey, who rewrote as quickly as he received the pages. When they were done, the editors had over two hundred changes for the story, the title of which was eventually shortened to "Hiroshima." According to a *Newsweek* article that ran shortly after the article was published, "no one outside Ross' office, except a harried makeup man, knew what was going on."

On his query sheet for the editorial department, Ross laid out some of his thoughts:

I am still dissatisfied with the series title.

All the way through I wondered about what killed these people, the burns, falling debris, the concussion—what? For a year I've been wondering about this and I eagerly hoped this piece would tell me. It doesn't. Nearly a hundred thousand dead people are around but Hersey doesn't tell how they died.

I would suggest . . . that Hersey might do well to tuck up on the time—give the hour and minute, exactly or roughly, from time to time. The reader loses all sense of the passing of time in the episodes and never knows what time of day it is, whether ten A.M. or four P.M. I thought of this halfway through annotation and mentioned it several times. If I appear to be nagging on the subject, that's why.

What Ross wanted was an exact chronicle of the events as they transpired in real time, much like a documentary movie crew tracking six characters without any subsequent edits. Whenever Hersey got ahead of the story, or referred to something that the characters weren't experiencing at that specific point in time, Ross suggested he take it out.

Hersey introduces all six characters by describing exactly what they were doing at the moment of the bomb blast, thus giving his narrative an unsettling specificity. The story begins,

At exactly fifteen minutes past eight in the morning on August 6, 1945, Japanese time, at the moment when the atomic bomb flashed above Hiroshima, Miss Toshiki Sasaki, a clerk in the personnel department of the East Asia Tin Works, had just sat down at her place in the plant office and was turning her head to speak to the girl at the next desk.

Hersey's story becomes a struggle for the characters to reclaim normalcy in the teeth of an atrocity, and he sticks to the particulars of the struggle, the small acts of self-sacrifice and resourcefulness that become crucial to his characters' survival. What makes "Hiroshima" a crucial New Journalism antecedent, among other things, is the way Hersey assiduously describes his characters' internal reactions, the thoughts racing through their heads when the "noiseless flash" makes its appearance over Hiroshima. Mrs. Hatsuyo Nakamura, the seamstress, finds herself spared from the total destruction of her house, but the disaster quickly impinges upon her, and she acts quickly.

> Mrs. Nakamoto . . . came across the street with her head all bloody, and said that her baby was badly cut; did Mrs. Nakamura have any bandage? Mrs. Nakamura did not, but she crawled into the remains of her house again and pulled out some white cloth that she had been using in her work as a seamstress, ripped it into strips, and gave it to Mrs. Nakamoto. While fetching the cloth, she noticed her sewing machine; she went back for it and . . . plunged her symbol of livelihood into the receptacle which for weeks had been her symbol of safety—the cement tank of water in front of her house, of the type every household had been ordered to construct against a possible fire raid.

"Hiroshima" is not a celebration of the extraordinary heroism of ordinary people. It's far too grim for that. For a magazine that tended to hold to a somewhat genteel line, it's extremely graphic ("their faces were wholly burned, their eye sockets were hollow, the fluid from their melted eyes had run down their cheeks"), but its tone is calm and measured. Without undue hysteria, Hersey limns an apocalyptic landscape from precise description, internal monologue, and constantly shifting points of view.

"Hiroshima" was a radical piece of writing for 1946, only a year after the war's end. It gave a voice and a sense of the tragic to the enemy, and its powerful imagery resonated with those who had never given a thought to—or who had even dismissed outright—the plight of the bomb's victims. In 1999 New York University's department of journalism named "Hiroshima" the most important news story of the twentieth century.

Another *New Yorker* writer, Lillian Ross, shared Hersey's affection for an unadorned storytelling style. A native of Syracuse, New York, Ross's writing career began auspiciously; as a teenager, she was already a regular contributor to the literary magazine *P.M.* under the stewardship of editor Peggy Wright. Lillian Ross came to the attention of *The New Yorker* when the magazine offered Wright a job and Wright, who was getting married, instead suggested the services of her young star writer.

Ross believed in functioning as a reporter by proxy and letting her subjects tell the story for her. She relied heavily on direct quotations, her keen observational instincts, and an elegant, uncluttered prose style to move her readers briskly through a piece. "I don't believe a reporter has the right to say what his subject is thinking or feeling," she wrote in her 2002 book *Reporting Back: Notes on Journalism.* The 1948 *New Yorker* story "Come In, Lassie!" was the first magazine article to chronicle the climate of paranoia that had overtaken Hollywood in the wake of Senator Joe McCarthy's ongoing Communist witch-hunt and the blacklisting of the Hollywood Ten (the story's title referred to the only actor in town whose politics were unassailable). Ross gained access to some of the city's most prominent players and used her material to lay bare the conflicting attitudes toward McCarthy and Communism. The story contains entire scenes in which little more than dialogue is used, but with material this rich, Ross didn't need embellishment. Here is an exchange between Humphrey Bogart, Edward G. Robinson, and John Huston on the set of the film *Key Largo:*

> Bogart nodded. "Roosevelt was a good politician," he said. "He could handle those babies in Washington, but they're too smart for guys like me. Hell, I'm no politician. That's what I meant when I said our Washington trip was a mistake."
>
> "Bogie has succeeded in not being a politician," said Huston, who went to Washington with him. "Bogie owns a fifty-four-foot yawl. When you own a fifty-four-foot yawl, you've got to provide for her upkeep."
>
> "The great chief died and everybody's guts died with him," Robinson said, looking stern.
>
> "How would you like to see your picture on the front page of the Communist paper of Italy?" asked Bogart.
>
> "Nyah," Robinson said, sneering.

"Come In, Lassie!" was to provide the model for every subsequent Ross story of the next half century. " 'Come In, Lassie!' taught me how to watch and wait for the interactions of my characters," wrote Ross in 2002. "I learned how to set the stage with facts, find the essential characters and their dialogue, and Go!" In 1950, Ross used the same technique for a *New Yorker* profile of Ernest Hemingway called "How Do You Like It Now, Gentlemen?" Ross provided a real-time account of two days spent with Hemingway in New York City—dining with the writer and his wife in the Sherry-Netherland Hotel, shopping for a jacket, looking at cherished paintings in the Metropolitan Museum of Art. By not sanitizing her prose or "cleaning up" her quotes—a common practice among journalists who want their subjects to sound more articulate than they are—Ross stripped away layers of myth to reveal a willful eccentric enamored of both boxing and beluga caviar, whipsawing between mannered cultivation and crude machismo.

His dialogue is a strange patois in which articles and verbs are dropped (Ross later referred to it as his "joke Indian language"), baseball metaphors are liberally applied, and flashes of insight into his creative process are judiciously revealed ("The test of a book is how much good stuff you can throw away"). Ross is a presence, but she keeps herself in the shadows of the narrative; her writing is pure, Hemingwayesque stage direction that pushes Hemingway's compelling monologues into the foreground. Ross achieved a drawing room intimacy with Hemingway, a casual rapport and candor, that no reporter had ever been able to pull off. What's most remarkable about Ross's interviewing technique is that she considers tape recorders anathema and relies on her memory and extensive note taking in her 3×5-inch spiral Claire Fontaine notebooks to record dialogue. Considering the peculiarities of Hemingway's speech and the prolix nature of his sentences, "How Do You Like It Now, Gentlemen?" is a remarkable triumph of transcription.

"How Do You Like It Now, Gentlemen?" was received with a mixture of perplexity and revulsion by some *New Yorker* readers when it ran in the May 13, 1950, issue. Ross had simply recorded what she saw and heard, and she was pilloried for it. In a preface to the Modern Library edition of the profile, Ross theorized that readers "didn't like Hemingway to be Hemingway. They wanted him to be somebody else—probably themselves." Ross also claims that Hemingway loved the profile and defended Ross against her critics. In a series of letters written to Ross after the piece was published, he reassured her that she had done an admirable job ("About our old piece—the hell with them!"). Perhaps Ross, in her own nonjudgmental fashion, had moved a little too close to the truth.

Although "How Do You Like It Now, Gentlemen?" benefits from Ross's desire to simply get it all down without embellishment, the story suffers from an amorphous structure; in her determination to not change in any way the shape of her raw material, Ross lets the story trail off unsatisfyingly. For her next assignment, a profile of the film director John Huston, Ross didn't have such problems.

At a time when the inner workings of Hollywood filmmaking were still a mystery to the general public, Ross had full access to one of the great directors as he adapted Stephen Crane's Civil War novel, *The Red Badge of Courage*, for MGM. She was friendly with Huston, and that would open any and all doors for her in California (Ross never had any compunction about cultivating friendships with her story subjects, perhaps because she was not the muckraking type). As Ross began soaking up information in story meetings and observing the production on Huston's ranch in the San Fernando Valley, it became apparent that her story was something else entirely: a primer on how a film really gets made in Hollywood. "As I spent time with the characters involved in the making of the picture," Ross wrote in her memoir *Here but Not Here*, "I became more and more excited about their relationships with one another, the development of the action, the drama of the story. It was like a novel unraveling right in front of me."

In a letter to Shawn, Ross remarked, "Huston as a person is almost too interesting to be true—he's complicated, funny, colorful, lonely, generous, crazy, driven, talented and outside of the conventional pattern of Hollywood, yet drawn and held by it, and the people in the business are attracted to and held by him." Ross suggested that the story be written like a novel: "I don't know whether this sort of thing has ever been done before, but I don't see why I shouldn't try to do a fact piece in novel form, or maybe a novel in fact form."

As Ross continued to observe, the story coalesced in her mind. She would focus on four main characters: Huston, MGM vice president in charge of production Dore Schary, producer Gottfried Reinhardt, and studio head Louis B. Mayer, and present their story as a microcosm of the way things got done in Hollywood. It was a propitious time to undertake such a writing project, as the old studio system was about to crumble and television would soon challenge film's hegemony as the country's leading entertainment medium.

Ross was excited about the story, which she felt seemed to be unfolding for her benefit alone. Her subjects were comfortable around her, so much so that they answered just about every question she posed to them. During her first meeting with Gottfried Reinhardt, the producer explained the nature of Hollywood's office hierarchy: "I'm on the first floor, Dore Schary is two floors up, right over me. L.B. is also two floors up. I have a washbasin but no shower in my office. Dore has a shower but no bathtub. L.B. has a shower *and* a bathtub."

The production was complicated, with large-scale battle sequences involving hundreds of extras. The trick was to bring the film in on budget and thus prevent Mayer, who had objected to the film from the very beginning, from meddling with the final product. After one battle sequence had been shot in Chico, Ross overheard the following conversation:

"Well," Huston said as we started off. "How much ahead of schedule are we, Gottfried?"

"A day and a half," said Reinhardt. "Reggie says if we had done that shot of the river crossing in the tank at the studio, it would have cost twelve thousand dollars more than this did. Albert, the box of cigars. Under my coat next to you."

"We can have the river crossing on the screen for a minute," Huston said.

"That long?" asked Reinhardt, who was driving.

"It's worth it," Huston said.

As the production progressed, an inevitable clash between art and commerce emerged. Mayer wanted to add narration to clarify the protagonist's thoughts. Huston didn't budge. When the film was finally completed, it tested poorly in two sneak previews, and Mayer felt he had been vindicated. During a meeting with MGM producer Arthur Freed, Mayer makes an impassioned pitch for good old-fashioned escapism:

The Red Badge of Courage? All the violence? No story? Dore Schary wanted it. Is it good entertainment? I didn't think so. Maybe I'm wrong. But I don't think I'm wrong. I know what the audience wants. Andy Hardy. Sentimentality! What's wrong with it? Love! Good old-fashioned romance!" He put his hand on his chest and looked at the ceiling. "Is it bad? It entertains. It brings the audience to the box office. No! These critics. They're too tony for you and I. They don't like it."

Mayer then proceeds to tell a bizarre story about a female critic-turned-screenwriter who used to knock MGM's films:

"I see Howard Strickling running across the green. You know Howard." Mayer huffed and puffed to demonstrate how Strickling ran across the green. "'Why are you running?' I ask Howard. He tells me the girl tried to commit suicide. I go with him, just as I am, in my golf clothes. In the hospital, the doctors are pushing her, trying to make her walk." Mayer got up and acted out the part of the girl. "Suddenly, she sees me, and she gives a cry! 'Oh!' And she walks. And this is what she says: 'Oh, Mr. Mayer, I am so ashamed of myself. When I think of how I used to knock the movies, I am ashamed.'"

That was the end of Mayer's story. Freed looked puzzled.

"You knock the movies, you're knocking your best friend," Mayer said.

Ross learned the true lesson of filmmaking as a collaborative art: those who pay the bills have the last word. When *The Red Badge of Courage* was finally released, it had been bowdlerized and watered down, beaten back into some gray area between art film and war picture. But Ross still needed an interview with the man who had green-lighted the film: MGM president Nicholas B. Schenck, who was based in New York. He could provide her with an ending, give her some kind of postmortem on the project. When Ross returned to the city, Shawn insisted that she stake Schenck out in the lobby of MGM's offices at 1540 Broadway—arrive at 8 A.M., and then wait for as long as it took for Schenk to show up. Schenk materialized on Ross's first try, pulling up in a stretch limousine. Ross introduced herself and explained the nature of her project, and asked if Mr. Schenk could spare a little time. Schenck didn't hesitate and, accompanied by his press agent, Howard Dietz, escorted Ross into his office:

> "*Red Badge* had no stars and no story," said Dietz. "It wasn't any good."
>
> "They did the best they could with it," said Schenck. "Unfortunately, that sort of thing costs money. If you don't spend money, you never learn." He laughed knowingly. "After the picture was made, Louie didn't want to release it," he said. "Louie said that as long as he was head of the studio, the picture would never be released. He refused to release it, but I changed *that*."
>
> Schenck puffed quickly on a cigarette. "How else was I going to teach Dore?" he said. "I supported Dore. I let him make the picture. I knew that the best way to help him was to let him make a mistake. Now he will know better. A young man has to learn by making mistakes. I don't think he'll try to make a picture like that again."

Ross's story, "Production Number 1512," ran in five issues of *The New Yorker*, beginning with the May 24, 1952, issue. When it was published in book form as *Picture* the following year, it was hailed as a breakthrough, a meticulously rendered chronicle of realpolitik within Hollywood's corridors of power. Ernest Hemingway called it "much better than most novels." It was the most novelistic book-length piece of journalism since *Down and Out in Paris and London,* leavened by Ross's light and lucid prose, her elucidation of character through description, and the dialogue-heavy interactions between the main players.

When novelist Truman Capote traveled to Garden City, Kansas, in November 1959 at the behest of *The New Yorker* to investigate the murder of Holcomb wheat farmer Herbert Clutter, his wife, and two of his children, he had to piece together a story that had only two living witnesses, as it turned out—the murderers themselves.

Capote at first refused to camouflage himself within the local milieu, to meld seamlessly into the sleepy rhythms of the midwestern town. In his sport jacket and bow tie, his epicene features set off by a pair of horn-rimmed glasses, Capote was every inch the northeastern bon vivant–cum–bookish nerd. No one recognized him or his work; of the entire population of Holcomb, only two high school teachers had ever read any of his books. Many of his interview subjects asked to see his credentials, which turned out to be a single letter he obtained from the president of Kansas State University. Capote, whose work had taken him all over Europe, Asia, and the Caribbean, felt like an alien. "It was as strange to me," he said at the time, "as if I'd gone to Peking."

"Truman was a little out of his element," said Bill Brown, the former editor of the *Garden City Telegram,* whom Capote enlisted to help him track down interview sources. "The first time I met him, he walked in in a fur-lined women's coat and hung out a limp hand. But while I think a lot of people may have laughed behind his back, they were cooperative with him."

As Capote investigated the mystery of the Clutter murder, he became an informal assistant to Alvin Dewey, the Kansas detective in charge of the case, as they both tried to piece together the motives behind the murders. Working with his friend Nelle Harper Lee, who functioned as Capote's stenographer, Capote traversed the state, lending an empathetic ear to everyone who would consent to talk to him.

"Harper was a genuinely friendly person, and if people were put off by Truman, they felt they could talk to her," said Herb Clutter's former attorney, Clifford Hope, who became the executor of the Clutter estate. "If someone would be talking to Truman, Harper would be behind him, taking notes, getting everything down on paper."

Capote never tape-recorded any conversations and never jotted anything down in a notebook during the entire six years it took for him to research the story. After each interview was complete, Capote would quickly retreat to his room at the Warren Hotel and type everything from memory and Lee's notes, then file it and cross-reference it. "People who don't understand the literary process are put off by notebooks," Capote told *Life* in 1966. "And tape recorders are worse—they completely ruin the quality of the thing being felt or talked about. If you write down or tape what people say, it makes them feel inhibited and self-conscious. It makes them say what they think you *expect* them to say." If Capote felt that he had missed some crucial information the first time around, he went back and interviewed the same subjects over and over again, until he had it right.

Capote for years had claimed that he had taught himself to be his own tape recorder. As a memory exercise, he would have friends read or speak into a tape recorder as he listened; then he would quickly write down as accurately as possible what he had heard and compare it to the tape. Over time, Capote claimed, the differences between what was on the tape and what he had had written became negligible.

Capote had to tread lightly when, a month after arriving in Kansas, two drifters named Dick Hickock and Perry Smith were arrested for the Clutter murders. Using his dispassionate and gently probing approach, Capote achieved a rapport with the killers that had eluded everyone working on the case. The writer spent hundreds of hours with the killers, who in turn used their jail quota of two letters a week to start a long correspondence with the writer. Capote kept them supplied with books, particularly the works of Thoreau and Santayana, which Perry favored, and they in turn filled him in on their backgrounds, their six weeks as fugitives, and the brutally clinical details of the murders. "It wasn't a question of my *liking* Dick and Perry," Capote recalled. "That's like saying, 'Do you like yourself?' What mattered was that I *knew* them, as well as I know myself."

In March 1960, Smith and Hickock were sentenced to death for the Clutter murders, but Capote didn't yet have his story. Three months of appeals would delay delivery of his manuscript to William Shawn at *The New Yorker*, but the wait was well worth it. On the eve of the execution, Perry and Hickock requested that Capote serve as an eyewitness. Thus the writer would be privy to the terminus of both his and the killers' story—holding up cigarettes for the visibly shaking Perry and Hickock on the gallows, receiving a will from Perry that bequeathed all his possessions to the writer, hearing a final "Adios, amigo!" from Perry right before his neck was snapped by the state.

Capote now had his ending, and he knew just how he wanted the story to play out. With such a great wealth of material, a mere by-the-numbers retelling of the story wouldn't suffice; it was just a small-town murder, after all, nothing inherently special or unique about that. What Capote had in mind was a narrative that would burrow deep into the lives of everyone who was touched by the murder—not only the Clutters, but Perry and Hickock, Al Dewey and his team of detectives, the citizens of Holcomb and Garden City. Using John Hersey's *Hiroshima* as a model, Capote would re-create the events using the omniscient voice of a novel—or, to use Capote's memorable phrase, a "nonfiction novel."

"My theory," said Capote, "is that you can take any subject and make it into a nonfiction novel. By that I don't mean a historical or documentary novel—those are popular and interesting but impure genres, with neither the persuasiveness of fact nor the poetic altitude of fiction. Lots of friends I've told these ideas to accuse me of failure of imagination. Ha! I tell them *they're* the ones whose imaginations have failed, not me. What I've done is much harder than a conventional novel. You have to get away from your own particular vision of the world. Too many writers are mesmerized by their own navels. I've had that problem myself— which was one reason I wanted to do a book about a place absolutely new to me—one where the terrain, the accents and the people would all seem freshly minted."

Indeed, Capote was venturing into unknown territory for *The New Yorker,* writing about events that he hadn't witnessed, dialogue that he received secondhand, interior monologues that required a fair amount of creative license on his part. Take as an example this passage from the first third of the book, when Al Dewey investigates the crime scene:

> During this visit Dewey paused at an upstairs window, his attention caught by something seen in the near distance—a scarecrow amid the wheat stubble. The scarecrow wore a man's hunting-cap and a dress of weather-faded flowered calico. (Surely an old dress of Bonnie Clutter's?) Wind frolicked the skirt and made the scarecrow sway— made it seem a creature forlornly dancing in the cold December field. And Dewey was somehow reminded of Marie's dream. One recent morning she had served him a bungled breakfast of sugared eggs and salted coffee, then blamed it all on "a silly dream"—but a dream the power of daylight had not dispersed.

Shawn was skeptical of such fanciful speculative prose; how could Capote possibly know what Dewey had been thinking at that moment? Or anyone else's thoughts, for that matter, especially those of the dead Clutters? In point of fact, Capote couldn't vouch for the Clutters, but everything else panned out; the *New Yorker* fact checker found Capote to be the most accurate writer whom he had ever worked with.

"There were inaccuracies, sure," said Hope. "He had events happening in different locations and so forth, but none of that really bothered me. What bothered me was that he overplayed certain characters, such as Al Dewey, but I think that Al perhaps let himself be used by Truman in a sense." Bill Brown thought that Capote's portrayal of the Clutters was so off the mark as to be virtually unrecognizable.

The 135,000-word story ran in four parts in four consecutive issues of *The New Yorker* beginning with the September 25, 1965, issue; the series was a hit, busting all previous sales records for the magazine. When Random House published it in book form as *In Cold Blood*, it heralded the arrival of a new form, what Capote called the "nonfiction novel," and netted its author $2 million in paperback and film sales.

Even after the story was published to great fanfare, William Shawn remained uncomfortable with the decision to run it in *The New Yorker*. For a magazine that prided itself on ironclad accuracy, there was too much unsubstantiated fact, too much fanciful speculation on Capote's part. Many years later Shawn would still rue the day he gave the green light to Capote's notion.

2

THE GREAT AMERICAN MAGAZINE

"Tiny Mummies" notwithstanding, there was a time when Clay Felker worshiped *The New Yorker*. In the forties, when Felker was in high school, *The New Yorker* was word-perfect, everything he could ever ask for in a magazine. The narrative nonfiction of Hersey, Ross, Liebling, and other *New Yorker* contributors represented the apex of creative journalism, the way good stories should be written. It was also a literary refuge from the local newspapers, which he found intellectually listless and uninspired. Growing up in Webster Groves, Missouri, an affluent bedroom suburb ten miles southwest of St. Louis, Felker had to make do with the *St. Louis Post-Dispatch,* a paper that had fallen mightily in the decades since former owner Joseph Pulitzer worked his magic. Felker, a baseball fan, stuck with the paper's sports pages.

Clay Schuette Felker was born on October 2, 1925 (for years he claimed it was 1928), and reared in a household with two University of Missouri journalism school graduates. Felker's father, Carl, a nonpracticing lawyer, was the managing editor of the *Sporting News,* at that time exclusively a baseball magazine, as well as the editor of the *Sporting Goods Dealer,* a monthly trade publication. His mother was a former newspaper editor who had quit her career to raise her family. Felker wasted little time in establishing himself as a budding publisher, setting up his first newspaper at the age of eight—"the publishing equivalent of a lemonade stand," he recalled.

Felker's earliest exposure to professional journalism came during high school, when he served as an informal apprentice at the *Sporting News*. He loved the way the paper's words were converted into print by the Linotype machine, and the emphatic clank of the typewriter keys. Felker also accompanied his father to St. Louis Cardinals games, where he watched the city's baseball writers frantically tap out their deadline stories in the press box in time for the morning edition. He buzzed on the energy of reporting, its frenetic industriousness, and he knew he wanted to make journalism his life's work.

Felker assumed that he would matriculate at the University of Missouri's journalism school; three generations of Felkers had graduated from there. But his parents objected; journalism was not something that can be taught, they said, but was drawn from the raw material of life experience, and it was better to get a solid general education at a quality school. One day Carl came home bearing an armful of college catalogs and spread them before his son. Clay regarded them for a while, then chose the Duke catalog—mainly because it had the most graphically pleasing layout.

Felker entered Duke as a freshman in 1942 and made a beeline for the school newspaper, the *Chronicle*, where he landed a job as a reporter. In 1943 he enlisted in the navy, pulling double duty as the sports editor and contributing writer for the navy paper, the *Blue Jacket*. In 1946, a year after the war's end, Felker returned to Duke and eventually assumed the editorial duties of the *Chronicle*. He imposed his will on the paper, increasing the frequency from weekly to twice weekly and taking on stories that had national import. In 1948 Walter Reuther, the powerful head of the United Auto Workers union, was shot in the right arm in an assassination attempt by an unknown assailant and taken to Duke University Hospital for treatment. Reuther's hospital room was sealed off from the press; no one could get near him. But Felker wanted that interview desperately. He recruited fellow student Peter Maas, the editor of Duke's humor magazine, *Duke and Duchess,* and an occasional *Chronicle* contributor, to get in there somehow and land the scoop of the century. But how to do it? Felker found a pile of textbooks sitting on a desk and handed them to Maas. "You'll walk into the hospital with these books, and they'll think you're a student," he told Maas.

The plan worked. Maas walked in without a hitch and found Reuther in an unguarded room, willing to talk. Maas got his interview, which was picked up by the Associated Press, and Felker's reputation as a ballsy newspaper editor spread to other campuses. "Oh man, when Felker and Maas got that Reuther interview, we all knew about it," said Robert Sherrill, who was writing articles for Wake Forest University's paper *The Student* at the time and would eventually work beside Felker at *Esquire*. "That became a legendary story among college newspaper writers."

The trajectory toward professional glory was gracefully arcing upward, but Felker's career at Duke was jeopardized by a missed curfew. In the fall of 1948 he was kicked out of school for staying out too late with his girlfriend, Leslie Blatt, and found himself prematurely thrust into the marketplace.

Which turned out to be salutary, because it allowed Felker to get some real-world experience. Newly married to Blatt and scrambling for work, he found a job through a friend as a statistician for the New York Giants baseball team, where he and Blatt double-dated with the team's star, Bobby Thomson. Felker also wrote stories for papers that didn't have a traveling correspondent to cover the team, and he contributed to the *Sporting News,* writing the first major story about a young minor-league phenom named Willie Mays. Felker found that he was comfortable among baseball players; he radiated self-confidence and easy charm, and he found that it opened doors for him, endeared him to those in positions of power.

Felker eventually returned to Duke in 1950 and graduated the following year, eager to conquer New York. In 1952 Felker was hired at *Life* as a sportswriter. There was little substantive work at first; Felker's job mainly involved gathering stories for other staffers to write. But he got his big break by virtue of a scoop. Felker managed to obtain the Brooklyn Dodgers' scouting report on the New York Yankees, which contained a smoking gun: Joe DiMaggio's throwing arm was shot, he could no longer throw anyone out at home. The Yankees never forgave him, but *Life* was mightily appreciative. Felker was now writing features, among them a long profile of Casey Stengel that he expanded into a book called *Casey Stengel's Secret* in 1961.

Felker thrived in Time-Life's buttoned-down culture. "There was a high degree of professionalism at Time-Life," he said. "The morale was unbelievable." He socialized comfortably with the executives at Time-

Life; even Henry Luce became a tennis partner and an occasional guest at Giants games. "Luce was an amazing man," said Felker. "One day he told me, 'You have to have a mission when you're publishing, otherwise you have nothing.' I took that to heart." A competent reporter, Felker quickly discovered that he had a greater aptitude for editing. "I enjoyed writing, but it wasn't my real ability," he said. Felker was really more of an idea man, someone who could generate countless story ideas and concepts for new magazines. He was a brilliant listener above all, collecting tidbits on cocktail napkins and eliciting information from dinner companions that could be used in editorial meetings. *Life* put him to work on special projects, such as an issue on the new moneyed class that he put together with four other editors. Felker also began to develop an idea for another magazine, which he called "a *New Yorker* with pictures." "*The New Yorker* at that time was the biggest bore in the world," he said. "So formulaic." Felker wrote a memo to Luce outlining his idea, and even worked up a dummy issue with the magazine's art department, but nothing came of it. Felker also worked on the prototype for what became *Sports Illustrated*, receiving a crash course in magazine start-ups that he would apply a few years down the line.

When Peter Maas turned down an editor's job at *Esquire*, he suggested that his old college friend Felker apply for it.

Although *Esquire* was no longer the cultural arbiter it had been in the 1930s, it was still a title that carried considerable cachet. The magazine was cofounded in 1933 by Arnold Gingrich and Chicago entrepreneur Dave Smart, who made his money producing display posters for retailers and something called *Getting On*, an eight-page leaflet about money management that savings banks passed along to their customers.

The idea for *Esquire* came from a freelance artist named C. F. Peters, who walked into Smart's offices one day with a drawing for *Apparel Arts*, one of the four fashion booklets Smart published. Before unwrapping the drawing, Peters mentioned in passing that one of his clients, clothier Rogers Peet, was wondering if Smart was thinking about producing more booklets, perhaps something that he could sell to his customers for a small fee. The Christmas season was coming up, and they could sure use the publicity.

Smart and Gingrich began pasting up fashion pages, trying to rethink a formula that they had milked, it seemed, in every conceivable permutation. Fashion pages alone couldn't carry a new title; they would need some editorial content to break it up. Smart began scribbling headlines on a piece of paper: "Gene Tunney on Boxing," "Bobby Jones on Golf," "Hemingway on Fishing." The title—*Esquire, the Quarterly for Men*—came fairly quickly. The magazine would function as a kind of *Vanity Fair* with men's fashion, and Smart would charge a premium price—50 cents—because if men were willing to pay $50 for a suit, they could certainly plunk down two quarters for his magazine.

But Ernest Hemingway? How would they attract writers of his stature to the magazine? As it turned out, Gingrich, an avid book collector, had been engaged in a correspondence with Hemingway for some time and had even sent him a few items of clothing. Now Gingrich had an offer of work for him, and Hemingway agreed. He would write pieces on the sporting life for *Esquire* at a rate that was agreeable to both parties.

Other writers followed in short order: John Dos Passos, Theodore Dreiser, F. Scott Fitzgerald. Smart and Gingrich had positioned *Esquire* as a must-read for the male urban sophisticate. But *Esquire* was also, in Gingrich's words, all about "the new leisure," and that meant male fashion spreads and well-crafted lifestyle pieces about fly fishing and automobiles. It was a golden formula; by the end of 1937, *Esquire*'s circulation had risen to 675,000. When paper rationing hit the magazine publishing business during World War II, Gingrich figured out a novel way to get the War Production Board to give *Esquire* bigger paper allotments: print pinups for the boys on the front. *Esquire* thus became known as a literate skin magazine, but Gingrich and Smart didn't care as long as circulation figures continued to escalate.

Esquire's winning mix of highbrow fiction, breezy reportage, and cheesecake collapsed after the war, when Gingrich retired at forty and handed over the editorial duties to Smart, who, despite his keen business acumen, was never the best judge of good writing. Under the clunky stewardship of new editor Frederic A. Birmingham, the magazine soon devolved into an unfocused mélange of breathless "amazing tales" pulp and dime-store detective fiction. Smart needed an infusion of new energy, and he convinced Gingrich, who had returned from temporary exile in Switzerland to edit a magazine called *Flair* one floor above *Esquire*'s offices at 488 Madison Avenue, to return to *Esquire* on any terms he wanted. That meant total creative autonomy, the chance to once again mold the magazine in his image as both publisher and editor. Gingrich agreed, and the magazine was back on track.

Dave Smart died three months after hiring back Gingrich, leaving *Esquire*'s assets in the hands of his youngest surviving brother, John. Without Dave Smart's steady hand, John, a publishing neophyte, wisely deferred to *Esquire* veteran Abe Blinder to run the magazine's financial affairs. Fritz Bamberger, an Australian with a doctorate in philosophy, would serve as editorial consultant, installing a research department and a thorough fact-checking system.

Gingrich cleaned house in a hurry. He promoted Henry Wolf, an Austrian who had studied with legendary teacher and *Harper's Bazaar* art director Alexey Brodovitch, to create a cleaner and bolder new look for the magazine. Gingrich also restored some of the magazine's literary luster by bringing writers such as Hemingway back into the fold. He fired Birmingham and went on a hiring binge. What was needed, in Gingrich's view, was young men with unlimited creative energy who could recruit new voices and imprint their vision on the magazine while still remaining true to the spirit of what he had built. He found three perfect candidates for the job, the trio that Gingrich referred to as "the Young Turks": Clay Felker, Ralph Ginzburg, and Harold Hayes.

Harold Hayes's and Clay Felker's paths had first crossed years earlier, during their tenures as ambitious young college newspaper editors. In 1950 Felker organized a seminar on journalism at the Washington Hotel, near Duke's campus, in Durham, North Carolina. Among those who showed up was Hayes, who made the two-hour trip from Wake Forest University to rub shoulders with the panel that Felker had assembled, which included the editor of the New York *Daily News*. But according to Felker, the two regarded each other skeptically, and barely talked. It was to set the tone for their subsequent professional relationship at *Esquire*, where Felker and Hayes battled for supremacy while they were shaping the most influential magazine of the 1960s.

The men had much in common. The son of a Southern Baptist minister, Harold T. P. Hayes was born in Elkin, North Carolina, and briefly lived in Beckley, West Virginia, until his family moved to Winston-Salem, North Carolina, when Harold was eleven. A fan of jazz music and all the great twentieth-century American novelists—Hemingway, Fitzgerald, James T. Farrell, John Steinbeck—Hayes fancied himself a novelist in training, and wrote short fiction during high school and as an undergraduate at Wake Forest.

Hayes was an indifferent student: "I floundered around for four or five years through a variety of courses, flunking some and passing enough to leave without total disgrace." Shortly before graduating, Hayes endured a brief stint in the navy, where he was stationed at New-berry, South Carolina, and played trombone in the jazz band. Hayes enrolled in a short-story class and found to his delight that it brought him some academic approbation. Encouraged by his professor, Hayes joined *The Student,* Wake Forest's literary magazine, where he became editor in short order. Hayes had found his métier, and he thrived at *The Student*—generating story ideas, working closely with the best writers on campus, making *The Student* one of the best college magazines in the South.

Hayes returned to military duty during the Korean War, serving two years as an infantry officer in the Marine reserve in 1950 and 1951. Shortly before his discharge, Hayes traveled to New York seeking job opportunities in the magazine business. He wrangled a meeting with *Pageant* editor Harris Shevelson, who suggested that Hayes submit a critique of the magazine. Hayes's detailed, astute memorandum impressed Shevelson enough to hire the young southerner as an assistant editor of the magazine, a kind of benign general-interest publication for those who might also subscribe to *Reader's Digest* and *Life.*

Years later, Hayes would look back upon his tenure at *Pageant* as a crucial apprenticeship. He had tremendous respect for the way Shevelson managed to pull together a quality magazine using limited financial resources. "His persistent refusal to accept an ordinary approach to conventional material caused his staff considerable discomfort," Hayes wrote, "but managed, I believe, to improve the level of individual performance." Hayes left *Pageant* in October 1954 and joined the staff of *Tempo* as a feature editor. During his off hours Hayes developed a concept for a new venture to be called *Picture Week,* a monthly news picture magazine. Working with a bare-bones staff, Hayes was given the go-ahead to start up the magazine, and it was here that he began to develop his taste for unconventional stories that would prick the prejudices of his readership and create a buzz. Among the stories Hayes assigned were "Twelve Southern Governors Answer the Question: When Will You

Allow Negroes in Your Schools?" "The Appeal of the Exposé Magazine," and "Perón Can Fall," all of which were picked up by the wire services for national distribution.

But Hayes's daring editorial policy didn't translate into healthy circulation numbers, and he and the entire staff were fired less than a year after launching the title. *Pageant* editor Laura Bergquist, who was friendly with *Esquire* publisher Arnold Gingrich, suggested that Gingrich interview Hayes as a possible editor. Armed with a portfolio book of the articles he had assigned for *Picture Week* and *Pageant,* Hayes impressed Gingrich, who put him in touch with Tom O'Connor, a friend of his from the *Flair* days. O'Connor hired Hayes to do some police reporting for a couple of small news digests he owned in Atlanta. For two years Hayes did the yeoman's work of beat reporter but kept in touch with Gingrich, just in case something materialized at *Esquire*. When the news digests folded, Gingrich hired Hayes as an editorial assistant. "This time," Gingrich wrote in his memoir, *Nothing but People,* "I took him in like the morning paper, knowing that in a southern liberal who was also a Marine reserve officer I had an extremely rare bird." Hayes would be "an anvil for which I would have to find a few hammers."

Those hammers, as it turned out, would be Felker and Ginzburg. An old friend of Fred Birmingham's, Ralph Ginzburg was a street-smart striver, a Brooklyn native who had engineered a meteoric rise in the publishing business. As an undergraduate at City College's school of business, Ginzburg edited the B-school's newspaper, *The Ticker,* and sold his first piece of writing, an article about Nathan's hot dog stand on Coney Island, while still in college. At the age of twenty-three, Ginzburg was hired as *Look*'s circulation promotion director, overseeing a $2 million budget and a staff of ten. In 1957 he was given an assignment from *Esquire,* whose offices were just a couple of floors below *Look*'s. The article was called "An Unhurried View of Erotica" and described in graphic detail the erotic literature to be found in the rare-book rooms of the world's greatest museums. *Esquire* never ran the story, but Fritz Bamberger was impressed with Ginzburg and hired him to be an articles editor.

Ginzburg, however, thought he was getting Birmingham's job as top editor; he didn't realize he was taking a big pay cut from his *Look* job until after he had signed the contract. It would not be the first time the young editor felt he was getting the bum's rush from *Esquire*. The same day he was hired, Felker was recruited to be features editor. Ginzburg would be *Esquire*'s articles editor, and Hayes the assistant to the publisher.

Ginzburg was furious. Not only had he been misled about his job title, but now he would have to share his duties with another editor. With the ambitious Hayes thrown into the mix, *Esquire* suddenly roiled with furious turf battles. All three editors desperately courted Gingrich in an attempt to gain leverage, but the veteran publisher kept himself out of it. "Arnold's removal from the heat of everyday editorial activity was accented by the physical distance of his office," Hayes wrote in an unpublished memoir, "a good ways down the hall and nestled securely between the offices of the president and the chairman of the board."

Hayes, Ginzburg, and Felker were wary of each other and took pains not to make any rash decisions; one false move, after all, could compromise a potentially promising career at *Esquire*. To Hayes, Felker and Ginzburg were young opportunists, comfortable in the requisite uniform of corporate upward mobility: "They wore the same kind of clothes: button-down shirts, horn-rimmed glasses (it was a short glasses phase for Felker; he wore them the first few weeks and then never again) and Brooks Brothers suits." In Hayes's view, Ginzburg was crude and unimaginative; his primary skill involved drumming up provocative cover lines and then matching the headlines with celebrities, who would be paired with ghostwriters to "draft" their stories.

Felker, on the other hand, was formidable competition. Hayes regarded him as an enterprising editor who was as sturdy as a starched collar, a gadfly with an abundance of intellectual energy and a special talent for collecting important people like Mont Blanc pens. "Clay was always wildly enthusiastic about writers and ideas," said John Berendt, a former editor at *Esquire*. "He could sniff out a developing story before anyone else. He was always out, going to parties, schmoozing, trying to match the right writers to the right stories. He had his finger on the pulse of things, just an amazing sixth sense about trends."

In his memoir *Nothing but People*, Gingrich referred to Felker as "our drinking editor, not because he had a more agile elbow that any of the rest of us, but simply because he was so party prone. Clay managed to get to more parties in a week than anybody else in a month. But in relation to the needs of the magazine at that moment he couldn't have made a better investment of his time."

Ginzburg was thoroughly unimpressed by Felker. "Clay would swipe ideas away from me," he said. "We would bat around ideas prior to meeting with Gingrich, then we'd go into the meeting and I'd pitch my idea. Gingrich would say, 'Why are you pitching this to me? Clay already told me about it.' I got on quickly to this. I played the game, but it was very ugly." As for Hayes, "he was an amanuensis for Gingrich; he was no editor. He was extremely hard-driving and ambitious, though. He should have been the sales manager of US Steel. He had no ability whatsoever to come up with ideas."

With Henry Wolf temporarily setting up shop in the vacant editor in chief's office, the three subeditors fervently jockeyed for the top position. Editorial meetings, which were held each Friday afternoon in Gingrich's office, became claw-and-scratch confrontations, with no clear consensus emerging as to which stories would ultimately make it into the magazine. The stories were supposed to be ratified by a vote between the three senior editors, fiction editor Rust Hills, and copy editor Dave Solomon, but according to Gingrich, it all came down to "a test of lung power, to see who could shout everybody else down."

Gingrich, for his part, kept himself at a remove from the power grabs that would occur after meetings. More often than not, the weekly editorial meetings were exercises in futility. It was often left for fiction editor Rust Hill to cast the deciding vote on which stories made the cut. When the subeditors decided, for the sake of propriety, to hold preliminary meetings prior to the official meeting, they nearly came to blows. The end result of this furious lunge for magazine space was a large pile of assigned but unpublished manuscripts.

Hayes and Felker's battle for editorial control was a clash of temperments. Hayes was a somewhat shy and reticent personality who cultivated a hail-fellow-well-met conviviality in the office, often inviting fellow editors and writers into his office for drinks on Friday afternoon. Felker maintained a more flinty abrasiveness; his editorial approach was more hit-and-run. While no one ever denied his unparalleled ability to weed out story ideas from his own social calendar, he often deferred to his writers to carry the ball. Felker would get wildly enthusiastic about a story but then move on to the next idea before properly nurturing the initial notion. "Follow-through was not something on which Felker placed a lot of emphasis," said John Berendt. "He had an inquisitiveness about things that weren't necessarily fully formed, which didn't make him a great manager. His office was a complete mess. He never knew where anything was. But they both were geniuses, just in different ways. Harold was not the kind of guy to pick up after Felker, and vice versa."

Felker's temper turned off more than a few staff members. "Clay would fly off the handle, he would really scream," said Berendt. "Harold didn't scream, he just fired off blistering memos. If staff members came in late to work, he would just make them generate ten story ideas. Hayes had a kind of cold fury, where Felker would pop off."

Even though Felker wasn't the most rigorous line editor, he had a knack for story structure, for finding the lead of a story buried in the twentieth paragraph of a piece. "What Clay did was very mysterious to me," said writer Patricia Bosworth, one of Felker's many protegés. "He was very much a conceptualist, and it always worked so beautifully."

Hayes was more inclined to take the long view with the magazine, generating a package of stories that would add up to a consistent tone and smooth editorial flow. "Harold's mantra was always tone, tone, tone," said Berendt. "Harold was much more methodical, but not quite as quixotic as Felker," said former contributing writer Brock Brower. "Clay would get an idea, press for the execution of it, and be off on the next thing, while Harold would always chaperone a piece though. Gingrich loved it, of course, because it stimulated the hell out of choices for the magazine. Harold would have his list, Clay would knock it down, and vice versa. They hated each other in the best of all possible ways."

Among the three editors, it became apparent in short order that Hayes and Felker were the hungier, more ambitious upstarts; thus, Ginzburg was the first to go. After he suggested that *Esquire* revert the rights of his erotica story to him in lieu of a pay raise, Ginzburg expanded the piece into a twenty-thousand-word essay and published it in book form with an introduction from drama critic George Jean Nathan. *Esquire* was uneasy about the enterprise from the start—they didn't want one of their editors to be so closely associated with such an unseemly piece—and when Ginzburg went on Mike Wallace's show *Nightbeat* to promote the book he was fired by John Smart. "I was depressed," said Ginzburg. "I thought I was doing some good work for the magazine, but the termination forced me to become my own publisher." Ginzburg would sell three hundred thousand copies of *An Unhurried View of Erotica,* but he would pay a dear price for success by serving eight months in jail for violating federal obscenity laws.

Felker and Hayes remained locked in mortal combat, but the push and pull of their energies began to yield some creative dividends in *Esquire* during the early sixties. The magazine was inching away from the innocuous celebrity profiles and sporting-life features and moving toward venturesome territory. Like two political adversaries from different parties who agree on the issues but have to manufacture dissent in order to distinguish themselves, Felker and Hayes were of the same mind about the editorial direction of the magazine—namely, that *Esquire* had to move beyond transcribed interviews with expository filler, or the "pictured essays" that the magazine liked to run with titles such as "How to Tell a Rich Girl" and "Castles for Rent." Gingrich was already making the magazine more of a repository for serious critical thought, hiring Dwight Macdonald to review films, Kingsley Amis to cover "art films," and Dorothy Parker to critique the latest fiction. Felker brought his college buddy Peter Maas into the fold to write features, as well as sociologist Paul Goodman, whose 1960 book, *Growing Up Absurd,* had mapped the incipient rebellion against established values that would culminate in the 1960s counterculture. Quality fiction had remained a constant, with contributions from such luminaries as William Styron, John Cheever, and Robert Penn Warren.

But Felker and Hayes wanted to move in another direction with the magazine's journalism. At Duke, Felker had trolled the library stacks in search of exciting precedents for him to follow at the *Chronicle* and came across Civil War–era back issues of the *New York Herald Tribune,* the great newspaper edited by the social reformist Horace Greeley.

"I spent the whole afternoon reading these things; I didn't even realize where the time went, because they were so gripping," said Felker. "They were written in a narrative structure. And I realized that they were so much more interesting than the newspaper stories I had grown up reading." The stories, with their vivid descriptions of life in the trenches, changed Felker irrevocably. American journalism had to move in this direction; reporters should be meticulous and exacting when describing events, have a novelist's flair for language, and enliven their stories with headlong momentum.

Ironically, the first great journalist of the Felker-Hayes era to fit this description had been a Ginzburg recruit. Thomas B. Morgan, the son of second-generation Polish Jews, was reared in an unlettered household in Springfield, Illinois. Although his mother was a graduate of Purdue University, "I don't think she read five books in her lifetime," and Morgan's father, a furniture salesman, hadn't made it past the second grade. Inspired by a high school English teacher who encouraged him to write fiction, Morgan earned an English degree at Carleton College in Northfield, Minnesota, before heading to New York in 1953 to find a job as a magazine editor in order to subsidize his fiction writing.

Morgan wrote eighteen letters to eighteen editors, but only one responded; Daniel Mich, the editor of *Look*, *Life*'s closest competitor in the "picture book" category. Morgan was hired as an associate editor, writing stories for the magazine on the side, and four years later was promoted to staff writer.

Morgan became *Look*'s young intrepid reporter, heading to locales as far-flung as Antarctica for stories. Morgan was eager to take on any idea that Mich tossed at him, and he was a quick learner, which made his stories ring with authority, even if they did adhere to *Look*'s pedestrian writing style, which stressed facts over flair. "The writing in *Look* was more or less ordinary journalism," said Morgan. "But it was an unbelievable education for me. It taught me how to be a reporter."

Morgan thrived at *Look*, but he had yet to write the novel he still felt he had in him. He quit his magazine job in 1957 to write two novels, but neither of them was published until years later, when Morgan had established himself as a freelance writer. Broke and casting about for magazine work, he knocked on the door of *Esquire*, which hired him to write picture captions and contribute stories.

Morgan found his true calling as a writer of profiles during his tenure at *Esquire*. Establishing a close collaborative relationship with Felker, Morgan was free to range across the landscape of public personalities, and wrote about whatever interested him at the moment. "Clay was just a great editor," said Morgan. "If you had an idea and called him up, you didn't have to go into a long dissertation about it, unlike Harold, who needed you to send a damn essay before he would approve an idea. Clay would just say, 'Okay, do it.' And you were on your way." Felker was attracted by the notion of smart celebrity profiles, if only because he knew *Esquire*'s readers would want to know about the private lives of public figures. But not puffery; he wanted Morgan to cut right to the bone and deconstruct these complex figures. "Clay was very commercial, but he wanted quality writing regardless of the subject matter," said Morgan.

Greatly influenced by Lillian Ross and her Hemingway profile, Morgan structured his pieces like short stories, with individual scenes and ample swatches of dialogue that would run on for paragraphs at a time. His profiles of Nelson Rockefeller, Roy Cohn, Gary Cooper, Alf Landon, and Teddy Kennedy established him as a Felker favorite and one of *Esquire*'s masters of the personality profile.

Morgan's 1959 profile of Sammy Davis Jr., "What Makes Sammy Jr. Run?" was Felker's idea, suggested after the editor had seen the performer on the *Ed Sullivan Show*. "What Makes Sammy Jr. Run?" was a portrait of a man being tugged by two impulses—the desire of a black entertainer to make it in a white man's world while maintaining some vestige of dignity. In Davis, Morgan saw a man working strenuously to assimilate himself into a world that clung tenaciously to Uncle Tom stereotypes:

> Early in his act, Davis comes on wearing a gray porkpie hat, black suit, black shirt, white tie, with a trench coat flung over his shoulder, a cigarette in one hand and a glass of whiskey-colored water in the other. He blows smoke into the microphone, sips the drink, and says, "My name is Frank Sinatra, I sing songs, and we got a few we'd like to lay on ya . . ." The audience applauds wildly and somebody is certain to cry out: "My God, he even looks like Sinatra," or words to that effect. A broken-nosed Negro does not look much like Sinatra, even though the latter is no work of art himself, but the illusion of Davis' voice and visage and movements . . . produces a kind of Sinatrian hallucination.

Morgan, who never cracked open a notebook in Davis's presence, stuck by him for seven days without a break: right after the nightclub act, when a euphoric but exhausted Davis feigned cordiality when greeting thirty or so well-wishing schmoozers while scheming with his agent about the next movie project; at four in the morning, closing a night-club by jamming informally with the house band; at the Sands Hotel in Las Vegas, plotting the after-show revelry ("Hey baby, call up Keely [Smith] and Louis [Prima] and tell them we'll be over after our show tonight. And chicks. Chicks, we need").

Morgan had a knack for retaining huge chunks of dialogue and detail in his head, which he would then frantically transcribe at the end of each session, so that he could re-create dialogue such as this without the benefit of a tape recorder:

> "Well, Dave, baby, it's a definite leave from here in two-oh minutes, maybe even one-five, followed by a definite cab, which will speed me to Danny's Hide-a-Way for a little din-din. Then it will be another cab-ola to the Hotel Fourteen, that is, one-four. After that, chickee, it is a definite lay-down with closed eyes, and Morpheus dropping little things in them for about forty winks, until I awake again, as myself—like refreshed—ready to go on. I mean, baby, is that clear?"

With the requisite reporter's tools out of sight, Davis shared confidences with Morgan, articulated insecurities to which no other reporter had ever been privy:

> "It takes a terribly long time to learn how to be a success in this business. People flatter you all the time. You are on all the time. And if you're a Negro, you find yourself using your fame to make it socially. Let's face it. The biggest deals with the big moguls are made in a social way, around the pool, that sort of thing. If you're not there, well you're not *there*."

Esquire had never run a profile as formally inventive or as revealing as "What Makes Sammy Jr. Run?" As a thwarted novelist, Morgan wanted to get as close as he could to the richness of fiction with his nonfiction, and in so doing he elevated his reportage into literature.

"Nobody had ever written serious pieces about entertainers at the time," said Morgan. "I earned Sammy's trust enough for him to open up to me about his life in a way that he hadn't to any reporter. He spent the weekend fishing with me and my wife at our summer home in Long

Island, and I earned his trust that way. I had the feeling that he had never had a friend who was a journalist before."

Morgan brought his careful observational prowess to *Look* in the winter of 1960 when the magazine assigned him to write a profile of Brigitte Bardot, the Parisian actress whose film . . . *And God Created Woman* had made her an international sex symbol four years earlier. Arriving for a noon appointment in Paris nearly five hours late, Bardot, accompanied by her husband, Jacques Charrier, opened their talk by asking Morgan, "Why are you here?"

"To see you."

"I do not wish to do any more interviews. I cannot talk to you. Sorry."

"But I've traveled all the way from New York to see you."

"Sorry."

Charrier told Morgan to wait in their apartment in the hopes that Bardot might change her mind. Morgan held a vigil for three days, catching only a fleeting glimpse of Bardot as she walked from one room to the next. He followed the couple to St. Tropez, practically stalking them to try to buttonhole the star for a formal talk. It took ten days before Bardot relented, but not until Morgan contrived a sob story about the enormous hotel bill he had run up at *Look*'s expense, and the fact that he would not get paid and might lose his job if he went back to New York empty-handed.

By the time Bardot acquiesced, the interview seemed an afterthought. Morgan was more intrigued by the actress's coy feints and parries, the way she made a game out of being unapproachable. "I had a hard time writing about Brigitte," wrote Morgan in the introduction to a 1965 anthology of his work. "Totally lost in herself, she brought the logic of impersonality to its ultimate conclusion—absurdity."

So instead, Morgan turned his Bardot quest into the subject of the story, making himself a character and leaving the formal interview out altogether.

Brigitte swung around the car again and again. She walked briskly with a completely un-self-conscious liquid motion of the hips. She came by, snapping French negatives, and passed on in the increasingly wider circles that finally took her 15 yards away from the car. I began to get the rhythm of her march and stopped talking when she was out of earshot. . . . On the eighth circumnavigation of the car, as suddenly as she had started, she stopped, smiled and said, "Get into the car. We go to my home."

Morgan earned a reputation for skillfully teasing out insights from recalcitrant interview subjects. When Felker assigned him a John Wayne profile for *Esquire*, Morgan had to cool his heels on a movie set for a week until Wayne agreed to talk to him, and then wound up writing a scathing portrait of a right-wing reactionary, wary of Kennedys and anti-American Hollywood subversives. For a profile of David Susskind called "Television's Newest Spectacular," Morgan observed a week in the life of the television producer as he skillfully negotiated his way through the worlds of television, theater, and film. Morgan structured the piece like a screenplay with the action prefaced by slug-lines, as in a shooting script:

TIME: *Afternoon*. Susskind, in his office, was just saying, "Look, when you're dealing with sponsors and an advertising agency you've got to come on—pow! They're like women. They keep shifting around. After you explain that you got lipstick on your collar kissing your mother, they accuse you of being late for dinner. So you have to handle them. I hate it, but you have to."

Morgan sketched a portrait of a man as unrepentant about tailoring his product to meet the conservative demands of corporate sponsors, but who also fancied himself a patron of high culture, remaking Broadway plays with B-level actors for television. Susskind was infuriated by the story, which ran in the August 1960 issue of *Esquire*. The impresario had somehow obtained an advance copy of the magazine and called Morgan at home, telling him he needed a psychiatrist and vehemently denying that he had ever used the word *fink* in a quote that Morgan had attributed to him. After thirty minutes of ceaseless haranguing, Susskind finally asked Morgan, "Why did you do it to me? Don't you see what it means? You've made it possible for the finks to get me!"

"I think Susskind thought I had fallen in love with him," said Morgan. "I just thought he didn't know who he was. The only thing David ever wanted more than anything was for somebody to say that he was important. I didn't hail him, and he wanted to be hailed."

Morgan was Felker's reclamation project, a frustrated novelist who had become *Esquire*'s best writer of profiles. Now the editor would turn the preeminent novelist of his generation into a magazine journalist. Felker's first encounter with Norman Mailer transpired at the Five Spot on Fifty-second Street during a performance by pianist Thelonious Monk. "Mailer was with his wife, Adele, there had been some drinking going on, and they were fighting," said Felker, who was friendly with the club's owner and thus availed himself of the chance to sit with Mailer. "I mean, I had never seen such fighting. They were hitting each other." It seemed an odd time to approach Mailer about writing for *Esquire,* but Felker took his best shot. After Adele stormed out of the club, leaving the two men, Felker asked Mailer, "Have you ever written about politics?" The 1960 Democratic convention in Los Angeles was approaching, and Felker asked if Mailer would like to cover it for *Esquire.*

Mailer had indeed written about politics for a brief time at the *Village Voice,* the weekly downtown New York paper that he had cofounded in 1958, and intermittently throughout his career. He made his fiction debut with the publication in 1948 of the World War II novel *The Naked and the Dead,* a book based on Mailer's own wartime experiences in the Philippines, and it had launched him to the top of the *New York Times* best-seller list at the age of twenty-five.

That book had immediately established Mailer as a major American novelist, but his energies were too protean for fiction alone, and his reputation as an unorthodox polemicist was beginning to take hold. In his 1957 essay "The White Negro" Mailer introduced the concept of the existentialist hipster hero, living outside the normal constraints of society in order to avoid annihilation by social conformity, abiding by the code of the Negro (who had been bred into a culture of oppression and danger), adapting his jazz, his marijuana, even his urge toward knife-edged violence. The hipster had therefore "absorbed the existentialist synapses of the Negro, and for all practical purposes could be considered a white Negro." The essay, which was published in Irving Howe's political quarterly *Dissent*, was discussed far more than it was actually read, but it turned Mailer into a lightning rod of controversy and a public intellectual.

In November 1959 Harold Hayes had purchased the serial rights to a chapter from Mailer's book *Advertisements for Myself*. "The Mind of an Outlaw" was a lengthy analysis of the troubled origins of his Hollywood novel *The Deer Park* and Mailer's struggles to write and publish it. Felker didn't like the story much, finding it long-winded and self-indulgent, and had objected to Hayes's suggestion that the magazine run it as a cover story. But *Advertisements for Myself*, despite meager sales, became a touchstone for Mailer as a public persona. The book was a self-annotated anthology of novel excerpts, essays, poetry, and social observations, a kind of "greatest hits" of a still-young career. It was the interstitial writing that Mailer used to introduce the pieces, written in a hubristic, self-regarding tone, that attracted the most attention. Here was Mailer positioning himself as the supreme thinker of his generation, a philosopher-king whose Herculean talents and keen turn of mind would change the world, elevate the national dialogue, and, most important, cure what ailed America. "The sour truth is that I am imprisoned with a perception which will settle for nothing less than making a revolution in the consciousness of our time," Mailer wrote at the beginning of the book.

"I really think the watershed book was *Advertisements for Myself*," Mailer would later say. "I thought that was, oddly enough, the first book written in what became my style. I never felt as if I had a style until that book. When I developed that style, for better or for worse, a lot of other forms opened to it."

Surely, Felker surmised, this was a writer who could bring something intriguing to bear to the national political scene. And now that the political landscape was changing, with a young, dynamic senator from Massachusetts bringing an element of Hollywood glamour to the Democratic party, surely Mailer's take on things would be provocative, perhaps even newsworthy.

Mailer welcomed the opportunity to expand his literary palette in the relatively untested waters of nonfiction, and Felker would give him his head, allowing him to write whatever, and however, he saw fit. *Esquire* would pay Mailer $3,500 for the piece; Felker would accompany Mailer to L.A. and introduce him to the right people.

As it turned out, Mailer didn't need Felker's help. His notoriety preceded him, and his Hollywood contacts, most notably Shelley Winters, whom he had met in the early fifties while adapting *The Naked and the Dead* as a screenplay, got him into all the best cocktail parties. It was, for the most part, politics as usual. Mailer had always been wary of Washington—all of those drab, unimaginative representatives setting the national agenda for the rest of us—but in Kennedy, he glimpsed the spark of something new. Not exactly a pinstriped insurrectionary, but perhaps someone who could reclaim some of the country's vibrancy. Peering over the balcony one night from his hotel room at the Biltmore, Mailer spotted Kennedy arriving via motorcade.

> He had the deep orange-brown suntan of a ski instructor, and when he smiled at the crowd his teeth were amazingly white and clearly visible at a distance of fifty yards. For one moment he saluted Pershing Square, and Pershing Square saluted him back, the prince and the beggars of glamour staring at one another across a city street, and then with a quick move he was out of the car and by choice headed into the crowd.

Mailer saw at once what Kennedy's election might mean for the country—a move toward some great reawakening of the American soul. "Eisenhower's eight years," he wrote, "has been the triumph of the corporation. A tasteless, sexless, odorless sanctity in architecture, manners, modes, styles has been the result." Kennedy could unleash the "subterranean river of untapped, ferocious, lonely and romantic desires" that had lain dormant during the two Eisenhower terms, reigniting the human potential that had been tamped down for so long. In his piece, which Mailer called "Superman Comes to the Supermarket," Mailer linked Kennedy's ascendance to the great American creed of unbridled adventure, virtue, and self-actualization; Kennedy's election could start a mission in earnest for the new frontier, returning America to its first principles.

It was perhaps too simplistic a dialectic to accept at face value; even Mailer was aware of that. But Mailer was canny enough to leaven his enthusiasm with a cold shot or two of skepticism; he didn't want the piece to read like Kennedy campaign boosterism. John F. Kennedy, after all, was the product of a smooth and efficient political machine whose patriarch, Joe Kennedy, had a criminal past. Was one witnessing "the fortitude of a superior sensitivity" or "the detachment of a man who was not quite real to himself"? Even Mailer couldn't say for sure.

It's Mailer's fresh combination of a reporter's detatchment with a novelist's vision—his ability to hold his subject up to the light and examine that person from every angle—that makes "Superman Comes to the Supermarket" the most insightful magazine article of the Kennedy era. The sheer intellectual expansiveness of the piece, coupled with Mailer's penchant for capturing the mood of the room with a few deft strokes, gives it the layered heft of great psychological fiction. His descriptions of the convention floor ("If one still smells the faint echo of a carnival, it is regurgitated by the senses into the fouler cud of a death gas one must rid oneself of"), Los Angeles ("a kingdom of stucco, the playground for mass men—one has the feeling it was built by television sets giving orders to men"), Lyndon Johnson ("When he smiled, the corners of his mouth squeezed gloom; when he was pious, his eyes twinkled irony"), and other aspects of the convention are first-rate, but his analysis of Kennedy and the social forces that conspired to make him a viable candidate—the link between Kennedy and the enduring American myths—was something new altogether. Certainly no other reporter had recognized so early the potential for a cultural renaissance with Kennedy in the White House, while at the same time openly acknowledging the potential dangers of a country submitting too readily to a seductive personality cult. The value of the piece is in Mailer's ability to hold those two opposing ideas in equipoise.

"Superman Comes to the Supermarket" was a new hybrid—think piece, personality profile, and polemic. It was unmistakably journalism, but a newspaper editor would be hard-pressed to place it. Years later, when the term "New Journalism" became commonplace, Mailer admitted that "Superman Comes to the Supermarket" fell squarely into that rubric of creative reportage. What Mailer had contributed to the form, in his view, was an "enormously personalized journalism in which the character of the narrator was one of the elements in the way the reader would finally assess the experience. I had felt that I had some dim intuitive feeling that what was wrong with all journalism is that the reporter tended to be objective and that that was one of the great lies of all time."

Felker loved the piece; Hayes and Gingrich had strong reservations. Never a fan of Mailer's to begin with, Gingrich considered scrapping the story, which he considered the scattershot jottings of an otherwise gifted writer. The magazine had reserved sixteen pages in the feature well for the story, and the issue had to be shipped to the printer by the end of August to make the newsstands on October 15. Felker, Hayes, and Gingrich fought it out for days, until it came down to the wire. "We had three hours to go before we shipped the magazine to the printers," said Felker. "Gingrich kept insisting it was the worst piece of dreck he had ever read, and I kept insisting otherwise." Felker eventually prevailed, and the story made it, albeit with one minor change, courtesy of Gingrich, who changed the title to "Superman Comes to the Supermart" without Mailer's consent.

That two-letter change from "Supermarket" to "Supermart" nearly sabotaged *Esquire*'s working relationship with Mailer for good. Mailer was furious when he saw it and fired off a letter to the editor, which was published in the January 1961 issue. Felker tried to mollify the writer, but to no avail. "Mailer for some reason thought that we hated the story," Felker recalled. "He just went bananas." Mailer stopped writing for the magazine for nearly two years.

Regardless of the title change, "Superman Comes to the Supermarket" had a seismic effect on American journalism. Pete Hamill, at the time a young reporter for the *New York Post*, could sense a sea change among his colleagues at the paper. "I could actually feel the impact of that piece in the city room at the *Post*," he said. "All the young guys were going, 'Holy shit, what the hell is this?' He just took the form and exploded it, and showed writers that there were other possibilities." Mailer knew that the story was good, perhaps even epochal, and he would devote more energy to journalism than to fiction over the next four decades.

Felker had pulled off a major coup, despite Gingrich and Hayes's protestations. It should have solidified his stature at the magazine, but instead his power was methodically being chipped away by Harold Hayes, who was endearing himself to Gingrich. By the summer of 1961 the battle lines were clearly drawn. Hayes was leveraging his position at the magazine by fielding offers from competing publications, which prompted Gingrich to act. He appointed Hayes managing editor in

July. Felker agreed to stay on as senior editor, but he started looking for other jobs.

"It reminded me of my days at Columbia, where you were either a Mark Van Doren man or a Lionel Trilling man," said former *Esquire* contributor Dan Wakefield. "Being a Greenwich Village guy, I took Felker to be more of an uptown dandy. I wasn't a part of that society life and I didn't admire it. Harold became my champion. He was one of those rare editors that didn't have writer's envy. At that time, a lot of editors wanted to be published, so there was a lot of tension and edge to them. Harold didn't have any of that."

Now that he had a proper title, Hayes began to steer the magazine with a firmer hand. To Gingrich, Hayes was like a film auteur, an editor who could masterfully organize all of the graphic and editorial elements of an issue into a pleasing, unifying whole that reflected his own tastes and sensibilities. But Felker knew that much of what made *Esquire* exciting could be directly attributed to him—not only the Mailer piece, but the hiring of David Levine, an artist he had discovered at a small downtown art gallery. Levine's distinctive line drawings of literary and entertainment figures in *Esquire* launched his long and distinguished career. He had also edited Tom Morgan, and brought in Peter Maas, who years later found literary fame as the author of the Mafia insider's account *The Valachi Papers*. But "Harold was very ambitious, and he was undermining me with Gingrich," said Felker. "He was a very good editor, but ruthless."

Hayes drafted a confidential memo to Gingrich, outlining his master plan to implement "a more active control of all our materials." According to the memo, *Esquire*'s separate editorial camps were creating an "inequitable distribution of work inside the editorial office." Hayes outlined a new top-down system in which he would oversee every aspect of the magazine. "It is very difficult—and even unfair of me—to assume responsibility and control over Clay's features so long as he has implicit authority from you to handle them as he sees fit. I am willing to do this, however—in fact I am willing to provoke a crisis of several megatons if that should be the best way to handle the problem." All story ideas would pass though Hayes's desk first, and the overall budget would be determined by him as well. Gingrich would interface only with Hayes, who would become the sole emissary of the editorial department. The idea, Hayes wrote, is to "maintain maximum autonomy with minimum anarchy."

Gingrich signed off on the memo, and Felker was left in the lurch. In June 1962 Felker was the apparent aggressor in a heated shouting match with comedian Mort Sahl shortly after an appearance by Sahl at the Basin Street nightclub. Sahl had taken issue with a story in the magazine that had referred to him as "the light that failed," and asked Felker if someone at *Esquire* had a personal animus against him. Felker's response was typically curt: "I don't like you, Mort." "Felker was quite drunk at the time," recalls Sahl. "I didn't take kindly to his tone." Then, according to legal papers filed by Sahl, Felker threatened to bury the comic in the magazine. Felker claimed that the incident had occurred in Sahl's dressing room; the editor had tried to convince Sahl to reconsider an interview with a writer the comic had initially rejected. When Sahl's lawyers began sending letters to the magazine hinting at a lawsuit, Gingrich, who had maintained a polite distance from all the infighting among his editors, couldn't allow Felker's short-tempered outbursts to continue if lawyers were now going to be involved. Forced to play his hand, he gave Felker the shove.

Felker's replacement, an editor at Time-Life Books named Byron Dobell, had the owlish aspect of a college professor and a lively intelligence that translated into unorthodox story ideas. "I moved right into Clay's office, which wasn't easy at first," said Dobell. "Despite what had happened with Gingrich, the staff liked him. I had to win everyone over by doing a good job."

Even as a newcomer, Dobell was unwilling to indulge the digressive whims of star writers, even if it meant a complete blue-pencil evisceration of a story. He favored reporting over think pieces and enjoyed the work of such dependable contributors as political correspondent Richard Rovere and Tom Morgan, whose Susskind piece "put my hair on end." As for Mailer, Dobell found him brilliant but long-winded: "He took his metaphysical insights to be God's truth."

Now that Hayes was securely in command, he had a few new writers he wanted to give a try. One of them, Gay Talese, was a *New York Times* reporter who was eager to spread his wings, push himself beyond the two- to three-column limitations of general assignment work, and really expand a story as far as it was willing to go.

The son of southern Italian immigrants, Gaetano "Gay" Talese was born on February 7, 1932, in Ocean City, New Jersey, near Atlantic City. Ocean City in the 1930s was a polyglot town where Irish coexisted with Italians, Catholics with Methodists, but there was little cultural common ground, and so little ethnic archipelagos formed. Talese was reared as an Italian Catholic, but he attended an Irish Catholic school. His father, Joseph, was a tailor and the owner of a dry cleaning business who dressed elegantly even for breakfast, thus bringing "the rakish fashion of the Continental boulevardier to the comparatively continent men of the south Jersey shore." His mother, Catherine, a stylish and fastidious but emotionally distant matriarch, ran a dress shop under the Taleses' apartment.

Talese at an early age was steeped in the sartorial codes of class and the ways in which wardrobe can connote sophistication; he dressed himself in suits and ties as early as high school. Thus he was cast out as a snob, reinforcing his own feelings of cultural isolation. "I was olive-skinned in a freckle-faced town," Talese wrote in his 1992 book *Unto the Sons*, "and I felt unrelated even to my parents, especially my father, who was indeed a foreigner—an unusual man in dress and manner, to whom I bore no physical resemblance and with whom I could never identify."

"My father was a miserable man during World War II," said Talese in an interview. "His brothers were in the neo-fascist army in Italy, but my father had a strong sense of patriotism. He joined a citizens' committee of patrolmen who looked out for enemy ships along the Jersey shore at night." Talese remained aloof from his volatile father during his childhood. "My father was a total prick all day long, but he'd go to restaurants with his friends and he'd be very happy."

Joseph ensured that his son, an indifferent student at best, made it all the way though parochial school by not charging the priests for dry cleaning their vestments; in exchange, Gay would get promoted to the next grade with an administrative nudge.

Sports saved his miserable childhood. Talese played baseball on his high school team and assiduously followed the fortunes of the Yankees, the Dodgers, and the Giants in the city's tabloid newspapers. That's when Talese became addicted to newsprint. At fifteen, Talese began covering his baseball team for the local paper, the *Ocean City Sentinel Ledger*. After only seven articles, Talese's assignment was expanded when he was given a column to cover general high school news for the paper. Talese's "High School Highlights" ranged across any number of topics, making it a kind of running commentary on the New Jersey enclave's academic life. Talese was free to write what he pleased, and he discovered that he could file quickly on tight deadlines. From 1947 to 1949 Talese wrote over three hundred columns.

He barely made it through high school academically, and so undistinguished was his academic record that even the principal advised against college. He was rejected by every local university, and all hope for higher education seemed lost until the family doctor pulled a few strings and got young Gay into his alma mater, the University of Alabama. But Talese could see the way clear to a path now; there was no question that his major would be journalism.

For Talese, journalism was an escape hatch—not only from the pinched circumstances of his childhood but also from his own personality, which tended toward reticence. "I didn't know who I was in those days," he said. "I had no sense of myself." Now a northeastern Italian Catholic in a southern school, Talese yet again found himself buffeted by ethnic and cultural differences, but writing would be his redemption. If he paid close attention to others, he could gain their confidence, and strengthen his own self-worth in the process. It was all about being empathetic, listening closely. It was a trait he had learned from his mother, who was always careful never to interrupt any of her customers. "I learned [from my mother] . . . to listen with patience and care, and never to interrupt even when people were having great difficulty in explaining themselves, for during such halting and imprecise moments . . . people are very revealing," Talese wrote in 1996. "What they hesitate to talk about can tell much about them. Their pauses, their evasions, their sudden shifts in subject matter are likely indicators of what embarrasses them, or irritates them, or what they regard as too private or imprudent to be disclosed to another person at that particular time."

At the University of Alabama, Talese thrived. His literary tastes matured, and he began reading a steady diet of American fiction, particularly John O'Hara, Carson McCullers, and Irwin Shaw. Talese admired McCullers for her empathetic depictions of the southern underclass and the ways in which she treated marginal characters with dignity and a minimum of sentiment. From O'Hara and Shaw, Talese learned how to sketch the peculiar mores of urban dwellers in clear, elegant prose. He began to structure his stories around individual scenes or set pieces, and he used more dialogue to bring his stories to life. In his junior year Talese was named the sports editor of the University of Alabama's *Crimson White* student paper, and created a sports column for himself called "Gay-zing," a forum that allowed him to further develop his literary storytelling skills.

By the time Talese graduated from the University of Alabama in 1953, his literary reporting style was fully formed. A college friend of his who was a cousin of the *New York Times* managing editor Turner Catledge suggested that Talese get in touch with Catledge and ask about potential work. Talese headed straight for the *Times*'s headquarters on West Forty-third Street and asked the receptionist if he could see Turner Catledge. Amazingly, Catledge invited Talese up to his office, and two weeks later Talese was offered a copy boy job.

Talese's first unsigned stories for the *Times* were unsolicited pieces that he wrote during his off hours and then forwarded to *Times* editors. A few of these, such as a story about the man who operated the ticker-tape billboard that curled around the Times Square building, made it into the paper, and soon Talese was getting assignments to write harmless general-interest stories. His earliest signed pieces—a story on the pedal-operated rolling chairs on the Atlantic City boardwalk, Sunday magazine features about Broadway star Carol Channing, the new bowling chic, and baseball-themed pop songs—were written in the prevalent *Times* style of the era, foursquare and structurally sturdy.

Talese's *Times* career was interrupted by a short stint in the Army Tank Corps in Fort Knox, Kentucky, where he wrote a column called "Fort Knox Confidential" for the base paper. It wasn't until Talese returned to the *Times* in 1956 and was assigned to the sports desk that his lucid writing style blossomed. Talese was especially drawn to boxing, because it was a metaphor for just about everything—personal redemption, race, celebrity, and especially the trying art of losing. An athlete's failures were more intriguing to Talese than his or her triumphs. "Sports is about people who lose and lose and lose," Talese said. "They lose games, then they lose their jobs. It can be very intriguing."

For a three-column profile of the Puerto Rican boxer Jose Torres, Talese sketched a portrait of a smart, ascetic loner beholden to a manager, the legendary Cus D'Amato, who wanted to transform him into an ethnic hero, despite Torres's trepidations.

> As the men talked, the prize fighter sat silently in a chair listening. Then he got up and went down a flight of stairs to Fifty-first Street and headed to Stillman's gymnasium. Puerto Ricans, recognizing the fighter, waved at him, and some followed him into the gymnasium to watch him spar. The fighter is a quick, clever puncher standing 5 feet 10 inches. His chest muscles twitched this way and that as he moved around the ring, jabbing at a sparring partner, without malice.

Talese's sharply etched portraits stood out, but he felt confined by the *Times*'s space limitations. "I was limited to two thousand words in the daily paper, and twenty-five hundred tops in the Sunday magazine," he said. "I wanted to know more than what the article could contain. I wanted to be a marathon runner of journalism." Talese was promoted to cover the Albany statehouse in 1959, but he felt even more bound by newspaper convention, and now his copy was being rewritten with impunity. When he was passed over for the job of writing the "About New York" column, a plum assignment he felt he deserved, Talese, with the paper's approval, started to pitch stories to Harold Hayes at *Esquire* in February 1960.

His timing was propitious. Hayes happened to be looking for New York stories for a special summer package the magazine was compiling. Did Talese have any good ideas? Talese jumped, culling various leads from his articles, rewriting them, and then stitching them together in a single article. "I am currently trying to gather unusual facts on people and things in New York," Talese wrote in his cover letter, "in the hope that someday I'll have enough for a good book . . . please excuse any typing errors."

Hayes bought the piece and ran it near the front of the issue. It began, "New York is a city of things unnoticed. It is a city with cats sleeping under parked cars, two stone armadillos crawling up St. Patrick's Cathedral, and thousands of ants creeping on top of the Empire State Building. The ants were probably carried up there by wind or birds, but nobody is sure; nobody in New York knows any more about the ants than they do about the panhandler who takes taxis to the Bowery; or the dapper man who picks trash out of Sixth Avenue trash cans."

Esquire paid $500 for "New York," and it established Talese as a comer, someone for Hayes to watch. After writing a few more stories in the vein of "New York" and a profile of New York mobster Frank Costello—a piece that *Village Voice* writer Nat Hentoff had told Hayes was the best he had ever read in a national magazine—Talese was becoming a favorite of Hayes. "I liked the toughness of Hayes, because I was tough," said Talese. His article fee was bumped to $850; Hayes felt that Talese had been invaluable in "forming a fairly specific *Esquire* point of view." But Talese still had a full-time job at the *New York Times,* which kept him busy from 1 P.M. to 7:30 P.M. every weekday except Friday, which was his day off. He had to squeeze the *Esquire* work in between filing stories for the paper, which left him with very little time for anything else—that is, until the New York papers went on strike in December 1962, providing Talese with a short break from his job and a chance to devote his energies to a feature story Dobell had assigned him: a profile of Broadway director Joshua Logan.

Dobell felt that Logan had coasted too long on an inflated reputation; it was time to set the record straight on this peddler of meretricious clichés and overblown productions, who was now in rehearsals for *Tiger Tiger Burning Bright,* Peter Feibleman's drama about African Americans in New Orleans. Dobell couldn't figure out Talese; the two had fought over what Dobell felt were disparaging remarks made by Talese about Hayes, the man who had turned Talese into a magazine writer. But he knew that beneath Talese's calm exterior there lurked "a bratty street kid" who would scrape and claw for a good story.

Talese, who had already staked out Logan during the premiere of his show *Mr. President* on October 22, was now free to observe to his heart's content. "I am a reporter who is forever in search of the opening scene," said Talese. "I never start writing until I have that scene, and then I become a man in search of a final scene. This all tends to take a lot of time."

Talese made good use of his time, sitting in the back of the Booth Theater with a notebook on his knee (Talese never used a tape recorder for fear that he would become too dependent on it) and watching Logan fulminate, cajole, and stage-direct while his actors slowly melted down from the heat of their director's temper tantrums. He spent days with Logan and the cast, recording all of their conversations, sparing no one. Then he blocked out all of the scenes on a large corkboard in his apartment, much like a film director uses a storyboard to direct the narrative flow of his film. The scenes alone would dictate the direction of his story; Talese would leave himself out of it.

In the story, "The Soft Psyche of Joshua Logan," Talese wrote of Logan's emotional attachment to Feibleman's play, how it reconnected him to his hardscrabble Mansfield, Louisiana, roots and the plantation where he was reared by a family of strong-willed females. Logan was identifying so strongly with the play, wrote Talese, that "it seemed he might be involved once again with Mansfield, the source of his old wounds and boyhood complexities; a trip, one might assume, that he could ill afford to make." Logan had a lot riding on the play, mostly the need to keep himself financially afloat: "Though Logan earns in the neighborhood of $500,000 a year, it somehow seems barely enough and one evening after a hard day's rehearsal of *Tiger,* Logan left the theatre and said, wearily, 'I work for gardeners and psychiatrists.'"

The piece continued in this vein, with Logan constantly tweaking the play to his satisfaction, culminating in a screaming match with his female star, Claudia McNeil. Dobell and Hayes thought the story might be a little too revealing, perhaps even libelous, but when Talese read back the story to Logan, the director vouched for every word.

"The Soft Psyche of Joshua Logan" would be a benchmark story for Talese and *Esquire.* Talese had perfected the profile-as-short-story technique that he had been working toward for the past decade. As Lillian Ross had done with her John Huston piece, Talese wrote the article in scenes, but he added a layer of psychological complexity with his depiction of Logan, a self-made man whose track record as a Broadway King Midas, and the attendant pressure to produce a hit every time out, had coarsened him, turned him into something monstrous and crude.

Talese was catching Logan on the downward trajectory of his career; he was a once-dominant cultural icon who had lost his golden touch. Fallen characters fascinated Talese, because they had to function in a world that once revered them but now looked askance. It was only in defeat that a man revealed his true self to the world. That's why boxers appealed to him. Talese had the corner on boxers at *Esquire;* as a *Times* reporter, he had profiled Jose Torres, Joe Louis, Ingemar Johansson, and Floyd Patterson. Talese had interviewed Patterson thirty-seven times, finding him to be unusually articulate, someone who could provide unique insights into his own psyche and the methodology of his technique. Talese had spent extended periods of time with Patterson at his training camp in upstate New York, and he came to know Patterson as intimately as a family member. "I had become almost an interior figure in his life," said Talese. "I was his second skin."

When Hayes assigned Talese a profile of Patterson in the winter of 1963, the twenty-nine-year-old former heavyweight champ had recently been knocked out a second time by his bête noire, Sonny Liston, and he was suffering from a severe bout of postmatch depression. Talese met him at his training camp, as he had done in the past, and it didn't take much prodding for Patterson to express feelings of failure and self-recrimination. In his article Talese presented Patterson as a loner, living in a desolate two-room apartment sixty miles from his family in Scarsdale, fighting with the demons that had haunted him in the weeks since Liston had KO'd him in the first round. The story was a first for Talese in that he would use large chunks of dialogue to tell his story; Patterson was so good at describing what it really felt like to be in the ring with Liston that Talese wasn't inclined to embellish.

> "It is not a bad feeling when you're knocked out," he said. "It's a good feeling, actually. It's not painful, just a sharp grogginess. You don't see angels or stars; you're on a pleasant cloud. After Liston hit me in Nevada, I felt, for about four or five seconds, that everybody in the arena was actually in the ring with me, circled around me like a family, and you feel warmth toward all the people in the arena after you're knocked out. You feel lovable to all the people . . .
>
> "But then," Patterson went on, still pacing, "this good feeling leaves you. You realize where you are, and what you're doing there, and what has happened to you. And what follows is a hurt, a confused hurt—not a physical hurt—it's a hurt combined with anger; it's a what-will-people-think hurt; it's an ashamed-of-my-own-ability hurt."

To Talese, Patterson seemed to be everything a professional boxer shouldn't be: sensitive, contrite, his personality tinctured with regret and world-weariness. When Talese accompanied Patterson on his Cessna plane as the fighter flew to Scarsdale to discipline some white kids who had been taunting his seven-year-old daughter, he found that Patterson, who had threatened to level the kids with a left hook, could not do anything more than deliver a gentle rebuke to the kids.

Later, Talese sat with Patterson as he returned to that night with Liston in Vegas, gently guiding him deeper into the recesses of his memory. When he wrote the piece, he chose to render this section as a running monologue, and placed it in italics as a framing device to alert his readers that they were inside Patterson's head:

> *"And so then you know it's time to get ready. . . . You open your eyes. You get off the table. You glove up, you loosen up. Then Liston's trainer walks in. He looks at you, he smiles. He feels the bandages and he says, 'Good luck, Floyd,' and you think, 'He didn't have to say that; he must be a nice guy.'"*

No journalist had ever pierced the facade of an athlete this way before, had ever gotten this close to what it felt like to be a champion who now felt like a coward. But Talese had earned this access over countless hours of hang time with Patterson across seven years, and it paid dividends when it counted the most. "The Loser," which ran in the March 1964 issue of *Esquire,* was a new high-water mark for the magazine, daringly innovative but suffused with empathy for its subject. Talese was now Hayes's pet writer, and their relationship would reap even greater rewards as the sixties progressed.

Clay Felker was missing out on all the fun at *Esquire,* but he wasted little time in establishing a new beachhead for himself. He returned to his newspaper roots and jump-started the New Journalism in an unprecedented fashion.

3

KING JAMES AND THE MAN IN THE ICE CREAM SUIT

By the time Arnold Gingrich showed Clay Felker the door, the editor was already plotting his next move, taking a consulting job at *Infinity*, a trade magazine for professional photographers, managing the film career of his wife, actress Pam Tiffin, and editing part time for Viking Press. He also unsuccessfully interviewed for a job at the *New York Herald Tribune*. The *Trib* was Felker's kind of challenge, a historical institution that was hemorrhaging money and readership and was looking for a fresh infusion of ideas to compete in the city's crowded newspaper market. Before long, Felker would get his chance at the *Trib* and lead it into its last great era.

The *Herald Tribune*'s lineage was one of the most distinguished in all of American journalism. It was created by the merger of two venerable newspapers, the *New York Tribune* and the *New York Herald*, in 1924. In the nineteenth century, under the stewardship of editor Horace Greeley, the *Tribune* was a leading advocate of social reform. A member of the pro-business Whig party until its dissolution in the 1850s, Greeley became a vocal supporter of the Republican party and helped engineer Illinois senator Abe Lincoln's nomination for the presidency in 1860. For the next eighty years, the *Tribune* continued to support Republican causes, advocating Wendell Willkie's nomination against Franklin Roosevelt in 1940 and championing Dwight Eisenhower's two terms as president in the fifties.

In 1872, the year of Greeley's death, the *Trib* was taken over by

Ogden Mills Reid, a former reporter for the *Cincinnati Gazette* and the managing editor under Greeley. Reid engineered his purchase of the paper with the help of Jay Gould, the notorious financier who cornered the silver market in August 1869. Thus began one of the great dynastic newspaper families; three generations of Reids would retain ownership of the paper for nearly a century.

A perpetual money-loser, the *New York Herald Tribune* was never a front-runner in the great New York newspaper wars of the early twentieth century, when as many as fifteen papers battled for readership, but its aggressive recruitment of great reporters made it a formidable editorial powerhouse. During World War II, correspondents Homer Bigart and Tex O'Reilly filed harrowing dispatches from the front lines from both the European and Pacific theaters; sports writers Red Smith and Grantland Rice honed their snappy prose styles while working for the *Trib*, while critic Virgil Thomson, a Pulitzer Prize–winning composer, critiqued classical music for the paper. Its news columnists were among the most widely read in the nation. Walter Lippmann, whom the Reids had poached from the *New York World* in 1927, was a Harvard graduate who had helped establish the *New Republic* as the leading periodical of the left before turning to newspaper work. Lippmann's column "Today and Tomorrow," which offered a pragmatic approach to national politics, was syndicated in a hundred newspapers, brought the *Trib* two Pulitzer Prizes, and ran for thirty years. During the postwar years Joseph and Stewart Alsop's column, "Matter of Fact, " which was syndicated in 137 papers during its twelve-year run, warned of the imperialist evils of the Soviet Union as it cut a swath through Eastern Europe, and argued for a renewed commitment to strengthening the U.S. military to meet the new Communist threat.

Despite the quality of its editorial content, the *Tribune*'s financial health was constantly in flux. During World War II, there had been a significant increase in ad revenue, orchestrated by Ogden Reid's wife, Helen Rogers Reid, and ad director William Robinson, but a newsstand price increase from a penny to a nickel in a quick-fix attempt to increase revenue in 1946 left the *Tribune* unable to boost its readership. When Robinson imposed a higher advertising rate, the *Tribune* found itself working from a position of weakness on both sides of the ledger. The *Trib* was charging three times as much for the same ad space as the *New York Times,* yet it had only 57 percent of the latter's circulation by 1950.

The paper continued to operate in the red throughout the decade, averaging a loss of roughly $700,000 annually. Without a white knight to save them, the Reids continued to burn capital, and by 1957 the situation had become desperate. Tex McCrary, the veteran newspaper columnist who was doing publicity for the *Trib,* suggested that the Reids approach John Hay (Jock) Whitney, the millionaire scion of a a vast railroad fortune who was now the U.S. ambassador to Great Britain, with the notion of buying in. Whitney, who had turned down an earlier offer of minority ownership from Helen's son Whitelaw Reid, was now more receptive to the idea if he could have a hand in the editorial content.

On the suggestion of Helen Reid's other son, Ogden Rogers Reid (known as Brown), Whitney provided the paper with a $1.2 million loan, enough to cover the deficit the Reids expected the paper to run through the end of 1958. Energized by Whitney's investment, Brown Reid, who had taken over the editorial reins of the paper, set out to remake the *Trib* into a more focused product, with eye-catching layouts and a stronger emphasis on newsy gossip. But nothing seemed to work; the *Tribune* lost $1.3 million in 1957, the biggest deficit in the paper's history, and its ad linage had dropped from 15 to 12.4 percent, while that of the *New York Times* had risen from 23.4 to 30.6 percent over the past decade. By mid-1959, the paper had burned through Whitney's loan and was on life support.

Instead of retreating, Whitney increased his commitment to the *Tribune,* with the proviso that some changes would be made. The first order of business was getting the Reids to give up their controlling interest in the paper. If Whitney was going to resuscitate the *Tribune,* he would have to do it on his terms, as a majority owner, and with his hand-picked team. Helen Reid made every effort to stave off the inevitable, searching in vain for a buyer who would allow the family to retain control, but time was running out. Finally Helen relented, and her family followed suit.

The search for an editor proved more difficult than Whitney or his closest confidant and business advisor, Walter Thayer, had originally envisioned. What the paper needed, in Thayer's view, was a severe shock to the system; in John Denson, he found just the man to administer it.

Among magazine insiders, Denson was already a legend for remaking

Newsweek into a formidable challenger to *Time*. He had done so by sprucing up the news package with zippy graphics—arrows, sidebars, highlighted pictures—and a breezy prose style that livened up even the most prosaic stories. As an editor, Denson had populist impulses; he wanted working stiffs and subway commuters to buy his magazine.

He wasted little time fulfilling his mandate to remake the paper. The standard vertical orientation of the broadsheet format was ditched; now stories might be splayed horizontally across the top fold of the front page, or a series of articles on the same subject—one providing the facts, the other offering perspective on the story—might run next to each other. The left column of the front page featured a section called "In the News This Morning," in which short summaries of the most important stories could be absorbed quickly. Stories were placed in boxes, newsweekly style, and headlines evinced a cheeky wit.

Denson's work yielded results; a month after his arrival in March 1961, circulation was up by forty thousand over the previous April. Although Denson had people buzzing about the *Tribune,* his scorched-earth policy was damaging morale. More important to Walter Thayer, his last-minute production tinkering cost too much to ignore, as the composing room began to rack up high overtime charges.

Though Denson had threatened to quit on at least eight occasions, only to relent each time, the day eventually came for Whitney to cast his lot with either his closest confidant or his mercurial editor. In October 1962 Whitney made his decision public. A prepared statement announced that Denson had refused "certain organizational changes" that had been proposed—a reference to Denson's rejection of a plan that would delegate the handling of production deadlines to editorial subordinates—and was no longer with the *Herald Tribune.* Jim Bellows, a veteran of the Naval Air Corps with previous stints at the *Columbus Ledger* and the *Miami News,* was named editor of the *Tribune.*

It seemed that the *Tribune* was destined to fail. No sooner had the paper gained some momentum than its editor was fired. Now a newspaper strike would shut the *Trib* down against its will. On December 8, 1962, the printers' union, led by ironfisted Bert Powers, closed shop after a prolonged negotiation between the union and the city's newspapers, including the *Trib* and the *Times,* had broken down. Whitney, for his part, was content to ride out the strike until the *Trib* could begin publishing again.

In the meantime, the paper would use its down time to its advantage. Bellows, who admired Denson's wayward creativity, wanted to continue to push the *Trib* in daring new directions. But instead of focusing on the front page at the expense of everything else, a tactic that proved to be Denson's undoing, Bellows would focus on the rest of the paper.

In a memo to national news editor Richard Wald, Bellows wrote that "there is no mold for a newspaper story" and that the truth behind a story often "lies in the way a man said something, the pitch of his voice, the hidden meaning in his words." Like Denson, Bellows believed the inverted-pyramid formula could be spruced up without sacrificing integrity for frivolity. Bellows had learned the lessons of his vanquished boss and began to recruit young writers to implement his ideas.

"I'd urge writers to open their eyes, to seek the new and different," Bellows wrote in his memoir, *The Last Editor*. "Because news is what is *unusual*. We think it's just *recording* things that take place. But it isn't. You've got to decide, with intuition and instinct, what is unusual here." For 114 days during the strike, Bellows and his brain trust, which included Wald and city editor Murray Michael "Buddy" Weiss, reconfigured the soul of the paper.

He also hired Clay Felker as a consultant in the fall of 1963. "Clay was hired because he was a social swinger, and he knew a lot of people in the city," said Bellows. "He also got along fairly well with people, and I thought he could contribute ideas that we could use."

To *Trib* staffers, Bellows was something of an enigma. Communication with his writers and editors usually involved a few muttered half-sentences, followed by some vague gesticulations meant to convey what he couldn't articulate verbally. "Bellows never finished a sentence," said Tom Wolfe. "You would get the gist of what he meant but you never got the end of it." If his writers didn't quite understand him when he spoke, they were clear about his mission to shake up New York with an aggressive newspaper war, just like the one he had waged in Miami against the *Miami Herald*. The *Trib* had existed for too long in the shadow of the *Times*, and Bellow, reveling in the underdog role, would hire young writers who shared his appetite for the main chance.

One of Bellows's most significant early hires came from an unlikely source: Jock Whitney's sister Joan Payson, who owned the New York Mets baseball team. In 1962, the Mets suffered the most abysmal season in baseball history to date by losing 120 games, an epic tale of ignominy that attracted a young sportswriter from the *New York Journal-American* named Jimmy Breslin, whose credo, like Gay Talese's, was "the loser is always more important than the winner." But Talese was intrigued by the free fall of fame; Breslin was more interested in the striving chump who never made it beyond the ladder's first rung.

The thirty-two-year-old Breslin, already a fifteen-year newspaper veteran, had interviewed Payson a few times for his book about the Mets, *Can't Anyone Here Play This Game?* In the preface to an early collection of his articles, Breslin remembered trying to buttonhole Payson at Penn Station just before the heiress was heading to Florida. "I get there and I can't find her nowheres. So I ask this guy, and he says, 'Sure, her train is over there in the corner.' God damn, she's got two private cars going to Florida, and there I was looking for her in the Pullman. How the hell was I supposed to know? So we get into this big goddamn drawing room with the servants in the other one and she offers me this drink and she has one, and before I knew it, I was stiff. I mean stiff. They threw me out at Trenton. And she just took it all in like it was part of life. Beautiful. What a broad."

Can't Anyone Here Play This Game? became a regional bestseller. Payson loved it and passed the book along to Jock Whitney. The *Trib* owner, too, was taken with Breslin's flinty prose style, the way he sketched the team's colorful characters using sharp-tongued quotes and roguish humor. Whitney brought the book to sports editor Hal Claassen and told him to inquire about first serialization rights. It turned out that assistant editor Lawton Carver had already broached the same idea to Claassen a week earlier. The *Tribune* acquired the rights, and Breslin's career at the *Trib* was launched.

Breslin had come a long way from his hardscrabble roots. He was born on October 17, 1929, in a gray frame house on 134th Street and 101st Avenue in Jamaica, Queens, the son of two alcoholics. James Earl Breslin, a piano player, abandoned the family when Jimmy was an adolescent. His mother, Frances, took a job as an elementary school teacher for a while, then found steady work as a supervisor in the city's welfare department in order to support Jimmy and his younger sister, Deirdre. She never got over her husband's abandonment and drank heavily. Breslin remembers one bender during which his mother put a gun to her temple and cocked the hammer. Mercifully, she didn't pull the trigger.

Breslin had a troubled relationship with his mother, an emotionally distant matriarch. But Frances was different at work—there she was a sympathetic supervisor who often invited black workers to her home despite the opprobrium of her Irish friends. From her, Breslin learned about basic decency and how the inequities of the city split along race and class lines.

A poor student, Breslin's solace was sports and sportswriters, particularly the great *New York Sun* columnist W. C. Heinz and *Chicago Tribune* writer Westbrook Pegler, whose anthologized collection of articles Breslin treasured. When he was eight, Breslin began collecting schoolyard gossip and hand-printing a one-sheet newsletter called *The Flash;* one issue featured the banner headline "Mother Tried Suicide." Breslin wrote to avoid dealing with real life; he could just sublimate it all though his work, use it an excuse to "keep all storms in my life offshore." He was never much of a book reader. "I read a Balzac novel once," he said. "It took me two years to finish it." Language was another matter; he loved playing with words and building sentences with them. After graduating from high school, Breslin hustled for newspaper work and found a job at the *Long Island Press,* attending class at Long Island University at night because "I needed it for my working papers. The *Long Island Press* was an incredible education for me, because I worked every desk—City, Sports, Night. It was incredibly hard work for no money, a backbreaking job."

Breslin moved up the newspaper chain quickly, taking sportswriting jobs at the *New York Journal-American,* a Hearst newspaper, and the Scripps-Howard syndicate. By the spring of 1963 the young reporter had grown weary of the sports beat, which was too circumscribed and a bit too easy for him. His first freelance column for the *Trib,* which ran in conjunction with the serialization of *Can't Anyone Here Play This Game?* was ostensibly a story about the Mets' first four-game winning streak, but it was really a gimlet-eyed portrait of a lovable no-goodnik, Mets first baseman Marv Throneberry:

Without Throneberry we would all be lost. His brand of baseball, as displayed last season, made the Mets. He had to be your hero. Anybody a little late paying a loan could understand Marvelous Marv when he went for, then usually missed, a pop fly. Only the bucket-shop operator, who specializes in old widows, didn't like Marvelous Marv.

One evening after work in May 1963 Whitney asked Breslin to meet him at Bleeck's bar, near the *Tribune*'s offices, to feel him out for a potential job offer. Breslin went into the meeting wanting no part of yet another low-paying newspaper gig; encouraged by the success of his Mets book, he was thinking about new book ideas and becoming a full-time freelancer. "Mr. Whitney, with all due respect, you can't pay me enough to work for you. I've had it with newspapers," Breslin barked, to which Whitney responded, "Well, what do you want?" Breslin knew that he had found a home and that Whitney was the kind of stand-up guy who would reward good work with proper recompense. He would be pulling down an annual salary of $125,000 within four years.

A few months after being hired as a sportswriter, Breslin was given his own column on the split page (the first page of the second section). The objective for Bellows was to neutralize the paternalistic tone of old-line columnists such as Walter Lippmann and the Alsops with a column that was written in the common-man cadence of a working-class readership that the *Trib* had been criticized for avoiding. "I never thought about how to do a column," said Breslin. "It just came naturally, I guess. It had a point of view and it had to spring right out of the news. Everything of the moment demands that it be done that day. Even when a few sentences don't work when you get to the deadline, there is an immediacy that makes the column fresh. Like you were covering the eighth race at Belmont. But no one was doing it when I started. That's why everyone thought it was new."

For Breslin, the greatest New York stories were to be found among the city's working class, the low-level wage earners who kept the city's industry churning. They worked in Manhattan, but they lived in the outer boroughs with another substratum of the working class: the shysters, the numbers runners, the small-time gangsters. Class was Breslin's big subject; he wanted to show readers what it was like "out there" across the bridges, among the dispossessed who had been ill served by the uptown New York media, maligned by their crude stereotypes. Mostly Breslin wanted to share his ardor for New York in all its multifarious, gritty glory. "New York is all I know," said Breslin. "It's all I care about." Like George Eliot or V. S. Pritchett, Breslin innately understood that everyone was interesting. They just needed someone to tell their stories for them. "On the surface, the *Tribune* was this dignified, Republican newspaper," said Tom Wolfe, who was hired as a general assignment reporter in 1961. "But it also gained this following of the cab drivers with the cap over one eye, and Jimmy had a lot to do with that."

A big, hulking Irishman who stood nearly six feet tall and weighed 240 pounds, Breslin resembled a Greco-Roman wrestler gone to seed. Add to that his voice—a reedy, adenoidal screech filtered through a heavy Ozone Park accent—and Breslin could easily insinuate himself into any scenario that had story potential. "It's news reporting, and that consists of using your two feet," said Breslin. "The only lesson, then, that you could give people is how to climb stairs, because there are no stories on the first floor. Anything you're looking for is four and five flights up."

Breslin, who never learned how to drive, conducted all of his research on foot. Often accompanied by his wife, Rosemary, he would just walk the streets, sniffing out stories in tenement buildings and Irish bars, making crucial contacts and a few lasting friends along the way. Equally as important was Breslin's ability to hold his drink. Breslin once remarked that the best story ideas were the ones that sounded good after the hangover had worn off. Breslin's story foraging frequently happened in bars, usually Pep McGuire's place on Queens Boulevard. Pep McGuire's was Breslin's salon, the meeting place where the reporter befriended the shady, Runyonesque characters who would people his columns for the *Trib*.

For many of his earliest columns Breslin used the raw material of his childhood: the kids in the neighborhood who "were a little poorer than some, a little more Irish than others, a little closer to the racetrack than most." "Marvin the Torch" was about a four-hundred-pound bookie friend of Breslin's who moonlighted as an arsonist, setting fire to money-losing businesses so that the owners could collect the insurance money. Like so many of Breslin's greatest pieces, "Marvin the Torch" was a short story disguised as a newspaper story; it read like nothing in the *Trib* or any other newspaper. Breslin wasn't interested in pat morality plays or the rote condescension that usually accompanied stories about petty criminals. His affection is obvious, but to Breslin, Marvin was just another working stiff, selling his services to the highest bidder. It began:

Marvin the Torch never could keep his hands off somebody else's business, particularly if the business was losing money. Now this is accepted behavior in Marvin's profession, which is arson. But he has a bad habit of getting into places where he shouldn't be and promising too many favors. This is where all his trouble starts.

Marvin is hired to torch a custard stand located "on the wrong side of an amusement park"; for kicks, he intends to "make the roof blow straight up into the air without bending the nails in it." Instead, a "good south wind" carries the fire out of control: "Marvin the Torch's favor job on the custard stand had also belted out most of a million-and-a-half-dollar amusement park." It was like something out of an old George Raft film, but it was happening in present-day New York, and Breslin could bring it to life with more verisimilitude and gallows humor than any other metro reporter in the city.

"Jerry the Booster" was the story of a small-time department store shoplifter, a charming rake with a propensity to stuff 42-regular suits down his size-60 pants.

"Yes, sir?" the salesman said. He said it the way he always says "Yes, sir?" to a customer. Only this time his nose was twitching.

"I would like a whole new wardrobe of clothes," Jerry the Booster said.

"I want a suit," a Providence boy called out from the right.

"Could I have a little service, please?" a Providence boy called out from the left.

"This looks nice," the third Providence boy, his hands all over a navy blue, said.

"Yes, sir?" the salesman said. But the salesman was not looking at Jerry the Booster when he said "Yes, sir?" The salesman, his nose twitching, was looking over Jerry the Booster's fat head. The salesman was trying to catch the attention of somebody who was someplace else in Goldwater's Department Store.

"The bum is trying to get a cop," Jerry the Booster said to himself.

Jerry the Booster pulled on the salesman's sleeve. "Say, mister," Jerry said to the salesman, "look what I know how to do."

Jerry stuck his tongue out at the salesman. Then he swiveled his shoulders around. His fingers flicked at his belt line. And, in one motion, Jerry's jacket slid off his back, and his pants dropped to the floor.

"Nyaaahhh," Jerry the Booster, tongue out, sang to the salesman.

Like Gay Talese, Breslin was using dialogue to elucidate character, but instead of pathos, Breslin went for laughs. Sure, Jerry the Booster was a crook, but Breslin knew that the city would be a very dull place without guys like Jerry around. "Jimmy was incredible, the greatest newspaper columnist of my era," said Tom Wolfe. "He turned out that column five times a week, and practically all of it was reporting. He introduced Queens to New York."

Breslin often didn't sit down at his typewriter until 4 P.M. or later, and then he'd make a mad dash to his 5:30 deadline. "When everyone else would be filing to the subway to go home, I'd be going in the opposite direction, headed toward my typewriter at the *Tribune*," said Breslin. "I felt guilty about it, but I never missed a deadline." Breslin would plunk himself down at a desk in the city room, hunching himself, according to Tom Wolfe, "into a shape like a bowling ball. He would start drinking coffee and smoking cigarettes until vapor started drifting off his body. He looked like a bowling ball fueled with liquid oxygen. Thus fired up, he would start typing. I've never seen a man write so well against a daily deadline." By the time he pulled the last page out of his typewriter, Breslin's desk would be covered in a sea of crumpled notes and Styrofoam coffee cups, his copy a spiderweb of handwritten cross-outs and scribbled revisions. Somehow the words always scanned on the page. Editor Sheldon "Shelly" Zalaznick characterized Breslin's deadline crunching as "absolutely heart-stopping, but I never remember him ever missing a deadline."

As someone who shared the same troubled origins as many of his interview subjects, Breslin skillfully endeared himself to even the most intransigent and cynical among them. A back slap and a few rounds of beers were effective social lubricants, but Breslin's avuncular demeanor closed the deal. He was just like them, another poor schmuck behind on his rent and his gambling debts. "Jimmy had the knack, he still does, of becoming your instant best friend," said former *Tribune* national editor Richard Wald. "And he was a very exacting reporter. He took reams of notes, until he had the name, rank, and serial number of everyone he interviewed."

Breslin's colorful reprobates were engaged in a commedia dell'arte of the city's underworld, the elaborate scheming and double-dealing of the criminal class. The *Trib*'s readers lapped it up; Breslin became the *Trib*'s first writing star of the 1960s, profiled in the national newsweeklies and envied by his colleagues. But Breslin's inside peek into a subterranean culture was regarded with suspicion by a number of his fellow journalists, mainly because the stories seemed too good to be true. Breslin's gifts as a writer were obvious, but did he make it all up?

The *New York Times*'s metropolitan editor A. M. Rosenthal thought so, so one day he went to Pep McGuire's to see for himself. Breslin column regular Fat Thomas was at the bar; another thuggish Breslin favorite nicknamed Cousin was in the office; Mafia figure James "Jimmy the Gent" Burke was nursing a beer a few stools away from Thomas. It all checked out.

One day in March 1964, Breslin was drinking in Bleeck's when an anonymous messenger boy walked in and told Breslin to meet Charlie Workman at the Port Authority that afternoon. This was a strange message to receive from a man Breslin assumed was behind bars. Workman, also known as Charlie the Bug, was one of Murder Inc.'s most prolific killers; his most notorious hit, the murder of Harlem kingpin Dutch Schultz, had landed him in the state prison in Trenton, New Jersey, for twenty-three years. When Workman, accompanied by his brother, Abe, and his wife, Catherine, met Breslin, he was only a few hours out of prison on parole. He wanted Breslin to be the first to know.

Breslin's editor, Buddy Weiss, had too much faith in Breslin's skill as a reporter to question his veracity, but he did allow him a certain degree of creative latitude regarding dialogue and the use of minor details to enliven some of his more fanciful set pieces. "Jimmy was so clearly over the top that you couldn't take it seriously," said Richard Wald. "And if the story wasn't serious, there wasn't the same amount of probity devoted to it. There was a lot of exaggeration in what Jimmy wrote, a lot of charged language and wild, crazy fabulations about the city, but he didn't invent the people. I met Marvin the Torch. Of course, his name wasn't Marvin."

But Breslin occasionally threw the names of people he knew into his stories, people who had no business being in there. For an article about a mob hit that had taken place on Queens Boulevard, Breslin implied that the real target of the murder, Joseph Buchwald, had had the good fortune of not being in town that day. Buchwald was the father of the *Tribune*'s Paris correspondent, Art Buchwald, and he had no connection whatsoever with Breslin's story. "That really upset my father, when Jimmy did that," said Art Buchwald. "He was implying that my father had something to do with the mob, when he didn't. But Jimmy just shrugged it off, and the people he worked for were delighted by this stuff."

Weiss knew that Breslin would often disguise the names in his stories to protect the guilty, but he would often take issue with some of the earthy language that Breslin used. As a man who could give as good as he got, Weiss wasn't cowed by Breslin, and the two would fight and yell at each other in the city room, making their arguments public spectacles, but Breslin never backed down. He wouldn't change his copy for anyone, not even the men who were cutting his checks every week. When Zalaznick, the editor of the *Trib*'s Sunday magazine supplement, tried to change a few words in a story, Breslin accused him of being underhanded in an attempt to "tunnel under me" and destroy his integrity. "Breslin was a bad guy to tangle with," said Zalaznick. "He could be very tough, but underneath it all I thought he was a very decent human being."

Pack journalism was anathema to Breslin; if a clutch of reporters was feverishly heading in one direction, Breslin would hightail it the other way, in search of the real story. The best examples of this were the series of stories he filed in the wake of President Kennedy's assassination on November 22, 1963. This was a story Breslin knew he had to cover; aside from his affinity for the nation's first Irish Catholic president, Breslin felt it crystallized, in one horrible moment, the nation's tendency toward senseless violence that had torn apart America's cities. Breslin arrived in Dallas on the twenty-second, just in time for the press conference with Kennedy's doctors, including Dr. Malcolm Oliver Perry II, the attending ER surgeon at Parkland Memorial Hospital, who had tried in vain to resuscitate the dead president. While the other reporters grilled the doctors about the chronology of events leading up to Kennedy's death, Breslin carefully probed Perry about his personal impressions, the thoughts that had raced through his mind when the president's lifeless body was wheeled into view. Perry was nonplussed by Breslin's line of inquiry; what direct bearing did it have on the tragedy at hand?

But the assassination itself was being covered amply from every conceivable angle; Breslin wanted to bring this national tragedy down to human scale, telescope it into the story of Dr. Perry's futility as he confronted a national tragedy. Breslin's dispatch, called "A Death in Emergency Room One," ran in the *Trib*'s November 24 edition, and began:

> The call bothered Malcolm Perry. "Dr. Tom Shires, STAT," the girl's voice said over the page in the doctors' cafeteria at Parkland Memorial Hospital. The "STAT" meant emergency. Nobody ever called Tom Shires, the hospital's chief resident in surgery, for an emergency. And Shires, Perry's superior, was out of town for the day. Malcolm Perry looked at the salmon croquettes on the plate in front of him. Then he put down his fork and went over to a telephone.
>
> "This is Dr. Perry taking Dr. Shires' page," he said.
>
> "President Kennedy has been shot. STAT," the operator said.

Breslin clinically enumerates Perry's usual operating procedure, the standard routine for gravely wounded gunshot victims, while Jacqueline Kennedy, "a tall, dark-haired girl in the plum dress that had her husband's blood all over the front of the skirt," stands nearby, observing it all with a "tearless . . . terrible discipline." Finally Perry defers to a priest for the last rites:

> The priest reached into his pocket and took out a small vial of holy oil. He put the oil on his right thumb and made a cross on President Kennedy's forehead. Then he blessed the body again and started to pray quietly.
>
> "Eternal rest grant unto him, O Lord," Father Huber said.
>
> "And let perpetual light shine upon him," Jacqueline Kennedy answered. She did not cry.

The story ends on Perry, alone with his thoughts in a hospital conference room:

> He is a tall, reddish-haired thirty-four-year-old, who understands that everything he saw or heard on Friday is a part of history, and he is trying to get down, for the record, everything he knows about the death of the thirty-fifth President of the United States.
>
> "I never saw a President before," he said.

With "A Death in Emergency Room One," Breslin created a charged narrative by relating the facts of Perry's experience as a real-time docudrama, using Perry's point of view and an occasional, unobtrusive detail to provide dramatic shading. It was the best column Breslin had written for the *Trib*, but it also brought to a head a long-running debate among Breslin's colleagues: had he papered over inconvenient facts and made up dialogue? "A Death in Emergency Room One" contained a number of niggling errors. Breslin had recorded the sequence of events incorrectly, for example. But even Perry himself had to admit that, despite Breslin's sloppiness, he couldn't have captured the story any better had he been present in the ER. "A guy's weight, the name of his mother," Breslin told *Newsweek* in 1963, "I'll blow it every time. But when it comes to a major insight, I don't think I miss very often."

Over the next two days, the *Trib* ran two more Breslin stories, this time from Kennedy's funeral in Washington, D.C.: "Everybody's Crime," in which the columnist observed dignitaries and citizen mourners as they passed by Kennedy's coffin in the rotunda of the Capitol, and "It's an Honor," the story of Clifton Pollard, the man who dug Kennedy's grave at Arlington National Cemetery. The second story developed as a result of Breslin becoming jittery amid the pomp of the presidential funeral, with its procession of world leaders and a bustling phalanx of international journalists. "I saw de Gaulle and Haile Selassie, who were great for the photographers, but I didn't make a living writing about people like that," said Breslin. Turning to his friend Art Buchwald, who was also covering the funeral, Breslin mentioned that he might ditch the funeral to interview the gravedigger. Buchwald thought that was a great idea, and Breslin left. "The story was about a dead body, after all," Breslin said.

Once again, Breslin brought the national tragedy down to the capillary level, the working-class guy with the dirt on his khaki overalls who is summoned from his Sunday bacon and eggs to do his duty:

When Pollard got to the row of yellow wooden garages where the cemetery equipment is stored, Kawalchik and John Metzler, the cemetery superintendent, were waiting for him. "Sorry to pull you out like this on a Sunday," Metzler said. "Oh, don't say that," Pollard said. "Why, it's an honor for me to be here." . . .

When the bucket came up with its first scoop of dirt, Metzler, the cemetery superintendent, walked over and looked at it. "That's nice soil," Metzler said. "I'd like to save a little of it," Pollard said. "The machine made some tracks in the grass over here and I'd like to sort of fill them in and get some good grass growing there, I'd like to have everything, you know, nice."

The country was in mourning, but a man still had to earn his pay. Breslin didn't have to elaborate or moralize, throw in some obvious paragraph about the quiet dignity of Pollard and the pride of a job well done. It was all in the telling—the careful reconstruction of the scene, the halting cadence of the dialogue.

If Jimmy Breslin was the *Herald Tribune*'s foremost chronicler of the dispossessed and overlooked, then Tom Wolfe was the paper's dazzling wordsmith of the decade's emerging status class, the new 1960s youth culture and its mores. Breslin and Wolfe were working opposite ends of the socioeconomic spectrum, but they shared the same uncanny flair for character and setting.

Wolfe, unlike Breslin, was not a product of New York, which was to his advantage; it gave him the gee-whiz enthusiasm of the outsider who found himself suddenly plunging headlong into a vibrant urban pageant. Thomas Kennerly Wolfe Jr. was born in Richmond, Virginia, on March 2, 1931. His mother, Louise Agnew Wolfe, was a landscape designer; his father, Thomas Wolfe Sr., was an agronomist, the director of a farmers' cooperative, and a professor at Virginia Polytechnic Institute. Wolfe senior was also the editor of the *Southern Planter*, a farm magazine with a literary bent. Tom Wolfe first became enamored of the writing life as he watched his father draft his farming articles in longhand, on yellow legal pads. "A couple of weeks later, there would be this nice, sparkling print in the magazine," said Wolfe. "I just thought that was great."

Tom Wolfe was reared in the Sherwood Park section of Richmond, an economically mixed neighborhood of academic types and working-class families. Wolfe's house, which was located about a mile from a railroad yard, would often be visited by tramps looking for a handout; his mother always graciously obliged with homemade sandwiches. Despite this, Wolfe looks back fondly on his childhood. "Even though it was the Depression when I was growing up, I was not very conscious of it," said Wolfe. "Doctors called that the old oaken bucket delusion. You just screen out everything around you that's unpleasant." He attended public schools until the seventh grade, when his mother, an educated woman who had once aspired to a career in medicine, enrolled him in St. Christopher's Day School, an Episcopal institution that educated the children of Richmond's elite farming families. He thrived there, becoming an honors student, chairman of the student council, and coeditor of the school paper. His column "The Bullpen" crackled with the earliest examples of Wolfe's Roman-candle prose. For an article on the school's men's basketball team, Wolfe wrote that "different spectators have suggested motorcars, bicycles and rickshaws for keeping up with Coach Petey Jacob's live-five."

At Washington and Lee, a private university in Lexington, Virginia, Wolfe, who had consumed books such as Jack London's *The Sea-Wolf* and L. Frank Baum's *The Wizard of Oz* as a child, had dreams of becoming a great American novelist. His parents had a couple of Thomas Wolfe novels on their bookshelf, and young Tom was convinced that the author of *Look Homeward, Angel* was a relative and that he could carry on his namesake's literary legacy. "My parents had the hardest time convincing me that I wasn't related to that Wolfe," he said. Wolfe wrote short stories when he wasn't filing sports stories for the school's paper and throwing curveballs for the school's varsity baseball team. He dreamed of becoming a big-league ballplayer: "You got no applause for writing. Lots of it if you played games." James T. Farrell's trilogy of Studs Lonigan novels had a profound influence on him; Wolfe was taken with the way Farrell used the raw material of a child's life to create a riveting coming-of-age story, written in the novelist's gritty, plainspoken prose. "Farrell got inside the minds of adolescents," said Wolfe. "Nothing of note happens in the books—Studs just watches his contemporaries rising and sinking in life—but it's riveting." Wolfe would eventually master Farrell's gift for writing convincing interior monologue, a talent that would serve him well at the *Trib*.

Wolfe was a solid student at Washington and Lee, but he kept his distance from the other students, mostly the rich sons and daughters of the southern gentry. "Tom was a bit of an oddball," said Professor Marshall

Fishwick, Wolfe's mentor in college. "He was much more intellectual than most of the students, who would come for a degree, rather than an education."

Wolfe published two short stories in *Shenandoah,* the college literary magazine that he coedited, stories that were hammered out in George Foster's weekly fiction seminars at the Dutch Inn pub off campus. It was in Foster's seminars that Wolfe learned to absorb harsh criticism, but he also realized that the write-what-you-know mentality of fiction was not necessarily what he had in mind for his own career. It was Marshall Fishwick's American studies course, which folded cultural, artistic, and sociological history into a kind of unified theory of American history, that radicalized Wolfe's attitude about his own writing. He learned about William James's pragmatism and Freud's theories of the subconscious, and it opened him up to new ways of thinking. "The impulse behind American studies was not to accept the dogma of scholars, but to use your own scholarship, to develop a healthy skepticism about things," said Fishwick. "Tom took that to heart. He wrote an early paper for me called 'A Zooful of Zebras,' which was about the lockstep conformity of academics. He was always very suspicious of that."

Wolfe earned a doctorate in American studies at Yale, studying under brilliant mavericks such as Norman Holmes Pearson, writing poetry, and reading big-screen social fiction such as John Dos Passos's USA trilogy. His dissertation was titled "The League of American Writers: Communist Organizational Activity Among American Writers, 1929–1942." Wolfe was offered a job teaching history at a small midwestern liberal arts college, but instead he tried to gather material for novels by taking a job as a furniture mover for a trucking company in New Haven. "Jack London of all people was my model," Wolfe said. "But I could see that the girls in the offices weren't impressed. Believe me, there is no insight to be gathered from the life of the working-class milieu."

Wolfe decided to pursue a career in journalism, if only because it would allow him to write steadily, without the uncertain financial vagaries of fiction writing. Wolfe wrote letters of introduction to 120 papers all over the country and received only one encouraging response, from the *Springfield Union* in Springfield, Massachusetts. "They hired me, mainly because they were curious about this guy with a Ph.D. from Yale who wanted to work on their paper," said Wolfe.

Wolfe was a general assignment reporter, sometimes working on five stories at the same time, covering the police beat on weekends, then commandeering the night desk, which would give him a $5 bonus on his $55-a-week paycheck. It was an invaluable apprenticeship—for the first time, Wolfe was exposed to the political and cultural machinations of a multiethnic community—but Wolfe was eager to make it in a major city. Delighted by the exciting portrayals of newspaper life to be found in films such as Lewis Milestone's *The Front Page,* he hungered for the competition and adrenaline rush of urban newspaper work, where reporters from four different papers might battle it out for a scoop. In 1959 Wolfe took a pay cut and landed a job at the *Washington Post,* working the city desk.

Wolfe chafed at the *Post*'s institutionalized, regimented approach to news gathering. "It was very much like an insurance office, with gray metal desks all lined up," said Wolfe. "You couldn't eat at your desk, and at one point, they even tried to ban smoking, but everyone just started climbing the walls." As a cub reporter, Wolfe was beholden to his editors, who tended to assign standard-issue stories to him, which he would then embellish out of sheer boredom, turning crime blotter items into rococo flights of fancy. One time when Wolfe was on night rewrite, a job that required him to write stories from facts fed to him by police reporters, he got a call from the *Post*'s Les Whitten about a homeless man in the Adams Morgan district who had been shot by a cop—the kind of two-paragraph story that might get buried in the paper. Wolfe pumped Whitten for information: Was the man's head in the gutter? What was the location of the bullet holes? From this, Wolfe fashioned a story that was pure Raymond Chandler, with a dramatic flourish about the five bullets in the man's chest forming the perfect shape of a heart.

Among his fellow reporters, Wolfe gained a reputation as a major talent who refused to abide by the *Post*'s assembly-line methods; he was constitutionally incapable of feeding the maw with merely serviceable copy. "The *Post* wanted everybody to march in lockstep, and Tom simply couldn't do it," said Whitten, who sat three desks away from Wolfe. Most days Wolfe could be found at his desk, leisurely reading the New York *Daily News* while editors Ben Gilbert and Alfred Friendly stewed and waited for the writer to turn in a story, which would invariably come in too late to run in the first edition. "A lot of us were delighted by that, because we didn't have the effrontery to do it," said Whitten. "We admired his fuck-all attitude."

Wolfe eventually branched out into international news, writing a long feature on Castro's newly hatched Cuban revolution "because none of the other writers felt like going to Cuba." Armed with a portfolio of presentable articles, Wolfe sent off a scrapbook of his clippings to the *Tribune's* Buddy Weiss in late 1961. He was hired on the spot at $9,000 a year as a replacement for departing reporter Lewis Lapham. Wolfe's supercharged copy, Weiss reasoned, was a fitting compliment to the *Tribune's* high-definition prose style. After a liquid lunch with John Denson at Toots Shor's, where the *Tribune's* editor made Wolfe pound five drinks at the bar, Wolfe realized that he had made the great leap into the world's capital of newsprint, and he could hardly believe his good fortune. "This must be the place!" Wolfe wrote a decade later. "I looked out across the city room of the *Herald Tribune,* 100 moldering yards south of Times Square, with a feeling of amazed bohemian bliss. . . . Either this is the real world, Tom, or there is no real world."

Wolfe may have stood out from the crowd at his previous two jobs, but he was running up against some formidable competition at the *Trib.* There was Breslin, but also Charles Portis, a gifted general-assignment reporter and fellow southerner from Arkansas who filed some of the era's best newspaper pieces on the civil rights movement, and Dick Schaap, who had quit his job as the city editor of the paper to write features. Portis and Wolfe would later become friendly when the two worked on the rewrite desk, much to the dismay of rewrite editor Inky Blackman, who felt the two writers bantered too much during lulls. There was also Sanche de Gramont, a French count who won a Pulitzer Prize on the rewrite bank while covering the death of Metropolitan Opera singer Leonard Warren, who in the autumn of 1960 had collapsed from a heart attack in midperformance. De Gramont, who changed his name to Ted Morgan, would later become an acclaimed biographer of Winston Churchill and Somerset Maugham, among others.

Wolfe was entranced by all the talent in that enormous, clattering, smoke-filled room, with its exposed "electrical conduits, water pipes, steam pipes, effluvium ducts, sprinkler systems all of it dangling and grunting from the ceiling," the walls painted in "industrial sludge . . . that grim distemper of pigment and filth." It was one "big pie factory, a landlord's dream," and Wolfe breathed it in lovingly. The southern initiate had found his Valhalla. "I still get a terrific kick out of riding down

Park Avenue in a cab at 2:30 in the morning and seeing the glass buildings all around," said Wolfe in 1974. " I have a real cornball attitude
towards [New York]."

Wolfe stood out from the rolled-up-sleeve culture of the *Tribune*
in more ways than one. At Washington and Lee, he had begun to wear
custom-tailored three-piece suits with pocket squares and extra-wide
ties–"Tom Sawyer drawn by Beardsley," one wag would later write. It
was a look Wolfe cultivated in part because his father had dressed that
way, and also because it set him apart in a respectably eccentric manner.
"I didn't have any other minor vices," said Wolfe. "I didn't belong to a
club, I didn't play tennis or golf or take vacations. My wardrobe budget
was the kind of money you spend on a hobby." Wolfe got his suits cus-
tom-made by a traveling employee of the esteemed Savile Row tailor
Hicks and Sons for $212. Now he was reporting for work at the *Trib* in
those threads, and it sent a little tremor of speculation throughout the
city room. Who was this guy, anyway?

"I think the thing that really annoyed people was the nipped-in
waist," Wolfe said. "That seemed unpatriotic, a real affectation. But my
contention is that all men are fashion-conscious; they just want to fit in.
I could have attracted more attention to myself–I could have worn a
dashiki, for example–but I wanted to be in the game. The important
thing was, I wanted them to say, 'Who in the name of God does he think
he is?'"

From the start, Wolfe's stories for the *Trib* were written in his hyperac-
tive style. Even for a paper that encouraged fanciful departures from the
usual gray reportorial formula, Wolfe's approach stood out. It didn't
matter what the story was about; Wolfe would Wolfeorize it. In a two-
column throwaway piece about bad winter weather, Wolfe described a
"mean, low-down cold streak, made up of practically every foul blow in
the book." In another early story, Wolfe wrote about frat boys, "with
eyes that looked like poached eggs engraved with a road map of West
Virginia, those guys who were trying to stumble, stagger, fall down,
grope, heave, lurch, list and tetter their way through the lines of an aria
called 'Dirty Lil.'"

Another early story, which ran on April 13, 1962, reported on a rent
strike by New York University students, and the activities of some of the
protesting students:

A willowy co-ed with Godiva-length blonde hair came forth from the throng and, to symbolize the approach of a new day, showed how she combed her lavish locks each morning: 20 runs from head to hips along each strand. Some applauded rhythmically and others chanted: Yes, yes.

The salient facts of the story weren't Wolfe's primary concern, although he always had them all in place; the idea was to set the scene with an accretion of peculiar details that other reporters might find tangential, but which were in fact crucial to the event in question—and to Wolfe's meticulously constructed mise-en-scène. "I learned that from Gay Talese, who was very good at reporting a story until you had the little things that helped bring the big things to life," said Wolfe. "You just had to be around, hang out."

Wolfe might hold off on the expository "nut graph" until the middle of the piece and forcefully guide the reader into the story from some other starting point, pulling back slowly to reveal the true subject. Wolfe's language was something else entirely, a vivid Technicolor vernacular that had editors scratching their heads and fellow *Tribune* writers wondering just what the hell he was doing. In Wolfe's stories, the East River was "chilled hogwash," paperback books were "white-meat slabs of revelation and culture," Grand Central Station was "the glamour depot of the East." The florid language was in part derived from Wolfe's love of southern patois, the rich, honeyed speech patterns of Virginia's native sons and daughters. But he also loved the gossip sheets and pulp magazines of his youth, the slangy prose of *Confidential* and *True Detective* magazines, with their playful double entendres, lurid metaphors, and adjectival sprees.

His main literary influence was a school of Russian avant-garde writers he had read at Yale called the Serapion Brothers, who came of age during the 1920s and were thus under pressure to produce agitprop for Stalin. Instead, they rebelled against literary conformity and pledged an ethic of absolute freedom from doctrine, state-sponsored or otherwise. The movement's leader, Eugene Zamiatin, was a brash and formally brilliant satirist, a naval engineer who also wrote plays, short stories, and novels. His major work, *We*, which was published in 1929, was a savage indictment of Soviet collectivist groupthink that presaged Orwell's

1984. But it was Zamiatin's prose that had a profound impact on Wolfe's work—the way he broke up sentences with ellipses in order to mimic nonlinear thought, and liberally used exclamation points. Wolfe's habit of writing stories in the historical present—a conceit that would become a trademark of his *Esquire* stories—was picked up from a popular biography of Napoleon by Polish writer Emil Ludwig that was published in the States in 1925. Wolfe became enamored of Ludwig's style as an eight-year-old, transcribing passages from Ludwig's book into his own heavily plagiarized biography of Napoleon.

He folded all of it into his articles—anything to avoid sounding like the "usual non-fiction narrator with a hush in my voice, like a radio announcer at a tennis match."

Jim Bellows worked him ragged, but Wolfe chafed at the space restrictions he was given in the daily paper. Not all of the subject matter was that interesting, either—writing stories about the new baggage carts at Grand Central or the increase in liquor tax wasn't going to rock the city to its foundations. He needed an outlet such as the one the *Times*'s Gay Talese had with *Esquire,* and he wouldn't have to look very far to find it.

Today's Living, the magazine supplement of the *Trib*'s Sunday edition, had been an Achilles' heel for years, but Bellows was open to new ideas. Working with editor Shelly Zalaznick and Clay Felker, Bellows mapped out some basic ideas for the magazine, which would be renamed *New York.* Each week Breslin and Wolfe would contribute a story. A staff of arts columnists, including classical music critic Alan Rich, film critic Judith Crist, and theater critic Walter Kerr, would be featured in the Lively Arts section. Design editor Peter Palazzo would create a classy template that would give the entire Sunday paper a nice lift. And, just to make sure everyone at least rifled through it, the TV listings would go in the back of the book.

Clay Felker, working closely with Shelly Zalaznick as an editorial consultant, orchestrated Tom Wolfe's transition from workaday general assignment reporter to magazine feature writer. "It's rare to find someone with real insight into good ideas, but Clay had the ability to match the right writer up with the story," said Zalaznick. Given Bellows's directive to come up with stories for Wolfe, Felker thought the reporter might be interested in a piece on the mad moneyed oglers who swarmed the art galleries every Saturday afternoon on Madison Avenue, the city's high-end retail artery. A shade over three thousand words long, "The Saturday Route" was the longest story Wolfe had filed for the *Trib,* and it started a run of pieces in which Wolfe observed the rituals of Manhattan's cultural tribes with a mixture of gentle mockery and the bemused wonder of a Virginia transplant:

> Is that Joan Morse, the fabulous dressmaker, over there on the curb? With that fabulous Claude yellow heath coat, those knee-high Rolls Royce maroon boots and the biggest sunglasses since Audrey Hepburn sunbathed on a cantilevered terrace in the Swiss Alps? Well, it *has* to be Joan Morse.
>
> "Joan!"
>
> And there at Madison Avenue and 74th Street Joan Morse, owner of A La Carte, which ranks in fabulosity with Mainbocher, swings around and yells: "Freddie! I saw you in Paris, but what happened to you in London?" . . .
>
> One is not to find out immediately, because the light has just changed. Joan is doing the Saturday Route *down* Madison Avenue. Freddie is doing the Saturday Route *up* Madison Avenue. But they keep on walking because they know they will meet sooner or later at Parke-Bernet and catch up on London.

Cinched in by the two-column stories he was filing for the paper, Wolfe's style took off like Air Force One in *New York.* Wolfe and Felker became the paper's trend spotters, with Wolfe filing stories on subjects that the *Trib* never would have taken seriously before: record producer Phil Spector, the Peppermint Lounge nightclub, stock car racing on Long Island. Two days a week, he was cranking out straight news stories as a general assignment reporter; the other three days were blocked off for a fifteen-hundred-word feature to run in *New York.* "Tom once told me that his body had taken more of a beating from writing than from playing baseball," said Elaine Dundy, a writer who dated Wolfe during the *Tribune* era.

In the *Trib* newsroom, opinion was divided as to whether the Virginian was a brilliant talent or just a facile trickster, a careerist with a marketing hook. Some, such as Jimmy Breslin, respected Wolfe as a dogged reporter who worked as hard as anyone to get his stories. "Everyone would make such a fuss about his clothes, but I knew he was a serious reporter, someone who did the legwork," he said. Others, including city reporter Dave Burgin, didn't understand what the fuss was about. "I didn't get it myself," said Burgin, who commiserated with a number of *Trib* writers who thought the paper's "Manhattan fop" was getting too much attention from Bellows. "Some guys were insanely jealous of him," said Burgin. "But no one, not even Bellows, could get him to take the punctuation out. I remember one guy, a business writer, told me, 'If I thought an exclamation point or two would get me a raise, I would have done it a long time ago.'"

Wolfe was fascinated by the insurgency of urban youth, largely because he felt it was the story of the decade, and he had the territory all to himself. "When I reached New York in the sixties, I couldn't believe the scene I saw spread out before me," Wolfe wrote in the *New Journalism* anthology. "New York was pandemonium with a big grin on."

What fascinated Wolfe were the myriad ways in which people with money were carving out new ways of living—novel approaches to leisure time, new choices in music, fashion, and film, and most important, new approaches to flaunting status. For Wolfe, New York was one big collection of "statuspheres," each with its own rules of engagement and hierarchies based on fame, style, and infamy, rather than archaic notions of an established social order. "When great fame—the certification of status—is available without great property," Wolfe wrote in the introduction to *The Pump House Gang,* his 1965 anthology, "it is very bad news for the old idea of a class structure. In New York . . . it is done for, but no one has bothered to announce its death."

As a southern outsider trying to carve his own niche in New York's hotly competitive newspaper world, the notion of self-made status appealed to Wolfe. "Wolfe is a kind of aristocrat, but he doesn't admit it," said Gay Talese. "He's southern gentry, but he's a classy man. The best manners I've ever seen. There is a combativeness about him, but Tom never spoke ill of anyone."

Esquire editor Byron Dobell had spotted a story that Wolfe had written, about the 1962 gubernatorial campaign between Nelson Rockefeller and district attorney Robert Morgenthau, and contacted him about writing pieces for the magazine. His first published piece for *Esquire,* a profile of heavyweight contender Cassius Clay called "The Marvelous

Mouth" that ran in the October 1963 issue, was trouble from the start. Clay wanted *Esquire* to pay him for the interview. Harold Hayes rejected that idea outright: most subjects were proud and honored to be interviewed by *Esquire*. Clay didn't want honor; he wanted cash. Hayes finally agreed to pay Clay $150—$50 when he met with Wolfe, $50 during the second interview, and $50 when Wolfe's time with him was completed.

During Wolfe's first meeting with Clay, which took place at the Americana Hotel in Times Square, Wolfe noticed that the champ wore the call letters of the New York radio station WNEW on his black tie—a small endorsement deal that paid him $150. Clay begged Wolfe not to mention it in his article. "As it turned out, the Louisville syndicate that handled Clay didn't want him to have any money, so he wouldn't wind up like so many boxers, with big entourages and distractions," said Wolfe.

Clay had so many reservations about Wolfe's questions that the formal sit-down interview was virtually useless. Wolfe soon realized that he would get his story by observing Clay in his element—the Gay Talese technique of "just hanging out." Trailing Clay to the Metropole Café, where the fighter was swarmed by goggle-eyed fans, Wolfe took notice of the quiet grace and dignity of the fighter, the unflappable cool. At one point the reporter noticed a white man, "obviously a Southerner from the way he talked," requesting an autograph:

> "Here you are, boy, put your name right there."
> It was more or less the same voice Mississippians use on a hot day when the colored messenger boy has come into the living room and is standing around nervously. "Go ahead, boy, sit down. Sit in that seat right there."
> Cassius took the Pennsylvania Railroad receipt without looking up at the man, and held it for about ten seconds, just staring at it.
> "Where's your pen?"
> "I don't have a pen, boy. Some of these people around here got a pen. Just put your name right there."
> Cassius still didn't look up. He just said, "Man, there's one thing you gotta learn. You don't *ever* come around and ask a man for an autograph if you ain't got no pen."

The notion for Wolfe's next *Esquire* story was inspired by the annual car show at the New York Coliseum, in which numerous examples of the latest custom cars—or "Kustom Kars," in West Coast insider's parlance—from Los Angeles were on display. Wolfe, who was covering the show for the *Tribune*, was fascinated by the cars—tricked-out hot rods with exposed engines, bold graphics, blue- and red-flake paint jobs, designed by little-known customizers such as Dale Alexander, George Barris, and Ed Roth. "It's the automobile that's the most important story today," Wolfe told *Saturday Review* in 1965. "The automobile dominates society. To incredible numbers of people, the automobile is a cult object." Wolfe pitched *Esquire* on a piece on custom cars—he would fly to Los Angeles and observe the phenomenon in its natural element, then write a feature with far greater scope than even *New York* magazine could accommodate.

Wolfe was overwhelmed by what he saw in L.A. It was the efflorescence of what he had witnessed in small doses in New York—the youth movement writ large. At the Teen Fair, an annual event in Santa Monica that functioned as a kind of pop-cultural World's Fair, produced by a few savvy businessmen, Wolfe witnessed the West Coast statuspheres—the surfers, the drag racers, the fruggers and twisters—converge on an event that combined rock music, teen product peddlers, and most important, the flamboyant custom cars of Barris, Roth, Von Dutch, and others. He went to Barris's shop, Kustom City, in North Hollywood, where Barris showed him how the cars were manufactured and then painstakingly painted and airbrushed. "Wolfe spent many hours, many days with me. He even came over to the house and cooked dinner with my wife," said Barris. "He wanted to know everything about the cars, and it was great for me, because of the publicity."

Wolfe had an abundance of interview material, but he was flummoxed as to how he should organize it into a cohesive story. What he lacked was a thesis, a compelling through-line that could justify three thousand words. He knew that the custom car subculture was unprecedented, but what did it represent? For a week he sat in front of his typewriter in his studio apartment in Greenwich Village, waiting for inspiration to strike, watching TV and doing sit-ups to keep himself occupied.

A call from Wolfe to Byron Dobell put the *Esquire* editor on alert that a story might not materialize after all. The magazine's art department already had a color photo of a Barris car from the New York show in place, and the magazine's production schedule dictated that stories with color art had to go to the printers first, before the rest of the issue. *Esquire*'s small budget couldn't accommodate a rewrite man to fashion the story from Wolfe's notes; if Wolfe couldn't make it work, then Dobell would write a few paragraphs to accompany the picture, and that would be the story.

"I was anxious to get something," said Dobell. "Wolfe always had difficulties with deadlines, but we were ready to roll without any text. I just asked him to tell me enough information so I could write the copy myself."

Wolfe was panicked. Starting at eight o'clock one night, he sat down and began typing a memo to Dobell that described everything he had seen in L.A., from the moment he first laid eyes on Barris's cars to the goings-on at the Teen Fair. Fueled on coffee (a habit he would kick a few years later) and an AM radio blaring Top 40 pop, Wolfe didn't stop typing until six-fifteen the next morning; by that time, the memo had swelled to forty-nine typewritten pages. He walked to *Esquire*'s offices as soon as the place opened at nine-thirty, and turned in his memo to Dobell.

"I read it and thought, 'Well, this is something new,'" said Dobell. "The story was there, even though Wolfe didn't know it. I walked into Harold Hayes's office and said, 'Don't worry, this is an astonishing piece.' It was well worth all of the strain and nervousness."

Dobell barely amended it, excising a few vernacular asides ("He had a lot of 'for Christ sakes' in there for some reason, little filler kind of things") and crossing out the "Dear Byron" salutation at the top of the memo. The throat-clearing headline—"There goes (VAROOM! VAROOM!) that Kandy-Kolored (THPHHHHHH!) tangerine-flake streamline baby (RAHGHHHH!) around the bend (BRUMMMMM-MMMMMMMMMMM . . .)"—was Dobell's.

A thesis had emerged from the accretion of detail that Wolfe had recorded in the memo, namely, that custom cars represented an overlooked episode in contemporary art history, the convergence of postwar prosperity with a new, ritualized formalism that wasn't beholden to, or even cognizant of, anything that had preceded it. "I don't mind observing," Wolfe wrote in the story, "that it is this same combination—money plus slavish devotion to form—that accounts for Versailles or St. Mark's Square."

"My definition of art is anything that you can take out of its natural environment and regard as something that's beautiful and significant unto itself," said Wolfe. "Customized cars were art, with those exposed motors and shiny chrome parts." In the story Wolfe made grand claims for custom cars as high art on a par with the works of Brancusi, Dalí, and Mondrian—perhaps even more significant. He called the Teen Fair a "Plato's *Republic* for teenagers" and wrote that the cars meant more "to these kids than architecture did in Europe's great formal century, say 1750 to 1850. They are freedom, style, sex, power, motion, color—everything is right there." Wolfe framed Barris and Ed Roth, the other major customizer in L.A., as outsider artists working under the cultural radar. "They're like Easter Islanders," Wolfe wrote of their custom cars. "Suddenly you come upon the astonishing objects, and then you have to figure out how they got there and why they're there."

Everywhere he looked on the streets of Los Angeles, Wolfe found vernacular art. The city's buildings were "shaped not like rectangles but like trapezoids, from the way the roofs slant up from the back and the plate-glass fronts slant out as if they're going to pitch forward on the sidewalk and throw up." Here was a New York–based writer giving serious consideration to West Coast culture in all of its magnificently gaudy (as in Gaudi) splendor. For *Esquire*, a magazine that regarded New York as the epicenter of just about everything, Wolfe's story was a revelation, evidence of life on the other side of the country.

"When I started writing in what became known as my style, I was trying to capture the newness and excitement of the West Coast thing," said Wolfe. "It's where all the exciting youth styles were coming from. They certainly weren't coming from New York. Everything I was writing about was new to the East Coast."

Hayes loved it, but Felker wasn't pleased that Wolfe was moonlighting for *Esquire* when he should have been writing his longer features exclusively for *New York*. Once again, Hayes and Felker found themselves at loggerheads, with Wolfe in the middle. "None of us were really pleased with the arrangement, especially Clay," said Shelly Zalaznick. "I hated the idea of Tom working for others, but it was something that Tom had worked out with Bellows, and so we really couldn't do anything about it."

For Wolfe, it was the best of all possible worlds. Not only did he have job security at the *Tribune,* but now he was making an impact on a national level, producing stories for the most talked-about magazine in America. He had never worked harder, but the six years Wolfe spent writing for both the *Tribune* and *Esquire* transformed him into a reporter–cum–cultural icon and produced some of the most vibrant journalism of the decade.

4

TOM WOLFE ON ACID

Tom Wolfe was juggling a monstrous schedule. Jim Bellows, Clay Felker (who had replaced Shelly Zalaznick as editor of *New York*), and Harold Hayes were tugging him every which way, and he willingly followed. After a few years of general assignment sloggery, he now had two prominent outlets that gave him a wide berth to write as he pleased. It came at a great time; everywhere Wolfe turned, he saw the old culture being plowed under and upended by new ways of living, thinking, playing. Wolfe was anxious to chronicle as much of it as he could—to write about all of it and become the authoritative voice of the decade's new vanguard. That every reporter in New York wasn't following suit was unfathomable to him.

In his features for the *Tribune* and *Esquire*, Wolfe cut a wide swath through the culture—the gambling rituals and psychiatric breakdowns of Las Vegas casino crawlers, new national pastimes such as drag racing on Long Island, teen cultural arbiters including popular radio DJ Murray the K and hipster habitué Baby Jane Holzer, and the "Nanny Mafia" of housekeepers among New York's upper class.

For *Esquire* stories that took him out of town, Wolfe traveled on weekends and wrote at night. "What I spent on those trips was always more than I ever earned," said Wolfe. "But the idea was to do more reporting than anyone had ever done before."

In 1964, *Esquire* editor Bob Sherrill suggested that Wolfe head out to Wilkes-Barre, North Carolina, to interview stock car driver Junior

Johnson, a colorful character whom Sherrill had first gotten wind of while working as a newspaper editor in Stanford, North Carolina. Johnson was a big deal in his home state, the subject of many local stories, but no one with Wolfe's skill had tackled him yet. Wolfe, ditching his white suit for green tweed this time in order to blend in a bit, made "countless, I don't know how many" trips to North Carolina, quietly insinuating himself with Johnson, a former bootlegger who had learned how to drive by keeping one step ahead of the feds. Wolfe had never worked harder on a story, but it was worth it. A 20,000-word epic, "The Last American Hero Is Junior Johnson, Yes!" was Wolfe's exegesis of the good-ol'-boy South. It was world's apart from the patrician South of his upbringing, but no less fascinating. Wolfe had done it again; coming into the subject cold, he had written the best magazine feature on stock car racing thus far.

In his *Esquire* story "Las Vegas (What?) Las Vegas (Can't Hear You! Too Noisy) Las Vegas!!!" Wolfe portrayed the Nevada gambling mecca as a netherworld of sleep-deprived psychosis and temporary euphoria, bathed in the bright, eternal glow of its neon signs: "Boomerang Modern, Palette Curvilinear, Flash Gordon Ming-Alert Spiral, McDonald's Hamburger Parabola, Mint Casino Elliptic, Miami Beach Kidney." Wolfe panned across the diverse cross section of Vegas dwellers, stopping to admire the "buttocks décolletage" of certain Vegas women, whose "bikini-style shorts . . . cut across the round fatty masses of the buttocks rather than cupping them from below, so that the outer-lower edges of these fatty masses, or 'cheeks,' are exposed." Here are the "old babes at the row upon row of slot machines," their "hummocky shanks" packed into capri pants, with a "Dixie cup full of nickels or dimes in the left hand and an Iron Boy work glove on the right hand to keep the calluses from getting sore." Wolfe leads the reader into the inner circles of Vegas hell, down into the county jail and the psychiatric ward of the county hospital, where those "who have taken the loop-the-loop and could not stand the centripity" come to heal themselves.

So eager was Wolfe to provide the definitive story on Vegas culture that his original draft was nearly twice as long as the final version that ran in the magazine; brevity was not his strong suit, and his stories often entailed massive paring and trimming.

Wolfe was pushing his language deeper into whimsical metaphor. His sentences were being pulled and distended to the edge of prolixity, and he was using onomatopoeia; Wolfe's pieces came with their own sound effects. The opening sentence of the Vegas story was a single word repeated 57 times: "Hernia, hernia, hernia, hernia, hernia, HERNia, hernia . . ." a device meant to convey the running drone of the stick men at the craps tables. In his Junior Johnson story, Wolfe wrote "Ggghhzzzzzzzhhhhhhgggggggzzzzzzzeeeeeong!–gawdam!" to simulate the sound of Johnson's car peeling out. In the lead paragraph for his story on Baby Jane Holzer, called "The Girl of the Year," Wolfe discovered another effective technique, the run-on enumeration of fashion details:

> Bangs manes bouffants beehives Beatle caps butter faces brush-on lashes decal eyes puffy sweaters French thrust bras flailing leather blue jeans stretch pants stretch jeans honeydew bottoms éclair shanks elf books ballerinas Knight slippers, hundreds of them, these flaming little buds, bobbing and screaming, rocketing around inside the Academy of Music Theater underneath that vast old mouldering cherub dome up there–aren't they super-marvelous!

The publishing world was taking notice. In the winter of 1965, Lynn Nesbit, a twenty-five-year-old junior agent, contacted Wolfe about taking him on as a client. "Lynn called me out of the blue," according to Wolfe, "and said, 'Don't you know you have a book here?'" Nesbit, who had started out as a secretary for leading agent Sterling Lord and thus came armed with a solid Rolodex, suggested to Wolfe that a collection of his stories might be something she could sell. "I was this fresh-faced girl from the Midwest, but Tom liked the fact that I was a straight shooter," said Nesbit. "He was actually thinking about writing a novel at that time, but I loved his work, so he took a chance on me, I'm not sure why."

Nesbit packaged the book of pieces along with Wolfe's novel proposal and sold a two-book contract to editor Henry Robbins at Farrar, Straus and Giroux for a solid four-figure fee–much to the dismay of Clay Felker, who was working as an editorial consultant for Viking Press and felt proprietary toward Wolfe and his work, particularly since he had shepherded many of the pieces into publication. "Clay Felker didn't talk to me for ten years because he didn't get Tom's first book," said Nesbit. And Tom Guinzburg, the editor in chief of Viking, was so furious at

Nesbit for not giving him the book that he refused to participate in the auction process that Nesbit had initiated.

Working with Robbins, Wolfe lightly edited a few pieces, then got back to the business of the novel. "Henry was a very sensitive literary person," said Wolfe. "I was very grateful that he and [Farrar, Straus and Giroux cofounder] Roger Straus found some merit in a book of pieces. Quite a few publishers had said, 'Look, you publish a real book and then we'll publish this one afterwards.'"

The Kandy-Kolored Tangerine-Flake Streamline Baby was published in July 1965. Reviews were mixed. Joseph Epstein, writing in a *New Republic* review titled "Rococo and Roll," called Wolfe an "intellectual slummer" who struck "a note of supreme reverse condescension" when writing about underclass bohos such as Holzer and the Twisters at New York's Peppermint Lounge. Yet Epstein found his satirical jabs at New York status-mongers, such as the "glamorosi" in his story "The Big League Complex," to be spot-on. Emile Capouya, writing in *Saturday Review,* found it "hard to be grateful for Mr. Wolfe's industrious researches, his eye for the characteristic triviality, and his very lively style," which is mostly "exclamatory and goes on too long."

No matter; the book was an immediate hit. A month after its July publication, it had already gone into its fourth printing. The success of *Kandy-Kolored,* coupled with Wolfe's savaging of *The New Yorker* in his *Tribune* stories, which ran in April of that year, made the writer the enfant terrible of American journalism, whose genteel disposition concealed a sharply subversive wit. Wolfe was being profiled in *Time* and *Newsweek,* interviewed on network television, and feted at parties from Richmond, Virginia, to San Diego, California, where, *Vogue* pointed out, "he appeared in a white-on-white suit kissing the ladies' hands."

The Kandy-Kolored Tangerine-Flake Streamline Baby expanded Wolfe's audience considerably. Now his pieces were being underlined and dog-eared by college students who felt the writer was providing an important forum for voices and cultural trends that had not been given their proper due in the mainstream media. If not quite a countercultural spokesman, Wolfe was certainly in consonance with the incipient cultural sea change. But he had written over 150,000 words in fifteen months, in countless features for both the *Tribune* and *Esquire,* and he wanted to try his hand at a book-length project—if not the epic social realist novel that he longed to write, then an epic nonfiction project with a compelling narrative at its center. "I had enough pieces for another collection, but I didn't want to keep turning out collections," said Wolfe. "I held off on publishing another one until I could get a real book done."

He found his book subject in July 1966, when he received a cache of letters from an anonymous sender. The letters, which were addressed to novelist Larry McMurtry, were written by author Ken Kesey, who had been busted for marijuana possession in April 1965 and again in January 1966 and had jumped bail to Mexico, where he was in exile. The letters had been passed along through the large network of Kesey's friends and followers. Ed McClanahan, a writer and editor who had known Kesey when the two were in Wallace Stegner's fiction writing class together at Stanford University, had sent the letters in the hope that Wolfe might want to write something about Kesey. "At the time," said Wolfe, "Kesey felt, quite correctly, that if you're in legal trouble, the bigger a celebrity you are, the better chance you'll have of beating the rap."

McClanahan had already tried once to get Kesey's story out there. Fellow Stegner alumnus Robert Stone had been assigned to write a story on Kesey for *Esquire,* but the magazine had killed the piece, so McClanahan published it in a literary anthology he was coediting with Fred Nelson called *One Lord, One Faith, One Cornbread.* But that was a little magazine for a little audience. "I knew that Bob's enterprise with *Esquire* had come a cropper 'cause they were too thickheaded to know what it was all about," said McClanahan, who had obtained the McMurtry letters through Kesey's lawyer, Paul Robertson, and felt they could be a great jumping-off point for a book. When Henry Robbins, who had signed McClanahan to a book contract, went to San Francisco to visit the writer in the summer of 1966, McClanahan suggested that Wolfe might be the perfect Boswell for Kesey. "I just thought Wolfe's style just went with what Kesey was doing," said McClanahan.

Wolfe was intrigued. The letters, he later wrote, were "wild and ironic ... written like a cross between William Burroughs and George Ade telling of disguises, paranoia, running from cops, smoking joints and seeking *satori* in the rat lands of Mexico." One Kesey letter provided some biographical background:

Once an athlete so valued he had been given the job of calling signals from the line and risen into contention for the nationwide amateur wrestling crown, now he didn't know if he could do a dozen
pushups. Once possessor of a phenomenal bank account and money
waving from every hand, now it was all his poor wife could do to
scrape together eight dollars to send as getaway money to Mexico.
But a few years previous he had been listed in *Who's Who* and asked
to speak at such auspicious gatherings as the Wellesley Club in Dah-
la and now they wouldn't even allow him to speak at a VDC [Viet-
nam Day Committee] gathering. What was it that had brought a
man so high of promise to so low a state in so short a time? Well, the
answer can be found in just one short word, my friends, in just one
all-well-used syllable: "Dope!"

Wolfe was drawn in by the wild head-charge of Kesey's writing, its
vivacity and gallows humor. He knew very little about Kesey other than
his book about corruption in a mental institution, *One Flew over the
Cuckoo's Nest,* a huge best-seller in 1962, and the follow-up about an
Oregon logging family, 1964's *Sometimes a Great Notion.* Wolfe was a big
fan of *Cuckoo's Nest*—he could tell that Kesey had done his homework,
New Journalism–style—but as it turned out, Kesey's life story was every
bit as intriguing.

Ken Kesey was raised on a farm that his father owned in Springfeld,
Oregon. Like Tom Wolfe Sr., Fred Kesey operated a collective, the
Eugene Farmers Cooperative, which he turned into one of the biggest
dairy operations in the state. A strapping athlete with literary aspirations,
eighteen-year-old Ken Kesey enrolled in the University of Oregon in
1953 and earned a bachelor's degree in journalism. In 1959 he received a
creative writing fellowship from Stanford to study with Wallace Stegner.
Kesey wrote during the day and worked the night shift at a psychiatric
hospital in nearby Menlo Park. He lived on Perry Lane, a small Palo Alto
bohemian enclave adjacent to the Stanford golf course, where he discussed literature and politics with the group of artists and writers that
had settled into the placid rhythms of the place.

His first exposure to hallucinogens occurred at the Menlo Park hospital when he volunteered to take part in experiments with LSD for sci-
entific research. Kesey's initiations into the world of psychoactive drugs

and mental illness provided the raw material for *Cuckoo's Nest* (Kesey wrote sections of *Cuckoo's Nest* while on peyote and LSD). The book's allegory about institutionalized repression resonated with young readers, and the book made Kesey enough money to live comfortably and support his future endeavors. He purchased a plot of land in La Honda, a mountainous rural outpost near Stanford, and began an experiment in communal living with fellow Stanford alumni and various other friends and family members.

The group would become known as the Merry Pranksters, with Kesey presiding over it all like a benign pasha. Meals were taken together, women were shared, and drugs were consumed in prodigious quantities. It was Kesey's firm belief that LSD was a portal to a higher consciousness; the Pranksters proselytized the good word with a series of Acid Tests that transpired all over northern and central California. Using an arsenal of bright, colorful electric lights, Day-Glo paint, and amplified music, Kesey and the Pranksters created a warmly communal atmosphere in which initiates would drop acid and burrow deep into their inner selves. This was the path to a new age of enlightenment, Kesey was convinced. "When they tripped, Kesey's instructions were, 'Whatever you are on your trip, that's who you truly are,'" said Wolfe. "If someone did something strange, or had a breakdown, that was their trip."

Wolfe wasn't so sure, but Kesey was a fascinating figure engaged, Wolfe felt, in no less than the founding of a secular religion. "At the time, I didn't know of the word *hippie*," said Wolfe. "The press saw the potential of these people, but they used terms like *acidhead*. To me, *acidhead* sounded like a corrosive battery. There was also the name *hippiedippie*, which brought to mind Christlike Renaissance figures." Kesey appealed to Wolfe's sense of fun and adventure, of forging new lifestyles from the effluvia of pop culture. "Unlike Timothy Leary, Kesey was influenced by comic books," said Wolfe. "He dressed in military outfits, used Day-Glo paint and acid rock as tools. Leary felt it was enough to just sit in your ashram and meditate. Kesey wanted people to move off of dead center. If you didn't do that, you were dead."

Wolfe decided he would go to Mexico City for the *Tribune*, hang out with Kesey, and file a story for *New York* about the author's eight months as a fugitive. But by the time Wolfe had booked his plane ticket, Kesey was already back in the States. Attempting to sneak across the border from Mexico, he had been arrested on the Bayshore Freeway south of San Francisco by the FBI. Wolfe decamped to the San Mateo county jail in Redwood City, California, where Kesey was being held pending his release on $35,000 bail.

At the jail Wolfe encountered a scene "like the stage door at the Music Box Theatre," with a colorful clutch of Kesey supporters sitting vigil in the waiting room, throwing the I Ching or silently praying. After haggling with the prison guards, Wolfe, accompanied by Ed McClanahan, was granted a ten-minute visit with Kesey. Although they were separated by thick plate glass, Wolfe was taken by the sheer mass and bulk of Kesey, his "thick wrists and forearms" and his "big neck with a pair of sternocleido-mastoid muscles that [rose] up out of the prison work shirt like a couple of dock ropes." Wolfe frantically flung questions at Kesey about some statements he had made in the local press about moving "beyond acid," and Kesey, through the lo-fi crackle of the phone, told him that "it's time to graduate from what's been going on, to something else." When Wolfe asked him why he had publicly announced his retirement from writing, Kesey told him, "I'd rather be a lightning rod than a seismograph."

Wolfe was drawn into Kesey's force field, taken in by the "strange up-country charisma" of the man. He traveled with some of the Merry Pranksters to an old pie factory on the ground floor of an abandoned hotel on Harriet Street in San Francisco, where they awaited their leader's return. Wolfe, wearing his white suit and wielding a reporter's notepad, witnessed men and women wandering around the vast space in white overalls with patches fashioned from American flags. Theatrical scaffolding lined the walls, with blankets filling in for curtains; there were mattresses strewn everywhere, and a school bus sat in the center of the warehouse, painted in a striking array of Day-Glo colors, "like a cross between Fernand Léger and Dr. Strange." Next to the bus, some Pranksters were painting a sign that read ACID TEST GRADUATION. Off to one side was Neal Cassady, the protagonist (as Dean Moriarty) of Jack Kerouac's 1950 novel *On the Road* and a Beat Generation icon, repeatedly flipping a sledgehammer in the air and dextrously catching it by the handle.

Three days later Kesey, who was out of jail on bail raised by his old Perry Lane friends, arrived to a hero's welcome and barely registered the fact that Wolfe was in his midst, which was only to the writer's advantage: he could observe Kesey and the Pranksters' exploits without getting in the way. "We were beyond being freaked out by appearances," said George Walker, a Merry Prankster and one of Kesey's most trusted confidants at the time. "Tom was this very patrician guy who I don't think ever got down to shirtsleeves the whole time he was with us, but we were too busy with our own stuff to pay any attention to him."

Even for a group as willfully unconventional as the Merry Pranksters, it made for a bizarre tableau—a dandy among the heads. Wolfe observed the Prankster preparations for something called the Acid Test Graduation, accompanying Pranksters George Walker, Kesey's former Stanford colleague Ken Babbs, and others on bus trips to Kesey's compound in La Honda. "Despite the skepticism I brought here," Wolfe would later write, "*I* am suddenly experiencing *their* feeling. I am sure of it. I feel like I am onto something the outside world, the world I came from, could not possibly comprehend, and it *is* a metaphor, the whole scene, ancient and vast." The Pranksters were a true mystic brotherhood, "only in poor old Formica polyethylene 1960s America without a grain of desert sand or a shred of palm leaf or a morsel of manna wilderness breadfruit overhead, picking up vibrations from Ampex tapes and a juggled Williams Lok-Hed sledge hammer, hooking down mathematical lab drugs, LSD-25, IT-290, DMT, instead of soma water."

After a while, Kesey began to test Wolfe, entreating him to put down his steno pad, drop acid, and join the Pranksters as a participant rather than an observer. "Ken usually believed, and he was often right, that through his magnetism he could bring you around to his way of looking at things," said Wolfe. "But he and I were on different wavelengths." Still, the communal nature of the Pranksters' great utopian experiment appealed to Wolfe. Once when the two were dating, Elaine Dundy asked Wolfe if there was any subculture of which he had written whose lifestyle appealed to him the most. "He said, 'If I could stop what I was doing, I would be one of the Pranksters.' As an only child, he was rather lonely, so I think a group like that, who gave up the world without really rebelling in any violent way and supported each other, was attractive to him."

At La Honda, on Kesey's compound nestled among the tall redwood trees of the Santa Cruz mountain range, Wolfe took in the full expanse of the Pranksters' mad technological swirl of sound and vision, the ecstatic mixed with the sophomoric. There were speakers mounted on the roof of the house and strung along the trees, blasting Ornette Coleman's angular free jazz and Bob Dylan's plugged-in folk. Strange mobiles hung from tree branches; abstract art was nailed to the trunks. Inside Kesey's vast log cabin, tape recorders and 8 mm cameras and projectors were strewn about. These were the documentary tools for the Pranksters' experiments in all-in-one consciousness, the Acid Tests.

A few Pranksters made some halfhearted attempts to rattle Wolfe. One afternoon George Walker took the writer for a spin in his Lotus, taking the curves around Menlo Park at ninety miles per hour. By the joy ride's end, Wolfe was ashen and visibly shaken; Walker was amused but admired Wolfe's stoic professionalism. When Kesey moved the Pranksters' operations to La Honda from Harriet Street, Wolfe tagged along with Ed McClanahan in his sports car. As McClanahan negotiated mountain roads "that were as crooked as a goat's hind leg," Wolfe interviewed him, scribbling shorthand on a legal pad situated between them. "Every story I told him was letter-perfect in the book," said McClanahan. "I couldn't believe how good he was at it."

The Pranksters were preparing for the Acid Test Graduation, in which Kesey would tell his followers to move beyond acid into a new level of being. What that might be, even Kesey didn't know for sure. "It was quite strange, the mysticism of it," said Wolfe of the graduation, which was held in a San Francisco warehouse. "As the hour grew late, people were getting pretty high. It became a religious atmosphere, not unlike that of snake handlers."

"Their faces were painted in Art Nouveau swirls," Wolfe wrote.

Their Napoleon hats are painted, masks painted, hair dyed weird, embroidered Chinese pajamas, dresses made out of American flags, Flash Gordon diaphanous polyethylene, supermarket Saran Wrap . . . A hell of a circus, in short, a whole carnival banner, a panopticon.

Neal Cassady was wearing a mortarboard and holding a bunch of rolled-up diplomas, while Kesey lurked in the shadows, wearing a white leotard, a white satin cape, and a red, white, and blue sash across his chest. "It's . . . Captain America! The Flash! Captain Marvel! The Superhero, in a word." But the great revelation never came. Kesey made some abstract comments about not going through the same doors, moving beyond "the Garden of Eden." The crowd was befuddled by this, and the presence of a handful of cops didn't help. The crowd thinned as Halloween turned into November 1, and at 3 A.M., Kesey's inner circle gatherered in the middle of the floor and huddled close together, touching hands with their eyes closed in an attempt at some mass trance. At five, Neal Cassady handed out the diplomas to those who had made it through the evening and early morning, the true believers in the Prankster faith.

The whole Prankster experiment seemed to be trailing off into an uncertain future that night. Weeks later, Kesey was sentenced to a prison work farm. It would provide a fitting climax to Wolfe's story. He now had his opening—Kesey returning to his followers after reentering the country—and his ending. But what he originally intended as a standard feature of a few thousand words had ballooned into a three-part epic that ran in three issues of *New York* in January and February 1967. "The first part, setting the stage, was O.K.," Wolfe wrote in the *New York Times*. "The second and third were pretty thin stuff. Certainly they failed to capture the weird . . . fourth dimension I kept sensing in the Prankster adventure."

Kesey wasn't particularly impressed. "They're all right," he told Wolfe. "They'll . . . intrigue people." What they lacked, according to Kesey, was the marrow, the real substance, of the Prankster ethos—Wolfe hadn't delved deep enough.

The series, which was illustrated with Ted Streshinsky's photographs and supplemented with incidents that Wolfe learned about through extensive interviews with the Pranksters, wasn't subpar by any means. They were thorough investigative stories, but written with a reporter's detachment that came no closer to explaining the Pranksters' reality than the early press coverage Wolfe had dismissed as hopelessly stodgy. Wolfe explains, but he doesn't really reveal. A typical passage such as this one, in which Wolfe describes the effects of LSD, had the paternalistic tone of an educational film:

So far nobody in or out of the medical profession knows exactly what LSD does in the body, chiefly because so little is known about the workings of the central nervous system as a whole. It is the blackout on this score that has left so much room for mysticism in the LSD life.

The stories were, in short, too straight. There had to be a better way to approach Kesey's story, but it wouldn't fly in *New York*. This, Wolfe decided, was going to be the next book on his contract with Farrar, Straus and Giroux. The question then became, exactly what *was* going to work?

He was stuck, just as he had been with the custom car feature for *Esquire*. How to capture the comic-spiritual nature of the scene without trivializing it? What Wolfe struggled with was the metaphysical aspect of the story; it was impossible to do justice to the Pranksters without really describing the effects of hallucinogens on the mind-set of the group.

"I froze," recalls Wolfe, "because I somehow thought that it had to be something much more magnificent than a newspaper article, and writer's block is the fear of not being able to produce what you announced, even if you've only announced it to yourself. I thought, is this so insignificant that I shouldn't spend another minute on it? I kept trying to fit it into a regular newspaper feature form, and it wasn't that kind of story. Finally, I just went through the process and got it done."

Wolfe needed to go back to the West Coast and gather more anecdotes, probe the inner lives of Kesey and the Pranksters more rigorously. "I had to follow the Pranksters' story to the end, no matter how long it took." He had his first chapter and the ending; now he needed to fill the space in between. The spring 1964 bus trip on the International Harvester bus the Pranksters called "Furthur," in which the group traveled to New York and Canada, would provide the bulk of the narrative. But the acid trips would provide the meta-narrative—or, rather, the metaphysical narrative.

This objective presented a new set of problems. Anything Wolfe didn't witness firsthand would have to be re-created from interviews and whatever else he could get his hands on. So he went back to La Honda, tracked down Pranksters such as Ed McClanahan and Stewart Brand, and interviewed them at length about what acid really felt like, what visions they might have had on the drug, and how it altered their perception of the world. Because the Pranksters were so attuned to the use of multimedia, Wolfe had the advantage of a tremendous amount of audio and visual documentation, particularly films of various Acid Tests, which Kesey screened for him.

But the story itself was changing, and the truth was uglier than Wolfe had anticipated. There was a dark side to the Prankster experience for those who weren't as psychologically strong as Kesey and who looked to LSD as a palliative that might make them whole again. Sandy Lehmann-Haupt, Wolfe's primary source, was the saddest case of all. A sound engineer from New York, Sandy had been introduced to Kesey through his brother Carl, a colleague of Kesey's at Stanford during the Perry Lane era. Among the Pranksters, Sandy Lehmann-Haupt had a reputation for erratic behavior and manic-depressive tendencies—the life of the party who could without warning succumb to his worst impulses and turn against everyone, including Kesey, with whom he had a tempestuous relationship. "Sandy could be extremely ingratiating in his manic mode," said George Walker. "But he could also be an extreme drag."

Lehmann-Haupt's experience with Kesey had been marked by paranoid episodes and bad drug experiences. He had endured an unusually frightening trip on the powerful hallucinogen DMT during the Pranksters' visit with Timothy Leary at the LSD guru's Millbrook estate in upstate New York, as well as a series of unsettling flashbacks. When the Pranksters traveled to the Esalen Institute in Big Sur, California, Lehmann-Haupt, suffering from paranoid delusions, ran away to Monterey, fearful that Kesey had initiated a plot to kill him. Lehmann-Haupt eventually rejoined the Pranksters, but he incurred Kesey's wrath during the 1964 expedition, when he stole audio equipment from Kesey and headed back to New York on his motorcycle.

Despite his separation from Kesey, Lehmann-Haupt was still enamored of him for years afterward. "At the time that Tom talked to Sandy, I don't think he would have been averse to getting back in [with the Pranksters]," said Sandy's brother Christopher, who had retrieved Sandy from prison in Monterey when he was arrested for disturbing the peace. "He was very much hung up on Kesey, though I was very negative about the whole thing from the beginning." It was Sandy Lehmann-Haupt who, in a series of interviews with Wolfe in New York, provided Wolfe with the specifics for a number of important scenes, most crucially Kesey's primitive jungle existence as a fugitive in Mazatlán and Manzanillo, Mexico, his trip back to the States, and his subsequent arrest, as well as some of the intimate details of Kesey's extramarital relationship with Carolyn "Mountain Girl" Adams.

There was another disturbing undercurrent to the Prankster experience: their uneasy relationship with the Hell's Angels motorcycle gang. For information about Kesey and the Pranksters' encounter with the Angels at La Honda over Labor Day weekend, 1965–a toxic culture clash that would result in a gang rape–Wolfe turned to another writer, Hunter S. Thompson, who had spent considerable time with the motorcycle gang for his own book, *Hell's Angels: A Strange and Terrible Saga*.

Wolfe and Thompson's relationship had started inauspiciously. In 1965 Thompson was a struggling freelancer who was starting to make a name for himself as, among other things, a roving foreign correspondent for the *National Observer*, a newsweekly published by Dow Jones. When *The Kandy-Kolored Tangerine-Flake Streamline Baby* was published in July 1965, Thompson embraced it as a revolutionary step forward for American journalism and wrote a rave review of the book for the *Observer*. The magazine's book editor, however, was not a fan of Wolfe's writing; like so many traditional journalists, he felt Wolfe was bastardizing a time-honored tradition. When the magazine killed the review, an enraged Thompson severed his ties with the *National Observer* for good, thus cutting off what was at the time his most reliable and remunerative outlet.

In a letter to Wolfe from San Francisco that accompanied the unpublished review, Thompson explained what happened:

> I owe the *National Observer* in Washington a bit of money for stories paid and never written while I was working for them out here, and the way we decided I'd work it off was book reviews, of my own choosing. Yours was one; they sent it to me and I wrote this review, which they won't print. I called the editor (the kulture editor) the other day from the middle of a Hell's Angels rally at Bass Lake and he said he was sorry and he agreed with me etc. but that there was a "feeling" around the office about giving you a good review. I doubt this failure will do you much harm, but it pisses me off in addition to costing me $75, so I figured the least it could do would be to send the carbon along to you, for good or ill.

Thompson and Wolfe were unlikely allies. Thompson also was from the South, a liberal firebrand from Louisville who abhorred authority and lived his life in a perpetual state of conflict with just about everyone in his personal and professional life. Wolfe, on the other hand, held to a more conservative philosophy, skeptical and wary of the liberal political movements of the decade. What bound them together was their break from conventional journalism, the feeling that they were both fighting the good fight for new ways of reporting. "I never competed with Wolfe," said Thompson. "We were fellow travelers."

A few days prior to Labor Day, Thompson had run into Kesey in San Francisco at the studios of KQED, where they were both being interviewed, and the pair wound up having a few beers afterward at a nearby bar. Thompson talked up the Angels, and Kesey felt a surge of fellow feeling coming on—the outsider's empathy for a rebel gang that also existed on the lunatic fringe. He tagged along with Thompson to the Box Shop, a de facto clubhouse in San Francisco, and, according to Thompson, "several hours of eating, drinking and the symbolic sharing of herbs" prompted an invitation from Kesey for a party at La Honda.

After reading *Hell's Angels: A Strange and Terrible Saga*, Wolfe wrote to the author asking him to send any material that might be useful for Wolfe's book. Thompson complied with some interview tapes and audio recordings of the Hell's Angels at La Honda. Wolfe now had the Labor Day party scene in hand, as well as the rape, which Thompson had also written about in his book.

Using Thompson's research as well as Kesey's extensive archive—diaries, photographs, correspondence, the Acid Test movie reels, and a forty-five-hour mass of film of the Pranksters' tour on the Furthur bus from La Honda to New York—Wolfe would meticulously piece the story together like Margaret Mead among the Samoans. "The movies that Kesey had were hardly great cinema," said Wolfe. "But they allowed me to describe scenes, the clothes that people were wearing. And those strange diaries were quite useful, too."

But just as Wolfe was about to start the book, Tom senior was hospitalized with asymptomatic myocardial endocarditis, an inflammation of the lining of the heart. In order to help out with his father's convalescence, Wolfe took a sabbatical from the *Tribune* and moved home to Richmond. Three daily hospital visits left him little time to write, but "there's something about not having much time that makes you say, 'I better put the hours in between to good use.'"

The writing process was fraught with indecision, however. Wolfe had mastered features for magazines, but this was a considerably larger canvas. "I initially had to think of each chapter like a separate article," he said. "That way, I could work my way through the book without worrying too much about it." More often than not, Wolfe didn't start writing until the early evening, churning out pages until two or three in the morning. "At first, I was trying to turn out ten triple-spaced pages a day, or fourteen hundred words," said Wolfe. "But soon I was experiencing these long sieges where I would produce twenty pages a day, about three thousand words, and I just held steady to that page rate."

He wrote nine hundred manuscript pages in four months, an astonishing rate even for a fast writer such as Wolfe. Just about everything he had written in the *New York* series was reworked. The prose style was a complete departure, even for a fanciful stylist like Wolfe. He stuck to the narrative he had mapped out: the Pranksters' bus trip to New York and all of the intriguing detours along the way, including a trip to a Beatles concert, the Hell's Angels party, and the meeting with Timothy Leary. But the Pranksters didn't function in conventional narrative time, not with all those drugs, and the book couldn't work if it was restricted to a linear storyline. So he fractured the story like a Braque painting. Instead of the omnipresent third-person voice, Wolfe shifted point of view, using interior monologues when necessary, thus taking the fictional trope of the unreliable narrator to unprecedented extremes: "Whomever I had as a source, I would try to be inside their skulls."

Wolfe rearranged his words in nonlinear fashion and used punctuation as a graphic element, like E. E. Cummings on a mescaline bender. He was fond of ellipses, because his subjects talked in elliptical patterns, even thought in them. Punctuation, Wolfe discovered, allowed him to control the pace and timing of a scene, so he could write the way people on hallucinogens actually think. By subverting his language, he was in effect dosing his prose. Everyone's reality was a subjective construct anyway, according to Kesey—a "movie" only they could see. Wolfe, in essence, was tailoring his style to accommodate Kesey's. In his recounting of Sandy Lehmann-Haupt's DMT flashback, Wolfe captures his paranoid, hallucinatory visions:

> Certain vibrations of the bus would trip his brain somehow and suddenly bring back the sensation of the rocketing DMT trip and it would be necessary to speed up and *keep moving.* The sweet wheat-

fields and dairy lands of America would be sailing by beauty rural green and curving, and Sandy is watching the serene beauty of it . . . and then he happens to look into the big rear-view mirror outside the bus and—the fields are—in flames :::::::::: curve and curdle straight up in hideous orange flames :::::: So he whips his head around and looks way back as far as he can see and over over to the horizon and it is nothing but flat and sweet and green again, sailing by serene.

Wolfe kicked off chapters with poetry:

> *A very Christmas card,*
> *Kesey's new place near La Honda.*
> *A log house, a mountain creek, a little wooden bridge*
> *Fifteen miles from Palo Alto beyond*
> *Cahill Ridge where Route 84*
> *Cuts through a redwood forest gorge—*
> *A redwood forest for a yard!*
> *A very Christmas card.*

He stacked words like children's building blocks:

Miles
　　　Miles
　　　　　Miles
　　　　　　　Miles
　　　　　　　　　Miles
　　　　　　　　　　　Miles
　　　　　　　　　　　　　Miles
　　　　　　　　　　　　　　under all the
good vegetation from Morris Orchids and hearing visions of
Faces
　　　Faces
　　　　　Faces
　　　　　　　Faces
　　　　　　　　　Faces
　　　　　　　　　　　Faces
　　　　　　　　　　　　　Faces

In describing the rape scene, Wolfe wrote with a spectator's veri-similitude.

[S]ome blonde from out of town, one of the guests from way out there, just one nice soft honey hormone squash, she made it clear to three Angels that she was ready to go, so they all trooped out to the backhouse and they had a happy round out there. Pretty soon all the Angels knew about the "new mamma" out in the backhouse and a lot of them piled in there, hooking down beers, laughing, taking their turns, making various critiques. The girl had her red and white dress pushed up around her chest, and two or three would be on her at once, between her legs, sitting on her face in the sick ochre light of the shack with much lapping and leering and bubbling and gulping through furzes of pubic hair while sweat and semen glistened on the highlights of her belly and thighs and she twitched and moaned, not in protest, however, in a kind of drunken bout of God knew what and men with no pants on were standing around cheering, chiding, waiting for their turn.

This passage bothered Kesey when he read it in Wolfe's book. He felt Wolfe was pulling his punches by not naming names and revealing the malefactors. "Certain passages—such as the Hell's Angels gangbang—would have been stronger if he had used the names of the real people that participated," Kesey said years later in an interview with Paul Krassner. "Kesey thought that I made a tragic moment look like farce," said Wolfe.

It was the sole discordant note in the book, the point at which Wolfe's prose style uneasily intersects with an event that might have benefited from a more restrained approach. It worked far more effectively when Wolfe got into Kesey's head during an acid trip:

The ceiling is moving—not in a crazed swirl but along its own planes its own planes of light and shadow and surface not nearly so nice and smoother as plasterer Super Plaster Man intended with infallible car-penter level bubble sliding in dim honey Karo syrup tube not so foolproof as you thought, bub, little limps and ridges up there, bub, and lines, lines like spines on crests of waves of white desert movie sand each one with MGM shadow longshot of the ominous A-rab coming up over the next crest for only the sinister Saracen can see the road and you didn't know how many subplots you left up there, Plaster Man, trying to smooth it all out, all of it, with your bubble in a honey tube carpenter's level.

For passages like this, Wolfe would revert to a "controlled trance" (Wolfe's term). Before writing each chapter, he would review his notes, then close his eyes and try to imagine himself in the mental states of his characters—a process of intellectual "sense memory" that he felt was akin to Method acting. But even that didn't get him as close to the source as he really wanted to be. Wolfe had been hesitant to drop acid when Kesey urged him to do so at La Honda, but no amount of research could get him close enough to the feeling of an acid trip unless he experienced it first-hand. He traveled to Buffalo, New York, where a friend of his had access to LSD, and dropped 125 milligrams. "I felt like my heart was outside my body with these big veins," he said. "As I began to calm down, I had the feeling that I had entered into the sheen of this nubby twist carpet—a really wretched carpet, made of Acrilan—and somehow this represented the people of America, in their democratic glory."

Fortunately for Wolfe, such specious insights didn't make it into *The Electric Kool-Aid Acid Test*. The reviews of the book, which was published in August 1968 on the same day as his second collection of articles, *The Pump House Gang*, were far more enthusiastic than the notices for *The Kandy-Kolored Tangerine-Flake Streamline Baby*. "*The Electric Kool-Aid Acid Test* is an astonishing book," wrote C. D. B. Bryan in the *New York Times Book Review*. "Wolfe is precisely the right author to chronicle the transformation of Ken Kesey from respected author of 'And One Flew Over the Cuckoo's Nest' [*sic*] to an LSD enthusiast. . . . Wolfe's enthusiasm and literary fireworks make it difficult for the reader to remain detached." *The Nation*'s critic Joel Lieber wrote, "You get excited reading this history. Its words reach as close to the feverishness of the thing itself as possible."

Such reactions were just the thing Wolfe had been aiming toward—to bring the reader as close to the Prankster experience as he possibly could without becoming an active participant. With his one-two publishing punch, Wolfe had scaled the heights of literary fame, but "I didn't have enough money to be a celebrity." His total income before taxes that year was only $17,500.

5

THE CENTER CANNOT HOLD

Tom Wolfe's dispatches from the West Coast for the *Tribune* and *Esquire* were field reports for a readership that maintained at best a disdainful attitude toward the youthquakes that were rewriting the Social Register, turning class into an easily acquired accoutrement rather than a privilege of birthright. The lifestyle experiments transpiring in Los Angeles and San Francisco as typified by Kesey and the Pranksters were so foreign to the primarily Republican *Trib* readership as to be more suitable for *National Geographic*. Wolfe was doing his level best to introduce West Coast culture to New York, and he did so with the enthusiasm and optimism of the initiate stumbling onto some Edenic glen where new social paradigms were washing away fusty domestic rituals and arrangements that had lain dormant for years.

But not every writer covering the youth movement was as enamored of the tectonic shifts occurring in California, and one in particular would always maintain a detached skepticism that bordered on existential dread. Joan Didion, unlike Wolfe, was a child of the West. She was born in 1934, but her ancestors had migrated to California in the nineteenth century from points east such as Virginia, Arkansas, the Carolinas, and Illinois, places where the failed dreams of financial bounty led to a great migration to where the crops were rumored to grow as tall and hearty as poplar trees. They had endured long, grinding treks by covered wagon across the Oregon Trail and barely survived the Humboldt Sink in Nevada (where the Donner-Reed party met its garish end; Didion's great-great-great grandmother Nancy Hardin Cornwall was a Donner party member), settling in California's Central Valley, whose vast, flat, alluvial plains seemed to hold the promise of eternal prosperity.

As a young child Didion heard the stories of her ancestors and their great struggles to tame this unsettled territory, forging new identities as farmers from the soil of the last undeveloped region in the country. Sacramento, where Didion was raised by a homemaker and an Air Force officer who served on the local draft board and then drifted into local real estate, was an exurb adrift in uneasy suspension from the rest of the state. But by the late forties, it seemed to Didion that the stories she had been told of the crystalline rivers and majestic plains had already been supplanted by the new narrative of unchecked corporate development, the colonization of the city by aerospace firms and other commercial enterprises. This new boomtown development coexisted with the old Sacramento in ways that gave Didion intimations of the impermanence of things in California, the chimerical nature of the great western dream that her ancestors had dreamed.

Even Sacramento became a mirage for Didion as she was jostled from base to base during her father's tenure in the Air Force. So Didion withdrew deeper into herself, finding solace in the novels of Hemingway, Conrad, and James. "I tended to perceive the world in terms of things read about it," she recalled in 1979.

She wrote her first story at the age of five. "I wrote stories from the time I was a little girl," Didion recalled, "but I didn't want to be a writer. I wanted to be an actress. I didn't realize then that it's the same impulse. It's make-believe. It's performance. The only difference being that a writer can do it all alone." In high school, Didion worked as a stringer for the *Sacramento Union,* saving up enough money to buy herself an Olivetti Lettera 22 typewriter; she taught herself how to put sentences together by typing passages from her favorite books.

Didion didn't know that this shape-shifting image of California that she maintained throughout her young life would become the raw material of her greatest work as a writer when she left Sacramento to attend the University of California, Berkeley, as an English major. After winning a writing contest for a story on the San Francisco architect William Wilson Wurster, Didion left for New York after graduating in 1956 and found a job at *Vogue* writing captions for editor Allene Talmey. Didion eventually graduated to stories about country homes, clothing designers, and other personalities, where a high premium was placed on getting the finer details of the products just right while avoiding the extraneous adjective or verb, the unnecessary descriptive word.

Didion fell in love with New York as only a rural initiate could love it. "Nothing was irrevocable," she would later write, "everything was within reach. Just around the corner lay something curious and interesting, something I had never seen or done or known about." New York was an "infinitely romantic notion, the mysterious nexus of all love and money and power, the shining and perishable dream itself."

And yet the West maintained a powerful grip on her; she missed the region terribly. Even as Didion was moving up the masthead at *Vogue*, eventually becoming an editor, she dreamed of Sacramento and the great silted rivers in which she had swum. Her first novel, *Run River*, which was written after hours while Didion was still working at *Vogue*, was a paean to the Sacramento Valley as it existed in her dream life, "the way the rivers crested and the way the tule fogs obscured the levees and the way the fallen camellias turned the sidewalks brown and slick during the Christmas rains." But it was also a novel that pitted the encroachment of modernity against the disturbances of rural life; in the novel, the protagonist Lily McClellan's mother sells off parcels of her land to make way for tract housing, while the body of her daughter Martha is inexorably exhumed from its grave by the swelling river.

Didion was making it in the city that was the big brass ring for journalists who came of age in the 1950s, but eventually the great media culture clamor—the endless cocktail parties, the enforced bonhomie of an intensely private person impelled to become a public one—sent her back to California. Newly married to John Gregory Dunne, an ambitious young writer at *Time* who longed to write novels and with whom she had adopted a baby girl they named Quintana Roo, Didion moved to Los Angeles in 1966.

The paradise of her youth had been wiped clean; a new generation of exiles had laid claim to the freedoms and opportunities that had brought Didion's forebears across the Midwest in the 1800s, and the Dust Bowlers in the 1930s after them, to a golden land that was wide open and unfettered by entrenched notions of class and tradition or the heavy baggage of historical continuity. This is the place where Tom Wolfe had seen new statuspheres spring up from nowhere, but Didion longed for that old continuity. In its absence, chaos and anarchy were free to roam.

For Didion, geography was destiny. Just as the land on which she was reared had shaped her view of the world as indeterminate, so her subjects in her earliest magazine stories were shaped by the natural laws of California, a state that, despite a postwar population boom that was unprecedented in American history, was still a wild, untamed desert that could tamp down the heartiest souls with obdurate force. Like previous migrants in search of some elusive destiny in the West, Didion's subjects were drawn by the Hollywood myths, only to encounter the same dust and desolation.

Didion saw disorder at every turn in California: in the hollowed-out eyes of the drug-addled hippies in the Haight, in suburban housewives staring down hope and losing, in the sun-baked concrete enclaves far away from the Pacific breezes. Shortly after moving back West, Didion became "paralyzed by the conviction that the world as I had understood it no longer existed. If I was to work again at all, it would be necessary for me to come to terms with disorder."

In her story "How Can I Tell Them There's Nothing Left?" which ran in the May 7, 1966, issue of the *Saturday Evening Post,* Didion chronicled in chilling detail the story of Lucille Miller, the child of strict Seventh-Day Adventists, who was reared in Winnipeg, Manitoba, and "came off the prairies in search of something she had seen in a movie or heard on the radio." Instead, Miller found herself in San Bernardino, a city "haunted by the Mojave just beyond the mountains, devastated by the hot dry Santa Ana wind that comes down through the passes at 100 miles an hour and whines through the eucalyptus windbreaks and works on the nerves." Miller's story, which Didion had read about in the *Los Angeles Times,* seemed ripped from the pages of a James M. Cain pot-boiler. On October 7, 1964, "a night when the moon was dark and the wind was blowing and she was out of milk," Miller, deep into an illicit affair with a local attorney named Arthwell Hayton, immolated her dentist husband alive in his VW Bug in an attempt to collect on his life insurance.

For Didion, Miller's story seemed to typify the desperation of all those lonely lower-middle-class strivers out on the fringes of L.A., the

California "where it is possible to live and die without ever eating an artichoke, without ever meeting a Catholic or a Jew. This is the California where it is easy to Dial-a-Devotion, but hard to buy a book." Miller expected one thing and got something else.

Didion seemed an unlikely writer for such a tawdry story. A painfully, almost pathologically shy interlocutor, Didion somehow made her reticence work to her advantage. "Most of my sentences drift off, don't end," she said. "It's a habit I've fallen into. I don't deal well with people. I would think that the appearance of not being very much in touch was probably one of the reasons I started writing." Instead of pushing and prodding her subjects into revealing themselves, Didion let them fill in the awkward silences, discreetly jotting it all down in her spiral notebook. In this fashion, she achieved a rapport with her subjects that eluded most traditional reporters.

For this story, Didion interviewed Miller, her friends and family members, and the prosecuting and defense attorneys, and meticulously pored over court transcripts to carefully piece together the timeline of the murder and its aftermath. The story is structured like a film noir; Didion skillfully unfurls the narrative without tipping her hand. The reader learns the facts as they are revealed to the protagonists in the story itself, culminating in a courtroom climax that leads to Miller's incarceration and a final visit to the Millers' vacant house on Bella Vista Road, with the television aerial "toppled on the roof, and a trash can [was] stuffed with the debris of family life: a cheap suitcase, a child's game called 'Lie Detector.'"

Didion's omnivorous eye ranged over the San Bernardino courthouse during the Miller trial, catching the small but revealing details that elevated the story beyond a true-crime tale into a morality play, the battle between darkness and light that seemed, for Didion, to permeate every aspect of contemporary California life. "So they had come," Didion wrote,

> to see Arthwell, these crowds who milled beneath the dusty palms outside the courthouse, and they had also come to see Lucille, who appeared as a slight, intermittently pretty woman, already pale from lack of sun, a woman who would turn thirty-five before the trial was over and whose tendency toward haggardness was beginning to

show, a meticulous woman who insisted, against her lawyer's advice, on coming to court with her hair piled high and laquered. "I would've been happy if she'd come in with it hanging loose, but Lucille wouldn't do that," her lawyer said.

Lucille Miller's was not an isolated case; it was emblematic of the dislocations of a region that obliterated its past as fast as it constructed new myths to replace it, withholding all of the golden dreams that it so tantalizingly proffered, a culture that granted its residents permissiveness as it if were an inalienable right but extracted a pound of flesh in return.

Didion saw this all so clearly in San Francisco, with the countercultural revolution in full bloom. Where others preferred to see a new community of the young rising like daisies from the cracked sidewalk streets, Didion saw a village of lost children, the fallout of a fractious society with a high divorce rate, where "adolescents drifted from city to torn city, sloughing off both the past and the future as snakes shed their skins, children who were never taught and would never now learn the games that had held the society together."

Didion embarked for San Francisco in the spring of 1967 on assignment from the *Saturday Evening Post*. She had only the flimsiest of conceits—to take the measure of the hippie scene—and even flimsier contacts. So she hung around awhile and insinuated herself with some of the kids she met on the street, and they invited her into their crash pads, offered their drugs and food to her.

What Didion witnessed was a far cry from the pie-eyed exuberance of the Merry Pranksters that Tom Wolfe had chronicled so gleefully in *The Electric Kool-Aid Acid Test*. Instead, these were runaways living on handouts and day labor, organizing their lives around acid trips, selling the acid they didn't ingest, scurrying around in search of some identity that would stick.

Debbie is buffing her fingernails with the belt to her suede jacket. She is annoyed because she chipped a nail and because I do not have any polish remover in the car. I promise to get her to a friend's apartment so that she can redo her manicure, but something has been bothering me and as I fiddle with the ignition I finally ask it. I ask them to think back to when they were children, to tell me what they had wanted to be when they were grown up, how they had seen the future then.

Jeff throws a Coca-Cola bottle out the car window. "I can't remember I ever thought about it," he says.

"I remember I wanted to be a veterinarian once," Debbie says. "But now I'm more or less working in the vein of being an artist or a model or a cosmetologist. Or something."

Ken Kesey's dream to "move beyond acid" never took hold in the Haight; drugs just became an end in themselves, permeating everything like toxic fallout. Didion paints a bleak picture of a would-be utopia curdling into a dystopian nightmare, and not even the very young are immune. The conclusion of the piece, which Didion called "Slouching Towards Bethlehem" (from the Yeats poem with the line "things fall apart; the center cannot hold"), is an image of a five-year-old girl named Susan

wearing a reefer coat, reading a comic book. She keeps licking her lips in concentration and the only off thing about her is that she's wearing white lipstick.

"Five years old," Otto says. "On acid."

Wolfe's words seemed to tumble out in a logorrheic rush, but Didion's prose was spare, honed to a fine edge. She strove for directness, a clear and uninflected rhythm, just like her literary hero Hemingway. She credited her *Vogue* apprenticeship with teaching her how to sculpt sentences down to the bone. "Every day I would go into [Allene Talmey]'s office with eight lines of copy or a caption or something," she recalled. "She would sit there and mark it up with a pencil and get very angry about extra words, about verbs not working."

Didion did place herself into some of her reported pieces, but only as a dispassionate observer; she never recorded her own impressions in Maileresque fashion, leaving that for her personal essays. If anything, Didion followed the tenets of Lillian Ross, framing stories in scenes and relying on her moral instincts to provide the undercurrent of tragedy that pervaded so much of her sixties output.

Didion's profile of John Wayne, which appeared in the *Saturday Evening Post* in 1965, was a close cousin of Ross's *Picture*. In it, Didion hung around the set of director Henry Hathaway's *The Sons of Katie Elder* outside Mexico City and carefully observed the interaction between the veteran cast and crew, which included Dean Martin and Earl Holliman. Wayne had been Didion's embodiment of the frontier man of action, the hero of her young dream life. Now Wayne was ill with cancer but still possessed that same stolid vigor of legend; he still had something of the cowboy's maverick code in his creaky carriage.

> Hathaway removed the cigar from his mouth and looked across the table. "Some guy just tried to kill *me* he wouldn't end up in jail. How about you, Duke?"
> Very slowly, the object of Hathaway's query wiped his mouth, pushed back his chair, and stood up. It was the real thing, the authentic article, the move which had climaxed a thousand scenes on 165 flickering frontiers and phantasmagoric battlefields before, and it was about to climax this one, in the commissary at Estudio Churubusco outside Mexico City. "Right," John Wayne drawled. "I'd kill him."

Because Didion's main outlet at the time was the *Saturday Evening Post,* a general-interest magazine not particularly known for its creative nonfiction during this era and headed toward its dissolution in 1969, her work didn't receive the kind of notice that Wolfe and Gay Talese garnered with their *Esquire* stories. But when Henry Robbins—Wolfe's editor at Farrar, Straus and Giroux—compiled the San Francisco and John Wayne pieces, as well as a handful of other essays from *Esquire,* the *American Scholar,* and *Holiday,* in a book called *Slouching Towards Bethlehem* in the summer of 1968 (summer traditionally being a down time for high-profile books), it was immediately hailed as the work of an exciting new voice in American letters. So unrecognized was Didion as a major talent that Dan Wakefield felt compelled to preface his *New York Times* review of the book with the qualifier that "Joan Didion is one of the least celebrated and most talented writers of my own generation." Wakefield continued: "Now that Truman Capote has pronounced that such work may achieve the stature of 'art,' perhaps it is possible for this collection to be recognized as it should be: not as a better or worse example of what some people call 'mere journalism,' but as a rich display of some of the best prose written today in this country."

6

MADRAS OUTLAW

In 1971, on the verge of becoming the most infamous journalist in America, Hunter S. Thompson unloaded a fusillade of playful vitriol in an essay that was meant to distinguish Thompson's balls-out approach from that of his closest rival, Tom Wolfe. "Wolfe's problem," Thompson wrote, "is that he's too crusty to participate in his stories. The people he feels comfortable with are dull as stale dogshit, and the people who seem to fascinate him as a writer are so weird that they make him nervous. The only thing new and unusual about Wolfe's journalism is that he's an abnormally good reporter; he has a fine sense of echo and at least a peripheral understanding of what John Keats was talking about when he said that thing about Truth & Beauty."

In short, Wolfe was a very artful stenographer, always keeping a discreet distance and never sullying his suit. Thompson, on the other hand, was a man willing to throw himself into the breach and risk his well-being, if necessary, to get the story. As much as Thompson admired *The Kandy-Kolored Tangerine-Flake Streamline Baby* and was willing to stand by his opinion of the book at the expense of his own livelihood, he regarded it as a brilliant exercise in simulacrum. It was Thompson, after all, who had been present during the Hell's Angels gang rape at La Honda, providing Wolfe with audiotapes that captured the scene for *The Electric Kool-Aid Acid Test*. No story was worthy for Thompson unless he could immerse himself, body and soul, and come out on the other side with a piece of writing tinctured with his own blood and sweat.

Hunter Stockton Thompson was born in Louisville, Kentucky, on July 18, 1937, the eldest son of Jack Robert Thompson and Virginia Davidson Ray. Jack was an insurance engineer for First Kentucky Fire Insurance Co. The marriage was Jack Thompson's second; his first wife, Garnett Sowards, had died of pneumonia in 1923. A stern disciplinarian and a veteran of World War I, Jack was fifty-four years old when his son Hunter was born. That age gap militated against any significant bond between father and son, and so Hunter gravitated to his mother, who nurtured his love of literature, the ripping picaresques to be found in the books of Mark Twain and Jack London.

Thus at a very early age Hunter was cultivating an image that was equal parts aesthete and roughneck. It was as if the warring impulses of the South's two great traditions—its regional pride forged in blood and its literary heritage—merged to make an uneasy alliance in Thompson's psyche. "I've always felt like a Southerner," said Thompson. "And I always felt like I was born in defeat. And I may have written everything I've written just to win back a victory. My life may be pure revenge."

As a teenager, Thompson cultivated his taste for adrenaline kicks—verbally provoking his schoolmates into fistfights, knocking over mailboxes, or engaging in war games with BB guns by the creek near his house, using animal life—and other kids—for target practice. "I had a keen appetite for adventure, which soon led me into a maze of complex behavioral experiments that my parents found hard to explain," Thompson wrote in his 2002 memoir *Kingdom of Fear.* "I was a popular boy, with acceptable grades & a vaguely promising future, but I was cursed with a dark sense of humor that made many adults afraid of me, for reasons they couldn't quite put their fingers on."

He lived to get under people's skin, to be unpredictable and hairtrigger dangerous, but he was also rakishly charming, and too smart to ignore. As a student in Louisville Male High School, his scabrous essays impressed English teacher Harold Tague enough for him to recommend Thompson to the Athenaeum Literary Association, an exclusive student organization at "Male" whose members contributed pieces to the association's annual yearbook, *The Spectator.* Thompson's contributions revealed a taste for playful polemics. "Security," one of his *Spectator* essays, laid out Thompson's philosophy of choosing a life of excitement over dull complacency:

Turn back the pages of history and see the men who have shaped the destiny of the world. Security was never theirs, but they lived rather than existed. . . . It is from the bystanders (who are in the vast majority) that we receive the propaganda that life is not worth living, that life is drudgery, that the ambitions of youth must be laid aside for a life which is but a painful wait for death.

In June 1956, right before he was to graduate, Thompson, along with two schoolmates, was arrested for violently harrassing a couple in their car for cigarettes and was sentenced to six months in Jefferson County Jail. By enrolling in the electronics program at Scott Air Force Base in Belleville, Illinois, Thompson was able to reduce his sentence to only thirty days. After his graduation from the program, Thompson was assigned to Eglin Air Force Base in Fort Walton Beach, Florida, where he finagled a job as the sports editor of the *Command Courier*, the base's newspaper. "In short," he wrote to his old high school friend Gerald Tyrrell, "we both know that I'm no more qualified for a post like this than I am for the presidency of a theological seminary," but as was often the case, Thompson's chutzpah compensated for his inexperience.

Thompson's tenure as the *Courier*'s sports editor was backbreaking and exhilarating. A virtual one-man staff, he not only wrote and edited all the stories and his weekly column, "The Spectator," but also was responsible for copyediting, page layout, and paste-up. Often working around the clock to whip the section into shape, Thompson consumed twenty or more cups of coffee and ran through four packs of cigarettes a day, a habit he eventually curtailed when he switched to a pipe. When he wasn't working on the paper, Thompson was taking speech and psychology classes at nearby Florida State University, leaving precious little time for the kind of drinking and carousing he had grown fond of in high school.

Nonetheless, Thompson made time, forming a large network of on- and off-base contacts that would help him make a smooth transition to citizen-writer when the time came—including the debutante daughter of Lieutenant Colonel Frank Campbell. "I met all kinds of people in Fort Walton, which has the most beautiful beaches in all of Florida," said Thompson. "I became part of Café Society, hung out with Bart Starr and Max McGee, guys like that. It was a rush. Looking back on it now, I don't see how I could have done all those things and done them successfully."

But the life of a professional journalist was pure liberation; for the first time, he wrote to his half-brother Jack, "no one is hanging over me saying, 'my oh my Hunter, just see what you can do when you apply yourself.'" There was no question in his mind: he would make journalism his life's work.

And he was hungry for more. In January 1957 he sold his first story— a two-hundred-word piece on the base's wrestling team, to the *Playground News,* Fort Walton Beach's civilian newspaper. Not long after it was published, the paper offered Thompson the job of sports editor. Despite Air Force regulations that forbade *Command Courier* staffers from taking civilian jobs, Thompson accepted, using the pseudonyms Thorne Stockton and Cuubley Cohn to keep the Air Force off his trail. "The whole thing," he wrote to his childhood friend Porter Bibb at the time, "tends to make my eyes water with wonder at my sudden eruption of ambition."

Thompson's idyll didn't last long. His snide swipes at the establishment and his broad-stroke send-ups of high-ranking military officers in the *Courier* didn't sit well with the Air Force's Information Services Office's chief, W. S. Evans; his savage eviscerations of cultural icons such as Ted Williams and Arthur Godfrey were thought of as heretical. His "rebel and superior attitude," Evans wrote in a letter recommending a discharge to Thompson's personnel officer, "seems to rub off on other airmen staff members. He has little consideration for military bearing or dress and seems to dislike the service and want out as soon as possible."

The Air Force had also found out about his *Playground News* gig. Thompson, chafing at the Air Force's stiff-necked protocol, wanted out anyway. After being demoted to the Communications Squadron, Thompson was given an honorable discharge in October 1957. Finally he was free to pursue the culturally rich and remunerative career of a professional reporter. Or so he thought.

The *Jersey Shore Herald* covered the cities of Lock Haven, Williamsport, and Jersey Shore, Pennsylvania, and did a poor job of it. A small-circulation daily where expediency trumped quality, located in a dreary urban area, it was the diametric opposite of his *Command Courier* experience. Thompson was miserable there. "If this path leads up," he wrote to his friend Larry Callen, "then I'd rather go down." He didn't last two months in the job. Instead he took the northward migratory path of so many other journalism aspirants, such as Wolfe, Clay Felker, and Harold Hayes, and headed to New York City to try his luck. On Christmas Eve, no less.

With only $110 to his name, Thompson called on a local YMCA in the city, only to be told it was full. He then lived for a short time in a flophouse in Secaucus, New Jersey, until his old Air Force buddy Jerry Hawke, who was attending Columbia Law School, agreed to put Thompson up at his apartment at 110 Morningside Drive until the young writer found gainful employment. In early January 1958, after experiencing his fair share of "sustained fear," Thompson, using the flimsiest of family connections, landed a plum job as a $50-a-week copy-boy for Henry Luce's mighty *Time*.

The *Time* job was to be an invaluable experience, a ground-level peek at the inner workings of one of the largest news-gathering organizations in the world. "Shit, that was a gravy train of access and perks," said Thompson. "What an education that was, all pumped into me in a year and a half."

Despite Thompson's eagerness to prove himself with Luce's best and brightest, the inner reprobate, which had been patiently lying in wait, pounced only weeks into his tenure. One night after the magazine had closed production and everyone had gone home, he snuck into the office of Henry Grunwald, the magazine's managing editor, and stole a case of "the best scotch money could buy." He also had a tendency to filch books and office supplies. Incidents such as these led to a number of run-ins with editors and other Time-Life employees; at one point during a cocktail party for new executives, he called the magazine's business manager a "fat lecher." At his apartment at 562 West 113th Street, Thompson engaged in other mischief, throwing a garbage can down five flights of stairs and turning a fire extinguisher on a couple of unsuspecting neighbors. It was all he could do to maintain some levity at a time when he was working for meager wages and trying desperately to keep afloat financially in a city that didn't make it easy.

He wanted to leave New York and try to make it as a freelance writer, because "Ernest Hemingway had shown me that you could be a freelancer in this country and get away with it." Thompson was enthralled by Manhattan's frenetic cultural currents, but they also made him miserable. When he finally found his own place, a dingy basement apartment on Perry Street in the West Village, he wrote to an old girlfriend, "Do you realize that sunlight NEVER ENTERS MY APARTMENT?"

Thompson was fired from *Time* after only a year, but his stint at the magazine, along with a canny bluff about extensive reportorial experience, helped him land a job with the *Middletown Daily Record,* a two-and-a-half-year-old newspaper located in upstate New York with a staff consisting entirely of writers and editors under the age of thirty. It seemed a dream gig: for $70 a week, Thompson would work as a general assignment reporter, writing copy and even shooting photos for the paper when the situation called for it. But he didn't last three months. Fired in March 1959 for sending back food in a restaurant that advertised heavily in the paper and then putting his foot through the office candy vending machine shortly thereafter, Thompson was out on the street again. "It was no free ride in those days. I worked very hard at [making a living]."

He started a novel called *King Jellyfish* and submitted short stories to various magazines; when *Esquire*'s fiction editor, Rust Hills, failed to respond fast enough to a story called "The Cotton Candy Heart," Thompson reeled off a frustrated missive. "Goddammit, Hills, I don't think there's an excuse in the world for you people holding onto my manuscript this long." After sending countless letters of inquiry, he found a job in Puerto Rico on *El Sportivo,* a weekly sports magazine that emphasized bowling coverage, and he freelanced for the *Louisville Courier-Journal* on the side. *El Sportivo* went out of business shortly thereafter.

Thompson decamped to Big Sur, on the northern California coast, in order to start work on another novel based on his Puerto Rico adventures, to be called *The Rum Diary.* More important for Thompson's future prospects, he sold his first magazine story, a piece on Big Sur and its boho inhabitants, for $350 to *Rogue,* a downmarket *Playboy* knockoff. "It was not so much the money," he wrote to his new friend, *San Juan Star* editor William Kennedy, "but the feeling that I had finally cracked something, the first really valid indication that I might actually make a living at this goddamn writing."

As it turned out, the *Rogue* sale, while providing a much-needed morale boost, did not unleash the floodgates for Thompson; constant rejection and poverty still gnawed at him. He returned to New York in January 1962 and struggled to finish *The Rum Diary* while relying on the kindness of friends and patrons to pay his bills.

Finding little success cracking the freelance market in New York, he decided to try his luck in South America, a region where the socio-economic discrepancies and roiling political landscape, stoked by the United States' meddling political and economic policies, would no doubt provide him with lots of material for stories. "I am going to write massive tomes from South America," he said in a letter to his friend Paul Semonin. "I can hardly wait to get my teeth into it. . . . It is almost too big to deal with."

In Puerto Rico, Thompson hitched a ride to Aruba on a fishing boat, then jumped onto a smuggler's boat headed for Puerto Estrella, Colombia. He had sent some clips to Clifford Ridley, the editor of the Dow Jones newsmagazine *National Observer,* and Ridley was open to the possibility of Thompson contributing to the magazine. His first piece, "A Footloose American in a Smuggler's Den," described his journey from Aruba to Puerto Estrella, and his experiences with the Guajiro Indians, mostly drinking smuggled scotch:

> As it turned out, three things made my visit a success. One was my size and drinking capacity (it was fear—a man traveling alone among reportedly savage Indians dares not get drunk); another was the fact that I never turned down a request for a family portrait (fear, again); and the third was my "lifelong acquaintance" with Jacqueline Kennedy, whom they regard as some sort of goddess.

The early stirrings of Thompson's mordant wit can be found in the *Observer* pieces, which are among the era's most incisive dispatches from South America. Just as he had done at Elgin, Thompson familiarized himself with the power structure of the places he found himself in—in South America, particularly the embassy circuit and the religious orders—in order to dig deeper than the intellectually torpid American reporters he found there. "There were a lot of reporters doing show pieces about the leadership in these countries, but they didn't talk to the people," said Thompson. "Some of the writers had their own drivers, for

Christ sakes. There was an embedded structure, but there was room for those who weren't working strictly by the book."

Endearing himself to the locals ("I used to hang out with the Jesuit priests in the mountains. The best scotch in any country was always available in the monasteries") was Thompson's MO, whether he was sniffing out the roots of anti-American sentiment in Cali, Colombia, describing the ways in which Peru's dictatorial tradition blotted out democratic reforms, or chronicling the benign neglect of the disenfranchised native Indians in Cuzco.

After a year and a half as the *Observer*'s de facto South American correspondent (he was still freelancing), Thompson found himself in familiar territory—broke and desperate for work. Shortly after marrying recent Goucher College graduate Sandy Conklin in Louisville in May 1963, Thompson moved to San Francisco, where he scrounged for magazine work. When Thompson pitched the *Observer* a story about the emerging Free Speech Movement at the University of California, Berkeley, Ridley refused, and Thompson, following a now-familiar career script, stopped pitching stories to the *Observer*.

Thompson, fed up with the penurious grind of freelance journalism, made an effort to finish *The Rum Diary*. "I tried driving a cab in San Francisco, I tried every kind of thing," Thompson told *Playboy*. "I used to go down . . . and line up with the winos on Mission Street, looking for work handing out grocery-store circulars and shit like that."

But circumstances had changed; now that Thompson had been writing regularly for a national magazine, the doors to national outlets creaked open a bit. Carey McWilliams, legendary editor of the liberal political weekly *The Nation,* was impressed by Thompson's South American coverage and wanted him to contribute to his publication.

In December 1964 McWilliams wrote Thompson a letter soliciting the writer's interest for a story on the insurgent band of motorcycle outlaws called Hell's Angels. It was a great time to assign a piece on the Angels: California attorney general Thomas C. Lynch had recently polled law enforcement agents around the state and distilled the information he received into a fifteen-page document called "The Hell's Angels Motorcycle Clubs," which listed eighteen major crimes and countless other infractions in clinical detail. A reporter for the *New York Times* wrote a story on the report, followed in short order by *Time* and

Newsweek, and soon the Hell's Angels were a full-blown national menace. McWilliams, who had obtained a copy of the Lynch Report, suspected that Thompson, with his keen talent for sniffing out stories that fell beneath the radar of more conventional journalists, might be an ideal candidate to get the real dirt on the motorcycle club, to tell the story from the Angels' point of view rather than Lynch's.

Thompson dug into the Hell's Angels story enthusiastically. After querying a few functionaries in the attorney general's office, he determined that no one working for Lynch had ever made any contact with any Hell's Angels member. Thus the real story had yet to be written, and Thompson had grand plans for it. "To my mind," he wrote in a letter to McWilliams, "the Hell's Angels are a very natural product of our society. Just like SNCC or the Peace Corps . . . But different people. That's what I'd like to find out: who are they? What kind of man becomes a Hell's Angel? And why? And how? The mechanics."

McWilliams was willing to pay $100 for the story, a tiny fee even by 1964 standards, but enough to cover Thompson's rent on his apartment in the Haight: "I would have speared sharks in San Francisco Bay for rent." He arranged a meeting with the Angels' Oakland chapter president and club leader, Ralph "Sonny" Barger, and a few other members through Birney Jarvis, a police reporter for the *San Francisco Chronicle* and a Harley-Davidson enthusiast who was an honorary lifetime member of the club.

Thompson showed up at the bar of the DePau Hotel in San Francisco's waterfront industrial district, where the Angels were having a meeting. In his madras jacket, wing-tip shoes, button-down shirt, and a tie, Thompson was every inch the geek. "I didn't have any other clothes, nor did I have a bike at the time," Thompson said. "I told them I was a writer, not a biker, and that I wanted to take a few notes—what else could I do? The fact that I had no bike didn't seem like too big a thing."

The Angels regarded the writer like a 4H Club member. Thompson felt he was in imminent danger—until they all started drinking, that is. "After a few dozen beers, things started to loosen up a bit," said Thompson. "We found common ground through the consumption of alcohol."

At the 2 A.M. closing time, Thompson invited five of the Angels, including Ping-Pong, Filthy Phil, and Frenchy, back to his apartment on 318 Parnassus Avenue, armed with a case of beer and a cheap box of red wine, much to the consternation of his wife, Sandy, who was "quietly hysterical for five hours." He cued up *The Freewheelin' Bob Dylan* on the stereo and proceeded to make merry with the Angels until morning broke through the windows. A bond, however tenuous, had been established.

The next day, Thompson met the Angels at their de facto clubhouse across from the DePau, a transmission repair garage owned by Frenchy called the Box Shop, but now the air in the room wasn't so stifling. He developed a tenuous rapport with Barger, who thought the tall, lanky reporter from Louisville was some kind of overeducated hayseed. "He was a typical Kentuckian," said Barger. "Not an Okie, you know, but straight from the hills." Once Barger understood Thompson's intentions—to provide an accurate portrait of the Hell's Angels, without the smoke-screen of media hype and moralizing—Barger opened up to him. "Sonny was a very powerful leader, charismatic in a quiet way," Thompson said. "We weren't friends, but there was a mutual respect that he acknowledged. We made our peace with each other."

Thompson's original intention for the *Nation* story was to provide an unvarnished look at the Angels from an eye-level perspective, but the resulting story, which was called "The Motorcycle Gangs: Losers and Outsiders," was in fact a meticulous debunking of the Lynch Report, with tantalizing allusions to Thompson's initial meetings with Hell's Angels members used for corroboration. Thompson couldn't resist a few digs at the mainstream press: "The difference between the Hell's Angels in the papers and the Hell's Angels for real is enough to make a man wonder what newsprint is for." But the story doesn't really deliver on its insider's promise, offering only teasing glimpses of the Angels' culture. The overall tone of the piece is measured and expository, as if Thompson had reluctantly tethered himself to the magazine's house style.

Still, "The Motorcycle Gangs: Losers and Outsiders" was the most accurate portrait of Hell's Angels yet to appear in a mainstream publication, and Thompson had the distinct advantage of conducting his research firsthand, which didn't go unnoticed. "We liked the article, because it was pro-us," said Sonny Barger. "We always thought any press was good press, but that article in *The Nation* was well written."

Shortly after the May 17, 1965, publication of the story, Thompson was inundated with offers from publishers to expand the article into a book. He finally accepted a $6,000 advance from Bernard Shir-Cliff, an editor at paperback publishing house Ballantine Books. "The moral here," he wrote his friend William Kennedy, "is never knock *The Nation* just because they paid $100. All that stuff I wrote for the *Observer* apparently died on the vine, but this one job for *The Nation* paid off in real gold."

Using his initial $1,500 payment, Thompson purchased a BSA 650 Lightning, "the fastest goddamn bike on the road," so he could endear himself to the Angels and, he hoped, ride along with them. Jim Silberman, the Random House editor who bought the hardcover rights to *Hell's Angels* on Shir-Cliff's recommendation, remembers meeting Thompson at a café in the North Beach district of San Francisco, trying to wrest the writer's attention away from his parked bike. "I don't want anyone to steal it," he told Silberman. When Thompson offered Silberman a ride, the editor politely declined. "I told him that [author] Richard Fariña had been killed on a motorcycle just weeks before," said Silberman. "So Hunter said, 'Okay, you take a cab and I'll race you to my place.'" Thompson won.

Thompson thought his Lightning would give him the street cred he felt he needed, but Barger and his fellow Angels scoffed at his fancy machine. "It was an insult to them for someone to just come along with a bike and expect to ride with them," Thompson said. For one thing, it wasn't the requisite Harley-Davidson, and the fact that it could outrun their hogs only made matters worse. "That was just a stock BSA," said Barger. "You could tie it to two Harleys back to back with chains on them, and it would rip that bike apart."

"They wanted to sell me a hot bike for $400," said Thompson. "I wasn't comfortable with that." Thompson reluctantly agreed to strip the bike down to the chrome, and he even removed the mufflers to give it that Harley growl. He compensated for his bike faux pas with his balls-out driving technique. "They thought I was a crazier driver than any of them," he said. "I fit in, oddly enough."

Thompson thought he might hang out with the Angels on their own turf, get a feel for the milieu. The earliest meetings took place at El Adobe, a dive that the Angels had made their official watering hole, as well as the Box Shop. The Angels remember Thompson as fidgety, conservative in dress and manner, and eager to test his constitution for heavy drinking if it meant getting the access he needed. "I remember these yellow-and-white striped button-down shirts," said Oakland chapter member Marvin Gilbert (Mouldy Marvin). "The first time I met him, he walked in with a couple of cases of beer, which was a good move. I liked him, but he was a little scatterbrained. But I didn't like the fact that he was writing a book about us. I didn't feel we needed something like that."

There was a difference in kind between the Hell's Angels two northern California chapters. The San Francisco Angels embraced the counterculture, or at least that aspect of the scene that reveled in psychoactive drugs, free love, and psychedelic rock. The Oakland chapter hated the hippies across the bay and were wholly committed to their bikes, to the exclusion of everything else. Thompson gravitated to the San Francisco Angels, if only because they shared an affinity for the same music and were more accessible as interview subjects. A few of the Angels, such as Frenchy and Terry the Tramp from the bohemian North Sacramento chapter, became frequent guests at Thompson's apartment and primary sources for his research. "I only invited the ones I thought I could control," said Thompson. "Very few of them took to the rock and roll life." Terry the Tramp "got along with Hunter very well, better than any of us," said Barger. "Hunter's apartment became a place for him to get free drinks and stay overnight."

Parties in Thompson's apartment became commonplace. They were boisterous affairs stoked by stolen cases of beer and Benzedrine, revels that usually didn't end until early the next day. "My wife was very pretty and very vulnerable when the Angels came over," said Thompson. "Things went well for the most part, but I recognized that they could go next door and kill somebody." The Angels didn't take half measures when it came to their partying; it was an all-or-nothing proposition, a bacchanal.

"We would party right down to the ground, take a few reds, blister our minds," said Gilbert. "Hunter liked to drink but couldn't keep up with us. If he got too loaded, he would just sneak off somewhere." Thompson didn't want to come off like another square reporter, so his small gun collection was frequently pulled out and demonstrated. "For reasons that were never made clear," Thompson wrote in *Hell's Angels,* "I blew out my back windows with five blasts of a 12-gauge shotgun,

followed moments later by six rounds from a .44 magnum. It was a prolonged outburst of heavy firing, drunken laughter and crashing glass."
The Angels found little humor in Thompson's reckless firearms displays,
frequently absconding with his guns and hiding them from him. "He
was trying to convince us he was a big, bad motherfucker," said Barger.
"He tried to intimidate people into thinking he was a tough guy, then
he'd turn to me later and ask me if I could get his gun back."

A week prior to the Fourth of July weekend in 1965, Thompson
asked the Angels if he could join them on their annual holiday run to
Bass Lake, a camping area near Yosemite Park in the Sierra Nevadas. The
Angels were wary about bringing a reporter along; the negative press
about the Angels had put the cops on high alert in the area, and a large
police presence was expected. Thompson's request was granted, but he
had to ride in his own car instead of on the BSA Lightning, the better to
avoid getting into any legal trouble by association.

Barger told Thompson to meet the Angels at 8 A.M. on July 3 at El
Adobe, from where members of the Oakland and San Francisco chapters
would ride to Bass Lake. "I overslept," Thompson wrote, "and in the
rush to get moving I forgot my camera. There was no time for breakfast
but I ate a peanut-butter sandwich while loading the car . . . sleeping bag
and beer cooler in back, tape recorder in front, and under the driver's
seat an unloaded Luger. Press cards are nice things to have, but in riot situations a pistol is the best kind of safe-conduct pass." He missed the
Angels by twenty minutes; driving over the Bay Bridge, he spotted the
Gypsy Jokers, a rival motorcycle club that was also headed to Bass Lake,
"grouped around a gray pickup truck with a swastika painted on the side.
They seemed to materialize out of the fog, and the sight was having a
bad effect on traffic."

Thompson joined up with some of the Hell's Angels, and finally the
posse headed out across the Central Valley toward Bass Lake, attracting
local oglers all along the route. The situation was fraught from the start.
Once they arrived at Bass Lake, the bikers discovered that a roadblock
had been erected by the local police, preventing them from entering the
lake area. A restraining order had been in effect against the Angels since
1963, when a group of bikers had invaded a vacant local church and
walked out wearing vestments and priests' frocks. Without a lakeside
camping area, and with limited beer supplies, the Angels were touchy
and not prone to conciliation. Thompson was of two minds: he was

eager to chronicle the discord, to be right in the thick of it, but careful to distinguish himself as a civilian, lest he get caught in the crossfire. "When I went on runs with them, I didn't go dressed as an Angel," said Thompson. "I'd wear Levi's and boots but always a little different from theirs: a tan leather jacket instead of a black one, little things like that."

The Angels moved to placid Willow Lake, where they could swim in their grease-stained jeans without any trouble (though at a considerable remove from the area's tourists). Thompson had brought a cooler of beer with him, but it was all appropriated by the Angels before the end of the first day. "When we made that [Roger Corman] film *Hell's Angels '69*, we drank the whole crew's beer in one day," said Sonny Barger. "To Hunter, a case or two of beer was a big deal, but we had forty people or so." After the Angels collected a little over $130 between them, Hunter volunteered to buy more beer for the Angels at a general store near the post office in town. Once there, however, he was accosted by a loose gang of local vigilantes bearing weapons, and the situation heated up in a hurry. Getting beaten by a mob, Hunter wrote in *Hell's Angels*, is "like being caught in a bad surf: there is not much you can do except try to survive." "Hunter was a real stone coward whenever things started heating up," said Sonny Barger. "But he always wanted to be part of the action, wherever it was. When things started heating up, Hunter jumped into his trunk."

The situation was neutralized when Sheriff Tiny Baxter redirected Thompson and a few Angels to a general store miles away from the main tourist site, where they encountered not vigilantes but looky-loo tourists. The beer finally secured, Barger and crew were temporarily mollified. Thompson, for his part, had crossed the Rubicon into the Angels' antiestablishment camp; the strong-arm intimidation tactics they had encountered had stirred up his latent indignation, and now "I was so firmly identified with the Angels that I saw no point in trying to edge back to neutrality." By nighttime, his car had become the locus of the party, stocked with beer and surrounded by a circle of Harleys. The Angels prided themselves on pulling all-nighters during the first evening of a run, but even a prodigious partier such as Thompson couldn't hack it. Whenever he tried to steal sleep in his car, he would be awakened by the sound of prying hands reaching inside the window, trying to pop the trunk for another six-pack.

With a few minor exceptions, the Bass Lake run came off with little incident. Mercifully, Thompson didn't have to contend with any epic brawls between the Angels and their enemies. "He was trying to outdo Hemingway by living the life he was writing about," said illustrator and frequent Thompson collaborator Ralph Steadman. "His attitude was, if you buy the ticket, you have to take the ride."

Thompson figured he'd be on safer ground when he brought some of the Angels, including Barger and Terry the Tramp, to a Labor Day gathering at Ken Kesey's La Honda compound. Despite Thompson's reservations about bringing the Angels to La Honda ("I knew violent freaks when I saw them"), the Angels had in fact already spent some time there. A few months prior, Barger and a handful of fellow Angels had provoked the cops into a mad cat-and-mouse chase through the woods en route to Kesey's place; when the bikes passed through the La Honda gates, the Pranksters closed them instantly, shutting out the heat.

Kesey, who was out on bail pending his trial for the two marijuana busts, had returned to La Honda like a man unburdened and eager to resume his position as the titular leader of the Merry Pranksters. For an ex-fugitive staring down the possibility of a long prison term, Kesey's relationship with the Angels was a risky provocation, considering the close tabs the cops were keeping on the gang. In *Hell's Angels,* Thompson claims to have introduced the Angels to the Pranksters; Tom Wolfe, in *The Electric Kool-Aid Acid Test,* relates the same story. But a handful of the Angels had in fact known Kesey since the late 1950s, when he lived on Perry Lane.

At the 1965 Labor Day gathering, Thompson was accompanied by Sandy and his baby boy, Juan, along with a number of San Francisco Angels, including Terry the Tramp, Frenchy, and Barger. It was a surreal scene: a phalanx of Madera County cop cars stood watch on the edge of Kesey's property, their headlights illuminating the cliff at the edge of the road leading to Kesey's compound like lighthouse sentries. Undaunted, Kesey hung a fifteen-foot sign in front of the property that read THE MERRY PRANKSTERS WELCOME THE HELL'S ANGELS. For many of the Angels, the La Honda party was their initiation into psychoactive drugs, particularly LSD, which was still legal and always in abundant supply.

The Angels took to LSD readily, but its effects varied. "They were wandering around, counting the number of cosmos that could be seen on the head of a pin, and contemplating the philosophies of various Nazis," said Ken Babbs. A few members, such as Terry the Tramp and

Magoo, had paranoid delusions. One night, Thompson writes in *Hell's Angels,* Terry "was convinced that he'd died as a person and come back to life as a rooster which was going to be cooked on the bonfire just as soon as the music stopped. Toward the end of every dance he would rush over to the tape recorder, shouting 'NO! No! Don't let it stop!'" Despite Thompson's claim in the book that "most of the Angels became oddly peaceful on acid," Sonny Barger remembers a few nights in which the going got rough. "The Pranksters weren't fighters, and so sometimes they would say things they shouldn't say. A lot of Pranksters got beat up at times."

Despite the occasional flare-up, the Angels consorted well with the Pranksters; Barger became friends with Ken Babbs and Carolyn Adams, aka "Mountain Girl," Kesey's mistress. Thompson, for his part, tended to keep his distance from the Angels at the La Honda parties, partaking in the merriment but chronicling it all on his tape recorder, including the gang rape that both Thompson and Wolfe would recount. "Hunter was an unassuming guy in those days," said Ken Babbs. "He was just lurking around, collecting material for his book, though we really didn't know what he was up to at the time."

By the winter of 1965 Thompson had accumulated enough material on the Angels to begin writing the book. He now occupied a strange position in the Angels' universe: an outsider on the inside. Thompson had become something of an unofficial publicist for the club, a go-between who fielded interview requests from reporters. Sonny Barger, who was well aware of the kind of scoop Thompson had on his hands, and that his book would be more accurate than anything previously published, was starting to demand recompense. First Barger asked for money, but when Thompson assured him that he was nearly broke, it became a keg of beer. "Hunter just didn't understand me at all," said Barger.

Thompson stalled on the keg; he wasn't about to pay the Angels for their time. He stopped hanging out at El Adobe, shut himself into his apartment, and sat down at his rented IBM Selectric typewriter. It took him six months to write the first half of the book, far longer than he had anticipated; occasionally the stray Angel would drop by to drink his beer and have a look at some manuscript pages. Thompson didn't want to step on anyone's toes; although the book wasn't necessarily an authorized history of the Angels, accuracy was crucial, lest he get his head stomped in. As his deadline loomed, Thompson panicked. He assumed the contract would be canceled if the book wasn't turned in on time. So he packed up his typewriter and a case of Wild Turkey and started driving north on the 101 freeway until he found a suitably isolated motel near the Monterey peninsula where he could work. Hunkering down, he wrote about forty thousand words in four days.

The book was completed, but there were other matters that still rankled, such as the book cover that Random House's art department had cooked up, which Thompson ranked among "one of the worst goddamn covers of any book I had ever seen." It would have to be reshot, but Thompson would do it right this time, with his own camera. He negotiated a deal with his publishers whereby they would pay for his traveling expenses and film if he could get the Angels to pose for a suitable photograph. It was time for another run, but unlike Bass Lake, which had transpired in the middle of Thompson's yearlong tenure with the club, this time he was going in cold, having been out of touch with most of the Angels for almost six months. He gassed up his car and headed out to Squaw Rock near Mendocino, where the Angels were spending their Labor Day weekend.

At first things proceeded as they had at Bass Lake. The Angels conducted their usual rituals—staying up all night on the first night of the run and getting looped on beer and bennies, swimming in the lake fully clothed, pawing their mammas. Thompson kept up with them every step of the way this time, his camera around his neck and primed for the perfect cover shot. But Thompson's comfort level turned to complacency. "I had violated my own rules about staying out all night on a run," said Thompson. "But I had shot a lot of film that day, and I got lazy." When Hell's Angel Junkie George got into a dispute with his girlfriend and hit her across the face, Thompson barked that "only punks beat up girls." Before he knew it, Junkie George had rabbit-punched him on the back of the head, and other Angels, including Frisco and Papa Ralph, piled on. "It was the ancient and honorable Angels ethic—all on one, and one on all," said Thompson. As Thompson described it to *Playboy* magazine:

> When I grabbed the guy, he was small enough so that I could turn him around, pin his arms and just hold him. And I turned to the guy I'd been talking to and said something like, "Jesus Christ, look at this

nut, he just hit me in the fucking face, get him away from here," and the guy I was holding began to scream in this high wild voice because I had him helpless, and instead of telling him to calm down, the other guy cracked me in the side of the head—and then I knew I was in trouble.

Just as Junkie George was about to apply the finishing touch—a boulder aimed straight for Thompson's skull—Tiny the Tramp intervened. Thompson ran to his car and drove to the nearest police station, bleeding profusely like a hockey player after a vicious check, only to be told to leave because he was making a mess. He had to drive sixty miles out of town to a doctor he knew in Santa Rosa, but it turned out the doctor was vacationing in Arizona. Thompson made a beeline for the ER at the local hospital and found a number of Gypsy Jokers in the waiting room, laid out with broken bones and blood everywhere—the result of an altercation earlier in the day with a number of Hell's Angels. Thompson, his nose completely out of whack, had no time to wait for a doctor with a backlog of bikers. So he drove to the nearest general store, bought a six-pack to anesthetize himself, and proceeded to reset his nose, "using the dome of the rearview mirror, trying to remember what my nose had looked like."

Thompson's editor at Random House, Jim Silberman, wasn't at all surprised when his writer told him what happened. "I told Hunter, 'Your method of research is to tie yourself to a railroad track when you know a train is coming to it, and see what happens,'" he said. "He wants a story in which something like that will happen. He's looking for a provocation. He needed that ending, because he was really struggling with an ending for the book."

Sonny Barger regarded the incident as a chance for Thompson to close out his book with a rousing and shocking climax. "He was there for a specific reason, to get beat up," he said. "Hunter had been around long enough to know that's what's gonna happen if you get out of line, how far you could push it." Thompson admitted that "at the time, I recognized it was valuable for the book," though he denied that he was there specifically to provoke a fight. "Being stomped sort of goes with the territory, but I was pissed off when it happened."

Hell's Angels: A Strange and Terrible Saga was published in February

1967. Early reviews were effusive. The book, Richard Elman wrote in the *New Republic,* "asserts a kind of Rimbaud delirium of spirit for nearly everybody to which, of course, only the rarest geniuses can come close." The *New York Times*'s Leo Litwak praised Thompson's sure-handed control of his material: "His language is brilliant, his eye is remarkable, and his point of view is reminiscent of Huck Finn's."

Sales were brisk right off the bat. By April over fifty thousand copies were in print. Demand was such that Random House couldn't print books fast enough, much to the dismay of its author. A handful of the bookstores that Thompson visited on his thirty-five-day publicity tour had sold out and had neglected to order more copies, leaving its author shilling a product that wasn't available. "I didn't realize it was a hit," said Thompson. "I thought that Random House had fucked up. They had dingbats and interns handling the publicity, so I was worried that no one was receiving copies."

Thompson lashed out at Jim Silberman, who assured him that the book was indeed being placed in stores and selling briskly. "The sales force was very enthusiastic about the book," said Silberman. "And the book advanced in stores pretty well. It was a success from the beginning. In those days, before the chain stores, you might run into a situation where certain stores didn't have the book, but no one was surprised when it hit the bestseller list. It was a hot topic, and a brand-new voice."

It was a curious way to sell a book: using the sensational tabloid hook ("long hair in the wind, beards and bandanas flapping, earrings, armpits, chain whips, swastikas and stripped-down Harleys flashing chrome, jamming crazy through traffic at 90 miles an hour like a burst of dirty thunder," the paperback jacket copy screamed) for a story that didn't resort to cheap scare tactics. The Hell's Angels had been exploited in so many ways—by the mainstream media, in tawdry B-movies and pulp novels—but only Thompson had bothered to work his way through the fabrications, to hang in there long enough to gain their confidence and ask them questions. As if to prove the veracity of his reporting versus the distortions of the press, Thompson devoted the first third of the book to a systematic debunking of Angels myths—the Lynch Report in particular, which Thompson called "a piece of gold that fell into my lap." In Thompson's view, the Lynch Report poisoned the well; its fallacies were taken as gospel truth by reporters who were all too eager to perpetuate them.

"There is not much argument about basic facts," Thompson writes in regard to *Newsweek*'s distorted coverage of an Angels run to Porterville, California, "but the disparities in emphasis and content are the difference between a headline and a filler in most big-city newspapers." If the public perception of the Hell's Angels as an authentic menace proved anything, it was "the awesome power of the New York press establishment."

Thompson went back to George Orwell's 1931 book *Down and Out in Paris and London*, one of his favorites, in which Orwell recounted his experience living among London's poor. There is a clear-eyed candor at work in Orwell's reportage, a reluctance to pass judgment or moralize, that Thompson took to heart, even if it seemed that the Angels would be a thornier subject with which to empathize. Thompson wanted neither sympathy nor opprobrium from his readers; he just wanted them to respect the truth, to understand the Angels in their proper historical context as a peculiar phenomenon of American history.

The Hell's Angels didn't emerge fully formed out of nowhere. Rather, they were a product of the country's nomadic forebears: the Dust Bowlers of the 1930s in search of arable land, the World War II vets who opted out of the G.I. Bill for something less settled and predictable, in short the whole western tradition of boundless exploration and adventure. The Angels weren't un-American but rather "as uniquely American as jazz . . . a human hangover from the era of the Wild West." Cowboys with hogs instead of horses.

But where there's danger, there's excitement—vertiginous, full-throttle excitement. Thompson was able to capture in his mad-dog prose what the Angels knew all along: that a speed trip down an empty freeway on a motorcycle is something like an ecstatic awakening, or a very good drug experience:

Into first gear, forgetting the cars and letting the beast wind out . . . thirty-five, forty-five . . . then into second and wailing through the light at Lincoln Way, not worried about green or red signals, but only some other werewolf loony who might be pulling out, too slowly, to start his own run . . . then into third, the boomer gear, pushing seventy-five and the beginning of a windscream in the ears, a pressure on the eyeballs like diving into water off a high board . . . Bent forward, far back on the seat, and a rigid grip on the handlebars as the bike starts jumping and wavering in the wind. Taillights far up ahead coming closer, faster, and suddenly—zaapppp—going past and leaning down for a curve near the zoo, where the road swings out to sea.

Despite his best efforts not to oversell the Angels, many readers felt a strong kinship with them. Thompson received countless letters from fans inquiring about club membership. To one teenage fan, Thompson provided strong cautionary words. "The best of the Angels," he wrote in a letter dated July 6, 1967, "the guys you might want to sit down and talk to, have almost all played that game for a while and then quit for something better. The ones who left are almost all the kind who can't do anything else, and they're not much fun to talk to. They're not smart, or funny, or brave, or even original. They're just Old Punks, and that's a lot worse than being a Young Punk."

The Angels reveled in the attention, particularly since Thompson had at least some of their story right. "That book was helpful in putting us on the road to where we are today," said Sonny Barger, "but he embellished." There are indeed touches of gloss throughout. Thompson describes Barger as a "six-foot, 170-pound warehouseman from East Oakland" when in fact Barger measured five foot nine and weighed 140 pounds. Thompson also described the initiation ritual as a dousing of a prospective member in dung and urine collected from other members, but no such ritual existed. Those were niggling facts, however; by completing the rough draft of the Angels' history, Thompson had produced a riveting chronicle of an American tribe without a homeland, displaced by the mainstream and lost in perpetual exile. By doing so, he had brought himself out of freelance exile, finally; magazine editors would know who the hell he was, all right.

7

INTO THE ABYSS

To the small coterie of countercultural trendspotters on the left, the Hell's Angels were right out there on the front lines of social revolt. But they represented a blank slate upon which idealists such as Kesey could fill in whatever notions of rebellion appealed to them. As an outsider who had stumbled into an uneasy role as the Angels' emissary to the mainstream, Hunter Thompson knew better. He had spent too much time with them, witnessed too much ugliness, to think of the Angels as anything but unenlightened thugs. The Angels' final break with Kesey, and by extension the counterculture, came on October 16, 1965, when Sonny Barger and a handful of bikers crashed a Get Out of Vietnam rally at the Oakland-Berkeley line, a formal protest in which both Kesey and Beat poet Allen Ginsberg participated.

In recounting the incident near the end of *Hell's Angels*, Thompson wrote:

> The existential heroes who had passed the joint with Berkeley liberals at Kesey's parties suddenly turned into venomous beasts, rushing on the same liberals with flailing fists and shouts of "Traitors," "Communists," "Beatniks!" When push came to shove, the Hell's Angels lined up solidly with the cops, the Pentagon and the John Birch Society.

The fragile alliance between the Pranksters and the Angels was torn apart by sharply divergent attitudes toward the Vietnam War. In a few years' time, that conflict would fan out across the country like brushfire.

From the start, the nature and scope of the United States' involvement in Vietnam had been shrouded in secrecy and obfuscation. The Southeast Asian country had been repeatedly jostled by the tides of history. The area that came to be known as South Vietnam was conquered by the French in 1863, and France grabbed control of the North in 1883. In 1940, the Japanese occupied mainland Southeast Asia, including Vietnam. After the Japanese surrendered to Allied forces in 1945, control of North Vietnam was ceded to Ho Chi Minh, the leader of a band of Communist insurrectionaries who formed a provisional government, with the French stubbornly clinging to the South.

The balkanization of Vietnam was, for the most part, transpiring under the news radar; the majority of Americans at the time couldn't even locate Vietnam on a map. In the fall of 1961 President Kennedy, under the guise of a counterinsurgency policy called Project Beef-Up, sent advisors, including a detachment of the 440th Combat Crew Training Squadron, to fight alongside the Army of the Republic of Vietnam (ARVN) against the newly formed National Liberation Front, or Viet Cong. Most news organizations barely flinched, but a handful of correspondents sensed that Vietnam might become an important Cold War crucible. "We have to confront them," Kennedy confided to the *New York Times*'s Washington bureau chief, James Reston. "The only place we can do that is in Vietnam. We have to send more people over there."

"You couldn't believe anybody," the *New York Times*'s Homer Bigart recalled years later. "Half the time the Americans didn't even know where they were, let alone know what to tell you, and the South Vietnamese government made the Kremlin look like an open society." The information embargo imposed by military leadership considerably hampered efforts to piece together the most fundamental news stories. American field advisors, disgruntled over the fact that the military rank and file was ignoring their negative reports on the war's progress, turned to journalists to get the word out. Military subterfuge was now being countered by a kind of press-driven counterinsurgency conducted by stealth and prodigious legwork.

In short, it was an ideal reporter's war. The official line diverged so sharply from reality that it left enterprising journalists a lot of material to work with; every aspect of the war was fair game and open to debate.

Hundreds of reporters converged on Saigon, setting up camp in the two de facto press lodgings in Saigon, the Hotel Continental Palace and the Caravelle Hotel, and each one set out to stake his or her own claim on a story so rich in intrigue that it verged on the mythic.

In the early years of America's involvement, events in Vietnam were shape-shifting at a rapid rate, and early correspondents—including David Halberstam, Neil Sheehan, and freelancer Stanley Karnow—had the story to themselves. Halberstam's earliest dispatches for the *New York Times* were hugely influential among his contemporaries, straightforward assessments of the war's grinding futility straight from the newspaper of record.

Harold Hayes was both a fan and a casual friend of Halberstam's, and assigned a profile of the writer for the January 1964 issue of *Esquire*. Written by George Goodman, "Our Man in Saigon" included an introductory sidebar called "Background for Revolution" that summarized developments for uninformed readers and pointed out that Halberstam's dispatches were not regarded as gospel by a large portion of the mainstream press. Old-line flag-flyers resented Halberstam's seditious reporting. Hearst columnist Frank Conniff called Halberstam's work a "political time bomb" that could mislead the president and destabilize the war effort on the battlefield. Never mind the twisted logic of a news reporter somehow nudging policy makers into ill-informed decision making; Halberstam, according to Conniff, was subverting the inexorable progress of civilized democracy.

With its three-month lead time, *Esquire* couldn't possibly keep pace with the news developments in Vietnam, particularly the chaotic period leading up to and following South Vietnamese leader Ngo Dinh Diem's assassination. Nor did Hayes and Gingrich view the magazine as espousing any political point of view. Hayes thought of Vietnam as a minor skirmish, a war that would quickly resolve itself. "I never heard Harold passionately discuss politics," said George Lois, the design guru behind *Esquire*'s great covers of the era. "I considered him a liberal, but he wasn't a very vocal liberal. We used to have arguments about Vietnam, because he was convinced that it would be a short skirmish, and he was worried about running covers on the war that might be out of date by the time they were published."

For *Esquire*'s Christmas issue in 1962, Lois suggested that the magazine run a picture of the one hundredth GI killed in Vietnam, but Hayes resisted the idea. "What if we wind up with egg on our face," Hayes asked Lois, and the war was over before the issue ran? The cover was killed.

But Hayes threw Vietnam into the editorial mix just the same, treating it much the way *Esquire* treated all of the incipient developments of the decade—with a heavy dose of irreverent humor. Early satirical pieces such as "An Armchair Guide to Guerilla Warfare" were snarky attacks, *Catch-22* style, against the very absurdity of war itself.

"Well, I don't think any of us were too heads-up about the war at first," said former senior editor Robert Sherrill. "But it wasn't like we were sitting around laughing our heads off about it, either. That kind of funny skepticism can be a very effective weapon." Former editor Tom Ferrell felt that the magazine spread "an overlay of irony" over its early war coverage, a safe and tenable position for both Hayes and the magazine's advertisers. It was easy at the outset to treat Vietnam as Lyndon Johnson's folly, but by 1965 the United States had committed two hundred thousand troops to the war, and Operation Rolling Thunder, the three-year air bombing campaign against North Vietnam, had begun in earnest. America had both feet in now.

For John Sack, the Madrid bureau chief for CBS News, the notion of going to Vietnam as a correspondent was an appealing one. George Goodman's profile of Halberstam left a lasting impression on him. Sack had been Halberstam's friend when the two attended Harvard together in the early fifties. They had shared girlfriends and their dreams of literary glory. Now the image of Halberstam was staring at Sack from the pages of *Esquire:* in country and on combat patrol, waist-deep in the mud, looking over his shoulder at the camera with a satisfied grin as if to say, "Ain't this the life?"

"Of course I'd read that [George Goodman story] about David, and that picture of David crossing a swamp with the hat on and turning back to look at the camera," said Sack. "A pang of nostalgia, maybe even jealousy, went through me, and I thought: I'm supposed to be there."

The Korean War had been a pure adrenaline rush when Sack, fresh out of Harvard, covered the western front for the Army newspaper *Stars and Stripes* as a volunteer infantryman. He loved diving in and out of foxholes, driving his jeep to Seoul and back, fraternizing with the soldiers in the cold, and then rushing back to his barracks to get it all down in his stories. The CBS job was steady income, but it had become a bit sleepy, and now the network was downsizing, leaving Sack with even less work than usual. When Sack returned to New York from Spain in September 1965, he found himself with little to do but read magazines, which in his view provided a trussed-up Hollywood version of warfare in Vietnam that didn't square with his experiences. In a pitch letter to Harold Hayes proposing a different approach, Sack articulated his beef with the mainstream press:

> This week's *Time* has [the soldiers] getting off their troop ship "lean, laconic, and looking for a fight," and in *Esquire* they're "cool" and they sound so. And here in the afternoon paper: one of them is quoted saying, "I heard I was going to Vietnam. I liked the idea. I wanted to get some action."
>
> Look, this is the army, I've got to assume that a couple of things are still snafu, that the cooks are getting eggshells in the scrambled eggs, that the back-of-the-barracks conversation is about making it with girls, that a sergeant's most awful anxiety is over the sheen of his combat boots . . . that a certain number of them haven't the foggiest of where Vietnam is or why they're going there.

Where, Sack wondered, were the "sad sacks, boneheads, goldbricks, loudmouths, paranoiacs, catatonics, incompetents, semi-conscientious objectors, malingerers, cry-babies, yahoos, vulgarians, big time operators, butterfingers, sadists and surly bastards"?

Sack, who had written one piece for *Esquire* in 1959 and had published pieces in *The New Yorker* and *Harper's*, proposed to Hayes that he attach himself to an army company, travel with them by troop boat to Vietnam, and head into combat—"combat with all of its wild inanities, and I'd like to write about it my way. I'd have to get a leave of absence from CBS for this; I think I could." Sack thought only of *Esquire* for his story, because it was the only magazine that would empathize with his approach (he once sent a darkly humorous and utterly factual story on Andora, Italy, to *The New Yorker*, but the magazine held the story for six months because the editors couldn't decide if it belonged in the fact department or the fiction department; Sack sold it to *Playboy* instead).

Hayes responded: "Jesus Christ, how much would all this cost?" Not much, according to Sack: $145 for airfare to San Francisco, then a $664 ticket back to Manhattan from Vietnam. The troop boat would be free, room and board taken care of. "These would be the only expenses outside of Bamoubia beer." (In fact, the final tally was close to $5,000.) All Sack would need from Hayes was an introductory letter to the Pentagon so that he could get his press credentials. Hayes agreed, and Sack was on his way to Vietnam.

In December Sack flew to Arlington, Virginia, to determine which infantry company would provide him with the best cross section of soldiers. Despite Sack's reservations about Fort Dix, New Jersey—he had trained there for Korea and was worried that it would be loaded with white kids from New York and Boston—Pentagon brass assured him that he would find what he was looking for there. Company M, with almost a month of training ahead of them before they would be dispatched, seemed the perfect fit.

Sack arrived at Fort Dix on January 3 on CBS vacation time, just to test the waters and determine if indeed there was a story to be written. Going to Fort Dix and interviewing the soldiers before they headed into the jungles of Southeast Asia was essential for Sack; if readers were going to care about who lived and who died, then he had to establish them clearly beforehand, set up the social dynamic, and get a feel for the leadership hierarchy. It was the first rule of all great war stories: readers had to identify with the soldiers to the extent that they cared about what lay in store for the young men. This wasn't going to be a boilerplate story about military strategy; Sack simply wanted to show *Esquire*'s readers what the soldier's life was really about, the complex matrix of military, social, and economic factors that come into play. Sack was intimate with war, and bloodless heroism had very little to do with it.

Sack was put up in the guest quarters at Fort Dix and took all of his meals in the officer's mess. Every day he would wake up at 4 A.M. with the soldiers and stay with them until 9 P.M., when they turned in for the night. Interviewing the soldiers was easier than Sack had anticipated, but there were skeptics. Most of the members of M Company thought of *Esquire* as a fashion magazine, and why would a fashion rag care about them? But Sack was one of them, a veteran, and they opened up readily to him. A few of them mistook him for a father confessor, an unintended consequence of the *C* emblazoned on his black armband. The *C* stood for *correspondent,* but some of the soldiers thought it stood for *chaplain*. "I remember that I felt that I had fallen into a goldmine," said Sack. "As I was writing the notebooks, clutching onto these notebooks, thinking it's gold, it's gold. People were tremendously accessible in the army."

What struck Sack immediately was the fact that no one at Fort Dix talked about Vietnam. No one even alluded to it. It only confirmed what he already knew, that writing the story for *Esquire* was the only approach that made sense. His bosses at CBS wouldn't accept such tight-lipped nondrama. They would probably send someone like Charles Kuralt to stick a microphone and a camera in the faces of M Company's soldiers and ask them how they felt about Vietnam, and thus manufacture responses that way. But their silence *was* the story—Sack knew it in his bones. Roughly 105 of them, or half the company, would be sent to Vietnam, but none of them knew who among them would be so chosen. The ultimate decision had already been made in Arlington, among the "stiff IBM cards the size of a British pound note, one apiece for every soldier in M." A Pentagon functionary had fastened those cards to other white cards that denoted where the soldier would be assigned, and that's how M's fate was determined. Sack had witnessed this process firsthand at Arlington and was thus equipped with the terrible knowledge of knowing who was going before M Company did.

The army tried to spin the story for Sack's benefit by replacing M Company's Sergeant Shaw, a hard-nosed bad-ass, with a charmer named Doherty, but the army eventually stopped thinking about him, and he melted into the scenery. Armed with only a notebook, Sack took everything in, furiously scribbling notes that he would decipher and organize every night until at least one in the morning, and sometimes much later. "I didn't have a tape recorder, and I was scribbling notes, and I sometimes had to scribble so fast all I could scribble were notes on the notes, notes to remind me of the notes," said Sack.

He watched M Company endure the rigors of training, and sat with them after hours, when they pined for their girls back home or imagined themselves confronting the unknown enemy. Soon a few major characters began to materialize out of the more than two hundred soldiers Sack was interviewing and recording detailed notes about: Demirgian, the Armenian roughneck who wanted more than anything to be discharged, and offered twenty dollars to the first man who would break his jaw; Smith, the good Christian son who enlisted in the army because it was

God's plan; Mason, the street-tough Harlem kid; Sullivan, the cocksure ladies' man. The story was laying itself out for him like a tidy Hollywood movie, Sack thought, with a cast that represented a cross section of class and social attitudes, but he knew better than to prematurely impose neat parameters on it.

M Company's training regimen was a triumph of cold military logic, but given the impending fate of those who would be shipped off to Vietnam, it seemed to Sack an exercise in illogic, a futile imposition of protocol for a war that followed no clear rules of order. In two full months of basic training and two of infantry training, no sergeant had addressed a basic tenet of warfare: how to avoid dying. Here is how Sack described a typical barracks inspection conducted by a sergeant named Malloy, "the purist for whose sensibilities all of M's craniums had to be austere as the pyramids, its footlockers parallel as the pedestals of Karnack."

> "Peoples, all of your khaki shirts. I want everyone get himself an iron and iron the left sleeve," because in the wall lockers that is the plenary sleeve, the plenipotentiary sleeve, the sleeve that the Captain or Major would see as he trotted by—the *be-all* and the *end-all* sleeve. No names, but Mallory knew of footlockers in M whose immaculate toothbrushes lay in their permanent showcase like a little Cellini necklace, totally untouched by human teeth. Far from being peeved at a boy whose secret workaday toothbrush might be the shape of a poodle's tail or the color of kelp, Mallory was pleased with the boy's expensive initiative.

After three weeks, 105 members of M Company were assigned to Vietnam, and Sack flew with them into Saigon. The first operation involved going behind enemy lines into a Michelin rubber plantation, a place where "the Vietnamese in the village did the tapping, providing American motorists with rubber tires and killing American lieutenant colonels evenings." M's mission was a cut-and-dried search-and-destroy job, "to kill, wound, or capture its negligent enemy or drive it into the western river like a pack of distracted lemmings." Sack watched Demirgian throw hand grenades into thatched huts where "a sniper or two might inconceivably lurk," but no such snipers ever materialized. M Company was fighting an enemy it couldn't see, but the omnipresent *clump clump* of distant fire became the soundtrack of their mission, the persistent footfall of impending danger.

As Sack moved with M Company into thick jungle territory, observing them torching rice caches and hamlets where no VC lurked, the morale of the soldiers hardened into something feral and irrational. "In actual fact, the cavalry's big lieutenant colonel had given the order, *insure that positive identification be made:* a sniper in the house destroy it, otherwise spare it. But through the iteration of imperatives . . . and a wise apprehension that the colonel couldn't be serious, his order was almost unrecognizable when it got through channels to Demirgian's Sergeant Gore. Gore heard the order as, 'Kill everything. Destroy everything. Kill the cows, the pigs, the chickens—everything.'"

Then M Company finally notched its first casualty.

A cavalry sergeant, seeing a sort of bunker place, a hut above, hole below, and hearing some voices inside it, told Demirgian to throw a grenade in. Demirgian hesitating, ___, a solider we have met before, though not by name, jumped from his APC and flipped in a hand grenade himself. It rolled through the door hitting a sort of earthen baffle before it exploded and ___ gasped as ten or a dozen women and children came shrieking out in their crinkled pajamas: no blood, no apparent injuries, though, and ___ got onto his carrier again, it continued on. Yoshioka aboard, drove up to this hovel, and a Negro specialist-four, his black rifle in his hands, warily extended his head in, peering through the darkness one or two seconds before he cried, *"Oh my God!"*

"What's the matter," said a second specialist.

"They hit a little girl," and in his muscular arms the Negro specialist brought out a seven-year-old, long black hair and little earrings, staring eyes—*eyes,* her eyes are what froze themselves onto M's memory, it seemed there was no white to those eyes, nothing but black ellipses like black goldfish.

The writer, who had always felt strongly about America definitively resolving any war that it entered, and who felt that Vietnam was a just cause worth dying for, had now borne witness to a pointless exercise in civilian savagery. But surely, Sack thought, it had been an anomaly.

When he returned to the first brigade of the first division, he contritely explained to Colonel Sam Walker that it was his intention to cover the operation and file his story. The operation had turned into a big mess, but Sack was stuck with his story. "I know it isn't typical," Sack told Walker, "but I have to do my job." Walker paused for a few seconds and then told Sack, "It's typical."

Sack was incredulous. "I couldn't believe that with this vast army in Vietnam . . . with this huge thing going on . . . that all it was resulting in was the occasional death of seven-year-old girls."

Sack returned to the Continental Hotel in Saigon and wrote up his twenty-seven-thousand-word story. In early June 1966 he sent copies to Hayes and his literary agent, Candida Donadio, in the hopes that she might see the potential to turn it into a book. Donadio turned him down, and Sack was despondent. What was missing? Sack thumbed through some other Vietnam articles in the army library and came across another story on Fort Dix in *Holiday* magazine by a young writer named Michael Herr, a former assistant editor at the magazine. What struck Sack about the article, called "Fort Dix: The New Army Game," was his powerful command of language and character, the way Herr infused everything he wrote about with tremendous dramatic power. Herr described things, whereas Sack just reported the facts. Sack was taken by the way Herr wrote about happy hour in the officers' club and how the senior officers resembled "Rotarians, perhaps highly skilled laborers—lathe operators out for dinner before a night of bowling." Sack was intent on writing in scenes—that's the way he had structured the TV documentaries he had made for CBS—but it wasn't enough to simply string dry scenarios together. Herr's story made him go back and look harder, push himself to elevate his prose to Herr's level.

The next day, after touring an aircraft carrier, Sack returned to the Continental to check his mail and found a telegram from Harold Hayes informing him that his story would take up the entire feature well for the next issue. A second telegram read: "Send any and all pictures of company M both in training and combat. Vitally important please do your best. Hayes."

Sack was ecstatic, but he had not taken a single picture during his time with M Company. He would have to go on another operation, possibly risking his life, to get the shots he needed. Borrowing a camera from Associated Press photographer Horst Faas, Sack joined M on something called Operation El Paso, hopping a helicopter along with Dimirgian and a few other soldiers. When the copter landed in enemy territory, Sack quickly jumped into a shell hole so that he could get shots of M disembarking from the helicopters. It turned out to be a cold landing zone—no VC to be found anywhere—but M formed a perimeter, and Sack had a perfect photo op to take advantage of.

When he returned to Saigon, he had over seven hundred pictures, and he sent them along to Hayes. The *Esquire* editor was now hearing rumblings from the magazine's legal department that the story could perhaps trigger an avalanche of libel lawsuits. Sack's portrait of army life in Vietnam left nothing out; his protagonists' most closely held thoughts about the war, marriage, combat, leadership in the field—it was all in there. Perhaps, Hayes suggested, Sack could go back into the field and get legal releases from his ten most prominent characters? That way, if anyone else complained about Sack's story, the magazine would have some leverage.

Sack agreed, but his mission to track down M Company would be considerably more difficult this time. They were now in war zone C, right on the Cambodian border, an area so dangerous that no helicopters would go near it. Sack's only recourse was to take the press helicopter, with a pilot who was under orders to fly anywhere an accredited journalist told him to go, but he needed five passengers in order to reserve it. Sack's girlfriend, a French baroness named Anne Rousseau de Prienne, was eager to break in her tailor-made camouflage outfit and agreed to join him. Sack had learned that M Company was going to burn a huge cache of rice, the largest yet found, in Zone C, and he convinced Dan Rather to bring his crew along.

That made five, but when Sack showed up at 7 A.M. to fly over, the helicopter pilot begged off: it was too risky. Sack pleaded with him, and they cut a deal: the helicopter would touch down, allowing them just enough time to disembark, but it would take off right afterward. They would have to make it back to Saigon on their own.

No sooner did they get close to Zone C than they were hit by machine gun fire; a .50 caliber bullet pierced the helicopter blade as they touched down. M Company was surrounded by VC, but Sack had a job to do. The baroness and Rather and his crew headed down the road to see the rice burn, leaving Sack to get his releases signed. Dimirgian, Sullivan, and a few other subjects were there, and Sack made swift work of it. He spotted a brigadier general in a bubble helicopter and hitched a ride back to Saigon that way, leaving Rather and the baroness to fend for themselves.

Hours went by, and still no sign of Rather or the baroness. At five that afternoon Sack retired to the bar of the Hotel Continental, where correspondents gathered daily for an informal happy hour, and he regaled his friend Dan Minor, a radio journalist, with the day's adventures. Minor found it worrisome that Sack would just leave his girlfriend and Rather in the lurch like that. Sack told him, "Don't worry, she'll prance in here shortly saying, 'How could you do this to me?'"

"I'd be worried," said Minor.

Sack told him, "No, I promise you."

A half hour later the baroness trudged across the square in her tiger suit, stomped into the Continental, and screamed, "How could you do this? I have dinner tonight with the French ambassador at seven. It's a dress party. I need to put my makeup on, I need to fix my hair, it is six o'clock, and I don't have time to put on my dress or makeup!"

When Sack returned to New York in June, he sent his longer, revised piece to Candida Donadio. This time she was sold, and made a book deal at publisher David Segal's New American Library. Sack spent the summer adding scenes to the book at his aunt's house in Ocean Bay Park on Fire Island while Hayes and the *Esquire* staff prepared the publication of his story.

In the end, none of the pictures that Sack snapped in Vietnam would be chosen for the piece; the story would have no accompanying art at all. Sack's notion for the cover—pasting Beetle Bailey's face over the heads of real soldiers—was rejected outright by Hayes, who told Sack, "You don't understand your story at all."

The cover would break ranks with the usual whimsical mockeries that *Esquire* had become famous for ever since it hired George Lois in 1962. Lois—whose firm, Papert, Koenig, Lois, had revolutionized American advertising with its sharp-witted, graphically bold designs for all manner of consumer products—was a master of bitter irony and the use of typography as a graphic element. The September cover had showed a male underclassman applying lipstick, with the headline "How Our Red-Blooded Campus Heroes Are Beating the Draft." That was the old *Esquire* approach to Vietnam. The October headline augured something darker and more menacing, the new twisted reality of the war. It was a slightly altered quote from Sack's story, written in white letters against a black background—a device that Lois had previously used in a cough syrup ad:

"OH MY GOD — WE HIT A LITTLE GIRL"
The True Story of M Company, from Fort Dix to Vietnam

"I just plucked out the line," said Lois. "Putting people in harm's way—that's what the war was all about." When Lois first presented the cover to Hayes, "Harold nearly fell to the floor. It was the first antiwar cover in a mainstream magazine." Lois warned Hayes, "You're gonna lose a lot of advertisers over this." Hayes paused, look up at Lois, and whispered, "You nailed it."

It was the first mainstream magazine article to discuss civilian casualties at any length, but not everyone at *Esquire* was thrilled with Sack's impressionistic technique. Bob Sherrill felt that it was a "fucking good story" that got "mired up in detail." He took issue with Sack's lead, which began, "One, two, three at the most weeks and they would give M company its orders—*they* being those dim Olympian entities who reputedly threw cards into an IBM machine or into a hat to determine where each soldier in M would go next, which ones to stay there in the United States, which to live softly in Europe, and which to fight and to die in Vietnam." It was in Sherrill's view too fanciful, designed to "lead you away from the story instead of getting right into it."

Among the editorial staff, Sherrill was a minority of one. Hayes loved the story so much that he threw a party in Sack's honor at the *Esquire* offices. "It's a much better story because you were for the war," Hayes told Sack. "If you were against the war, it wouldn't have come across as strongly."

Published by New American Library in February 1967, *M* was the first great Vietnam book, and it's unquestionably the first great New Journalism war book. Layer by layer, Sack peels away M Company's thin veneer of resolve and courage, because it was absurd to pretend that soldiers in Vietnam were somehow made of sterner stuff. Soldiers weren't superheroes; they were just unfortunate conscripts, forced to endure ungodly privations and accept death as a given of wartime life. Sack's grunts were scared, they were vulnerable, they cared a little too much. This was a major break from the time-honored tradition of war report- age, especially that of the World War II correspondents who pumped up the heroism of our boys on the front until they effaced every vestige of realism.

Guadalcanal Diary, Richard Tregaskis's chronicle of the U.S. Marines' crucial strategic battle in which an undermanned division defeated the Japanese and gained control of the Pacific island, was a massive bestseller when it was first published by Random House in January 1943. Tregaskis, a correspondent for the International News Service, attached himself to the First Marine Division during the six-month campaign, the only jour- nalist to do so. Tregaskis's narrative is a smooth upward trajectory of victo- ries both small and significant, building to a final, victorious crescendo. Tregaskis doesn't linger too long on the injured and the maimed soldiers; they are just the prelude to a successful counterattack. His soldiers are no different from those cardboard cutouts Sack had referred to in his query letters to Hayes—lean, mean, and looking for a fight.

> [T]he Marines had fought with the greatest ferocity. Corp. George F. Grady (of New York City) had charged a group of eight Japs on Gatuvu Hill, by himself. He had killed two with his sub-machine gun; when the gun jammed, he used it as a club to kill one more Jap, and then, dropping his gun, had drawn the sheath knife he carried on his belt and stabbed two more of the enemy, before he himself was killed by the three Japs who remained unharmed.

The book is a diary of everything Tregaskis saw or heard, written in a clipped, straightforward style. Any speculative attempts at taking the emotional temperature of the situation are limited to Tregaskis's own observations. Sack, in contrast, removes all mediation between reporter and reader; the story is not his, and thus not for him to tell.

"I don't put myself in the story," Sack said. "I don't want the reader to even be aware that I'm there. . . . I want [the reader] to feel they're get- ting undiluted reality—that they're getting absolutely objective report- ing. Of course, this is a trick—because I have my own values, as to what's important, what's worth saying, and what isn't worth saying. I'm choos- ing what I want to write, and I'm choosing the order it goes in, so though it pretends to objectivity it's really subjective, and this is a trick on the reader."

For Sack, reportorial objectivity was one of the great myths. "If one million people threw roses at Khrushchev when he came to the States, and one person threw an egg and hit him, the Russian press would say one million threw roses, and the American press would say one threw an egg . . . and both of them would think they were being objective." It was all about sifting through the information and choosing your own version of the truth.

To merely describe the activities of M Company in the verdant thicket of Laikhe was insufficient, because inertia and boredom was the story. The enemy was a wraith, unseen but omnipresent. Campaigns became tense waiting games, followed by a flashpoint cataclysm. This, Sack discerned, was slowly driving the members of M Company to seek refuge inside their own heads, which were being cross-wired by the confusing nature of their mission.

When M did encounter the Viet Cong, the army's rules of engagement faded into insignificance. The intuitive, improvised tactics of guerilla warfare left M Company confused and frayed, with no other recourse but to "burn, burn, burn" everything within reach.

"Burn, burn, burn," Demirgian's captain said. "Yes, that'll get old Charlie out."

"Yes, sir," the lieutenant said.

"Charlie's got no place to hide now. Charlie don't like open spaces," the captain said.

"No sir, that Charlie don't," the lieutenant said.

"That's the way to end this war. Burn villages—burn the farms," the captain said. "Then the Charlies'll have to come in planting and rebuilding instead of just stirring up trouble."

Demirgian got the worst of it in-country. After he narrowly escaped an ambush, his animus curdled into something irrational and murderous—and Sack probes his running inner monologue, a continuous reel of malevolence.

Charlie tries to creep up on me, Demirgian wistfully said to himself—
*Charlie ever tries that and I'm just going to lie here—yeah! Let him get ten
meters from me, the stupid little son-of-a. Yeah, and I'll have my hand
grenade and I'll pull the pin—Charlie you're about to have had it! k-k-k!*

Sack wasn't present during such incidents, but he didn't make anything up, either. The use of interior monologues in the work of Sack and
other New Journalists would become a common complaint among the
genre's critics: how can a writer know what his or her subject is thinking
at any given moment? The answer is that the writer merely has to ask. "I
hate to use the word *reconstructed* because the word *reconstructed* means
that I make up the conversation," said Sack. "But I just mean that . . .
every conversation is something somebody told me they said, and I'm
putting that together with what somebody else has told me."

The critics had another phrase to describe *M:* "documentary novel."
"Sack manages to make M Company both vivid and human, deeply
human," wrote Leonard Kriegal in *The Nation.* "He has written a superb
book." The *New York Times*'s Neil Sheehan had problems with Sack's
"hyperbolic" style but still found plenty of "fine" and "often powerful"
writing. *Publishers Weekly* was taken with the "satiric bite" of M's Vietnam
experiences; Sack's "quietly written" humor, the anonymous reviewer
wrote, packed "a cumulative punch."

M was a watershed story for *Esquire,* both formally and thematically.
Harold Hayes would no longer flinch at confronting the horrors of Vietnam in the pages of the magazine. And the worst was yet to come.

8

HELL SUCKS

The positive critical response to M convinced Harold Hayes that covering Vietnam without tears or irony was the right thing to do. Troop levels had escalated to 485,000 by the winter of 1967; military casualties had doubled from the previous year, to 11,153, with over 100,000 North and South Vietnamese civilians dead. Hayes didn't want *Esquire* to tip too far in the direction of far-left publications such as Warren Hinckle's *Ramparts* magazine or Paul Krassner's *The Realist*, but the magazine's gentle mockeries of the war were clearly untenable now. John Sack had seen to that.

No writer was as eager to go in-country as Michael Herr. He wanted not only to cover the war but to produce a modern-day *Nostromo*. He wanted to write the greatest book to come out of the war. Herr, whose Fort Dix story for *Holiday* magazine had compelled John Sack to become a better writer, was a native of Syracuse, New York, who had attended Nottingham High School with John Berendt, who would become an editor at *Esquire*. Herr was charismatic, a natural-born leader, elected president of the student body in his senior year. "Michael was brilliant in high school, already a terrific writer," said Berendt. "Even then, he had a way of expressing himself that made it clear he was a talent to be reckoned with."

The son of a jewelry store proprietor in Syracuse, Herr's great ambition in life was to become a literary eminence. Herr graduated from Syracuse University in 1961; after a six-month stint in the army reserve, he did some freelance writing, mostly movie reviews for the *New Leader*—from which he was fired for writing positive notices on films that his editors disliked—and travel stories for *Holiday* magazine.

Herr applied for an editing job at *Esquire* in 1962, only to lose out to his former Nottingham classmate Berendt. He was probably better off not chained to an editor's desk; the urge to travel to far-flung areas of the world and write about them was too strong. He got his wish after a short tenure as an assistant editor at *Holiday* when the magazine made him a roving correspondent.

Herr's global dispatches for *Holiday* were competent efforts but hardly an indication of his special gifts. Herr was *Holiday*'s intrepid adventurer, filing stories from Guam, the Amazon jungle (where he interviewed a snake hunter), Venezuela, Taipei, and elsewhere—solidly written stories redolent of atmosphere and finely attuned to the rituals and folkways of the people. But it wasn't until Herr observed basic training at Fort Dix in early 1966 at a time when conscription for Vietnam was being ramped up considerably that his latent skills emerged.

For Herr, Vietnam was *the* story, but a benign general-interest magazine such as *Holiday* wasn't exactly the right forum for what he wanted to do. Aside from *M,* which Herr admired, no one had really tackled the war by writing what Herr called "higher journalism." In a May 1967 pitch letter to Hayes, Herr talked of writing "the best kind of journalism" from Vietnam to "make it seem more real." Herr had a number of potential approaches: perhaps a story on the press in Vietnam, or General Westmoreland, or the Green Berets. He wanted to be *Esquire*'s man in Vietnam, roaming the country for stories that could be published in a monthly column: "extended vignettes, set pieces, geographical sketches, personality portraits . . . even battle reportage." What Herr wouldn't touch were straight news stories—the piles of statistics and body-count roll calls that explained nothing and which, Herr thought, made "conventional propaganda look innocent." If *Esquire* wanted the real news, then Herr would tease it out from the players in a format unmediated by army censors or the dictates of wary editors.

Herr didn't regard himself as a journalist in the conventional sense. "I don't have a journalist's instincts and have absolutely no training or discipline as a journalist," he once told an interviewer. Herr could respond to events in the fullness of time and free of odious deadline pressure, sniffing out the hidden currents at work, the subterranean angle. Herr would later write:

> Conventional journalism could no more reveal this war than conventional firepower could win it; all it could do was view the most profound event of the American decade and turn it into a communications pudding, taking its most obvious, undeniable history and making it into a secret history. And the very best correspondents knew even more than that.

"As an overwhelming, unavoidable fact of our time," he wrote Hayes in the summer of 1967, "it goes deeper than anything my generation has known, even deeper, I'm afraid, than Kennedy's murder. No matter when it ends or how it ends, it will leave a mark on this country like the trail of slime that a sand slug leaves, a lasting taint."

Esquire wouldn't even have to advance that much money for Herr's trip; *Holiday* magazine had assigned him another story, and he had a little advance check from a contract that his agent, Candida Donadio, had sold for a Vietnam project. The press accreditation would allow him to travel with the military, roaming freely as he saw fit. Berendt vouched for Herr, and Hayes figured it was a risk worth taking.

It took four months for Herr to get to Saigon. *Holiday* kept holding off on his money, but Herr welcomed the delay; he needed to steel his nerves, gird himself for the big plunge. He bought a gun while staying with some friends in San Francisco, then flew to New York in November. In a November 15 cable to Hayes from Taipei, Herr confided, "This lapse of four months since leaving New York has made me sit bolt upright in the middle of the night, all sweats and bad nerves, more times than I care to remember."

Herr left for Vietnam on December 1, 1967. "I was twenty-seven years old when I went there," he recalled, "and I had spent all the time previous traveling and writing pieces about places, but not writing what I felt I should be writing. So I believed before I ever got there that that was the time and the place and the subject. I was very ambitious for the work and had large expectations for it."

During the first month of Herr's stay, things went pretty much as he had anticipated. He tagged along on a few offensives, hung out with the infantrymen, and gathered material for his first column with virtually no interference from the military brass. But on January 30, in the early hours of the Vietnamese lunar new year, more than one hundred South Vietnamese cities, including Danang and Qui Nhon, were rocked by a series of North Vietnamese mortar attacks. Saigon, the country's safe house for the press, was attacked the following day. The Tet Offensive, as it came to be known, was a well-coordinated and overwhelming show of force that laid waste to any assurances of an imminent U.S. victory. Herr was in a compound in Cantho with the Special Forces when the Tet offensive was launched, and he knew at once that the first column he had filed, as well as a Vietnam establishment chart similar to the establishment charts that *Esquire* had run in the past, in which a hierarchy of civilian power brokers would be mapped out in a splashy graphic, would be of little use now.

"Tet changed everything here, and made the material I'd filed seem like it had been written from a different war. . . . I'm sick about it (I never worked harder on anything in my life, and I think the text was good), but I don't see any real alternative to crapping it," Herr wrote to Hayes on February 5. "As for the column, or that mess of stuff I sent in as a column, I'd rather not see that run right now, either. It is not the same war, not in any way. Before the Tet offensive, the war had a predictable rhythm and tone, and the two month lead time wasn't an issue. . . . Now, all the terms have changed, all the old assumptions about the war, about our chances for even the most ignoble kind of 'victory' in it, have been turned around."

After enduring five sleepless nights when he couldn't even find the time to slip his boots off, Herr found his way back to Saigon, where about fifteen hundred Vietcong troops were occupying much of the city that had until then provided a buffer zone between the correspondents and the war. He sent a cable to Hayes laying out the situation in some detail, but the mails had been suspended, and Herr wasn't even sure if Hayes had received it. After a few days of "getting my head together," Herr traveled to the city of Hue, where he was caught in the crossfire between ARVN and North Vietnamese forces for control of the city.

Though he had "passed through so many decimated towns and cities that they all get mixed up in my mind," Hue was even worse. "The destruction has been incredible, air strikes knocking out whole blocks of the one really lovely city in Vietnam, destroying the university, the walls around the Citadel [an ARVN military headquarters], and, probably tomorrow, the Citadel itself."

While Herr's jeep was passing through the district of Cholon, a mortar round exploded ten yards away, burning a four-inch piece of shrapnel into his backpack, which he was wearing. Another shrapnel fragment blinded the jeep's driver in his left eye. Everywhere Herr looked, there were desperate scenes of sickening destruction and human displacement—refugees wandering aimlessly away from burned-out homes while South Vietnamese soldiers looted abandoned businesses. Herr chalked it up to U.S. hubris and arrogance, the government's persistent underestimation of the enemy. "Where we have not been smug," he wrote Hayes, "we have been hysterical, and we will pay for all of it."

There were scores of civilian casualties sprawled across the countryside: a little girl who had been killed while riding her bike, an old man hunched over his straw hat. In Hue, Herr saw a dead Vietnamese man whose skull had been sheared off by shrapnel debris, so that the top of his head resembled an open flap loosely hinged to the back of his head. The image spooked him. "I knew that if I stayed here he would drift in over me that night, grinning and dripping, all rot and green-black bloat." Herr now viewed Vietnam as a bifurcated war: "There are two Vietnams, the one that I'm up to my ass in here and the one perceived in the States by people who've never been here. They are mutually exclusive."

Herr was appalled at the cognitive dissonance that existed between the cushy major press outlets in Saigon, with their lavish budgets and extensive R&R excursions, their "$3,000 a month digs at the Continental or the Caravelle," and the horrors that were taking place within the city and nearly every other major city in the South. "I have colleagues in the press corps here, some of them incredible fakes, fantastic hacks, who live so well on their expense accounts that they may never be able to adjust to peace."

Herr, on the other hand, was out of money and begged Hayes for at least a small stipend to tide him over for a while: "I'm not after a lot of money, only enough." Hayes complied via Western Union, and Herr traveled on to Khesanh and Danang, two cities that were caught in a death struggle in the conflict between North and South Vietnamese forces. He finally made his way back to Saigon, the cosmopolitan city that was now a hollowed-out war zone, its streets besmirched with human feces and dead foliage. American engineers and construction workers, "who were making it here like they'd never made it at home," were now openly brandishing AK-47s and .45 Magnum pistols, "and no mob of Mississippi sheriff's boys ever promised more bad news."

Herr had seen too much to bring it all into focus in a single story, but he had to file another piece for *Esquire* now that the other column was being spiked. "For all the talk about Vietnam being a television war, I never believed it was television's war," Herr recalled years later. "I always believed it was a writer's war. And in my arrogance and ignorance I wanted to be the one to prove it." The truth, as Herr saw it, was that the entire country had been engulfed and absorbed by the war as if by a virulent viral strain.

> We know that for years now, there has been no country here but the war. The landscape has been converted to terrain, the geography broken down into its more useful components; corps and zones, tactical areas of responsibility, vicinities of operation, outposts, positions, objectives, fields of fire.

The Tet offensive, he wrote, had changed everything, "made this an entirely different war, made it Something Else . . . Before Tet, there was some clean touch to jungle encounters, some virtue to their brevity, always the promise of quick release from whatever horror there was . . . Now, it is awful, just plain awful, awful without relief."

Herr described what he had seen in Hue with graphic clarity: the refugees huddled against the side of the road heading toward nowhere, the bombed-out houses, the ARVN looting. In south Hue, Herr had accompanied the Marines across a large public park along the banks of the Perfume River, where the university had been totaled and the picturesque colonial-era villas destroyed. Crouched with the troops behind a crumbling villa that served as flimsy cover, Herr watched the Marines, who had secured the central south bank of the river and were now moving westward, try to capture the Citadel, the headquarters of the First ARVN Battalion, which had been commandeered by the Vietcong during the Tet offensive.

It stayed cold for the next ten days, cold and dark, and that damp gloom was the background for the footage that we all took out of the Citadel. The little sunlight there was caught in the heavy motes of dust that blew up from the wreckage of the East Wall, held it until everything you saw was filtered through it. And most of what you saw was taken in from unaccustomed angles, prone positions or quick looks from a crouch; lying flat out, hearing the hard dry rattle of shrapnel scudding against the debris around you, listening to the Marine next to you who didn't moan, "Oh my God, Oh Sweet Jesus, Oh Holy Mother save me," but who sobbed instead, "Are you *ready* for this? I mean, are you *ready* for this?"

Herr wrote about the friendship he had cultivated with an unidentified general, a veteran of the Indochina war and a lover of Beethoven and Blake, a fellow adrenaline addict, like Herr, repelled by but also drawn into the war.

The eyes are ice-blue but not cold, and they suggest his most interesting trait, an originality of mind that one never associates with the Military, and which constantly catches you off balance.

The general chides Herr for his morbid obsession with death: "'That way lies you-know-what,' he says, tapping his temple."

"If you hate this all so much, why do you stay?"

He has me there. I wait a moment before answering. "Because, General, it's the only war we've got."

And he really smiles now. After all that talk, we're speaking the same language again.

The South Vietnamese eventually took back the Citadel at Hue, but it was an inconsequential notch in the holster, another bloody battle with no appreciable net results. While Herr's empathy for the infantrymen comes through, his version of the quagmire was relentlessly bleak, more bleak than in *M*, even—a corrective for what Herr felt was the anesthetizing slow drip of the television and mainstream print press, with its refusal to break through the distancing "fourth wall" of objectivity. "I think the [television] coverage turned the war into something that was happening in the media wonderland that we are all increasingly living in," Herr said. "Unless we keep ourselves extremely alert, we're going to be utterly consumed by that horribly homogenized, not real and not unreal, twilight world of television."

Hayes was blown away by Herr's story, passing it on to Arnold Gingrich with a note that praised Herr's "extraordinarily perceptive and thoughtful battle report." This "John Sack–type sleeper" was obviously not going to work as a column; "better as a straight piece," he wrote to Gingrich. Fiction editor Bob Brown captured the tone of the piece with his headline, swiped from something that one of the grunts scrawled on his helmet: "Hell Sucks."

The magazine's legal department vetted the story, but they were troubled by the last section, Herr's conversation with the unnamed general, the one who Herr wrote "was seen . . . leaving the house of a famous courtesan in Dalat, driving off in a jeep with a Swedish K across his lap." Hayes circled this passage and scrawled "No—if the general is identifiable" in the margin of Herr's manuscript. Could the writer reveal his source?

From Hong Kong, the writer sent a wire to the lawyers and a cable to Hayes with an explanation. "He's fiction—I hoped that that would be obvious—made up out of a dozen odd types I've run into around Vietnam, most especially a Special Forces colonel I knew in the Delta who was a Persian scholar and a fanatic about things like the late Beethoven quartets ('The purest thing in all of music!'). There were others, too, the party intellectuals of the Vietnam war, and they all went into the General."

Hayes signed off on it. *Esquire*'s policy on scene reconstructions and composites remained consistent during this period, when the magazine's best nonfiction writers were pushing their reportage into murky territory where creative interpretation mingled with straight documentation. The approval of composites was largely a matter of trust in the writers themselves and of the editorial staff's instinctual sense that the copy being sent in was not made up out of whole cloth. Composites had to be constructed from the raw material of interviews and observation, lest the reporting move uncomfortably close to pure fiction. "Harold was a good lie detector," said Bob Sherrill. "He knew almost immediately if something was bullshit."

The soldiers at Hue of whom Herr had written approved as well. Shortly after "Hell Sucks" was published, a number of Marines gave Herr an inscribed cigarette lighter as a token of their appreciation.

Herr's next two articles took on a darker cast as he told the grim story of Khesanh, the combat base for the Twenty-Sixth Marine Battalion perched in the Highlands along the Laos-Vietnam border. Khesanh had been under siege by North Vietnamese troops since the summer of 1967. A continual series of attacks against the NVA's entrenched positions had done little to squelch the enemy's firepower or resolve, and the North's attacks only ratcheted into heavy artillery offensives against the Khesanh base. As reinforcements poured into Khesanh by the thousands, the Vietcong fortified their positions in the surrounding hills and along the nearby infiltration routes.

Assigned to a base whose medical detachment was planted "insanely close" to an airstrip that had been repeatedly shelled, with no solid intelligence regarding the Vietcong's troop strength or their precise location, the troops at Khesanh were hiding in plain sight and blindly groping for whatever small victories they could muster.

Khesanh was even worse than Hue. Herr sensed an existential dread that had spread like pestilence: exhausted soldiers narcotizing themselves with dope and booze, "animals who were so spaced out that they began taking pills called Diarrhea Aid to keep their walks to exposed latrines at a minimum." Body bags were covered with flies, and the debris of aircraft lay sprawled near the dangerous airstrip; the jury-rigged medical detachment looked like a rickety lean-to with no air cover whatsoever. The Highlands were "spooky, unbearably spooky, spooky beyond belief." Long, sustained silences were interrupted "only by the sighing of cattle or the rotor thud of a helicopter, the one sound I know that is both sharp and dull at the same time."

If all the barbed wire and all of the sandbags were taken away, Khesanh would have looked like one of those Columbian valley slums whose meanness is the abiding factor, whose despair is so palpable that for days after you leave you are filled with a vicarious shame for the misery you have just tripped through. At Khesanh, most bunkers were nothing more than hovels with inadequate overhead cover, and you could not believe that Americans were living this way, even in the middle of a war.

In Khesanh Herr witnessed some savage scenes. While ducking for cover in a trench during an air attack, Herr watched a solider get hit in the throat, "making the sounds a baby will make who is trying to work up the breath for a good scream." Another grunt nearby was "splattered badly across the legs and groin." Herr pulled him into the trench; when Herr told him that he was not a fellow grunt but a correspondent, the soldier replied, "Be careful, mister. Please be careful."

Herr was a magazine writer; he had no deadline pressure, no mandate to file daily dispatches. His intention from the start was to somehow get a book out of his experiences, even if he hadn't made his intentions explicitly clear to Hayes, and he positioned himself at a remove from the other journalists. After the triumph of "Hell Sucks," Hayes gave Herr his head to write whatever he pleased. "My ties to New York were as slight as my assignment was vague," he would write. "I wasn't really an oddity in the press corps, but I was a preculiarity, an extremely privileged one."

He had little use for the daily press briefings by the military brass—what the press corps referred to as the Five o'Clock Follies, an "Orwellian grope" through the day's events. While his writer acquaintances, such as the *New York Times*'s Bernie Weinraub and Peter Arnett of the Associated Press, would head to their respective bureaus at day's end to write their stories, Herr would retire to the Continental Hotel to grab a drink, write some leisurely notes, maybe not write anything at all. He was drawn to what *Esquire* writer Garry Wills regarded as a key tenet of New Journalism, the centrifugal instinct . . . to "get to the sidelines and watch," and that yielded his best material.

"A lot of us never really knew what Michael was up to," said Weinraub. "Everyone else had a work rhythm that they were into, and Michael had this long lead time, and he was a little bit on the fringe. All the newspaper, newsweekly, and wire guys hung out together, but Michael was so much more offbeat than all those guys. To be a freelancer in Vietnam was to have no home base, as it were, no support system in the field. So you had to be pretty unusual to want to do that."

Years after the fact, Herr admitted that, going in, he "had no idea what the subject was." But the latitude that Hayes had given him allowed Herr to roam freely and indulge his literary whims, which meant inventing composite soldiers whose personas were stitched together from what Herr observed during many zonked-out late-night bull sessions over cheap scotch and locally procured marijuana, the psychedelic rock of the Jefferson Airplane and the Grateful Dead pounding out of radios and soundtracking this dreadful episode in the soldiers' lives.

For the Khesanh stories, which were really designed for the forthcoming big Vietnam book, Herr invented a black soldier who called himself Day Tripper (so named because he hated going out on night missions) and his white running buddy Mayhew, two worn-out grunts whose devil-may-care fatalism squared with Herr's attitudes about the detached confusion that Khesanh had bred in its entrenched troops. They were a far cry from John Sack's disillusioned idealists, who, Demirgian notwithstanding, had been careful to keep their insurrectionary tendencies in check with a measure of cautious optimism. Day Tripper and Mayhew bore a closer resemblance to the deserting soldier in Stephen Crane's *Red Badge of Courage,* subjugating their fear into a demotic sense of the absurd.

Herr portrayed Day Tripper and Mayhew as the dark side of Abbott and Costello. The soldiers' plainspoken, schoolboy jive was a shot across the bow to all those deadline humps writing about the "lean, laconic fighters" that John Sack found so distasteful in *Time* magazine's coverage. When Mayhew signs up for a four-month extension, Day Tripper lays into him:

"You jus' another dumb Grunt. What I gotta talk to you for? It's like you never hear one word I say to you, ever. Not one word. An' I *know* . . . oh man, I jus' *know* you already sign that paper."

Mayhew didn't say anything. It was hard to believe that the two were around the same age.

"What I gonna do with you, poor f—er? Why . . . why you jus' don' go running out over th' wire there? Let 'em gun you down an' get it over with. Here, man, here's a grenade. Why you jus' don' go up backa the shithouse an' pull the pin an' lie down on it?"

"You're unbe*lie*vable! It's just four months!"

"Four months? Baby, four *seconds* in this whorehouse'll get you greased."

Herr captured perfectly the slangy cadence of the soldiers' speech—and their coarsened psyches as well. Instead of soldiers sending pictures of themselves to their girls back home, Herr wrote of a grunt sending back "a gook's ear," soldiers procuring clandestine pot from Vietnamese dealers, men grabbing snatches of haunted sleep that provided no reprieve from their waking nightmares. It was rough stuff, but Hayes let him keep all of it, except for the *fuck*s and *motherfucker*s, many of which had to be excised.

The specifics of warfare weren't as crucial to Herr as what it *really* felt like to be in that godforsaken place, fighting a meaningless war. The ominous crepuscular sounds, the smell of death everywhere—Vietnam was a pincer movement on the senses, and it was enough to slowly drive strong men mad. But television couldn't convey that feeling sufficiently in two dimensions, and daily journalism never had the time or the space for it. Having internalized the horror, Herr used a savagely poetic style that appealed to the reader's emotions rather than his intellect.

Herr knew that, like John Sack, he was shooting down well-worn myths about the implacable stoicism of upright American soldiers, but it was the only reality he saw fit to report. He also knew that his whip-saw prose, which darted around on a Benzedrine bender, was radical even for *Esquire*. "I say to myself, 'Oh, no, you can't say that! It isn't done,'" he said. "'You can't move from this to that. So and so never did it. And since he never did it, you can't do it.'" But you reach a point where you realize that of course you can do it. You can do anything. You just have to issue yourself a license to do those things. And then you do them."

Herr carried the voices of the soldiers in his head long after he had arrived back in New York. Herr regarded himself as a literary person, almost to a fault, but the grunts' words had moved him more profoundly than the most powerful war literature. He didn't have to unduly probe, or ask them leading questions; they would locate the stories on their own, and it was all so terribly eloquent, so eloquently terrible. The dialogue in the Khesanh stories wasn't directly transcribed from notes; the scenes were drawn from the hazy, half-lit dream world of Khesanh that still burned in Herr's subconscious. Herr readily admitted that his version of Vietnam was some mutant hybrid of fiction and reportage, but however outrageous it might have read on the page, it was all culled from what he had seen and heard. "Everything . . . happened *for* me, even if it didn't necessarily happen *to* me," he said.

The Khesanh stories, as well as his April 1970 *Esquire* story "The War Correspondent: A Reappraisal," were ostensibly a jumping-off point for the book that Herr always intended to write, and even *Esquire,* in its "Backstage" column of September 1969, had announced that a volume was imminent. Herr was indeed writing, but it wasn't coming quickly. Shortly after Herr had left Vietnam, photographers Sean Flynn and Dana Stone, two of his closest compatriots in Vietnam, were killed in Cambodia. Herr had been full of hubris and the weird, jangly energy of the war when he returned in the summer of 1969; he felt confident that he could channel all he had witnessed into the book. But now the weight of all that horror was pressing down on him, and he fell into a debilitating clinical depression—what Herr called a "massive collapse"—that led to writer's block.

"Sometimes I was crazy in a very public way," Herr recalled, "and after I crashed, I was crazy in a very private way. Except during the very worst of it, I always knew that it was redeemable. There was a certain point at which I realized that whatever I thought I was doing, I wasn't completely conscious of what I was actually doing. So as long as I didn't know what I was doing, I would do whatever came up. I always believed that there was another door on the other side of me that I could go through and come out of with a book under my arm."

Herr experienced a "complete paralysis of fear"; he felt like the blocked writer in Stephen King's *The Shining,* just writing the same sentence over and over again, filling up endless pages with unusable material. He had the meat of the narrative in hand—the *Esquire* stories—but no notion of where to start the book and how to resolve it satisfactorily.

Herr went into psychoanalysis and struggled for six years before the words finally came. "I had trouble adjusting to the seventies," he told Tom Morgan, who profiled Herr in 1984 for *Esquire.* "We got fucked up in Vietnam. Lost some dear friends. We didn't get away all that clean." In an unpublished passage from Herr's 1976 *Esquire* story "High on War," the writer seemed to be working through his lingering feelings about the war:

This is already a long time ago, I can remember the feelings but I can't still have them. A common prayer for the over-attached: You'll let it go sooner or later, why not do it now? Memory print, voices and faces, stories like filament through a piece of time, so attached to the experience that nothing moved and nothing went away.

Herr didn't publish his Vietnam book until 1977, but the long delay didn't mitigate its impact. *Dispatches* was recognized as a classic of war literature, one of the few nonfiction Vietnam books that rose to the level of great fiction. "Quite simply," the *New York Times* critic C. D. B. Bryan wrote, "*Dispatches* is the best book to have been written about the Vietnam War. . . . Herr's literary style derives from the era of acid rock, the Beatles' films, of that druggy, Hunter Thompson once-removed-from-reality appreciation of The Great Cosmic Joke."

Dispatches was nominated for the 1978 National Book Award, and it has never gone out of print. The book's echoes reverberated in all of the great films made about the war, from the surreal mindscape of *Apocalypse Now* (for which Herr wrote the voiceover narration) to the unrepentant brutality of Oliver Stone's *Platoon*. Herr couldn't get away from Vietnam. Even when he moved to London in 1980 "because I didn't want to become some kind of horrible media personage," he continued to receive letters from vets and countless offers from magazine editors to cover some war or another. He turned them all down. "Any more wars? Never again, man," Herr told Tom Morgan. "Shit, man, every time there's a shot fired around the world, I get a call from some magazine to go. I don't want to see it ever again. I don't want to, man."

9

HISTORY AS A NOVEL,
THE NOVEL AS HISTORY

In late May 1964, a time when the majority of Americans still supported the war in Vietnam, there appeared in the *New York Herald Tribune* an ad signed by 149 draft-age men stating that they wouldn't fight in Southeast Asia if called to do so. The ad attracted little attention; it was just a benign little cherry bomb, nothing more. The country's antiwar dissent had yet to coalesce into a critical mass.

The earliest antiwar protests, such as the teach-ins at the University of Michigan, Kent State, and Berkeley, were relatively modest in size and received only perfunctory news coverage. On July 3, 1964, the day that President Johnson signed the Civil Rights Act into law, a group of protesters led by activist David Dellinger and folk singer Joan Baez gathered at Lafayette Park to protest Vietnam. As a symbolic act of disobedience, the group then kneeled en masse in front of the White House, and found to their surprise that no one cared. The police made no effort to arrest anyone.

The early antiwar protests were fairly genteel affairs, orchestrated by earnest conscientious objectors, civil rights organizers, and nuclear disarmament activists whose combined ire was not enough to evoke more than a collective shrug by the large majority of Americans who still supported the war effort. Not every peacenik was a protester, either; it was one thing to voice one's concerns privately, quite another to carry a placard.

When President Johnson ramped up draft calls from 17,000 a month to 35,000 a month in July 1965, it triggered a wave of domestic protest that pulled in a large coalition of disparate groups, from students and businessmen to housewives and Social Security card carriers. Public figures were also starting to contribute their voices to the dissent. In 1967 the Bertrand Russell Peace Foundation sponsored the International War Crimes Tribunal, a plenipotentiary forum whose board members included novelist James Baldwin and existential philosopher Jean-Paul Sartre. Using extensive testimony from Vietnamese citizens, journalists, medical experts, and military leaders, the tribunal sought to reprimand the United States for its illegal use of chemical weaponry, particularly napalm, against the North Vietnamese, comparing it to the war atrocities committed by the Nazis during World War II.

The tribunal was great theater, a display of rhetorical fireworks and moving testimony. At one point Sartre branded tribunal no-show Secretary of State Dean Rusk a "mediocre functionary" and wondered how Rusk, "armed with the miserable arguments with which he amuses the press," would fare in a face-to-face debate with Bertrand Russell.

But the tribunal was being held in Stockholm, and its indignant cry was faint and indistinct in the United States, a series of small stories buried in newspapers. A few enterprising activists would bring the debate to the foreground in short order, however. Weaned on the civil rights battles of the early sixties, they were now transferring their energies to domestic resistance against the war, using their flair for street theater and human mobilization in ways that the first-wave protesters could not fathom.

Jerry Rubin, a former journalist and aspiring socialist who had participated in the earliest Free Speech Movement marches that had coalesced around the University of California campus in Berkeley, was the shrewdest agent provocateur of the antiwar effort. A founding member of the Youth International Movement along with Brandeis University grad and civil rights veteran Abbie Hoffman, Rubin in early 1965 was organizing two days of demonstrations to take place on the Berkeley campus, a call to action that would land Cal at the forefront of student-driven social activism in America. The idea was to bring the world's leading intellectuals to Berkeley, including Bertrand Russell and muckraking journalist I. F. Stone, to speak out against the war and thus generate big media coverage. The first name on Rubin's list of speakers was Norman Mailer.

Rubin's fellow members on the Vietnam Day Committee, particularly the New Left contingent, vehemently objected. For one thing, Mailer was too controversial, a poor role model for passive resistance. On November 19, 1960, in the waning hours of a party held in his Brooklyn Heights apartment, Mailer had stabbed his second wife, Adele, in the sternum and the back with a penknife, and was sent to Bellevue Hospital for seventeen days of psychiatric observation. That act of violence didn't sit well with the organizers, nor did Mailer's penchant for drunken fisticuffs and other petty demonstrations of hairy-chested machismo. A writer who craved attention and respect, Mailer tended to suck all the air out of a room. Not, in other words, a man of the people.

But Rubin knew better than to reduce Mailer to the sum of his scandals. He had been a fan of Mailer's journalism, which in Rubin's view had been the era's most probing social criticism written expressly for a mainstream audience. In Rubin's view, "Superman Comes to the Supermart," Mailer's *Esquire* dispatch from the 1960 Democratic convention, had nailed the dialectic between the Kennedy voters who wanted to see America return to its best version of itself—its crackling dynamism and hunger for social progress made flesh in their young candidate—and the dreary Nixonians who settled for flabby middle-class pieties. Rubin sensed that, given the proper forum, Mailer could articulate the rage and fear of the antiwar constituency with the same rhetorical brilliance he had displayed in that seminal *Esquire* piece.

Mailer himself wasn't so sure. He was, he once wrote when he was forty-four years old, an "embattled aging enfant terrible of the literary world, wise father of six children, radical intellectual, existential philosopher, hard-working author, champion of obscenity, husband of four battling wives, admirable bar drinker, and much exaggerated street fighter, party giver, hostess insulter." Mailer was a generation removed from the young firebrands of the New Left, whose radicalism had been forged in civil rights organizations like Tom Hayden's Students for a Democratic Society. Mailer was a World War II veteran who had seen action in the Pacific theater and had written what many still considered the definitive novel of the "good war," *The Naked and the Dead*. But that book was nearly two decades old, and since then, Mailer's literary reputation had waxed and waned.

The Deer Park, his 1955 novel about spiritual rot in Hollywood for which he had struggled to find a publisher, received some of the most vituperatively negative reviews of Mailer's career. He was perhaps the most famous writer in America but, in the VDC's view, for all the wrong reasons. "Mailer has grown a great deal in power of language since he wrote *The Naked and the Dead*," wrote *Saturday Review* critic Granville Hicks in 1967. "Why, then, has he been writing trivia and tripe for the past ten years or more?"

"There had been all too many years when he had the reputation of being a loser," Mailer would self-reflexively write. "It had cost him too much. While he could hardly, at this stage of his career, look back on a succession of well-timed and generally established triumphs, his consolation in those hours when he was most uncharitable to himself is that taken at his very worst he was at least still worthy of being a character in a novel by Balzac, win one day, lose the next, and do it with boom!"

Rubin knew better. Mailer had been an early champion of the Beats, a major theorist of "hip" culture with his essay "The White Negro." Mailer agreed in principle with the impulses and objectives of the antiwar movement, but he had never been a joiner, not to the extent that he could commit himself to activism in earnest. Deep in his bones, he still thought of himself as a literary establishment figure, an Edwardian of sorts who kept himself at an Olympian remove from organized social movements. Even when he was dabbling with Marxism with his friend Jean Malaquois in the forties, its appeal was largely that of an intellectual construct, a mode of thought to toss around for a while. Karl Marx's *Das Kapital*, he felt, "helps you to think better, but I never thought Marx was right, as far as Communism would solve all our problems."

When Rubin called him, Mailer demurred; he had never addressed a large crowd before—Rubin estimated that as many as twenty thousand demonstrators might turn out. Mailer's chosen forum was not oratory but the written word. And would the young crowd respond to him in any meaningful way or just dismiss him as an old-guard anachronism? Mailer told Rubin he would think about it.

A week later, he called Rubin back with an offer to present a speech on LBJ; it would be an opportunity to air some grievances against the president that Mailer had been pondering for a while. Some members of the Vietnam Day Committee wanted to screen the speech, but Rubin wouldn't have it; it was absurd to think that Mailer would agree to that kind of scrutiny. The idea, Rubin argued, was to provide a forum for the march's participants to offer any viewpoint they so chose. Rubin threatened to quit the VDC unless Mailer was given free rein, and eventually the VDC relented.

Accompanied by novelist Don Carpenter and poet Michael McClure, Mailer encountered bedlam at every turn at Berkeley—protesters packed shoulder to shoulder on the steps of Sproul Hall, hanging over the balconies and rooftops of the surrounding buildings, chanting pro-NVA slogans and brash incitements to stop the madness. Paul Krassner, the editor and publisher of the underground paper *The Realist*, who was emceeing the event, introduced Mailer to thunderous applause. Mailer, dressed in a three-piece suit, addressed the crowd:

> [L]isten, Lyndon Johnson, you have gone too far this time. You are a bully with an Air Force, and since you will not call off your Air Force, there are young people who will persecute you back. It is a little thing, but it will hound you into nightmares and endless corridors of nights without sleep, it will hound you ... they will print up little pictures of you, Lyndon Johnson, the size of postcards, the size of stamps, and some will glue these pictures to walls and posters and telephone booths and billboards ... These pictures will be sent everywhere. These pictures will be pasted up everywhere, upside down.

Rubin claimed it was the first time that any major public figure had actually made fun of the president, reduced him to a grotesquerie—the emperor as unholy fool (Krassner published the speech in *The Realist*). Don Carpenter chalked it up to Mailer's uncanny prescience: "He knew that by telling everyone to turn LBJ's picture upside down he was going to make political history." So successful was Mailer's speech that after he walked away from the podium, Dick Gregory, the comedian turned activist who was the next scheduled speaker, turned to Carpenter, and said, "I ain't gonna follow that shit."

The Berkeley speech ratified Mailer's alliance with the counterculture, much to the dismay of his literary contemporaries in New York, who, despite their vehement objections to the war, didn't abide by the broad-strokes insurrectionary antics of Rubin and Hoffman; a pull-out from Vietnam would not solve either country's problems. When the

Parisian Review published a series of essays on the war in the spring of 1965 with contributions from literary critic Alfred Kazin, writer Norman Podhoretz, and others, along with a joint antiwar statement signed by the writers that tempered criticism of the war with skepticism as to whether the complete withdrawal of U.S. troops would leave the South Vietnamese to an uncertain fate, Mailer led off his contribution with a handwritten note: "Three cheers, lads, your words read like they were written in milk of magnesia." "A Communist bureaucrat," he reflected in his essay, "is not likely to do any more harm or destroy any more spirit than a wheeler-dealer, a platoon sergeant, or a corporation executive overseas." He was distancing himself from the hand-wringing equivocations of the northeastern literary establishment and aligning himself with the front-runners of the youth movement, even if their guerilla-style grit didn't necessarily square with his own idiosyncratic ideas about public comportment.

Mailer's affinity for the VDC's grand ambition to change the consciousness of the country was consistent with what the writer had been trying to do with his writing, particularly his journalism: to burrow into the diseased marrow of American life and restore it to health. Mailer regarded himself as a writer pitched somewhere between the mystic and the rationalist, trying to elevate his readers' attitudes about justice and virtue through his impassioned prose. Like Rubin and the rest, he agreed that there was a cancer eating away at the country, with its architecture "under the yoke of a monstrous building boom" which "gave promise of being the ugliest in the history of man," a pharmaceutical industry whose proliferation of "wonder drugs" could trigger a "mass poisoning," and most important, a military-industrial complex whose Cold War realpolitik could strengthen the very thing it wished to vanquish: "Prosperity was Communism's poison, but attack from capitalism was its transfusion of blood."

The Berkeley speech was a transformative experience for many of those activists who were skeptical of Mailer. The truth was that this middle-aged literary eminence could articulate their discontent more eloquently and coherently than could many of the titular leaders of the movement, including Rubin and Hoffman, whose to-the-barricades war chants lacked Mailer's nuance and moral heft. If Mailer could provide a bridge between the World War II generation and the baby boomers, it would only help their cause.

Mailer, as it turned out, needed the movement as much as it needed him; his involvement in the antiwar cause became a creative super-charger. For a writer whose entire published oeuvre had given off a strong whiff of paranoia over the nefarious workings of powerful Ameri-can institutions (the anticapitalist rants in the second half of his novel *Barbary Shore,* the shady CIA operatives and their pernicious intentions in 1963's *An American Dream*) and a healthy ambivalence about what it meant to be a "good American," the Vietnam War provided a wealth of source material; he would get three books out of it in three years.

Two of those books were nonfiction. Although Mailer's overarching goal as a writer was "to hit the longest ball in American letters" and perhaps even snag the Nobel Prize, he had moved effortlessly between fiction and nonfiction since the mid-fifties. Journalism was instant grati-fication for quick pay, a forum for expressing opinions about events that were still playing themselves out, a chance to work through ideas that didn't necessarily belong in his novels. "Moving from one activity to another makes sense if you do it with a hint of wit or a touch of grace— which I don't say I've always done, far from it," Mailer told *Playboy* in 1968. "But I think moving from one activity to another can give momentum. If you do it well you can increase the energy you bring to the next piece of work." Although he thought of nonfiction as stopgap work, his journalism would be Mailer's greatest literary achievement of the 1960s.

Mailer addressed the Southeast Asian conflict, albeit in highly oblique fashion, in his novel *Why Are We in Vietnam?* published by G. P. Putnam in September 1967. The book's narrator is Ranald "D. J." Jethroe, an eighteen-year-old shit-kicking Texan and "disk jockey to the world" with a head full of free-associative jive about the corporation as secular religion, the life-giving properties of horny women, and the emasculation of the Anglo-Saxon male in the face of the Negro's sexual prowess (shades of "The White Negro"). D. J. and his pal Tex embark on a bear hunt along with D. J.'s father, Rusty, an executive with a plastics company and "the cream of corporation corporateness," the three of them engorged with bloodlust as a sublimation of unfulfilled sexual urges.

One of Mailer's pet theories during this period was that malignancy of mind and body could be attributed to the subconscious being out of sync with the conscious. In this case, it is the latent homosexuality of the two boys—their hopelessly displaced sexual energies masked by studly posturing—that makes a perverse fetish out of violence. The war isn't mentioned until the last page of the book, but it doesn't need to be; employing a highly discursive, hipster-slang prose style that reads like a prim Burroughs, Mailer seems to be enamored of the notion that the Anglo-Saxon male's inability to come to grips with his own maleness leads to porno-violent cataclysms such as Vietnam.

Why Are We in Vietnam? is a tough slog; aside from the sludgy prose style, Mailer tries too hard to use graphic sexual descriptions as a cudgel to shock his reader. The book was so out of character that critics tended to be either confused or annoyed; the *New York Times*'s Anatole Broyard called it "a third-rate work of art, yet it's a first-rate outrage to our sensibilities." Years after its publication, Mailer still regarded it as one of his best books, a successful bid to "transmute myself and create a somewhat ongoing, rampant, inflamed, sort of mad ego."

A month after the publication of the book, which sold anemically, Mailer received a call from novelist Mitch Goodman. An old Harvard classmate and the husband of Beat poet Denise Levertov, Goodman had made headlines seven months earlier when he organized a protest at the National Book Awards ceremony due to the presence of the ceremony's guest speaker, Vice President Hubert Humphrey. Goodman wondered if Mailer might participate in a rally and march on the Pentagon that was going to take place in a few weeks' time.

The march was the brainchild of David Dellinger, a veteran antiwar protester and protégé of A. J. Muste, a pacifist who had been arrested twice during World War II for refusing to enlist. The son of a successful Boston litigator, Dellinger had been the driving force behind the 1964 Lafayette Park demonstration and had met both Rubin and Mailer during the Berkeley teach-in in 1965. Now Dellinger would turn to Rubin to help him organize the Pentagon march, despite their vastly different approaches. Dellinger was averse to centralized leadership and the use of figureheads as protest symbols, and he disdained any provocations that might lead to violent scenes with cops. The idea was to provide spiritual uplift and some meaningful reflection, an approach that was antithetical to Rubin's confrontational finger-pointing.

But Rubin had a proven track record for mobilizing large groups and drawing media attention with guerilla theater. Four months earlier, Rubin, Abbie Hoffman, and a handful of others had sneaked their way to the third-floor gallery of the New York Stock Exchange and ranted about the corporate sponsorship of the war. After the speech, they tossed fistfuls of cash down to the floor, sending traders into a frenzied scramble that was supposed to symbolize the "death of money" and the corrosive effects of greed on American capitalism. Dellinger couldn't even conceive of dreaming up such a scheme, but Rubin's in-your-face style was an asset to the movement.

Mailer had met Dellinger in Berkeley, and Rubin had been his champion there, but two years later activist fatigue had set in. Since the LBJ speech had turned him into a de facto spokesman for the anti-war movement, Mailer had been inundated with requests for speeches and monetary contributions for the cause, and he wanted to woodshed a little, get back down to the business of writing. He was also anxious to edit his self-financed film, *Maidstone,* a loosely structured morality tale about crime and punishment. There was no time for long-winded oratorical marathons, which Mailer found insufferably, terminally dull. As he would write later of himself,

> Mailer received such news with no particular pleasure. It sounded vaguely and uneasily like a free-for-all with students, state troopers, and Hell's Angels flying in and out of the reports—exactly the sort of operation they seemed to have every other weekend out on the Coast.

But this march would be different, Goodman assured Mailer; they were going to storm the halls of the Pentagon, shut it down, and immobilize the machinery of military savagery. Mailer conceded that it sounded like an ambitious objective, perhaps the most ambitious operation in the short history of the antiwar movement. "Mitch, I'll be there," Mailer told his college friend, "but I can't pretend I'm happy about it."

A week later, Mailer received another call, this time from Ed de Grazia, a free-speech lawyer who was organizing an evening of talks at the Ambassador ballroom in Washington two days prior to the march on the Pentagon. Mailer also accepted this invitation with great reluctance.

The impulse behind de Grazia's event, which was called Artists of Conscience, was to raise bail money for those who might be arrested during the march, but it was also a chance for a few members of the Old Left to make themselves heard before the march. Joining Mailer would be the brilliant *Esquire* film critic and leftist firebrand Dwight Macdonald, Pulitzer Prize–winning poet Robert Lowell (who had been a conscientious objector during World War II), and author Paul Goodman, whose book *Growing Up Absurd* had criticized the stifling "organized systems" of American culture and their deleterious effects on youth.

But waxing platitudinous about the evils of U.S. imperialism was not what Mailer had in mind. The Ambassador event was a starchy circus, a processional of well-behaved liberals reaffirming each other's assumptions. It was just another academic colloquy, Mailer thought, and thus impotent in the face of the potential violence that thousands of protesters would be confronting over the weekend. A spokesman for the antiwar movement but hardly a card-carrying member of the radical left (he classified his political views as "left conservative"), a major cultural figure but a controversial public one, Mailer felt at loose ends, unsure of his role.

So he got drunk. The drinking began at the dinner party held prior to the Artists of Conscience event, and continued well after the event had started. By the time the six hundred audience members had filed into the Ambassador, a former movie palace that had been retrofitted to accommodate rock concerts, Mailer was nowhere to be found. De Grazia, who had offered Mailer the opening speech, could hold off on starting, but only for so long.

Mailer wasn't the only one drinking; Lowell was in his cups too, and so were a few other scheduled speakers. De Grazia characterized the atmosphere as "kind of up in the air, chaotic—which was characteristic of the whole movement—but the situation onstage was . . . well, everyone was just going to do his thing." An hour after the scheduled start time, de Grazia approached the podium and introduced Goodman, "because he was the soberest." Mailer entered the auditorium during Goodman's speech, clutching a copy of *Why Are We in Vietnam?* in one hand and a tin mug of bourbon in the other. And he had to pee, badly. He staggered to the men's room and, despite missing the commode and relieving himself on the bathroom floor, made it through the packed crowd and walked onstage.

Mailer was enraged that de Grazia hadn't waited for his opening remarks, as they had agreed, and he lit into the lawyer before approaching the podium. "He used me as a foil to play off his grandiosity," said de Grazia. "He liked to do stuff like that because it made him feel alive. Mailer was most comfortable with combative relationships."

His ensuing speech was the rhetorical inverse of his great address at Berkeley—frustratingly discursive, hostile, sodden. Instead of invoking LBJ as a figure of ridicule, Mailer himself became Johnson's bête noir, his "dwarf alter ego." Using a thick southern accent, Mailer unleashed a profane tirade that sounded like an outtake from his last novel. "I pissed on the floor," he bellowed, sans microphone, at the crowd. "How's that for Black Power full of white piss? You know all those reporters are going to say it was shit tomorrow. Fuck them. Fuck all of them." Mailer's performance was received with catcalls and boos. "I think Mailer was afraid that the crowd was going to throw bottles at him," said de Grazia.

The next day, a hung-over Mailer arrived late for the draft card demonstration that was being staged outside the Justice Department prior to the official Pentagon march. As the students and academics gathered up their cards in a pile before they were to be proffered to the attorney general, Mailer felt a queasy twinge of self-pity and generational displacement:

> He was forty-four years old, and it had taken him most of those forty-four years to begin to be able to enjoy his pleasures where he found them, rather than worry about those pleasures which eluded him—it was obviously no time to embark on ventures which could eventually give one more than a few years in jail. Yet, there was no escape.

Because the Vietnam War was "an obscene war, the worst war the nation had ever been in," its "logic might compel sacrifice from those who were not so accustomed." Yes, Mailer would be committed to the event, even risk a few hours in jail, but only to a point. There was a party in New York on Saturday night that he really wanted to attend, so it was best to get arrested early so that he could be released in time to catch a plane back to the city. Despite Mailer's hand-wringing, it seemed that the latent New York establishment gallivanter in him would prevail.

The march, as David Dellinger and Jerry Rubin had envisioned it, would start with a mass rally at the Lincoln Memorial and then work its way across the Potomac via the Arlington Bridge to the Pentagon. A short rally would be held, with speeches from dignitaries such as Noam Chomsky and Benjamin Spock, followed by the blockade of the building and an "exorcism" of the Pentagon led by Abbie Hoffman.

But the crowd that day was bigger than the organizers had anticipated—some news reports estimated that as many as 250,000 had traveled to Washington for the march—which meant that the relatively short distance from the memorial to the Pentagon would take hours and require reserves of patience and fortitude. Mailer, marching in his dark blue pinstripe suit on the front lines along with Lowell, Chomsky, Macdonald, and Goodman, sensed unease and restlessness in the atmosphere:

> Picture then this mass, bored for hours by speeches, now elated at the beginning of the March, now made irritable by delay, now compressed, all old latent pips of claustrophobia popping out of the crush, and picture them as they stepped out toward the bridge, monitors in the lead, hollow square behind, next the line of notables with ten, then hundreds of lines squeezing up behind, helicopters overhead, police gunning motorcycles, cameras spinning their gears like the winging of horseflies, TV car busting seams with hysterically overworked technicians, suns beating overhead—this huge avalanche of people rumbled forward thirty feet and came to a stop in disorder, the lines behind breaking and warping and melding into themselves to make a crowd not a parade, and some jam-up in the front, just what no one knew, now they were moving again. Forty more feet. They stopped.

The huge mass disgorged itself in the Pentagon's North Parking lot, an area so "large and empty that any army would have felt small in its expanse." A festival-like atmosphere fell upon the gathering, and the formal invocation to exorcise the Pentagon of its demons had begun in earnest with spontaneous chants of "Out, demons, out!" Mailer found himself whispering the words almost in spite of himself. He was emboldened and heartened by this display of wild, seditious energy. Now was the time to transgress whatever police barricade he could find and get himself arrested, before he had to endure any more boring polemics. In a grassy area between the lot and the Pentagon, he found two ranks of military police spaced about ten yards apart standing in front of a low-hanging rope. With little fanfare Mailer climbed over the rope and walked almost directly into the waiting arms of a couple of officers. "Mailer had the guts to get himself arrested when a lot of other celebrities at the march didn't," said Ed de Grazia. "The idea was not only to demonstrate but to put your body on the line as well, and he did that."

Nonplussed, with his hands stuffed into the pockets of his suit, Mailer was led into a Volkswagen camper that drove him to an army truck filled with other protestors, but none of his marching comrades were present, no Lowell or Macdonald. The plan had been for everyone to get arrested, and make news. Had they copped out at the last minute?

Mailer and his vanmates were next corralled onto a yellow school bus, which brought them to a post office that would be used as a makeshift holding pen for the protestors. At one point, a unusually rabid protestor started hurling horrid epithets in Mailer's direction, yelling "You Jew bastard" repeatedly, to which Mailer dished it right back, with a few "dirty Krauts" thrown in for good measure. If he was going to offer himself as a prize prisoner on the altar of justice, he was damn sure going to defend himself with both fists cocked.

Most of the detainees were processed through quickly, with small fines and a promise not to engage in any protest activities near the Pentagon for six months. With $200 in his pocket, Mailer began to hand out bail money to the kids who were broke. While the others were arraigned and released, Mailer remained, and his hopes of making the New York dinner party dimmed. "In jail," he wrote, "a man who wished to keep his sanity, must never anticipate, never expect, never hope with such high focus of hope that disappointment would be painful. Because there was no place for disappointment to go in prison, except back into one's cells. Prison was frustration."

After interminably tedious hours of waiting, word came down that Mailer would be processed not in Washington but in a workhouse in Occoquan, Virginia. Here he was given a ratty cot on which to sleep, but the bright lights obviated any chance of rest. Joining Mailer in Occoquan were Noam Chomsky, Tuli Kupferberg, a fixture of the Greenwich Village underground and co-leader of the Fugs, a folk-rock agitprop group that had played in the Pentagon parking lot during the rally, and David

Dellinger. "He was being treated worse than anyone else in jail," said Kupferberg of Mailer's incarceration. "They kept him to the last to be arraigned, so he had to wait an extra day, and it was obvious they were gonna make an example of him. No one was urging Norman to stay. Very few people were gonna stay, and I didn't know what he was going to do."

Kupferberg refused to cop a plea, which would have resulted in a five-day suspended sentence; it was too convenient, he reasoned, and would make his arrest seem like the obligatory gesture of an antiwar dilettante. Mailer was struck by Kupferberg's depth of commitment; perhaps his arrest too could become something more meaningful than a hollow symbolic gesture. He decided to plead guilty as well. He would not give himself up and thus confirm for himself the doubts that had dogged him from the very beginning of his engagement with the antiwar movement—that he was a middle-aged man with middle-class values, a writer who could articulate the rage of the outlaw in his writing but couldn't become an outlaw himself.

Despite a nolo contendere plea, Mailer's sentence was the harshest yet meted out to the public figures that participated in the march: thirty days, of which twenty-five would be suspended. That meant five days in jail. A hastily handwritten appeal was immediately filed, and after much wrangling with the public prosecutor, Mailer was released on his own recognizance.

The arrest had been a crucible for Mailer, a test of his own resolve to fight the power, but in the end, he was resigned to his role as belletrist rebel. Even Jerry Rubin had to admit that "there was a part of me that knew he would have lost his effectiveness if he'd become a Yippie. Norman was better being Norman Mailer."

Mailer didn't go to Washington with a specific magazine assignment, but when he returned to New York it occurred to him that there was a story to be written, perhaps a major piece. He called Midge Decter, the executive editor of *Harper's,* and asked her if she would be interested in something. Mailer and Decter's relationship dated back to the late forties. *Commentary,* the liberal politics and arts monthly created by Decter's husband, Norman Podhoretz, in 1945, had raved about both *The Naked and the Dead* and *The Deer Park,* and Mailer had contributed occasional pieces to the magazine since the early sixties.

Harper's editor, thirty-two-year-old Willie Morris, had become the youngest editor in chief in the magazine's 117-year history in 1967 when John Fischer resigned over a dispute with publisher John Cowles over the magazine's finances. A native of Jackson, Mississippi, and a Rhodes Scholar, Morris was a writer (his memoir *North Toward Home* was published to great critical acclaim in 1967) and an editing prodigy. He landed his first publishing job in 1960, as editor of the muckraking biweeekly *Texas Observer,* at the age of twenty-five.

Morris and Decter, along with senior editor Bob Kotlowitz, had quickly transformed *Harper's* from a sleepy and irrelevant literary monthly ("as fuddy-duddy a magazine as you could imagine," said Decter) into a lively and essential forum for arts and political coverage, with contributions from such writers as David Halberstam, Elizabeth Hardwick, Neil Sheehan, Alfred Kazin, Gay Talese, Joan Didion, Irwin Shaw, Bernard Malamud, and Philip Roth. Mailer knew he would be in good company, and Decter was thrilled that Mailer had thought of the magazine. Morris, who had first met Mailer in Austin in 1961 when was editing the *Texas Observer,* felt Mailer was "in many ways a literary genius," and he was equally as enthusiastic about bedecking the revamped *Harper's* with Mailer's byline. There had been past attempts by Morris to get Mailer to contribute to the magazine during his tenure as associate editor, but Mailer's fee was too exorbitant, and John Fischer had never been a fan. When Morris argued vociferously for *Harper's* to publish an excerpt from Mailer's 1966 anthology *Cannibals and Christians,* Fischer rejected it.

Now that the opportunity to publish Mailer had again presented itself, there was no way Morris was going to let the writer walk. Morris sensed this would be a watershed piece, "one that would strike to the taproots of all that was happening at that moment in the nation." In order to get Mailer his rate without forcing *Harper's* to pay an exorbitant amount, Mailer's agent, Scott Meredith, had the idea to sell the Pentagon story as a book as well. Mailer would be given a wide berth to write long, perhaps twenty thousand words, more than enough to justify a smallish but timely title.

Morris and Decter arranged meetings with a number of publishers. When the editor in chief of Macmillan had the temerity to ask Decter about the sales figures for *Why Are We in Vietnam?* the meeting was peremptorily cut short. Meredith eventually handled the sale of the book for $25,000 to Bob Gutwillig at New American Library; *Harper's* would pay $10,000 for the article, a fifty-cents-a-word bargain. But Mailer would have to move fast; NAL didn't want to sit on a book whose subject matter would go stale in a few months' time, and *Harper's* needed to close their issue in less than eight weeks. The story, it was agreed, would run in the February 1968 issue.

The money was in place, but Morris had yet to have a single conversation with Mailer, who, according to Meredith, was in seclusion at his beach house in Provincetown. It was a trick of fate that found Mailer, who was accompanied by the boxer Jose Torres, face-to-face with Morris one afternoon on the corner of Forty-fourth Street and Seventh Avenue near the Algonquin Hotel, where Morris was having drinks with a reporter from the *Memphis Commercial Appeal*.

"We just closed the deal," Morris told Mailer.

"I know, I know. This one could be kind of good. I'll be in touch."

Two weeks later, Morris received a phone call from Mailer. The story was getting long; he would need more time. The February issue wasn't tenable now; Morris would try to run it in March instead, with a final printer's deadline of January 10.

The writing came slowly at first. Mailer's reporting at the Pentagon was circumscribed by his role as a participant; any pretense of a full-scale accounting of the event was out the question. He was unsure about the tone and scale of the piece; what was required was a deeper understanding of the counterculture's political landscape, the inner workings of the various factions and how they responded to each other. From his assistant Sandy Charlebois, an activist and insider who had spent a fair amount of time with the Diggers' Emmett Grogan in San Francisco and had helped create the name "Yippies" with Rubin and Hoffman, Mailer received deep background on the origins of street theater as political outreach. Mailer dispatched Charlebois to interview Rubin extensively, and Mailer himself grilled Paul Krassner, Dellinger, and other participants in the Pentagon march.

Given the ambitious scope of the project at hand, Mailer's domestic situation provided a constant source of distraction. His already parlous relationship with his wife, actress Beverly Bentley, was disintegrating into violent bouts of recriminatory, boozy verbal strafing. At one point during the writing process, Beverly claimed that Mailer had performed voodoo on her stereo system because the needle had unaccountably dropped off when he had left the house one night. "You're evil!" she screamed. The piece, Mailer recalled, "was written in a towering depression. I did it in two months and those were some of the worst weeks of my life. I would come home each night and think it was terrible."

After attempting a number of approaches, Mailer as a last resort tried the third person; the "I" would become a character called Norman Mailer. Even then, he wasn't confident that it was the right way, but it carried him deeper into the story than he had managed thus far. After ten thousand words and a great many bouts of self-reproach, he was convinced it was clicking.

Writing about yourself in the third person, particularly within the context of nonfiction, was a rare and highly eccentric device to use in 1967, but it had a distinctive literary precedent. Journalist Henry Adams—the grandson of John Quincy Adams, the son of a U.S. ambassador to Great Britain, and a Harvard graduate who would teach medieval history at the university—rejected in 1877 the appurtenances of privilege and title that had been his birthright to devote himself to extensive travel and a rigorous, years-long study of American history, the centerpiece of which was a nine-volume history of America under the administrations of Jefferson and Madison. But it wasn't until Adams sat down to record the events of his own life that he forged an unprecedented approach to historiography—fusing social criticism with larger historical currents in the form of a memoir. *The Education of Henry Adams* was self-published by its author in 1907, one hundred folios that Adams sent to the country's best and brightest in the hope that it would spark sweeping social reform.

Mailer wasn't a particularly close reader of Adams's book, but a chapter had been assigned in his freshman English class at Harvard: "I remember thinking at the time what an odd thing to write about yourself in the third person. Who is this fellow, Henry Adams, talking about himself as Henry Adams?" Adams's influence was latent; he remained in Mailer's mind "as a possibility, the way a painter might look at a particular Picasso or Cezanne and say to himself, 'That's the way to do it.'" "On the one hand, it seemed interesting to speak of a protagonist named

Norman Mailer," he said. "On the other, it was odd. It's a very funny way to look at oneself."

The third-person technique liberated Mailer from the reductive "housing projects of fact and issue" that he felt prevented traditional reportage from examining the often complex matrix of impulses and root causes behind a mammoth act of resistance such as the march on the Pentagon—its decentralized command structure, the prevarications among the nonstudent academics and fellow travelers among Mailer's tweedy contemporaries, and the warring philosophies between Dellinger and Rubin that threatened to derail the objectives of the march. But more important, it freed up Mailer to write about himself in a clinically detached way—to map his own complex motives, emotions, and impressions as carefully as he might delineate a character in a novel. He would become a "true protagonist of the best sort . . . half-heroic, and three-quarters comic."

Once Mailer began writing as "Mailer," the words came at a furious clip. The third-person device enabled him to transition freely between public events and interiority and write as discursively as he pleased. After six weeks of work in Provincetown, he called Decter and told her, "It's getting long."

But the magazine's deadline was approaching, and Mailer was still writing. If the story was going to make it into the March issue, then Morris and Decter would have to trudge up to Provincetown and start preparing the still incomplete manuscript. Shortly after the first of the year, Decter and Morris flew up the Cape in a puddle-jumper that gave Decter wretched flight sickness. The two editors arrived at Mailer's three-story redbrick retreat on Cape Cod Bay, where a hothouse atmosphere of industriousness prevailed. Sandy Charlebois was dutifully typing Mailer's handwritten story, while the writer, who was ensconced in his office on the second floor for twelve- to fourteen-hour stretches, produced more pages. In six weeks, Mailer had produced almost eighty thousand words—a messy and frequently amended assemblage, with countless notes scribbled in the margins and serpentine sentences wrapped around paragraphs. A makeshift distribution system was put into place: Charlebois retrieved the pages from Mailer and typed. Mailer made corrections and handed the manuscript pages to Morris, who made his notes. Decter then read the pages, rewriting Mailer's crabbed handwritten changes in legible type to eliminate the need for another draft. Mercifully, the editing was minimal. "The kind of editing one does with him is to say, 'In this part here you really should explain a little more. You go over that a little too fast—it's hard for the reader to follow the point you're making,'" said Decter. "That kind of stuff, but that's not editing, and he was never testy about any of these suggestions. Mailer's an absolute pro."

A third of the way into Mailer's manuscript, Morris knew he had something special on his hands. But it was far longer than the original projection of twenty thousand words. When Decter and Morris did the final count, it topped out at ninety thousand. Morris called Kotlowitz:

"It's marvelous."
"That's great. How many words?"
"Ninety thousand."
"Ninety thousand?"
"About that."
"You think we should run it in installments—two, three?"
"I think we should run it all at once."
"All of it?"
"I really do."
"Well, why the hell not?"

When Kotlowitz finally read the story, he was "mesmerized and stunned. There was no question we had to do it in full. I didn't think the piece was inflated by a single word. The momentum and propulsion of the piece was so powerful. I was so excited; it was an editor's dream. I knew that no one, upon reading the story, would forget this issue."

John Cowles wasn't so sure. The conservative publisher of *Harper's*, whose family owned the magazine as well as the *Minneapolis Star-Tribune* newspaper, felt the story was far too long and too enamored of the leaders of the left as front-runners in a social revolution. "He was bewildered by it," said Kotlowitz. "Nor did he advocate devoting an entire issue to a single piece, because it would set a bad precedent for other writers wishing to do the same."

Even some *Harper's* staffers were bewildered by the piece. When a copy editor questioned whether the crude language was suitable for a mainstream magazine, and sarcastically wondered how Mailer might write when he was sober, "Willie told her to sit down, shut up, and not say a word," according to Decter. But even Mailer had second thoughts about the use of so much scatology. When the editing was finally complete and Morris and Decter were about to head back to New York, Mailer turned to Morris and asked, "What will my father think?"

"The Steps of the Pentagon," which ran in the March 1968 issue of *Harper's*, was a dazzler, the greatest sustained work of reportage that Mailer had written thus far—reportage in the Mailer sense, at least. "The Steps of the Pentagon" was a multihued tableau: a vividly impressionistic account of the march, a clear-eyed critique of the left and its leadership, a series of spot-on profiles of Lowell, Macdonald, and other prominent participants, and a self-portrait of the writer as an "ambiguous comic hero," constantly vacillating between doing the right thing and catering to his own questionable self-interests. In less capable hands, the story might have read as a confused jumble, but Mailer's ability to pleasingly syncretize the disparate parts lifted "The Steps of the Pentagon" into the realm of nonfiction literature.

Mailer's third-person device, which he had questioned from the very start, allowed him to write about himself as a protagonist in the march but also a character for whom he gives no quarter.

> Mailer was a snob of the worst sort. New York had not spoiled him, because it had not chosen to, but New York had certainly wrecked his tolerance for any party but a very good one. Like most snobs he professed to believe in the aristocracy of achieved quality—"Just give me a hovel with a few young artists, bright-eyed and bold"—in fact, a party lacked flavor for him unless someone very rich or social were present.

Mailer's gift for using careful observation as a psychological divining rod had never been utilized as effectively. Here's Mailer writing about Lowell's reaction to Mailer's soused speech at the Ambassador:

> Lowell looked most unhappy. Mailer, minor poet, had often observed that Lowell had the most disconcerting mixture of strength and weakness in his presence, a blending so dramatic in its visible sign of conflict that one had to assume he would be sensationally

attractive to women. He had something untouchable, all insane in its force; one felt immediately that there were any number of causes for which the man would be ready to die, and for some he would fight, with an axe in his hand and Cromwellian light in his eye.

Mailer resents Lowell for his confident command of the Ambassador audience during his poetry reading: "Lowell's talent was very large, but then Mailer was a bulldog about the value of his own talent. No, Mailer was jealous because he had worked for this audience, and Lowell without effort seemed to have stolen them." (Years later, Lowell would comment that Mailer's piece was "one of the best things ever written about me.")

Mailer views the marchers as artists in their own right, appropriating the iconic images of popular culture and subverting them into the pagaentry of a freak parade:

The hippies were there in great number, perambulating down the hill, many dressed like the legions of Sgt. Pepper's Band, some were gotten up like Arab sheiks, or in Park Avenue doormen's greatcoats, others like Rogers and Clark of the West, Wyatt Earp, Kit Carson, Daniel Boone in buckskin, some had grown mustaches to look like Have Gun, Will Travel—Paladin's surrogate was here!—and wild Indians with feathers, a hippie gotten up like Batman, another like Claude Rains in *The Invisible Man*—his face wrapped in a turban of bandages and he wore a black satin top hat . . . They were being assembled from all the intersections between history and the comic books, between legend and television, the Biblical archetypes and the movies.

Mailer is constantly shifting between enthusiasm and enervation in "The Steps of the Pentagon." Look to the feel of the phenomenon, Dwight Macdonald had told him; "If it feels bad, it *is* bad." Nothing is excised for propriety's sake, neither the pissing incident at the Ambassador nor Mailer's contempt for middle-class liberalism and its phony pieties ("He had no sense of belonging to any of these people. They were much too nice and much too principled for him"), his timidity in the face of law enforcement, his "gloomy hope" for the children of the march, "twenty generations of buried hopes perhaps engraved in their chromosomes, and now conceivably burning like faggots in the secret inquisitional fires of LSD." The march, Mailer agrees, was a just and proper demonstration of outrage, but is the left really any match for the infernal power of "technology land"? It was the same dialectic that Mailer pondered in "Superman Comes to the Supermarket": Can a nation beholden to consumer culture be transformed by a movement that wanted to banish its coarsening impediments to social reform?

Thus "The Steps of the Pentagon" worked on two levels: as an adroit disquisition on the events surrounding the march, but also a speculative essay about a nation that had sacrificed its ingenuity on the altar of technology and the corporation, and loosed its wild, untamed energies upon imaginary enemies using the Cold War as its organizing principle.

> [T]he center of Christianity was a mystery, a son of God, and the center of the corporation was a detestation of mystery, a worship of technology ... The love of the Mystery of Christ, however, and the love of no Mystery whatsoever, had brought the country to a state of suppressed schizophrenia so deep that the foul brutalities of the war in Vietnam were the only temporary cure possible for the condition—since the expression of brutality offers a definite if temporary relief to the schizophrenic.

But there is also a generosity of spirit, however grudgingly offered, in Mailer's clear-eyed examination of both his motives and those of the other participants on both sides of the barricade. He's acutely observant *and* shrewdly self-aware. If the marshals seethe with malice, it's only because they are products of social engineering, the Pentagon's malleable instruments of power. He is capable of empathetic feelings for his enemies, even if they are merciless oppressors.

As for Mailer's own motivations, they are never reconciled. His short time as an imprisoned detainee presents him with a moral dilemma—to do right by the movement or by his family, to serve whatever sentence might await him or scramble back to the comforts of his middle-class life. Instead of the polemical flame-thrower, here is Mailer offering himself up as flawed and vulnerable to feelings of cowardice and shame. "To have his name cheered during a season at every deadly dull leftist meeting to raise money—he would trade such fame for a good hour's romp with the—yes, doomed *pater familias*—with the wife and kids."

When Mailer, after considerable negotiation on the part of his lawyers, is released on bail pending appeal, he feels cleansed and possessed of something virtuous, even beatific, at its core, "not unlike the rare sweet of a clean loving tear not dropped, still held." But to what extent had the protest and its aftermath impacted the consciousness of the country? Mailer isn't entirely sure. "Some promise of peace and new war seemed riding the phosphorescent wake of this second and last day's siege of the Pentagon, as if the country were opening into more and more on the resonance of these two days, more that was good, more that was bad."

"The Steps of the Pentagon" inspired more letters than any other article in the century-plus history of *Harper's*. Some readers of the magazine were outraged at Mailer's language and requested subscription cancellations. Others were delighted to find such a nuanced take on the present American crisis in the pages of the magazine. Mailer was taken aback by the avalanche of letters that had flooded into *Harper's* offices. "All these people sitting all over America writing these letters," he told Morris. "They're carrying on a conversation with a magazine as if a magazine itself were a human being."

Mailer had another section prepared for publication—"The Battle of the Pentagon," a thirty-thousand-word examination of the origins of the march, a careful analysis of the sectarian battles and failures of the Old Left and new guard, and the price paid in violence and bloodshed—but Morris rejected it for space reasons. In hindsight, he was right to turn it down; "The Battle of the Pentagon" lacks narrative punch because Mailer isn't in on the action as a character. Instead, Decter's husband, Norman Podhoretz, published it in the April issue of *Commentary*.

When New American Library published both articles in book form as *The Armies of the Night*, it brought Mailer the best reviews of his career since *The Naked and the Dead*. *The Nation*'s Alan Trachtenberg singled out Mailer's "brilliantly demonstrated coincidence between the objective event and the subjective experience" and regarded the book as nothing less than a "permanent contribution to our literature—a unique testimony to literary responsiveness and responsibility." Henry S. Resnik in the *Saturday Review* praised Mailer's "amazing stylistic virtuosity" and "breathtaking verbal cadenzas." In his lead review of *The Armies of the*

Night in the May 5, 1968, *New York Times Book Review,* Alfred Kazin compared Mailer to Walt Whitman, another writer who "staked his work on finding the personal connection between salvation as an artist and the salvation of his country." Kazin found Mailer's balancing act as a reporter of the personal and the political as dexterous an amalgam as Whitman's great Civil War diary, "Specimen Days." "Mailer's intuition in this book is that the times demand a new form," Kazin wrote. "He has found it."

In 1969, Mailer was awarded both the National Book Award and the Pulitzer prize in nonfiction for *The Armies of the Night.*

10

THE KING OF NEW YORK

For Clay Felker, "The Steps of the Pentagon" was the one that got away. In early 1966 he had offered Mailer an assignment for the *New York World-Journal-Tribune,* the awkwardly titled new iteration of the *Tribune* that had resulted from a merger of that paper, the *World-Telegram,* and the *Journal-American.* Felker's plan was for Mailer to file dispatches for the paper from Vietnam, reporting on whatever he saw fit. Mailer wasn't sure if he was up to it; it had been more than twenty years since he had seen the horrors of combat up close. Resorting to a familiar negotiating tactic that he used whenever he felt unsure about a prospective assignment, Mailer played hardball with Felker and Jim Bellows; none of his stories could be cut for space or content, and all of them had to appear on the front page of the paper. It was only fair, Mailer reasoned, for the *Tribune* to make some concessions if Mailer was going to risk his life for the paper.

Contracts were drafted, and Mailer was set to go, but Jock Whitney's paper, which had been losing money and readership to the *New York Times* and the city's tabloids since the early 1960s, folded on May 5, 1967, in the midst of a labor dispute involving the newspaper merger. Felker's great experiment in newspaper New Journalism seemed over as well.

Felker had been tipped off to the *Trib*'s demise by Jimmy Breslin, who called him the night before the announcement. Over drinks at the Monsignore bar, Breslin and Felker commiserated, toasted their achievements at the *Trib,* and pondered their next move. Breslin suggested that they somehow keep *New York* magazine afloat. Too much of their blood and sweat had gone into the supplement, Breslin said. They couldn't let *New York*, the best general-interest magazine in the city, die with the paper. *New York* was the best thing about the *Tribune*, the number one reason why nearly 83 percent of female readers and 75 percent of male readers bought the Sunday *Trib* every week. It was incumbent upon Felker to try to save it.

Felker was intrigued. Certainly no other newspaper would give him the creative latitude he had enjoyed at the *Trib*, and a return to the staid precincts of conventional journalism was unfathomable. "I saw the impact of the magazine," said Felker. "I was committed to it. And I knew the formula was right."

So he decided to take Breslin's advice and attempt to establish a stand-alone magazine that would retain *New York*'s spirit and, he hoped, the same cast of contributors. For Felker, it would be the fulfillment of a lifelong dream: to finally own a magazine. "I never thought about the risk," said Felker. "It had nothing to do with bravery. It was a dream I had and I couldn't live with myself if I didn't try."

In order to create a prototype, Felker enlisted Milton Glaser, the brilliant thirty-eight-year-old graphic designer who had contributed some freelance drawings to *New York* and had cowritten with Jerome Snyder a column called "The Underground Gourmet." A graduate of New York's Cooper Union and a Fulbright scholar, Glaser founded Push Pin Studios in 1954 along with fellow Cooper Union alumni Seymour Chwast, Ed Sorel, and Reynold Ruffins. Push Pin quickly established itself as a cutting-edge commercial design firm—"The Beatles of illustration and design," according to writer Steven Heller—eschewing more lucrative advertising commissions for venturesome magazine, poster, and album cover art work, anything that might offer a creative challenge for the erudite and imaginatively fecund team of Glaser, Ruffins, and Chwast. The operative word was *eclectic;* Push Pin found ideas anywhere and everywhere—comic strips, Art Deco, Italian Renaissance painting, Victorian typography, even their own medicine cabinets—combining disparate design elements into an aesthetic of funhouse formalism that transformed the design industry. Push Pin's images became lasting visual icons; Glaser's famous 1967 poster of Bob Dylan, which combined a chiaroscuro profile topped by a Technicolor tangle of hair, became the most famous rock poster of the decade.

Glaser was no stranger to magazine publishing; he had helped produce fifteen issues of the *Push Pin Almanack,* a compendium of the firm's work that was sent to potential clients as a bait for commissions. Felker thought of Glaser as the greatest designer of his time, an artist sensitive to the beauty and sensuality of typography, to how the careful juxtaposition of words and images could convey an attitude and a subtextual complexity that moved beyond the mere shilling of product. "Milton is a certifiable genius," said Felker. "Before he undertakes a project, he takes the time to understand what the potential market might be for whomever it is directed, what message the client is trying to convey. He is a man for whom design with a point of view is crucial."

The push and pull between Felker, the mercurial idea man, and Glaser, the oracular, intellectual guru, would result in one of the most fruitful collaborations between an editor and an art director in the history of American magazine publishing. "Glaser edited Clay in a way," said Pete Hamill, an early contributor to *New York.* "If Clay had an idea, Milton would say, 'That's great, but what's the illustration gonna be, what's the headline?' He helped Clay conceptualize notions into workable ideas."

The idea was to emulate the editorial and graphic template of the *New York* supplement, the assumption being that those *Tribune* readers who harbored goodwill toward the defunct paper would migrate to the newsstand edition. But there was a stumbling block; Felker couldn't use the name *New York,* which remained the property of Jock Whitney. Other names—*Metro, Gotham, The Express, The Metropolitan,* even *New York, New York*—were floated. Tom Wolfe suggested *New York Moon,* so when a new issue hit the stands, ads could proclaim, "The *Moon* is out!"

But Felker wouldn't give up on *New York* so easily. It took six months of negotiations with the *World-Journal-Tribune*'s president, Matt Meyer, to acquire the name, during which time Glaser and Felker, with assistance from Jimmy Breslin, freelancer Gloria Steinem, and other *Trib* writers, continued to tinker with a prototype to present to potential investors. Other *Tribune* alumni, such as *New York* managing editor Jack Nessel and Eugenia Sheppard, the most respected fashion writer in the country, whose *Tribune* column had been syndicated in over a hundred papers, would also join the fold. "We didn't know what we were doing at first," said Felker. "We had to design for a smaller page now, the logo had to be stronger. It took us nearly a year to figure everything out."

In November 1967 Meyer relented, and the name was purchased by Felker for the price of his severance pay–$6,575.00. With a mock-up in hand, Felker–accompanied in many instances by the comely Steinem, whom he used as a beard to soften up potential investors–began trying to raise money on Wall Street. The first targets were the lowest-hanging fruit. His old friend Armand Erpf, a partner in the investment firm Loeb, Rhoades and Co., had always been intrigued by the publishing world, and the two of them had idly discussed the idea of starting up a city magazine for years. Now Felker was ready for Erpf to ante up.

Erpf was a major power broker, which made him an appealing partner for Felker. A patron of the arts, Erpf lived lavishly among the spoils of his Wall Street fortune. His Margaretville, New York, mansion was filled with modern art; its sculpture garden, with its giant Henry Moore bronzes, rivaled any domestic museum's collection. "Armand was an utterly fascinating character," said George Hirsch, who joined the *New York* team as publisher from Time-Life's international division. "He used to have these dinner parties that were like salons, with people from the arts and finance coming together to discuss a wide range of subjects. He was a legendary figure in his time, and I don't use that word lightly."

Erpf and Felker made the rounds of Wall Street and the city's cultural elite and, after many months of appeals, accrued a group of $25,000-or-more investors: Loeb, Rhoades CEO John L. Loeb, Great Western United Corp. Chairman William White Jr., mergers and acquisitions specialist Alan Patricof, investment bankers Dan Lufkin and Bob Towbin, Joseph E. Seagram and Sons president Edgar Bronfman, Random House cofounder Bennett Cerf. All told, Erpf scraped together $2.4 million (Erpf himself contributed $100,000). The magazine was a limited partnership, with participations distributed among its board of directors. Felker, publisher George Hirsch, and Milton Glaser represented management on the board, while Erpf and Patricof represented the money. Token amounts of stock were also distributed to contributing editors Tom Wolfe, Jimmy Breslin, and "Adam Smith," the pseudonym of financial writer and portfolio manager George J. W. Goodman. Glaser cut Felker a deal for his time and office space: Glaser would work for $25,000 a year and provide rent-free offices for the magazine in Push Pin's walk-up townhouse at 207 East 32nd Street.

In October 1967 Felker and his eight editorial staffers moved in, bringing along some discarded furniture from the *Tribune*'s offices to fill it up, including John Whitney's conference room chairs and Helen Rogers Reid's mahogany desk. Felker and Hirsch worked out a production schedule that would allow them to begin publishing in April 1968. T. Swift Lockard was brought on as advertising director, and an aggressive direct mail campaign—with prizes as incentives, no less—was initiated in order to attract charter subscriptions. Half of the start-up investment was eaten up by the campaign, which resulted in sixty thousand subscribers.

"You get hooked on this city," Clay Felker wrote in a mission statement sent to potential advertisers. "You want to revel in it and rail at it. . . . You want to participate in this city because it is alive. . . . New York is the quintessence of urban civilization. . . . New York is, in fact, the capital of the world. . . . We want to be the weekly magazine that communicates the spirit and character of contemporary New York."

New York's strength would be good writing, according to Felker, because "it's what reading is all about." The magazine would provide a multifarious view of the city: "Jimmy Breslin's New York, and Tom Wolfe's New York, and Adam Smith's Wall Street, and Eugenia Sheppard's Seventh Avenue and Harold Clurman's theatres . . ."

Felker printed 250,000 copies of the first issue, which sold for 40 cents and featured a color-saturated cover shot by Jay Maisel of the Manhattan skyline as seen from the East River. It didn't stray far from the *Tribune* iteration of the magazine, but it had more heft. Lockard and his team wrangled up enough clients for the premiere issue to produce sixty-four ad pages, with advertisers paying $1,250 for a black-and-white page and $2,010 for a color page.

There were subtle but significant design changes. The elegant *New York* logotype, based on the Caslon typeface, became thicker and bolder; the "scotch rule" border that enclosed the logotype on the old *New York* was eliminated. Instead, Glaser placed one scotch rule above the logo, and left space above it for "teasers" that would clue in readers to the magazine's editorial content each week. The scotch rule would be used as a unifying design element within the magazine as well. Many of the popular features of the *Trib*-era *New York* were retained, such as Glaser and Snyder's "Underground Gourmet" column, which scoped out the best ethnic cuisine in the city; and the Felker creation "Best Bets," a two-page spread of coveted products that became the first destination in the magazine for many of its female readers.

Felker and Erpf decided to launch with a splash and held a breakfast party at the Four Seasons restaurant on Monday, April 1, a week before the publication date. Two hundred copies were distributed to press and local luminaries; Mayor John Lindsay spoke of the challenges of publishing a magazine that captured the pulse of the city. "The people here met that challenge once and now meet it again. We of the city are grateful today to salute the rebirth of the magazine . . . a magazine called *New York*."

But even as the city's best and brightest were toasting the second coming of *New York*, managing editor Jack Nessel felt his palms getting sweaty, his pulse quickening. Monday was not a day to fritter away; the staff was already a day behind on the next issue. While Lindsay sang *New York*'s praises, an anxiety-ridden Nessel sneaked out to draft the production schedule.

Felker's star writers picked up where they had left off at the *Trib*. Jimmy Breslin hopped on the commuter train that travels from Grand Central Station to Connecticut and wrote about the Harlem tenement dwellers that black-loafered commuters passed by every day on their way home; Tom Wolfe dissected the class distinctions of New York accents; Gloria Steinem retraced the New York travels of Ho Chi Minh; Adam Smith described the latest trend to afflict Wall Street heavies, car phones. Back-of-the-book reviews by classical music critic Alan Rich, movie critic Judith Crist, and theater critic Harold Clurman rounded out the issue, as well as a crossword puzzle by Stephen Sondheim.

"We were just trying to carry on the tradition of the magazine supplement by relying on the quality of writing we were offering," said managing editor Jack Nessel, who, post-*Tribune*, was working at radio station KFPA in Berkeley when Felker recruited him as employee number one for the new magazine. "With writers like Breslin, Wolfe, and Gloria Steinem, we had the advantage of publishing a high level of journalism right off the bat."

But Felker and his staff quickly learned that the key to making *New York* a success was not a question of editorial transposition—retrofitting the old *Trib* blueprint onto the new glossy pages. The magazine would have to stand or fall on its own merits now, and a point of view was necessary to compel readers to pay for it every week. "The first year we were really stumbling," said Milton Glaser. "We didn't know how the hell to do it, and we were too indebted to the Sunday supplement. Just running beautiful pictures on the cover unrelated to the editorial product, that didn't work. We needed cover stories that would grab readers by the lapel and say, 'Read this!'"

The magazine was starting up at a tumultuous time. On the day that the first *New York* hit the streets, Martin Luther King Jr. was gunned down while standing on a balcony of the Lorraine Motel in Memphis. There was no question that the magazine had to acknowledge the impact of King's assassination on the city, but the second issue had already gone to press, and the third issue was in galleys. Felker knew that King's death would send the biggest shock waves through the city's most politically engaged African American community, so he dispatched Gloria Steinem to "get the hell up to Harlem and just talk to people."

Steinem stumbled upon a great stroke of luck: Mayor Lindsay, as it turned out, was going to conduct a walking tour of Harlem and the city's other black neighborhoods. Steinem accompanied Lindsay as he talked to Harlem's citizenry and local leaders, assuaging fears and tamping down the insurrectionary fervor that had already led to riots in other cities across the Northeast. Felker then seamlessly merged Steinem's story with that of an African American freelancer named Lloyd Weaver, thereby providing perspectives from both uptown and downtown.

The piece, "The City on the Eve of Destruction," was an affecting and sharply etched examination of political crisis management as viewed from the perspective of a master conciliator. Steinem and Weaver started the piece with Lindsay taking in a play on Broadway, where he was alerted by an aide to the news of Dr. King's death ("He thought: *It's stunning, it can't be true; like Kennedy.* He thought: *A wild reaction, all over the country.* He thought: *And here.*") Lindsay vowed to calm his constituents by meeting with them, listening and responding to their concerns ("Somebody just has to go up there, someone white just has to face that emotion and say that we're sorry"). As Lindsay walked through the black neighborhoods of the city, Steinem and Weaver caught some of the tension in the air:

> Women stood with tears streaming down their faces. Groups gathered silently outside record shops where loudspeakers blared news of violence in other cities, or the speeches of Martin Luther King. Both

were frequently drowned out by sirens—a fire had started a few blocks away—or by the staccato of police calls from a nearby squad car. Small packs of teenagers were hanging back, laughing uncertainly, waiting. . . . "Man," said a big kid in an athletic jacket happily, "there's gonna be white blood in the streets tonight."

The writers depict Lindsay as a self-possessed mediator throwing down barricades and breaking up potential conflagrations, but mostly providing solace to an enraged and confused citizenry.

"Man, he only some itty-bit shorter than Wilt the Stilt!"
  "He ain't never gonna get killed, because we *like* him."
  "Thank you, Mr. Lindsay, we love you."
  He got back in his car, smiling.

"I didn't interview Lindsay for the piece," said Steinem. "The idea was to be a fly on the wall, a technique that I admired in the work of Lillian Ross." The story would become the first in a series of personality-observed stories that Steinem wrote for the magazine; over the next few years, she would turn her shrewd reporter's gaze to Eugene McCarthy, President Nixon, and football-star-turned-movie-star Jim Brown. "*New York* magazine in general allowed me to bring together my writing and my interest in politics—which had been more difficult before that because women reporters had a tougher time getting political assignments," said Steinem.

Eight weeks after Martin Luther King Jr.'s assassination, on June 5, Robert Kennedy was killed in the kitchen of the Ambassador Hotel in Los Angeles, moments after addressing a crowd of supporters who had cheered the news of his victory in the California primary. Gail Sheehy, a gifted young writer whom Felker had wrested from Eugenia Sheppard's women's pages at the *Tribune* to write for *New York*, was already working on an Ethel Kennedy profile for the magazine when RFK was killed. Now the piece would be refashioned as a meditation on RFK's widow and "the arithmetic of life and death."

Ethel Kennedy knows life from bullets and airplanes and maternity beds. She has brought life into the world ten times and has watched it go out violently seven times from close range. Now it is eight.

The piece, "Ethel Kennedy and the Arithmetic of Life and Death," was Sheehy's first cover story for *New York;* she would eventually write fifty stories for the magazine over the next nine years, making her the most prolific feature writer of the Clay Felker era.

Jimmy Breslin was also in L.A. the week of Robert Kennedy's death, writing about gun control for *New York.* Breslin had heard that Los Angeles had an abundance of storefronts selling .45 Magnums and automatic rifles like Florsheim penny loafers, and he wanted to see it for himself. On June 4 he was driven by Bert Prelutsky, a *Los Angeles Times* writer whom he had met through Jim Bellows, to a gun store in Fullerton, a mom-and-pop operation owned by a moonlighting working-class couple who hoped to make the store their full-time business, if only they could get their hands on some good Smith & Wessons. The next day, Kennedy was killed.

Breslin returned to New York enraged and disconsolate, and he wanted real answers. The biggest movie in the country that week was *Bonnie and Clyde,* a film that he found objectionable, a Hollywood gloss on violence. Written by former *Esquire* staffers David Newman and Robert Benton and starring Warren Beatty and Faye Dunaway, it was a stylish meditation on the notorious bank robbers, and Breslin wondered if that film's success wasn't somehow linked to certain cavalier attitudes about guns in America. If Hollywood could turn killers such as Clyde Barrow and Bonnie Parker into sex symbols, were Americans somehow inured to the real ramifications of guns? Accompanied by his friend and occasional driver Fat Thomas, Breslin took in *Bonnie and Clyde* one more time to give it a fair shake. Maybe there had been some nuances in the story or subtext that he had missed the first time around. Breslin had never thought of himself as a particularly sophisticated moviegoer, anyway.

A second viewing only confirmed his judgment that the film was a pretty picture about pretty criminals, a myth. The story that Breslin filed was ostensibly a critique of the film, but it was really an impassioned polemic against firearms and a plea for federally sanctioned gun control laws.

Right at the start, Warren Beatty, who plays Clyde Barrow, was standing on the street corner and he pulled out a pistol and showed it to Faye Dunaway, who plays Bonnie Parker. She began to run her hand on the black barrel of the pistol. Run her hand on it lovingly.

"That's a lot more than a pistol right now," I said.

"She gets one of them jammed into her back, she don't go around petting it, I guarantee her that," Fat Thomas said.

Gun stores and Hollywood movies didn't engender violence, Breslin wrote, but they made guns fetish objects for losers.

Armed robbery isn't a grin. It really isn't. Armed robbery is this old woman on Pitkin Avenue in Brownsville, Brooklyn, on the floor behind the counter of her husband's tailor shop clawing at the three bare-armed cops from the emergency squad who are trying to stuff her 72-year-old husband into a body bag. He is dead from three bullets in the head over a $10 stickup. . . .

You see, the movie is all about playing with things. Playing with yourself, really. And it is in tune with the times, *Bonnie and Clyde* is. We are not a violent society. This is actually a society of jerks and for some of them the gun has got everything to do with it.

Pieces such as "Bonnie and Clyde Revisited," which interwove elements of personal reflection, impassioned polemic, and reportage, made Breslin *New York*'s social conscience. "Breslin was such a natural that I began to think of him as a phony, but he wasn't," said former *New York* senior editor Shelly Zalaznick, another *Trib* alumnus Felker hired for the new magazine. "He wasn't a patrician trying to act like a regular Joe. He really was the guy he wrote about."

In the winter of 1969, Breslin and Norman Mailer made a quixotic bid for public office. The idea had germinated at an after-hours story meeting with Felker, Peter Maas, Gloria Steinem, and Jimmy Breslin. Felker had pointed to Jimmy Breslin and said, "You should run for mayor. We can get a story out of it, maybe a series of stories." Breslin wasn't against the idea in principle—he truly believed that he could cure the ailing city by empowering the working class—but he was a writer, not a politician. He had seen too much backroom blood sport, too much nasty chicanery in that world. But the momentum toward a run was already snowballing. Jack Newfield, a political columnist for the *Village Voice,* had endorsed a Breslin-Mailer ticket on a local radio show, with Mailer running as a mayoral candidate and Breslin vying for the job of

City Council president. When Newfield broke the news to Breslin over coffee, Breslin laughed at the absurdity of it, then wondered why Mailer was on the top of the ticket.

Mailer had floated the notion of running for mayor prior to the 1960 mayoral campaign but then, three days before he was to officially announce his candidacy, he stabbed his then-wife, Adele. "I wanted to make actions rather than effect sentiments," he said in a 1963 *Paris Review* interview. "But I've come to the middle-aged conclusion that I'm probably better as a writer than a man of action."

Mailer, of course, was the writer *as* man of action, and although he had written what was widely acknowledged as the definitive account of leftist politics in the age of Vietnam with *The Armies of the Night*, political office would give him a chance to ratify reforms that he had thus far only written about, to clear the decks of noxious corruption and start anew. The popular mayor John Lindsay was suddenly vulnerable after a series of punishing snowstorms had virtually immobilized the city, and the field of potential candidates, which included city controller Mario Procaccino and Bronx borough president Herman Badillo, was not insurmountable. There was perhaps an opening for a social theorist of the people to stake his claim.

Mailer wasn't quite sure of the enterprise himself at the start, and never settled into the avuncular comfort zone of a seasoned pol, for whom "a love of handshakes is equal to a writer's love of language." But all Clay Felker cared about was the fact that he had the inside scoop and a great cover grabber for *New York*.

A convocation of informal advisors gathered in Mailer's Columbia Heights brownstone in late March to determine the feasibility of a Mailer candidacy. Among those present were *New York* writers Peter Maas and Gloria Steinem, *Village Voice* writer Jack Newfield, Pete Hamill, Jerry Rubin, boxer and Mailer confidant Jose Torres, and Breslin. Mailer quickly learned a crucial lesson of politics: appeasement of one faction leads to alienation of another. Many wanted Breslin to join Mailer on the ticket as a candidate for City Council president, citing his empathy with the working class that resided outside Manhattan's zone of exclusion, but others rejected the idea. Mailer's candidacy might siphon crucial votes away from Badillo: a rising minority star, a favorite among the city's liberal elite, and a friend of Torres.

Mailer wanted Breslin on his team; Mailer could handle the cocktail party fund-raisers and the media ops, but he needed Breslin to stump for him in places such as Queens and Staten Island, the populist leavening Mailer's lofty rhetoric with common street sense.

Amazingly, for a ticket that had two of the city's best-known writers, no local press bothered to cover the story of the campaign at the outset. Only the *Village Voice* and *New York* deigned to take the Mailer-Breslin run seriously—*New York* being the in-house media organ for the campaign, with Breslin reporting on the action as it transpired. Photographer Dan Wynn snapped a shot of the candidates and Clay Felker ran it on the cover of the May 5 issue of *New York* with the headline "Mailer-Breslin Seriously?" The answer could be found inside. "I Run to Win," screamed the headline of Breslin's story:

> [T]he condition of the city of New York at this time reminds me of the middleweight champion fight between the late Marcel Cerdan and Tony Zale. . . . There were no marks to show what was happening. But Tony Zale was coming apart from the punches that did not leave any marks and at the end of the eleventh round Tony was along the ropes and Cerdan stepped back and Tony crumbled and he was on the floor, looking out into the night air, his face unmarked, his body dead, his career gone. In New York today, the face of the city, Manhattan, is proud and glittering. But Manhattan is not the city . . . and it is down in the neighborhoods, down in the schools that are in the neighborhoods, where this city is cut and slashed and bleeding from someplace deep inside.

As Mailer's platform evolved, it began to resemble an odd mélange of old-fashioned populism, radical progressivism, and Thoreau-like civility. Foremost among Mailer's ideas was the notion of bureaucratic emancipation. New York City should declare statehood, which would allow a new charter to be written that would create autonomous zones in the city, giving people greater control over their own neighborhoods. Private automobiles would be banned and day care centers would be built, methadone would be plentiful for the heroin addicts who needed it, and the quality of life in the city would acquire a simpler, more humane cast.

Mailer's common touch was more adroit than anyone could have fathomed. At a Brooklyn College forum, one student wanted to know how Mailer would handle an act of God such as a blizzard. What, he asked, would Mailer do if there was a big snowstorm and he was the mayor? "Sir," Mailer replied with a poker face, "I'd piss on it."

When the campaign got down to the business of retail politics, Mailer discovered that he wasn't half bad at it, and the city's citizenry seemed to respond to him favorably. His fame was a nonstarter anyway: a poll had determined that more than half the city's citizens didn't know who he was.

As the team was soon to discover, volatile mavericks aren't good at building constituencies, and Mailer's intemperance did irrevocable damage to the campaign. A disastrous town-hall-style meeting at the Village Gate nightclub, in which a drunk Mailer sprayed epithets at his supporters like buckshot, became a fatal body blow when Sidney Zion wrote about it for the *New York Times*.

Tensions between Breslin and Mailer increased at the campaign slogged on. Breslin didn't have the fortitude to adhere to a rigorous schedule of appearances, and Mailer was often left in the lurch. To say that Mailer's chances were slim would be understating it—when the votes were finally tallied, he barely mustered thirty-seven thousand votes, coming in fourth in a field of five. (Incumbent mayor Lindsay was reelected.) The final result, for Breslin, was more welcome relief than a disappointment. "After Norman Mailer and I finished seven weeks of a mayoralty campaign adjudged unlikely, I still came away nervous and depressed by what I had seen of my city," Breslin wrote in *New York*. "So when the business of the Democratic primary was over, I migrated naturally to a bar and found it fine sport, and then to another bar, which was even better, and I then plunged entirely into the toy world. Important things became Mutchie's face falling into a plate of spaghetti at 3 A.M., and Joe Bushkin playing the piano, and the horse Johnny Rotz was supposed to be on the next day. News bulletins were the score of the Mets game and Joe Namath's troubles."

A year after its rebirth, *New York* hadn't lost a beat. Wolfe, Breslin, and the rest were contributing the same high level of journalism to the magazine, but there were growing pains that needed to be addressed. The magazine's lively mix of politics, culture, and lifestyle coverage was strong, but not distinguished enough to stand apart from the other two weekly newspapers in town, the *Village Voice* and the *East Village Other*.

Felker knew he needed a sharper focus, a stronger point of view. The *Voice* and the *Other* were addressing readers who lived below Fourteenth Street; *New York* would have to be for Felker's crowd, those who lived tightly circumscribed lives on the upper half of Manhattan island—the privileged class who worried about building a nest egg to pay for private school tuition and struggled to pay their maintenance fees on co-op apartments, as well as the class-conscious strivers who longed to be tuned in to the vertiginous uptown whirl. Outwardly, Felker intuited, his readers might empathize with the tragedy of the South Bronx, but really they were enamored of status and power, the fossil fuel of the most important city in America. "We don't think of ourselves as a city magazine," Felker told *Newsweek*. "We are an elite magazine in the business of setting standards and attacking the conventional wisdom in all areas."

New York's new direction was announced with its January 6, 1969, cover story, "Going Private: Life in the Clean Machine." Written by Julie Baumgold, a twenty-two-year-old former columnist for *Women's Wear Daily* and a product of a private-school education, the story, which was Felker's idea, dared to explicate in print what was already an open secret among the denizens of Manhattan's white elite: the public school system in New York was a mess, and the path to success in the city went through its exclusionary private schools, which operated on fear and placed an untenable premium on social rank and fat bank accounts.

Baumgold was something of a writing prodigy. She went to work for Fairchild Publications right out of college, where her self-assured and wickedly clever writing style attracted the attention of Marion Javits, the wife of Senator Jacob Javits and a close friend of Felker's. Javits called up Felker, who hired Baumgold as an editorial assistant. "I was Clay's pet, so he had a temper with me," said Baumgold. "But he was also the person who completely found me and gave me great stories to write. He used to tell his writers, 'I'll make you a star,' but he really meant it with me. Clay demanded more from his favorites and rode them harder. He was always running after me, either because he was enthusiastic about something I had written or I hadn't gotten my copy in on time."

Baumgold, like so many writers of her generation, had been influenced by Tom Wolfe. She read *The Kandy-Kolored Tangerine-Flake Stream-line Baby* in college and emulated Wolfe's jazzy prose. "We were all influenced by Tom," said Baumgold. "Reading him was good training to be a novelist." Which meant that Baumgold was incapable of writing a straight piece of reportage. Baumgold wrote the private-school story in an ironically detached prose style that was Wolfe-like to the core.

A wistful Republican malaise has settled over Mother Goose's playground at East 72nd Street. Two young mamas, more *Vogue* than *Redbook*, rock spanky navy blue English prams. It is Wednesday, nurse's day off. The jungle gym is hung with scions and siblings, their Indian Walk soles taunting the skies. Pretty toy boys. Little girls who curtsy. Nothing elaborate, the babe bob of breeding. The mamas are rocking around and talking in the fairy tale playground. They are on private schools. Only they do not say the word "private." To them they are just plain *schools*. Assumptions of life. Spence versus Chapin. Trinity versus Collegiate. Buckley. Brearley. Maybe Dalton. But first the nurseries. Christ Church or Everett? The names flip from their tongues so easily. Those brief uncomplicated names. Nothing inspirational like Joan of Arc Junior High. Just the Trads (traditional schools) versus the Progs (progressives). And they love it. It's the most fascinating thing to come along since orthodonture talk. Really everyone's a Raving Expert. Now they are into how Bitsy's boy was rejected at St. Bernard's. They giggle over Maureen's disaster at Chapin. But the Mother Goose malaise gets to them.

Newsstand sales for the private schools issue went through the roof; publisher George Hirsch was incredulous. This wasn't a story by Breslin, Steinem, or Wolfe, the writers who usually hit the long ball for the magazine. This was an education piece by an unknown. When Hirsch approached Tom Wolfe to get his theory as to why it had been such a smash hit, Wolfe laid it out for him: "Well, of course, George! It's about status, and status is the number one concern of New Yorkers."

Felker had tapped into something essential about the city, and he knew it. Wolfe's big subject—status anxiety and its manifestations—would be the organizing principle of the magazine. Manhattan's inhabitants were obstinately proud to call themselves New Yorkers, but they were also urban survivalists; their self-preservation skills were a crucial test of their commitment to enduring the best city on the planet. *New York* would be a how-to guide for this white, upwardly mobile demographic segment.

A subscription solicitation that ran in the magazine in early 1969 trumpeted *New York*'s attributes. "We'll show you how to get a rent-controlled, semi-professional apartment, even though you're not a semi-professional person," the copy read. "We'll tell you how to go about getting your kid into private school with confidence, even though you graduated from P.S. 165." Previous issues had addressed status (the December 9, 1968, cover featured a white-collar beggar in a Burberry coat holding a tin cup and a sign that read I MAKE $80,000 A YEAR AND I'M BROKE), but now Felker would push it harder.

"We thought of ideas as our subject matter," said managing editor Jack Nessel. "People, to the extent that they embodied certain ideas, were interesting to us. Clay was really obsessed with the idea of power and who holds it. The power of influence and persuasion, of money, politics. That's what our readers responded to."

The magazine's content now squared with Tom Wolfe's status-conscious sensibility; his writing and worldview infected everything like an editorial strain. Felker's favorite writers—some of them *Trib* vets, but now mostly ambitious young cubs—made no claims to sober objectivity. It had always been Felker's belief that the best journalism germinated from a unique point of view, especially the idiosyncratic high style that Wolfe handled so deftly. Well-crafted stories were of no use to him if they were dull. Writers who thought they had nailed their subject would get their manuscripts handed back to them with a directive from Felker to "put yourself in the story."

When actress and aspiring journalist Patricia Bosworth was struggling mightily with a story assignment for Felker, the editor told her to just draw on her theater experience: "Writing is like performing," he told her, "except, when you write, you get to play all the parts." Felker demanded fearlessness from his writers, a willingness to muck around with form and content in order to make the story jump off the page.

Many of New York's best writers, such as Baumgold, Sheehy, Nora Ephron, and Steinem recruit Jane O'Reilly, were women—much to Jimmy Breslin's dismay. "Jimmy, when he was in another state of consciousness, often complained that New York had too many female writers," said Gloria Steinem. "That changed over time, due to his wife." At a time when female journalists were still trying to break out of the *McCall's-Redbook* ghetto and write about serious issues for mainstream general-interest titles, Felker hired numerous female contributors to write on a wide variety of subjects. He hadn't forgotten that his mother had given up a career in journalism to raise a family, something she regretted until the end of her life. "Women," he said at the time, "tend to have a more personal point of view about things than men, and I'm looking for an individual viewpoint first." There was a more practical reason as well; most men couldn't afford to write regularly for *New York*'s abstemious rates, which topped out at $300 for feature stories.

New York's best female contributors were some of its boldest prose stylists. Gail Sheehy had been born and raised in Mamaroneck, an affluent New York suburb. The daughter of a successful advertising executive, Sheehy graduated with a B.S. degree from the University of Vermont in 1958 and worked briefly as a traveling home economist for J. C. Penney. After a short apprenticeship as a fashion editor at the *Rochester Democrat and Chronicle,* where she worked as the fashion editor, Sheehy was hired by Jim Bellows at the *Tribune.*

Sheehy's first piece for the magazine, "The Tunnel Inspector and the Belle of the Bar Car," was a look at the white commuting class that converged on Grand Central Station every afternoon to disperse into the suburban diaspora. Unlike Breslin's earlier piece, which focused on the business class's willful ignorance of the poor neighborhoods they passed by in their trains every day, Sheehy's piece was more like a comedy of manners. She structured it much as she would many of her best stories for the magazine—as a series of set pieces propelled by wry dialogue exchanges and an unerring eye for character-revealing detail. Above all, it laid bare the striations of class in New York, the socioeconomic taxonomy that was mother's milk to Felker.

Upper-level trains carry $100,000-plus incomes down to $12,500, and that's probably the bartender. Golden men. In the summer they come off the trains with their cocoa panamas wrapped in rakish silk and consult the gold Omegas nestled in the golden foliage growing out of their tennis brown wrists. On rainy days they wash over Grand Central on a wave of beige poplin.

Sheehy became *New York*'s cultural anthropologist in residence, probing the inner lives of single mothers, speed addicts, and antiwar protesters, among other things. Her inside-out style of reportage made readers feel as if they were brushing up against their subjects, an intimacy achieved through a determination to leave nothing out.

George Goodman was another *Tribune* veteran who became a star at the new *New York*. Writing under the pseudonym "Adam Smith," Goodman's knack for turning the dry-as-dust field of economics into humorous pieces would make him the most famous financial writer in the country.

After attending Harvard and then Oxford on a Rhodes scholarship, St. Louis native Goodman skipped out on his graduate thesis (the subject was how totalitarian governments use languages) in order to write fiction. Returning to New York, Goodman, who had taken Archibald MacLeish's writing class at Harvard, felt reasonably sure he could make a living as a novelist. Much to his chagrin, he couldn't. His first book, *The Bubble Makers*, received glowing reviews but sold poorly. Strapped for cash, Goodman enlisted in the Special Forces unit of the army in 1954, then wrote another novel about an expatriate in Paris that also sold meekly.

Goodman had better luck with periodicals, nabbing a staff writing job with the weekly financial newspaper *Barron's* in order to support his book projects. He eventually broke through with a novel by selling his book *The Wheeler Dealers* to the movies, then landed a job with Sam Steadman at Loeb, Rhoades as a junior fund manager.

After selling two Talk of the Town pieces to *The New Yorker*, Goodman attracted the attention of Clay Felker at *Esquire*. When Felker left *Esquire* for the *Herald Tribune*, he brought Goodman with him to write a weekly column. After penning a scathing article about Motorola, Goodman got cold feet about using his own byline on the piece; it would compromise his good name as a fund manager, creating the appearance of conflict of interest. Goodman suggested the pseudonym Procrustes, the conniving thief of Greek mythology, but none of the editors liked that, and when Goodman picked up the paper, he saw another byline had replaced it: "Adam Smith," a name Shelly Zalaznick had come up with at the last minute. Goodman hated the name—another, far more esteemed economic theorist had already laid claim to it, and besides, it sounded corny to him. But it was a done deal.

At *New York*, Goodman created a rogue's gallery of Wall Street fund managers, brokers, speculators, and CEO fat cats—some of them real, others not—and spun fanciful stories that explained economic trends to New York's readers without resorting to jargon. In "Notes on the Great Buying Panic," Goodman's first story for the new weekly, he introduced Poor Grenville, the manager of a "swinging" fund, and Grenville's dilemma: how to spend $42 million of the fund's money to avoid an imminent stock market collapse.

> With his tall, blond, Establishment looks Poor Grenville is a Hickey Freeman model or an ad for the Racquet Club, not poor. One of Poor Grenville's great-grandmothers had a duck farm and part of the duck farm is still kicking around in the family. There aren't many live ducks on it anymore, since the duck farm ran roughly from Madison Avenue east, bounded by, say, 59th Street and 80th Street.

Goodman framed the entire story as a lunch-hour speculative selling frenzy in which Poor Grenville would unburden himself of his money while Adam Smith, ever the credulous outsider, watched the spectacle unfold. Numbers were of interest to Goodman only as they related to the unusual behavioral traits of those who controlled the numbers. From Breslin, Goodman acquired an acute feel for characterization; from Wolfe, he learned how to transform the foibles of the rich and powerful into arch satire.

"Well, I think we all influenced each other," said Goodman. "That Tom Wolfe piece, the one that started with 'Hernia, hernia, hernia,' that was a big influence on me. Tom really loosened the borders for all of us. *New York* was like a great varsity team, and we knew it, too."

Not that they got on too well at first. Goodman thought of Wolfe's Savile Row getups as an elaborate put-on: "People didn't wear white spats and white suits in New York." Goodman was annoyed by Breslin's abrasiveness and arrogance, and he thought Felker displayed passive-aggressive tendencies, even though he was the best editor he had ever written for. "Clay was not a good arbiter of arguments," he said. "He would just let us fight it out." During one such meeting, Goodman suggested that the magazine might explore politics in greater depth. To Wolfe, that was code for *liberal* politics; irate, he yelled, "Well, why don't you just go work for the *New Republic* instead?"

New York's office quarters did little to alleviate the tension. The cramped, 2,400-square-foot space, in which editors and writers worked with their desks jammed up against each other in some cases, was too cold in the winter and unbearably hot in the summer, the result of a constantly malfunctioning thermostat. "I sat in a puddle for two years because the radiator leaked," said Byron Dobell, who became a senior editor at *New York* in 1972. "I had to lay down newspapers so my shoes didn't get soaked." The gutters were never cleaned out, and eventually the entire office flooded during a rainstorm. Dobell had to come in on a Saturday to haul away the waterlogged magazines that had been destroyed in the basement. "It was a repellent mess of crap," he said.

Felker had one of two enclosed offices, but when he realized that yelling directives down the hallway would work more efficiently if he was actually *working* in the hallway, he moved his desk and turned his office into a conference room. The magazine was woefully understaffed from the start. Secretaries doubled as proofreaders and factcheckers, and no one ever went home early. "It was exhilarating, but it was really hard," said Jack Nessel. "We were always one step away from disaster." Most of the magazine's star writers were chronic deadline truants. Gail Sheehy was always late with her copy, as was Wolfe. Breslin would personally call the magazine's printer in order to determine exactly how long he could push back his drop-dead deadline. When Breslin finally consented to hand-deliver a manuscript, George Hirsch could hear him huffing and puffing up the stairs with Fat Thomas in tow, muttering expletives under his breath, along with an occasional "Why doesn't this fucking building have an elevator?" Despite his tardiness, Breslin demanded instant feedback from his editors. "Thirty seconds after turning a story in, he would ask me, 'Is it all right?'" said Shelly Zalaznick. "He was always eager to get it just right."

By mid-1969, *New York* was hitting its stride. Although the magazine had lost $2.1 million during the first year, Felker and Erpf had gone back for another round of financing with a public offering as Aeneid Equities, Inc., raising an additional $2 million, and the advertising revenue was starting to roll in. The magazine's circulation was 145,000 in August 1969, and 587 pages of ads had brought in $723,000 for the year. There was a compelling reason: *New York* had forged a distinct identity as a regional magazine. It had become an essential crib sheet for Manhattan snobs who would never cop to their parochialism. Felker and his staff struck a judicious balance between edgy service features (such as food critic Gael Greene's survey of the best Mafia restaurants in town); opinionated local political coverage from Steinem, Breslin, and Peter Maas; and insightful pop sociological reportage from Wolfe, Julie Baumgold, and Gail Sheehy.

The magazine didn't look like any other publication on the newsstand, either. The playfully savage illustrations of Edward Sorel and Bob Grossman quickly became the magazine's visual trademark, while Milton Glaser created a spare and elegant template for the editorial content. Glaser loved to leave some breathing room on a page; where others might gratuitously fill in a page of copy with busy imagery, Glaser and his associate art director, Walter Bernard, weren't afraid to leave in a large, vacant expanse, usually on the top third of the page. "Clay and Milton would have fights about leaving in so much blank space," said Jack Nessel. "Milton would eventually assuage Clay by telling him that 'we've got to let the story breathe,' that kind of thing."

By its third year of existence, Felker and his staff had succeeded in capturing the mad, scrambling ambition and creative energy of the most vital city in America between its covers every week. For the magazine's loyal readers, *New York* caught the gestalt of the city better than anything else. "Clay saw New York as Ambition City," said Tom Wolfe. "The excitement came from the collision of ambitious people. Status fascinated Clay."

Wolfe's attitude was more ambivalent. While New York City was the world's proving ground of power and privilege and thus supplied endless story ideas for him, he was disenchanted with the appropriation of radical politics by the city's liberal elite. The New Left, which had done so much to push the cause of civil rights into the foreground in the early sixties, had now, as he saw it, congealed into a faddish emblem of protest, an excuse for slumming activists to feel virtuous about their righteous indignation. But it was a codependent relationship. By embracing liberals in positions of power and influence, the leaders of the New New Left, which included the Yippees and the Black Panthers, received funding and media attention, while their newly converted supplicants could rub elbows with genuine insurrectionaries.

Wolfe was of two minds about the counterculture—writing admiring accounts of its lifestyle choices and artistic endeavors, yet criticizing its politics. Wolfe was amused by uptown matrons' embrace of the more frivolous aspects of sixties culture, but that same impulse had no role in serious considerations of race and economic disparity. One couldn't try on politics like a Pucci dress, only to discard it when it went out of fashion. "The left was on uncertain moral ground in those days," he said. "The New Left really took over in New York, but their followers were often wishy-washy about their motives. I felt there was a lot of hypocrisy in the movement."

A fund-raising party that Assemblyman Andrew Stein gave for striking California grape pickers on June 29, 1969, initially alerted Wolfe to these modish radical causes and their high-society partisans. The party, which spread far and wide over the lush expanse of Stein's father's Southampton beach estate, was a classic example of how New York's glittering left courted the lumpen proletariat and their working-class problems, and transformed real issues into the chitchat of festive cocktail parties. "The party was held in what is whimsically known as a cottage—in the Newport sense of cottage," said Wolfe in a prefatory note for "Radical Chic," which ran in the June 8, 1970, issue.

> It was all being done for the grape workers, at a time when the same group of people were doing little or nothing for Bedford-Stuyvesant or the Southeast Bronx. They would pick people 3,000 miles away who also had the advantage of being exotic because they were Latin, had a charismatic leader in Cesar Chavez, and wouldn't come back next weekend and knock on the door. . . .
>
> The difference between the people who give this sort of party and those who don't is the difference between people who insist on exoticism and romanticism (the grape workers, the Panthers, the Indians) and those who don't. There are two levels of sincerity. They are sincere about the issue, and they want to help, but at the same time they feel quite sincerely about their social position. They want to keep things going on both tracks.

Wolfe had never addressed these misgivings at any great length in print, but the opportunity to observe one of these parties firsthand presented itself one afternoon in the spring of 1970, during a visit to his friend David Halberstam's office at *Harper's*. Wolfe happened to see an invitation on Halberstam's desk for a fund-raiser that was to take place at Leonard and Felicia Bernstein's Park Avenue apartment. The event was to be given on behalf of the Panther Twenty-one, a group of Black Panthers who had been arrested on a charge of conspiring to blow up five New York department stores, New Haven railroad facilities, a police station, and the New York Botanical Garden in the Bronx. Wolfe thought he might write a book about this new tendency toward downward nobility, but with Bernstein—the dashing maestro of the New York Philharmonic, a true New York icon—now casting his lot with the radical left, the story suddenly had a compelling and timely angle. Wolfe would make this party the focus of a *New York* story instead. He surreptitiously scribbled the RSVP number on the back of a *Harper's* subscription card when Halberstam wasn't looking.

The *New York* reporter was a conspicuous presence at Bernstein's apartment that night, his white suit a studied contrast to the Panthers' black turtlenecks and Leonard Bernstein's all-black ensemble of sport coat and trousers. Felicia, too, was wearing a black cocktail dress, black being the de rigueur color of underclass solidarity. There were many luminaries in attendance, including *New York Review of Books* editor Robert Silvers, Barbara Walters, Otto Preminger, Sheldon Harnick, and Julie Belafonte. Wolfe wasn't the only reporter in attendance; the *New York Times*'s Charlotte Curtis was also taking notes. But the presence of the press didn't deter anyone in attendance from declaiming against the white power structure and its harassment of blacks in general, and the Panthers in particular.

Curtis's story ran two days after the party. "There they were," the *Times* reporter wrote, "the Black Panthers from the ghetto and the black and white liberals from the middle, upper-middle and upper classes studying one another cautiously over the expensive furnishings, the elaborate flower arrangements, the cocktails and the silver trays of canapés." The following day, a *Times* editorial criticized Bernstein for "elegant slumming that degrades patrons and patronized alike."

Bernstein was furious, but the story blew over and all was forgotten—until Wolfe weighed in nearly five months later. It took five months, because Wolfe also wanted to cover the Andrew Stein party, do supplemental interviews, and include a brief history of New York society and its recurrent strain of paternalism toward the lower class. The final draft topped out at twenty-seven thousand words. "We gave Tom a wide berth because we knew it would be worth it in the end," said Shelly Zalaznick. "He wasn't a prima donna; Tom was always dancing as fast as he could. But that was Tom's nature. He treated himself right."

Felker decided that Wolfe's novella-length feature would have the greatest impact if it ran in one gulp; the story took up the entire feature well of the June 8 issue. But it was Wolfe's phrase "radical chic" that nailed the folly of the "elegant slummers" that Wolfe eviscerated in his story. Above Carl Fischer's cover photo of three society matrons in their Yves Saint Laurent finery, their Black Power gloves raised in righteous defiance, was the *cri de guerre,* "Free Leonard Bernstein!" Inside, readers were confronted with a full-page portrait of Lenny and Felicia with Black Panther Don Cox, reclining on one of the Bernsteins' chintz wingback chairs. Wolfe opened the piece with an imagined vision:

> He could see himself, Leonard Bernstein, the *egregio maestro,* walking out on stage in white tie and tails in front of an orchestra. On one side of the conductor's podium is a piano. On the other is a chair with a guitar leaning against it. He sits in the chair and picks up the guitar. A guitar! One of those half-witted instruments, like the accordion, that are made for the Learn-to-Play-in-Eight-Days E-Z Diagram 110-IQ 14-year-olds of Levittown! But there's a reason. He has an anti-war message to deliver to this great starched white-throated audience in the symphony hall. He announces to them: "I love." Just that. The effect is mortifying. All at once a Negro rises up from out of the curve of the grand piano and starts saying things like, "The audience is curiously embarrassed." . . . Finally, Lenny gets off a heartfelt anti-war speech and exits.

Bernstein is getting played, a prize pawn in the Panthers' media game, and he doesn't like it a bit: "Who the hell was this Negro rising up from the piano and informing the world what an ass Leonard Bernstein was making of himself?" Actually, it was Wolfe who took it upon himself to announce to the world what an ass Bernstein and his guests were making of themselves. Here we find the Panthers mingling with the folks on the wrong side of the social ledger ("Do the Panthers like little Roquefort cheese morsels rolled in crushed nuts this way, and asparagus tips in mayonnaise dabs ... all of which ... are being offered to them on gadrooned silver platters by maids in black uniforms with hand-ironed white aprons") while Bernstein's invited guests try to expiate their Jim Crow guilt with histrionic verbal displays of self-flagellation and vigorous assent for the Panthers' anti-whitey rhetoric. Wolfe had hit the mother lode with Bernstein's party; it threw all the "status contradictions and incongruities" of the privileged class into bold relief, and there was no other subject, in his view, that better explained the motivations of certain powerful New Yorkers.

As usual, Wolfe, notebook in hand, absorbed every last detail: how the Panthers' Afros were authentic, "not the ones that have been shaped and trimmed like a topiary hedge and sprayed until they have a sheen like acrylic wall-to-wall—but like funky, natural, scraggly ... wild"; how Felicia Bernstein greeted her black nationalist guests with "the same tilt of the head, the same perfect Mary Astor voice" with which she greeted her usual après-concert guests. The Bernsteins, it must be noted, employed South American domestic help, therefore ducking the embarrassment of exploiting the very people they wanted to empower. "Can one comprehend how perfect that is, given ... the times?"

"Radical Chic: That Party at Lenny's" was Wolfe's most audacious hybrid yet—speculative fantasia, sociology lesson, and biting satire. Extended passages are devoted to wild riffs on the tortured inner lives of these well-intentioned liberals, who are prone to paroxysms of guilt about their exorbitant and extravagant lives, calibrating the right mix of "dignity without any overt class symbolism" for the Panthers' sake. Wolfe traces this tendency to ennoble the oppressed classes back to the nineteenth century. It was then known as *nostalgie de la boue*, or "nostalgia for the mud," when socialites in Regency England adopted the capes (the trucker's caps of their day) and bold driving styles of the coach drivers and the "reckless new dance" of the middle class, the waltz.

"Radical Chic" hit New York's chattering classes like a megaton bomb. Readers responded with both praise and criticism for Wolfe. Gloria Steinem and Jimmy Breslin felt that the piece cast a pall over fundraising in the city, creating a climate of fear for those who wanted to help worthy causes lest they become figures of ridicule. "I thought it was funny, but I was accused of putting up a big barrier to money for worthy causes," said Wolfe. "The Bernsteins assumed that, since I was there, I was sympathetic to their cause. It shocked some since I seemed to have a hip take on popular culture. Surely, I had to be on the Left somewhere! But I was quite prepared for the reaction, and quite pleased."

Bernstein was incensed. He was not, he insisted, a supporter of the Black Panthers, but a defender of due process and the rule of law as it applied to those who had been accused of crimes. "As an American and as a Jew I know that freedom of religion and the freedom of the citizen go hand in hand," Bernstein told his biographer Meryle Secrest. "Strike one and you have damaged the second." Bernstein's wife, who had thought to host the fund-raiser, was never again quite so public about her pet causes.

This was all just delicious icing to Felker. "Radical Chic" was the most talked-about article in the short history of *New York*, a piece whose title dissolved into the American vernacular, becoming a default phrase for pet causes of the rich and famous. In three years, Felker had not only resurrected *New York* but stamped it with his own thumbprint, turning his dream of owning a magazine that was inseparable from the life of the city into a self-fulfilling prophecy.

11

SAVAGE JOURNEYS

Hell's Angels had accomplished exactly what Hunter Thompson had hoped, which was to make him famous enough to get steady freelance work. In three years, more than eight hundred thousand copies of the book had been sold in both hardcover and paperback. *Esquire,* which had reacted coldly to Thompson's story solicitations in the past, ran an excerpt of the book in its January 1967 issue. But Thompson had yet to reap any significant financial windfall, which he blamed on his book's publisher, Random House, and his editor, Jim Silberman. "In 1968, I had only seen ten thousand bucks from the book. I assumed Silberman and the others were ripping me off. " So he continued to hustle up work. The *New York Times,* a publication that had turned down Thompson when he applied for a job there a few years before, now wanted the writer to provide an analysis of the counterrevolution that was taking root in San Francisco; "The 'Hashbury' Is the Capital of the Hippies" ran in the Sunday magazine on May 14, 1967.

Pageant magazine assigned him an interview with Richard Nixon on the eve of the 1968 New Hampshire presidential primary, when the former vice president was trying to present himself as less abrasive and more solicitous toward the press. Thompson was unconvinced. "I suppose it's only fair to say that this latest model might be different and maybe even better in some ways," he wrote in the piece, "Presenting: The Richard Nixon Doll." "But as a customer, I wouldn't touch it—except with a long cattle prod."

All was not lost, however: Thompson found, much to his delight, that Nixon knew football as well as Thompson did, and the two whiled away time in Nixon's limousine after a campaign appearance in Manchester, New Hampshire, discussing the upcoming Super Bowl matchup between Green Bay and Oakland. "Nixon had always claimed to be a big fan, but goddamn, the man really knew his stuff," said Thompson. "Shit, you could actually start to believe that he was a human being for a minute there."

Thompson no longer had to observe the reportorial proprieties of the mainstream press; he could just write stories as he saw fit, flinging barbs like nunchakus. If he wanted to disparage Nixon's political comeback as a bunko game, he could. "It was an exciting and wide-open time for me," said Thompson. "Shit, I always felt that I was right where I should be, and that's extremely vital."

Playboy magazine thought it had arranged the perfect marriage of subject and writer when it assigned Thompson to profile Jean-Claude Killy, the fair-haired French skier whose three gold medals at the 1968 Grenoble Winter Olympics had turned him into a household name in the States. Thompson went into the interview with an open mind, but when he met Killy in Chicago, he was appalled at how the skier was cheapening his own name for a quick buck. There was Killy and O. J. Simpson, pitching Chevrolet's latest models at the auto show like Fuller brush salesmen. When Thompson berated Killy for selling out to corporate interests, Killy got defensive. "You don't understand! You could never do what I'm doing! You sit there and smile, but you don't know what it is! I am tired. Tired! I don't care anymore—not on the inside or the outside! I don't care what I say, what I think, *but I have to keep doing it.*"

Playboy wanted a harmless profile, but there was another story, a story larger than Killy, in fact. Thompson turned in an eleven-thousand-word portrait of a cipher, a selling machine running on autopilot, accountable only to his greed and the executives cutting his checks—in short, the poster boy for the new breed of media-engorged, money-mad celebrity: "He is a handsome middle-class French boy who trained hard and learned to ski so well that now his name is immensely saleable on the marketplace of a crazily inflated culture-economy that eats its heroes like hotdogs and honors them on about the same level." Senior editor David

Butler killed the piece; had he approved it, there was no chance the story would ever run. Hugh Hefner had been trying to land the Chevrolet account for the past five years, and he wasn't about to run a story that alienated a potentially lucrative advertising client.

But Thompson knew the piece was a winner. He had successfully negotiated the space between "massive public opinion and taste and desires, and what people really say," and he was determined to place the story somewhere. As it turned out, a new magazine was starting up, and, more important, it was being edited by someone Thompson knew personally. Warren Hinckle was a San Francisco native, the product of a strict Catholic school education whose inbred skepticism and reflexive chafing at authority (he once chided the school library for not subscribing to *The Nation*) suited him for a career as a journalist-provocateur. As an undergraduate at the University of San Francisco, Hinckle edited the college paper, the *Daily Foghorn*, often creating sensational news when there was none to report. Once, in search of a story to fill an empty news hole, he had an accomplice burn down a guardhouse on campus.

Hinckle's *Foghorn* work had caught the eye of *San Francisco Chronicle* editor Scott Newhall, who was trying to reinvent the parochial newspaper as a vehicle for provocative writing. Newhall hired Hinckle as a general assignment reporter, but the writer hated the prosaic nature of daily beat reporting, the constant chasing after stories of little consequence. He left the *Chronicle* in order to open a public relations firm, but it failed miserably, and the tug of journalism pulled him back in.

Hinckle would find his true métier in the most unlikely of places, a Catholic reform quarterly founded by Edward Keating, whose wife was the heir to a vast San Francisco fortune. *Ramparts* was a liberal Catholic quarterly, a vehicle for Keating to challenge what he regarded as the hypocrisy and moral bankruptcy of the Catholic Church. An early story written by Robert Scheer criticized New York archbishop Francis Cardinal Spellman for his vocal support of the Vietnam War—a story that was so untouchable that only *Ramparts* was willing to publish it.

Hinckle convinced Keating to hire him as executive editor, then proceeded to redirect the magazine's editorial content. He hired Scheer, a former economics major from City College of New York and lecturer at the University of California, Berkeley, who had recently mounted an unsuccessful run for Congress, to be the magazine's political editor, and proceeded to make *Ramparts* a debunker of received wisdom in any form, particularly as Vietnam became the wedge issue of the era. *Ramparts* published a series of explosive investigative pieces, most notably an article by Sol Stern that revealed a connection between the CIA and certain student organizations at Michigan State with links to South Vietnam, which led to a fumbling campaign by the intelligence agency to discredit the magazine with bribes, wiretapping, the works. Hinckle, however, was wise to all of this skullduggery, and the magazine didn't back down from its story.

In a few short years, Hinckle had raised *Ramparts*'s profile considerably, but the magazine was hemorrhaging money too fast for the gains to make any appreciable difference. In the winter of 1970 Hinckle bailed out and moved to New York to start another publication, this time with a mandate to remain untethered from an outside publisher's purse strings (*Ramparts* would continue to publish until 1975). Together with former advertising executive Howard Gossage and attorney and former *New York Times* reporter Sidney Zion, Hinckle raised $675,000 in a public stock offering, then plastered the check on the cover of the first issue of the magazine, called *Scanlan's*. "Hinckle and Zion were a couple of shysters," said illustrator Ralph Steadman, an early *Scanlan's* contributor. "But they were good at what they did."

Scanlan's improved and refined upon *Ramparts*'s editorial blend of rigorous investigative pieces and sharp cultural criticism. Such august bylines as Richard Severo, Auberon Waugh, Joseph Kahn, and Murray Kempton graced its first issue; so did Hunter S. Thompson.

Thompson and Hinckle had met three years earlier, in the offices of *Ramparts*. Hinckle, who read *Hell's Angels* in galleys, invited Thompson up to the magazine's North Beach offices for an informal meeting. The two proceeded to tie one on at Vanessi's, a local bar and regular *Ramparts* watering hole. When they returned to the office a few hours later, the magazine's in-house spider monkey, Henry Luce, had dug into Thompson's stash of pills in his knapsack and rampaged through the halls of the building, wide-eyed and hopped on a toxic pharmacological cocktail.

Now, three years later, Thompson was looking for a home for his Jean-Claude Killy story. "Here is the Killy piece," he wrote to Hinckle in a December 6, 1969, cover letter accompanying his only extant copy of the manuscript, Xeroxed on puke-orange paper that rendered the type barely legible. "Some people dig it for the word-action; others hate it for the style and tone. The editors of *Playboy* really despised it: Their edit/memos ranged from 'This is a good *Esquire* piece' to 'Thompson's ugly, stupid arrogance is an insult to everything we stand for.'" Never in his ten-year career as a freelancer, Thompson wrote, had he been "shit on so totally" by a publication, which in his estimation was nothing but "a conspiracy of anemic masturbators." Although Thompson invited Hinckle to edit and amend the story at his discretion, he nonetheless had a list of things he preferred to have Hinckle leave alone—a list that included virtually every paragraph.

Hinckle agreed to retain the original lead that *Playboy* had cut, but Thompson strenuously objected when *Scanlan's* tried to excise the last ten pages of the story; only there did he set aside the pointed barbs and sardonic set pieces and home in on his thesis about Killy being a metaphor for America's celebrity culture worship. Hinckle, a man not prone to capitulation, relented, and the piece ran as Thompson intended.

This was a beautiful thing for Thompson, who had clashed with so many editors over editorial content and money that he had become inured to the routine. With Hinckle, he had found a kindred spirit, an editor who refused to put up obstacles before the far-flung excursions of Thompson's prose. "Hinckle is an editor that would do anything to get a story, including writing bad checks," said Thompson. "But I liked him as much as any editor I ever worked for. Whatever needed to be done, he would do it. I've always thought of him as a good offensive tackle. As long as he was blocking for me, even if it entailed questionable tactics, I valued it tremendously."

Now Thompson would embark on an original story for *Scanlan's*, a trip to the Kentucky Derby in his hometown of Louisville. Novelist James Salter, Thompson's friend and neighbor in Colorado, had first suggested the Derby to Thompson during a soused dinner one night, and Thompson immediately pitched it to Hinckle with a 3:30 A.M. phone call. The Derby was obviously a perfect fit for him, a chance to lay bare the idiotic celebration rituals of the South's ruling class and thus expose its reckless behavioral decadence.

Armed with a fistful of up-front expense money from Hinckle—a rare and pleasurable luxury—Thompson prepared for his trip, notifying his mother, Virginia, that he would be staying at her apartment. But one matter still needed to be sorted out. Thompson was confident he could describe the gaudy awfulness of the Derby in his story, but he felt that it might play better if it was accompanied by illustrations, like the classic satires from *Punch* magazine in England. He suggested Pat Oliphant, the Pulitzer prize–winning political cartoonist, but there was no way Oliphant's schedule could accommodate a trip to Kentucky. A few other illustrators were contacted, such as British artist Ronald Searle and photographer Rob Guralnick, but everyone was booked up.

Scanlan's managing editor, Don Goddard, had another idea. A British illustrator named Ralph Steadman had recently made an appearance in the office with his portfolio, and both Goddard and art director J. C. Suarès were impressed with his work, particularly his book *Still Life with Raspberry*, a selection of Steadman's provocative line drawings that had been published by the British publishing house Rapp and Whiting in 1969. A native of Wallasey, Cheshire, Steadman had been drawing steadily in his native country for the past decade as a political cartoonist, mostly for the satire magazine *Private Eye* and the *Times* of London. Heavily influenced by the German Expressionists Otto Dix and Max Beckmann, Steadman had a fine eye for the macabre and sinister in everyday life. His exuberant line and Boschian flair for locating the molten core of his subjects kept him in steady work in England, a country that has never spared its public figures the satirist's rod. Now he wanted to try his luck in the States, and make his long-deferred fortune. *Scanlan's* wasn't the pot of gold he was looking for, but it was a start.

Suarès called Steadman on Long Island, where the artist was staying with a friend during his fact-finding visit to the States.

"How would you like to go to Kentucky to work with an ex–Hell's Angel who shaved his head?"

"Is he violent?"

"Not that I know of. He's a writer."

"Yea, that would be good."

Thompson had no idea what Steadman was all about, nor was Steadman aware of Thompson's work, but they both shared a reflexive hatred of authority and unchecked power, and a conviction that they could change the state of things. "At that time, one was intent on bringing down the establishment and having a better world," said Steadman. "What a naive thing to think! *Scanlan's* had a great sense of what was necessary for the time; they were on a crusade, too."

No sooner had Steadman arrived in Louisville on April 30, 1970, and took the full measure of the Derby revelers in their white bucks and seersucker sports jackets than he knew he was in for the joy ride of his life. "I sensed the screaming lifestyle of America immediately," he said. "It was apparent that America was different in a very wayward way." It took two days for Steadman to track down Thompson, who had no press credentials and thus couldn't be contacted through the Derby press office. "I figured *Scanlan's* was a legitimate publication," said Steadman. "Surely, I would find their writer in the press office!"

Eventually, they did encounter each other in the press box. Steadman was expecting to see a Hell's Angels type, not a wild-eyed outdoorsman type. "His head was like a piece of bone," said Steadman. "He was built like a footballer, wearing this multicolored hunting jacket with a big sun hat that fell over his eyes, and here I was with a beard and tweed coat. We were like chalk and cheese."

Thompson set him at ease right away. "I've been looking for you for two days," Steadman told Thompson, to which Thompson replied, "Well, we've met now. You want a drink?"

They never stopped having drinks for a week. Beer with bourbon chasers, brandy, an occasional mint julep for good measure. "Oh, we went on a bender," said Steadman. "We were pissed the whole time. It was totally irresponsible of us as journalists, but we felt it was kind of a crusade. We thought we would put the world right with our shenanigans."

There was nothing subversive about a marathon drinking binge in Kentucky, however: they were merely blending in with their environment, "going native," as Steadman put it. To the artist, Churchill Downs was like a Brueghel tableau in the antebellum South, full of half-mad drunks falling into the mud, jockeying for position at the betting windows, frantically crashing and sloshing all over each other. The crush of the crowd was so intense that Thompson and Steadman never witnessed any of the race itself. Not that it mattered; the crowd was the story anyway. "Ralph was such an innocent audience," said Thompson. "I could take him anywhere and point something at him and he would make it interesting."

Steadman was entranced by the faces that swept by him all day and night, the ruddy complexions and jaundiced stares of the jowly reprobates. He never went anywhere without his sketchbook, drawing caricatures of anyone who caught his eye, which was nearly everyone. He had misplaced his colored pencils in a cab in New York and had to borrow eye shadow and lipstick from Don Goddard's wife, who was an executive at Revlon. It was the ideal medium for an event in which the mascara streaked and runnelled with beer and sweat. This led to some huffy scenes, much to Steadman's dismay. "Here was this limey drawing these denatured pictures of people, and they were taking it personally, like a personal insult. I got a few 'fucking limey's thrown my way."

Thompson insisted that Steadman cease and desist his "filthy habit" at once, but the artist persisted. One night after a few drinks, while Thompson and Steadman were having dinner at a local restaurant with Thompson's brother Davison and his wife, the artist got into an argument with another patron who objected to an unusually garish rendering that Steadman had drawn of him. "The drawing just kept getting ruder and ruder," said Steadman. "So it got kind of ugly in there." Thompson proceeded to pull out a can of Mace (he referred to it as "Chemical Billy") and sprayed it in the general direction of the waiter, then fled with Steadman. "You're a guest in our country," Hunter told Steadman. "I didn't want them to hurt you!" "I just accepted it as part and parcel of what the job entailed," said Steadman. "It didn't occur to me that it was completely nonsensical on Hunter's part. A lot of it was paranoia. It was purely in Hunter's head. He was very protective towards me."

Back in New York, Hunter had to file the story for *Scanlan's,* but he couldn't recall most of what had transpired. The trip was lost to hazy recollections of wild drinking bouts with Steadman, or short, cryptic notes written in red ink in his notebook. But he had missed his deadline and Goddard was screaming for the story. The rest of the contents of the fourth issue had already been shipped to the printer in San Francisco, leaving Thompson's feature as the only gaping hole. Warren Hinckle suggested that Thompson lock himself in a room at the Royalton Hotel on *Scanlan's* dime and not leave until he had the piece written.

With Goddard standing by, Thompson leaned hard on his notes

and cranked out what he remembered—the Rabelaisian adventures of a native son and a limey outsider adrift in the innermost circle of southern hell. Goddard edited on the fly, as the pages were ripped from Thompson's typewriter, cutting what Thompson referred to as "sociophilosophical flashbacks" and "weird memory jogs" in order to streamline the narrative.

"The Kentucky Derby Is Decadent and Depraved" was Thompson's revenge on the uptight, cosseted South that he had left behind in the 1950s, the first piece ever written about the Derby that was brave enough to admit that the ritual had little to do with ladies in sun hats fanning themselves with programs and men in seersucker suits sipping mint juleps. That stifling and hermetic culture of noblesse oblige wasn't charming, and it was so out of touch with the rest of America as to be completely severed from it. "In a narrow Southern society," Thompson wrote, "the closest kind of inbreeding is not only stylish and acceptable, but far more convenient—to the parents—than setting their offspring free to find their own mates, for their own reasons and in their own ways."

The Derby was a metaphor for the "doomed atavistic culture" of the South—its inbred racism and chauvinism, its willful disengagement from the civil rights struggles that it had engendered. No one talked about Vietnam, the better to ignore it. "Not much energy in these faces," Thompson wrote, "not much *curiosity*. Suffering in silence, nowhere to go after thirty in this life, just hang on and humor the children." Thompson and Steadman didn't bother to watch the race because no one at the Derby really cared, anyway: Churchill Downs was just a big bar with a bunch of desperate characters trying to stave off their inevitable obsolescence with enough booze to kill a pack of thoroughbreds. Thompson was convinced that the counterrevolution would just swallow them whole.

"The Kentucky Derby Is Decadent and Depraved" is a meditation on the moral decline of the South; it's also very, very funny. Here is Thompson encountering a hail-fellow-well-met Texan in the airport lounge:

> "I'm ready for *anything,* by God! Anything at all. Yeah, what are you drinkin'?" I ordered a Margarita with ice, but he wouldn't hear of it: "Naw, naw . . . what the hell kind of drink is that for Kentucky Derby

time? What's *wrong* with you, boy?" He grinned and winked at the bartender. "Goddam, we gotta educate this boy. Get him some good *whiskey*. . . ."

I shrugged. "Okay, a double Old Fitz on ice." Jimbo nodded his approval.

"Look." He tapped me on the arm to make sure I was listening. "I know this Derby crowd, I come here every year, and let me tell you one thing I've learned—this is no town to be giving people the impression you're some kind of faggot. Not in public, anyway. Shit, they'll roll you in a minute, knock you in the head and take every goddamn cent you have."

Thompson tells his drinking buddy that he's a photographer from *Playboy* and that his assignment is to "take pictures of the riot."

"What riot?"

I hesitated, twirling the ice in my drink. "At the track. On Derby day. The Black Panthers." I stared at him again. "Don't you read the newspapers?"

The grin on his face had collapsed. "What the *hell* are you talking about?"

"Well . . . maybe I shouldn't be telling you. . . ." I shrugged. "But hell, everybody else seems to know. The cops and the National Guard have been getting ready for weeks. They have 20,000 troops on alert at Fort Knox. They've warned us—all the press and photographers—to wear helmets and special vests like flak jackets. We were told to expect shooting. . . ."

"It's a shitty article," Thompson wrote in a letter to his friend Bill Cardoso after he returned home to Woody Creek, Colorado, "a classic of irresponsible journalism." It *was* irresponsible, in the traditional sense, but a scathing critique of a blinkered culture lay just under the surface of Thompson's humorous set pieces, a seriocomic tightrope act that no other journalist in America was capable of negotiating with as much panache. The harried journalist just might be nuts, but the good ol' boys and half-wits are much more dangerous.

"The Kentucky Derby Is Decadent and Depraved" ran in the June 1970 issue of *Scanlan's* with the bylines "Written under duress by Hunter

S. Thompson" and "Sketched with eyebrow pencil and lipstick by Ralph Steadman." Bill Cardoso called it "pure gonzo," so outrageous that it needed its own name. It became the most notorious Thompson dispatch since his Hell's Angels stories for *The Nation*. Journalists from the *New York Times* made the trip to Woody Creek to interview him, while Tom Wolfe sent Thompson a copy of his latest book, *Radical Chic and Mau-Mauing the Flak Catchers*, along with a personal note: "Dear Hunter, I present this book in homage after reading the two funniest stories of all time—J. C. Killy and The Derby. You are The Boss! Not the sheriff, maybe, but you are The Boss!"

Flattered and quite pleased with himself, Thompson wrote back, pointing out to Wolfe that "with the perhaps fading exception of Kesey, you're about the only writer around that I figure I can learn from." In its reckless disregard for proper reportorial decorum, its skillful blend of comic picaresque and moral tract, it mapped out the blueprint for all of Thompson's subsequent work of the decade.

Hinckle was so thrilled with the story that he gave Thompson and Steadman another assignment, the second of a projected multipart series about the strange mores of significant annual American events. The two would converge upon the America's Cup yachting race in Newport, Rhode Island, and provide a gonzo story similar to the Derby piece. Thompson had more artillery for this misadventure, namely, a large supply of psilocybin or "magic mushrooms." Steadman, who had progressed from bemused fellow traveler to Thompson's willing coconspirator, had never taken any drugs aside from an occasional marijuana toke and one acid trip, but he was game.

It didn't take long for the drugs to wend their way into the pair's adventure. While attending a party on a three-masted schooner in Newport harbor, Steadman fell ill with motion sickness, and after three hours of severe discomfort on board finally asked Hunter for a dose of magic mushrooms, thinking that it might alleviate his nausea. "Hunter was sleeping really well in Newport, and I thought the drugs might have the same effect on me," said Steadman. But after a while, "I started seeing red-eyed dogs emerging from the piano. My hair felt slick and I felt it coming down my forehead like Hitler. The psilocybin just gouged out my interior; it scraped it right out and hit my consciousness. It was terribly frightening."

Thompson had other ways of instilling fear in Steadman. "A friend of

mine had a dreadnaught that had parking privileges in the port, so I gave
him some *Scanlan's* money to let us aboard," said Thompson. "The security was tight, like military security, but I noticed that you could access
the boat from the ocean side." Thompson and Steadman rented a rowboat and armed themselves with several cans of spray paint; Thompson's goal was to deface a luxury yacht with some witty graffiti scrawl.

"Any suggestions?" Thompson asked Steadman.
"How about 'Fuck the Pope'?"

But the sound of the shaking paint ball inside the spray cans gave
them away; a sentry light found the rowboat just as Steadman was about
to do his handiwork. "I thought of everything except the paint ball,"
said Thompson.

It was a fool's errand; *Scanlan's* folded before Thompson and Steadman could make it back to New York. Hinckle and Zion had burned
through a million dollars in less than a year, leaving Thompson without
a regular outlet for his work. It was a bitter disappointment for Thompson, who enjoyed the creative freedom that Hinckle had given him—an
all-access pass to write as he saw fit about whatever subject came to
mind, despite his constant gripes about magazine work being no better
than "writing copy for [Ford Motor Company] pamphlets."

There were other projects to keep him busy, not the least of which
was another book, which he had held off for close to three years. After
floating a number of ideas past Jim Silberman at Random House, the
two agreed that Thompson would chronicle the death of the American
dream, the rogue reporter casting his jaundiced eye on the dry rot of
contemporary culture, as he had done in the Kentucky Derby piece. But
the idea was so broad and abstract that Thompson had trouble getting
his mind around it. What, exactly, was the death of the American dream,
and where was his entry point? "I wish I could explain the delay,"
Thompson wrote to Silberman in January 1970. "In a nut, my total
inability to deal with the small success of the H.A. book has resulted—
after three years of useless, half-amusing rural fuckaround—in just about
nothing except three wasted years."

There was plenty of material to work with, mostly research for abandoned articles about gun control and the oil industry, but Thompson

couldn't organize it all in a way that would cohere as a book. He suggested other approaches to Silberman—perhaps an anthology of pieces like Tom Wolfe's *The Pump House Gang* or Mailer's *Advertisements for Myself,* the latter a book that had been a formative influence on the young Thompson.

Thompson was thinking about a new composite form that would combine reporting and fiction in ways that blurred distinctions between the two: "a very contemporary novel with straight, factual journalism as a background." Thompson had been groping toward this style with the Kentucky Derby story—ratcheting up the clamor of the South's ignoble savages to a fever pitch—but now he wanted to delve into an invented persona and tinker with form. In doing so, he could get away with just about anything and become a man of action with no restrictions. He would call his alter ego Raoul Duke: "semi-fictional," he wrote to Silberman, "but just hazy enough so I can let him say and do things that wouldn't work in first person."

For months, Thompson grappled with the death of the American dream and Raoul Duke, but nothing came of it. In order to stave off the anguish of writer's block, Thompson turned his energies to extracurricular activities—shooting his .44 Magnum into the gloaming on his Woody Creek property near Aspen, Colorado, a ranch house he called Owl Farm; dropping mescaline and blasting the Jefferson Airplane and Dylan at ear-wrenching volume.

Politics became another diversion; it appealed to Thompson's desire to change the order of things. He marshaled his creative energies into the mayoral campaign of Joe Edwards, a twenty-nine-year-old Colorado lawyer and biker who was running in a three-way race against Leonard Oates, the hand-picked successor of Aspen's outgoing Republican mayor, Dr. Robert "Buggsy" Bernard, and local small business owner Eve Homeyer. Thompson viewed the race as a crucial battle for the agrarian soul of Aspen, which he felt was being destroyed by the rapacious greed of big real estate interests. The liberal Edwards would mobilize the "freak vote" in Aspen, the under-thirty hippies and heads who would put a stop to the unchecked growth and plant the seeds of reform.

Thompson devoted all of his energy to the race, which, unlike writing books, offered the promise of a quick and unambiguous resolution. Then he received a cold call from Jann Wenner, the editor in chief and owner of *Rolling Stone* magazine in San Francisco. Wenner had obtained a copy of *Hell's Angels* in galley form while working at *Ramparts* as an apprentice editor and consumed it in two days. "It knocked me out," said Wenner. "It was such a vivid piece of writing. I was so impressed with the fact that he had the balls to hang out with Angels. It seems tame now, but then it was the height of adventure and courage."

Now Wenner wanted Thompson to work for him. Thompson's style—irreverent, angry, anything but detached—would fit in perfectly with Wenner's young magazine, the only mainstream periodical that bothered to cover youth culture with rigor, taste and intelligence.

A graduate of the University of California, Berkeley, Wenner had scraped together $7,500, some of it from his future wife's parents, to start the magazine, relying on the sage counsel of his mentor, Ralph J. Gleason, the jazz columnist for the *San Francisco Chronicle*, to steer a steady editorial course. In three years, *Rolling Stone* had not only become the definitive magazine for rock music coverage—due in no small part to critics such as Jon Landau, Lester Bangs, and Greil Marcus—but also long investigative pieces on the Altamont killings and the Manson Family, the antiwar movement and the battle for environmental preservation.

Wenner was a native of Marin County. His father, Ed, was an engineer who had served in the Army Air Corps, a resourceful and avuncular man who tended to defer to his wife, Sim, when it came to taking disciplinary action against his three children. Sim was headstrong, a former Navy lieutenant junior grade during World War II who became the owner of a successful baby food business shortly after her discharge.

Jann caught Sim's entrepreneurial spirit early. In third grade he published a gossip sheet called the *Bugle*, printing all the dirt on his classmates, but the *Bugle* had to fold when a few too many kids threatened to shut Wenner's operation down with a bloody nose. When Jann was fourteen, he was sent to Chadwick, a boarding school outside of Los Angeles; his parents divorced shortly thereafter.

At Chadwick, Wenner threw himself into his own endeavors with brio and determination. He sang in the glee club, ran for office, acted in school productions (he was the lead in *Dr. Faustus*) and started up a newspaper called the *Sardine*. Wenner was a model student, if not exactly a typical boarding-school do-gooder. He wore his hair long and developed a taste for European art films and editorial insurrection, publishing critical articles about the school administration that resulted in stern warnings and expulsion threats.

In 1964, Wenner enrolled in the University of California, Berkeley, just as the school administration was about to come under siege by a clutch of student firebrands led by a brilliant twenty-one-year-old philosophy student named Mario Savio. Wenner, who was working as a stringer for NBC radio in between classes, was enthralled by Savio and the Free Speech Movement, volunteering his services for a "countercatalog" that rated college courses according to their political and sociological criteria. But Wenner had little use for political cant and the internecine battles between Berkeley's numerous leftist organizations. While he abided by their principles, he was not going to immerse himself in radical protest. Exactly what he was going to do with his life was not entirely clear to him, at least until he saw the Beatles' movie *A Hard Day's Night*.

It was an epiphany, the night Wenner found his life's purpose. The visceral energy of the Beatles' music sent a charge through him, conquered him head, body, and soul. From that point on, nothing would be as important to Wenner as rock and roll. It was more potent a cultural force than Savio or the FSM, more vibrant and alive—the thrilling sound of an emergent generation giving voice to itself.

Emboldened, Wenner ventured out beyond Berkeley to La Honda, where he experienced his first acid trip under the auspices of Ken Kesey and the Merry Pranksters. In San Francisco, where an alternative culture rooted in rock and roll was simmering, Wenner attended concerts at places such as the Fillmore and Longshoreman's Hall, reviewing the shows for the *Daily Californian* using the byline Mr. Jones—an homage to Wenner's musical hero, Bob Dylan. He met Ralph Gleason at one such show and proceeded to pump him for information about the publishing business.

Despite the generational differences—Wenner was nineteen, Gleason forty-eight—Gleason recognized in Wenner the same passion for music that had seized him upon attending his first Bunny Berigan concert in New York's Apollo Theater in 1945. Gleason, a soft-spoken man of somewhat patrician bearing who wore sport coats with elbow patches and smoked a briarwood pipe, was a jazz critic first and foremost, but he found merit in any musical genre that had integrity and soul. He was an early champion of Jefferson Airplane and the Grateful Dead, devoting extensive column inches in the *Chronicle* to both bands and other rock artists.

Gleason would be a crucial ally for Wenner when the Berkeley student dropped out of college during his junior year to try his hand in the publishing world. Taking the recommendation of Gleason, a contributing editor for *Ramparts,* Warren Hinckle hired Wenner to be the entertainment editor for a new Sunday edition of the magazine, but Hinckle had no empathy for the counterculture. In a cover story for *Ramparts,* he savagely decried the leaders of the movement, calling acid guru Timothy Leary "Aimee Semple McPherson in drag" and Ken Kesey a "hippie has-been." That attitude made no sense to Wenner, but the final straw came when editor Sol Stern took a trowel to Wenner's introduction to his Timothy Leary interview, making excessive changes to his text. Wenner tried to do an end run around Stern, inserting his original text into the edited version, and was caught. Hinckle reluctantly kept him on, but when the Sunday *Ramparts* folded, Wenner was gone.

He tried freelancing, writing a two-thousand-word review of the Beatles' *Sgt. Pepper's Lonely Hearts Club Band* for *High Fidelity* magazine that never ran. But the freelance life was too unpredictable. The days of toiling for editors, of being beholden to the capricious judgment of others, was over for him. It was as good a time as any to start his own magazine. Gleason would give him the credibility; the rest would be up to him.

The idea, as he had discussed it with Gleason, would be to combine the professionalism of *Time* and the hipness of the underground press with stories that would run as long as *The New Yorker*'s. But first he needed money, so he hit up everyone he knew. Gleason chipped in $1,500. Wenner's stepmother was in for $500. Sim Wenner contributed $2,000. The rest of the money came from the parents of Wenner's new girlfriend, Jane Schindelheim, whom he had met while working at *Ramparts.*

He used part of that money to rent an office on 625 Third Street in the warehouse district. He called the magazine *Rolling Stone,* which had a triple echo effect—it was the name of one of blues musician Muddy Waters's greatest songs, a name that had been appropriated by Wenner's favorite British band. His hero Bob Dylan had also kick-started his electric phase with a song called "Like a Rolling Stone."

Like Harold Hayes at *Esquire* and Clay Felker at *New York,* Wenner valued great writing more than political dogma; *Rolling Stone* was unapologetic about presenting itself as a "rock and roll newspaper" that framed its music coverage within the proper cultural context. Rock would never stray too far away from the foreground.

"We were off the map as far as mainstream magazines were concerned," said writer Timothy Ferris, who was *Rolling Stone*'s first New York bureau chief. "We had this high-minded notion that we wouldn't take any cigarette, alcohol, or car ads, but no one wanted to buy any, so it was beside the point. But we knew we were publishing innovative stuff, pieces that people just had to read because they were so good." Within three years of *Rolling Stone*'s first issue in November 1967, circulation jumped to a hundred thousand—a huge number for a magazine running on a shoestring budget.

Wenner was most interested in fresh voices—writers who were inexperienced and hungry, outcast freaks and former dope dealers with a flair for story structure, news veterans who had been beaten down by endless eight-hundred-word dispatches for late-edition deadlines. Recruiting Hunter S. Thompson would be a feather in his cap; here was an established author with a best-selling book under his belt, a master of the long-form story who had lost a crucial outlet with the demise of *Scanlan's* and was eager to fill the void quickly. "I wanted Hunter to write for *Rolling Stone* from the beginning," said Wenner.

Now Wenner had an assignment for Thompson: the obituary of Hell's Angel Freewheeling Frank. Alas, Thompson was too busy to do it, immersed as he was with the Aspen sheriff's campaign. Thompson had vowed that he would run for the office if Joe Edwards won his mayoral campaign. Edwards wound up losing by six votes, a margin that made the writer think he just might have a chance if he ran. Wenner told him to write about that.

"The Battle of Aspen" ran in the October 1, 1970, *Rolling Stone* and was a discursive and riotous account of the two Aspen campaigns. There was no question that Thompson had found a perfect vehicle for his turbocharged prose; even though he studiously avoided writing about rock explicitly, his flair for the gleefully subversive made him a natural ally of Wenner's publication. "It wasn't too difficult editing Hunter on that story," recalled Wenner. "He was far more resilient and easier to deal with in those days. I remember it being a fairly spontaneous affair."

The other staffers at *Rolling Stone* weren't so sure about Thompson. "None of us really knew what to think of Hunter at first," said former *Rolling Stone* copy editor Charles Perry. "I remember the first time I saw him in person. He was coming into the office to work with [editor] John Lombardi on a story, and he had this big box of hats and wigs with him. He would just keep changing into these wigs and hats every few minutes. John found this puzzling and somewhat disturbing. He quit a few weeks later." Fortunately for *Rolling Stone,* Wenner knew how to handle the writer. "Hunter needed an apocalypse going on all the time," he said. "But the writing was absolutely electric, and it was tremendous fun working and hanging around with him. I was resilient enough to handle him, but a lot of people were brutalized by him."

Thompson's next story for *Rolling Stone* would come from an old drinking buddy, a civil rights lawyer he had met through a mutual friend, Ketchum, Ohio, bar owner Mike Solheim. Like Thompson, Oscar Zeta Acosta was an Air Force veteran. After being honorably discharged, Acosta attended Modesto Junior College, near his hometown of Riverbank, a small, rural central California town that would eventually be gerrymandered into Modesto. The objective for Acosta was to distance himself from the minimum-wage drudgery that his father, Manuel, had endured for so long as a janitor, but just what that entailed, Acosta wasn't quite sure. At least a proper education would give him a leg up. He had literary aspirations, but despite a ferocious commitment to writing, including an unpublished novel, Acosta was unable to sell anything.

Following a short stint at San Francisco State University, Acosta enrolled in San Francisco Law School and struggled mightily to pass the bar, succeeding on his second attempt in 1966. But providing expensive counsel for corporate fat cats was anathema to Acosta. It was highly unlikely that any white-shoe law firm would hire him anyway; Acosta was a heavy user of LSD and other psychoactive drugs, which he felt were gateways to self-realization. "I think psychedelic drugs have been important to the development of my consciousness," Acosta wrote in an unpublished essay. "They've put me into a level of awareness where I can see myself and see what I'm really doing." As a Chicano growing up near the San Joaquin Valley, that vast agricultural expanse in central California in which most of America's produce is harvested, Acosta was well aware of the exploitation of immigrant laborers by white landowners, the brazen injustices imposed on illiterate workers who had no legal recourse. He would make it his business to help the disenfranchised among his people.

After a short stint working as a lawyer for the East Oakland Legal Aid Society, Acosta moved to Los Angeles in 1968, where the Chicano civil rights movement, known as El Movimiento, was gaining momentum. His brother Bob tipped him off to a large Brown Berets protest in L.A., and Acosta was intrigued by this Latino analogue to the Black Panthers. He was worn down by the workload and the menial pay of his Legal Aid job. His ambitions were too outsized for a civil service job, anyway. Armed with a bar license, Acosta wanted nothing more than to help foment a Chicano revolution. "Whenever he set out to do something, he went at it with full force," said Acosta's son Marco. "But he was never satisfied with any one thing."

During the next six years in L.A., Acosta was the legal point man for virtually every significant civil rights case regarding Chicano activists. In late 1968 he defended thirteen protesters who were indicted for conspiracy to disrupt the public school system after a teacher walkout. In 1969 he defended the Biltmore Seven, a clutch of radicals who were arrested for trying to firebomb the Biltmore Hotel while Governor Ronald Reagan was giving a speech inside. To Acosta, guilt or innocence was beside the point; due process should be accorded to anyone who had to defend him- or herself in a court of law. He became the Latino equivalent of white civil rights lawyer William Kunstler, who had defended the Chicago Seven in the wake of the violent clashes between cops and protesters at the 1968 Democratic convention.

Acosta first encountered Thompson just prior to his Los Angeles move, during a 1967 trip to Aspen. Beset by a chronic ulcer and distraught over the death of his secretary, Acosta was tipped off by his client John Tibeau to a cure located somewhere in Aspen, and hoped to relocate there and restore himself to health. But that didn't deter him from drinking. When he came into town, Mike Solheim arranged a meeting between Acosta and Thompson at the Daisy Duke bar. Dressed in chino shorts and an L. L. Bean sailor's cap with a bowie knife holstered to his waist, Thompson struck Acosta as a willful eccentric with a nasty contrarian streak. Thompson, for his part, didn't know what to make of Acosta either, but indifference certainly wasn't an option. As the booze flowed, Acosta became more animated and energized, loudly enumerating the ways in which he was going to redress America's racial inequities and bring down the *gabachos* who had oppressed his people (Charles Perry said that Acosta "talked much the same way Hunter wrote"). Thompson couldn't follow everything that Acosta was telling him—the latter's speech came in rapid-fire bursts—but he was certain he had found a kindred spirit. The fact that Tibeau had broken his leg while riding on Hunter's BSA motorcycle was broached and quickly forgotten.

"I recognized in Oscar [someone] who would push things one more notch toward the limit," said Thompson. "You never knew with Oscar what was going to happen next." They became brothers in arms, fellow troublemakers with a mutual disregard for propriety and authority. One night Thompson and Acosta dropped acid and went to the Whiskey a Go-Go in Hollywood, the hottest club on the Sunset Strip. As the music droned on and drug-induced psychosis began to set in, Thompson persuaded Acosta that the singer on stage was a lip-syncing fraud. At first incredulous, Acosta slowly began to buy into Thompson's bogus claim, until he finally stormed the stage and demanded that the band stop the sham at once. When they refused, Acosta reared back and punched the lead singer in the jaw.

Acosta and Thompson became fast friends, tying one on whenever they found themselves in the same city. In the winter of 1970, Acosta tipped off Thompson to the story of Ruben Salazar, a Chicano reporter for the *Los Angeles Times* who had been killed by an LAPD tear gas shell in an East Los Angeles restaurant during a civil rights protest. Although the death was officially ruled an accident by the Los Angeles County Sheriff's Department, Acosta and others felt that Salazar, an outspoken critic of the L.A. police and mayor Sam Yorty, had been intentionally killed, the investigation of his murder a clumsy coverup. Thompson pitched the story to *Scanlan's* and, using Acosta as his guide, went down to L.A. to conduct interviews. But when Sidney Zion rejected the piece (along with Thompson's $1,200 fee), Thompson sold it to *Rolling Stone,* with the proviso that Thompson would update the story and clarify some confusion in the timeline of the narrative.

Thompson moved to L.A., setting himself up in a fleabag hotel in East L.A. Racial tension in the city had spilled over into violence; the

LAPD reported scattered instances of hate crimes, and Acosta, a vocal critic of the Salazar investigation who had organized a protest outside the L.A. coroner's office, was now surrounded by amateur bodyguards to protect him from his enemies during public appearances. Thompson, who had endured the knife-edge hostility of the Hell's Angels and had traveled to some of the world's most dangerous places for stories, now found himself surrounded by a pincer movement of angry Mexicans whenever he encountered Acosta. It was one of the few times in his career where he felt that physical harm was actually imminent.

In order to separate Acosta from his phalanx of thugs, Thompson suggested they book a room at the Beverly Hills Hotel in order to discuss the Salazar case. But the metallic clang of jewelry on the dainty wrists of matrons lunching at the Polo Lounge was not quite the ambience Thompson was looking for. He had a better idea.

Tom Vanderschmidt, a senior editor at *Sports Illustrated* and an old friend from the *National Observer* days, had called up Thompson a week earlier to determine his availability for a story. The magazine needed a writer to provide accompanying text for a photo spread about a motorcycle race called the Mint 400, a rally sponsored by Del Webb's Mint Hotel in Las Vegas. Thompson initially hemmed and hawed, thinking that another assignment would compromise the complex Salazar story. But Vegas had always appealed to him as a potential story subject, and now he surmised that a trip there would be a great excuse for him and Acosta to distance themselves for a while from the madness in Los Angeles, grab some R&R, and get paid for it to boot.

Thompson approached the assignment much like he approached every other story—by the seat of his pants. No hotel reservations, no press credentials—just expense money and a vague mandate to report on what he witnessed at the race. Acosta rented a Chrysler convertible and acquired a prodigious supply of mescaline, speed, and booze, and Thompson pointed the car east toward the desert.

Jack Kerouac was in Hunter's head when he pressed his foot to the accelerator of the rented wheels, heading east on Interstate 15. Kerouac's books—*On the Road, Visions of Cody, The Subterraneans, The Dharma Bums*— were thinly veiled memoirs of an existential life in which mad sensation counted for more than reason. Kerouac's colloquial prose bounced across the page like a Charlie Parker solo; it was all sinewy brawn and earthy spontaneity. The trick was to steer clear of complacency and plunge headlong into the vortex of unreason, where life was truly, exuberantly lived.

Thompson internalized Kerouac's worldview with a close reading of the books, particularly *On the Road,* and he wanted his writing to resonate with that same flailing passion. The Vegas trip with Acosta would just be a continuation of his own antihero's journey, which commenced with the Hell's Angels and continued at the Kentucky Derby, the America's Cup, and the campaigns in Aspen. Thompson wanted to be this generation's Kerouac.

Like those earlier misadventures, Thompson knew the Vegas assignment certainly wasn't going to be a who-what-when-where reporting job. It couldn't be, with Thompson and Acosta running roughshod through Las Vegas. To ensure that events and scenes wouldn't be lost to the half-lit memories of a marathon drug binge, Thompson carried a notebook and a tape recorder with him at all times, recording every conversation with strangers, croupiers, cocktail waitresses. He hadn't the foggiest notion if his fieldwork would amount to anything, but Thompson had always been a conscientious collector of his own data, however haphazard his gathering methods might have been.

The Mint 400 was being held on a giant spit of dirt track that turned into a dust cloud when the race commenced. It was impossible to follow and just plain boring from a journalism standpoint. After wrangling mightily for press credentials and securing a driver to help him keep tabs on the racers, Thompson quickly abandoned the Mint 400 altogether.

Recklessly driving the convertible down Las Vegas Boulevard, Acosta and Thompson ducked in and out of various casinos with the observant dispatch of bomb sweepers, marveling at the downcast midway attractions at Circus Circus, then crashing a Debbie Reynolds performance at the Desert Inn. "Hunter came into Circus Circus when I was performing in the bar," said musician and friend Bruce Innes. "He wanted to see if he could buy one of the chimps from the Flying Wallendas. Alas, they wouldn't sell one to him."

"Hunter would call me up from Vegas, and there would be all this commotion," said *Rolling Stone* editor David Felton, who had been assigned to work on the Salazar story. "He would be yelling into the phone, 'David, Oscar's out of control, I don't know what to do.' I'd hear all these strange noises in the background, things breaking and crashing to the floor. I think they were high, but I also think it was an act for my benefit. Hunter liked to push things, but only to a point."

After a few days in Vegas, Thompson and Acosta skipped out on their hotel bill, which had snowballed to $2,000, and gunned it back to L.A. The Vegas trip had temporarily delayed Thompson's work on the Salazar story, and he was past his deadline. There was also the matter of writing a short piece for *Sports Illustrated,* but, having missed the race, he had little to write about. Thompson checked into a Ramada Inn near Felton's Pasadena apartment and tried to fashion a Salazar piece based on the information Acosta had provided. Keeping himself awake for days on end with a prodigious supply of speed, Thompson struggled with the complexities of the case, which folded issues of racism and class conflict within the context of a byzantine court case. It was the most complicated story of his career, and he struggled to make it something worthwhile.

During breaks from the story, he tapped out incidents from the Vegas trip on his IBM Selectric typewriter to keep himself sane. With the Rolling Stones' album *Get Yer Ya-Ya's Out!* blaring from his stereo, Thompson summoned the words easily; it was pleasurable, not like work. One paragraph became a page, then ten pages. By the last week of April, Thompson had written more than two thousand words on the Vegas trip. He turned in the manuscript to *Sports Illustrated*'s Tom Vanderschmidt, who summarily rejected it. He couldn't even extrapolate any captions out of the manuscript; it was of no use to the magazine. "Your call was the key to a massive freak-out," he wrote to Vanderschmidt. "The result is still up in the air, and still climbing. When you see the final fireball, remember that it was all your fault."

He decided to try his luck at *Rolling Stone.* "We were supposed to meet about the Salazar piece," said editor David Felton. "Hunter walks into my place with this paper in his hand and starts reading from the Vegas story. He was obviously very excited about it." Felton got excited too and Hunter forwarded the manuscript to *RS* editor John Scanlon and Jann Wenner, who upon reading it demanded that Thompson keep going.

But there was always the matter of scraping up enough money to keep going. A deal was also struck with Random House to publish the article in book form, with the proviso that Thompson write more material. Thompson eventually sold the project to Jim Silberman for a $100,000 advance and then drove back to Vegas (in a white Cadillac this time) to observe the National District Attorneys' Association conference on narcotics and dangerous drugs, which was scheduled to start on April 26. After that he returned to Woody Creek and tried to make sense of all he had seen and wrecked in Nevada.

Thompson invoked the rebel spirit of Kerouac when he sat down to write the rest of *Fear and Loathing in Las Vegas* in the cramped guest bedroom at Owl Farm that he called the "war room." The title was a play on Danish philosopher Søren Kierkegaard's book *Fear and Trembling,* though Thompson always denied it. "Kerouac taught me that you could get away with writing about drugs and get published," he told the *Paris Review* in a 2000 interview. "Jack Kerouac influenced me quite a bit as a writer ... in the Arab sense that the enemy of my enemy was my friend."

In *Fear and Loathing in Las Vegas,* Thompson, like Kerouac, cloaked real events in a mythic realm where the verisimilitude of journalism encounters the juiced-up rhetorical style that had become his trademark. It was journalism as bricolage: Thompson moved around freely in space and time, moving from internal acid monologues to brittle comic scenes, contrasting the high times on Parnassus Avenue in San Francisco with the gold-lamé depravity of Vegas, always searching in vain for the American dream. One morning, his friend and house guest Lucian K. Truscott IV came in at 1 A.M. and found Hunter pounding away. "What are you working on?" Truscott asked. Thompson handed him some pages; Truscott approved. "I don't know," Hunter said. "I'm just going to keep writing until it makes sense."

But if *gonzo* can roughly be defined as a provocation on the reporter's part to drive the story forward, then *Fear and Loathing in Las Vegas* doesn't exactly qualify. Acosta, as the manic, drug-ingesting Dr. Gonzo, is the driver of the story—a character of boundless energy and unrestrained temperament, testing every situation to the breaking point, a 300-pound Samoan with a severe amyl nitrate habit and a tendency to light up his hash pipe in public.

Thompson is Raoul Duke, an amalgam (derived from Fidel Castro's brother and John Wayne's nickname) that he had used in a *Scanlan's* story the previous year. Throughout the book, Thompson/Duke finds himself trying to negotiate a way out of the awful predicaments Acosta/Dr. Gonzo creates. Dr. Gonzo is a great Falstaffian force of nature, Raoul Duke his bemused foil.

"Certainly many of the character traits that Dr. Gonzo posesses had parallels to my dad," said Marco Acosta. "He wasn't Samoan, of course, but in the Samoan culture, the men tend to be large, and Hunter was trying to invoke my dad's dominant physical presence. There are many aspects of him that you don't see, but Hunter's goal was to be funny first and foremost."

Thompson wasted little time kick-starting his story into motion. From *Fear and Loathing*'s very first line, Thompson and Acosta are on the move, in search of . . . well, who knows what.

> We were somewhere around Barstow on the edge of the desert when the drugs began to take hold. I remember saying something like "I feel a bit lightheaded, maybe you should drive. . . ." And suddenly there was a terrible roar all around us and the sky was full of what looked like huge bats, all swooping and screeching and diving around the car, which was going about a hundred miles an hour with the top down to Las Vegas. And a voice was screaming: "Holy Jesus! What are these goddamn animals?"

The ostensible objective is a journey to Vegas to report on the Mint 400, but as in *On the Road*, the journey is the point. Raoul Duke wants to revel in the great gift of freedom that all Americans share; the Vegas trip was a "classic affirmation of everything right and true and decent in the national character. It was a gross, physical salute to the fantastic *possibilities* of life in this country—but only for those with true grit."

True grit, just like John "Duke" Wayne himself. But there was no wild frontier to explore in the West, just a "cluster of grey rectangles in the distance, rising out of the cactus." The sixties notion of a new age of enlightenment in the West, glimpses of which Thompson had encountered in San Francisco, had never taken root, "burned out and long gone from the brutish realities of this foul year of Our Lord, 1971." The Mojave Desert, the West's last untouched frontier, had been colonized by the greed-mongers, and nobody at the keno tables seemed bothered by the rising body count in Vietnam. For Sal Paradise/Kerouac, the characters on his cross-country trip are an affirmation of the beatitude and bedrock virtue of the underclass; the freak parade of humanity that Raoul Duke and Dr. Gonzo encounters is merely bestial and overfed on excess.

Raoul Duke/Thompson's cognitive dissonance in Vegas is most acute when he and Dr. Gonzo attend the National District Attorneys' Association conference on narcotics and dangerous drugs in the ballroom of the Dunes Hotel. Thompson, who was registered as an accredited journalist for the event, ducked out to score mescaline from a Vegas contact, only to return to a ballroom of fifteen hundred vehemently antidrug cops loudly deriding the use of controlled substances:

> Their sound system looked like something Ulysses S. Grant might have triggered up to address his troops during the Siege of Vicksburg. The voices from up front crackled with a fuzzy, high-pitched urgency, and the delay was just enough to keep the words disconcertingly out of phase with the speaker's gestures.
>
> "We must come to terms with the Drug Culture in this country! . . . country . . . country . . ." These echoes drifted back to the rear in confused waves. "The reefer butt is called a 'roach' because it resembles a cockroach . . . cockroach . . . cockroach . . ."
>
> "What the fuck are these people talking about?" my attorney whispered. "You'd have to be crazy on acid to think a joint looked like a goddamn cockroach!"

Thompson eventually does find the American dream, but it's been corrupted beyond recognition. Manifest Destiny is just a money grab now—drunk tourists in Vegas amusing themselves to death, throwing their money into a rabbit hole, where it is retrieved by greedy casino owners. As for the counterculture, it has been beaten into submission by a heavy load of drugs: "All those pathetically eager acid freaks who thought they could buy Peace and Understanding for three bucks a hit. But their loss and failure is ours, too." The dream was over, and there was no turning back now.

David Felton regarded the story as a eulogy for the dashed hopes of the sixties: "I think he saw the generation as falling apart long before most of us who were still trying to be practicing members. It was pure inspiration."

In a letter to Tom Wolfe that accompanied the first part of the story, Thompson explained his objectives:

> What I was trying to get at in this was [the] mind-warp/photo technique of instant journalism; One draft, written on the spot at top speed and basically un-revised, edited, chopped, larded, etc. for publication. . . . Raoul Duke is pushing the frontiers of "new journalism" a lot further than anything you'll find in *Hell's Angels*.

Fear and Loathing in Las Vegas: A Savage Journey to the Heart of the American Dream was the greatest achievement thus far of Thompson's fifteen-year career; with Wenner, he had found a sympathetic editor who gave him the space to push the throttle all the way and develop a "mind-warp/photo technique" that resulted in a new voice—antic, lysergic, blackly humorous, gently moralizing. Published in two parts in the November 11 and November 25 issues of *Rolling Stone* and illustrated with garish slash-and-burn ink drawings from Ralph Steadman, it created a huge stir among readers and envy from his peers. "I just thought it was phenomonally good," said Tim Ferris. "Something like that doesn't come along too often. It just had a bombshell effect."

William Kennedy, Thompson's old Puerto Rico running buddy, thought of it as a "totally original piece of work. It was so over the top, the result of morphing his fictional aspirations into his journalism." Tom Wolfe, whom Thompson regarded as his closest competitor, declared it a masterpiece of New Journalism, a "scorching, epochal sensation."

It should have been time for some well-earned gloating, but with critical approbation came a number of complications. First and foremost was the matter of recompense for the piece. Aside from the initial $300 that *Sports Illustrated* had forwarded him, Thompson had laid out the rest of the expense money for both Vegas trips on credit cards, an amount exceeding $2,000. When Thompson, in a frantic telegram from the Flamingo Hotel, had begged Wenner to send along some money, he received $500—but that was just his monthly retainer, as it turned out. The expense money would have to be absorbed by the story fee. "I think the thing to do is for you to *lend* me the 1K-plus to pay off Carte

Blanche," Thompson wrote in a letter to Wenner. "Fuck. Maybe I should. I'll never deny the thing was excessive. But I don't recall spending anything, out there, that didn't strike me as being *necessary at the time*. But this is a hard thing to argue or defend, it drags us into the realm of the preternatural."

Acosta wasn't getting paid a dime for providing all of that fodder for Thompson's story, which was all well and good until he read the piece. Being classified as a slovenly Samoan didn't sit well with him, and when the story was published in book form, he threatened a libel suit against both Thompson and Random House for defamation of character.

Thompson was baffled. He had thought he was doing the right thing—protecting his friend by using a pseudonym. But Acosta, who constantly feared disbarment and worried about how the story might affect his already shaky legal career, wasn't having any of it, especially since the book carried a back-cover photo of Thompson and Acosta in Caesar's Palace, sitting at a table strewn with drink glasses. "I've been mistaken for American Indian, Spanish, Filipino, Hawaiian, Samoan and Arabian," Acosta wrote in his book *The Autobiography of a Brown Buffalo*. "No one has ever asked me if I'm a spic or a greaser. Am I Samoan? Aren't we all? I groan."

Acosta made a deal with Alan Rinzler, the publisher of *Rolling Stone*'s book division, Straight Arrow: he would sign a waiver that dropped all liability claims against Random House in exchange for a two-book deal with Straight Arrow. The *Fear and Loathing* photograph, which had been a sore point for him, now was a prerequisite—the first Acosta book had to include the picture, so readers would know exactly who he was.

With all legal threats out of the way, Thompson was free to enjoy his good fortune. *Fear and Loathing in Las Vegas* eventually sold millions of copies, and Thompson could finally cool off a bit on the relentless hustling for assignments, perhaps even take on another big writing project: the upcoming presidential election, in which the incumbent, Nixon, would perhaps finally have to pay the piper for all of his malfeasance and double-dealing across his long political career. The hippie dream may have died on the craps tables at Caesar's Palace, but if Nixon was defeated, there was still a shred of hope for everyone.

12

FUN WITH DICK AND GEORGE

In December 1971 *Rolling Stone* held an editorial confab at the Esalen Institute in Big Sur, California. The ostensible purpose of the conference was to brainstorm ideas and plot strategy for the magazine; the unspoken agenda involved ingesting prodigious amounts of booze and weed. Jann Wenner had one key talking point for the conference: he wanted Hunter Thompson to cover the 1972 presidential campaign for the magazine, and not just the conventions—every primary from New Hampshire to the Republican and Democratic conventions in Miami, an eight-month reporting marathon.

It wasn't an obvious fit for the magazine. "There was a lot of big talent in that room," said Thompson. "But when it came to politics, I was the only one that raised my hand. No one wanted to touch it except me." A political project on the scale of what Thompson was proposing might turn off the magazine's core rock-and-roll readership—an audience that Wenner had been aggressively courting with a strong emphasis on rock-and-roll coverage to the exclusion of political coverage—but Thompson had become a favorite of the *Rolling Stone* editor, and this election, in Wenner's view, just might deliver on the long-deferred notion of a powerful youth electorate. There had been press coverage about the registration rolls swelling with twenty-five million young voters between the ages of eighteen and twenty-five who were perhaps ready to scuttle Nixon's chances at a second term. As the most influential print media outlet of that youth voting bloc, *Rolling Stone* might have an opportunity to nudge a national election to the left side of the ledger.

Only one other writer expressed any interest in covering the campaign, and he was the youngest and least experienced journalist in the room. Timothy Crouse was a Harvard graduate, the son of successful Broadway playwright Russell Crouse, and a Peace Corps veteran who had apprenticed as a cub reporter for the *Gloucester Daily Times* and the *Boston Herald-Traveler* before Wenner hired him to be a contributing editor in 1971. A presidential campaign for a young reporter such as Crouse was too exciting to pass up, and so Wenner mapped out a game plan: Thompson would handle the heavy lifting and record his impressions of the campaign, while Crouse would provide backup stories that would add factual ballast to Thompson's pieces. Thompson would file a new story every two weeks on the road; Crouse would carry bail money, in case Thompson got into any heavy trouble.

Trailing a U-Haul filled with books and a telefax machine that Wenner had procured for him, Thompson, his wife, Sandy, two Dobermans named Benji and Darwin, and his seven-year-old son, Juan, drove cross-country from Colorado to Washington in December, setting up shop in a two-story brick house on Juniper Street in the Rock Creek section of the city, a down-at-the-heels district far removed from tonier neighborhoods such as Georgetown, where many mainstream reporters resided. That's just how Thompson wanted it; he had contempt for the Washington press corps, who he felt coddled the city's power players at the expense of doing their jobs responsibly. It was unfathomable to him that a reporter with his eyes wide open could live in Washington and not deride it at every turn. The political process was corrupt and noxious, and Thompson was going to call it the way he saw it. "In twenty-eight papers," Thompson would write, "only the rarest kind of luck will turn up more than two or three articles of any interest . . . but even then the interest items are usually buried deep around paragraph 16 on the jump (or "Cont. on . . .") page."

In early February, Crouse and Thompson decamped to New Hampshire for the first Democratic primary. In his blue jeans, sneakers, hunting jacket, and blue-tinted sunglasses, *Rolling Stone*'s correspondent stuck out like a Klansman at a Rotary Club mixer. The press corps dressed much like the politicians they were covering—wing-tip loafers, Windsor-knotted ties, navy blue sport coats. Thompson thought they dressed like bank tellers, but he was also aware that professional attire and comportment were essential for access to the candidates.

He couldn't get press credentials for the White House ("Rolling what?" the press office had asked him), and his bid to join the press pool for the primaries was still being decided upon. This assignment would have to be handled like all the other stories in which Thompson couldn't obtain the traditional entrée to subjects—it would be a pure stealth operation, with Thompson and Crouse working by their wits, relying on Thompson's instinct for winding up in the right situations at the most opportune times.

That methodology was a far cry from the approach that Theodore H. White had pursued while reporting for his book *The Making of the President 1960*. White's project was a touchstone for American journalism—the first time that a reporter had canvassed the primaries and the two conventions and assimilated all of his information in a narrative that captured the dramatic sweep and suspense of a presidential election. White had initially forged his reputation as China bureau chief for *Time* during World War II. After the war, he lived in Europe and contributed articles on politics to just about every major American periodical, including the *Reporter*, one of the magazines where Thompson worked in the early sixties. By the time he covered the 1960 election, White was one of the most revered journalists in the country, a trusted guardian of sanctified facts.

When it was published in 1961, *The Making of the President 1960* was regarded as an insider's revelation, but history hasn't been kind to it. Granted, the book is as scrupulous a breakdown of the electoral process as has ever been published. White witnesses the quiet tension of the Kennedy team as they await the Wisconsin returns; follows Kennedy as he assures the coal miners of West Virginia that he will fight for their dignity in the White House; graphs the complex machinations behind the choosing of vice presidential nominees at the conventions, traces the historical voting tendencies of both parties through an accretion of socioeconomic numbers and statistics.

And yet reading White today, one feels that something is being held back, that cracks and fissures are being glossed over. While White was an astute judge of character (of Nixon he writes, "It was as if the changing unsettled society of Southern California in which he grew up had imparted to him some of its own essential uncertainty"), he regards politicians as essentially well-intentioned men, conducting the nation's business with probity and a stern stoicism. Despite his claims to objectivity,

White's regard for Kennedy as a fair-haired *Übermensch* is evident; the book's cardinal sin is perhaps its risible pretense of impartiality. (Not that it affected sales: The book shot straight to the number one spot on the *New York Times* bestseller list and stayed there for a year. White published subsequent volumes for the 1964, 1968, and 1972 campaigns, also big sellers.)

In 1961, most Americans didn't think twice about whether White's book was too hagiographic. When Kennedy was elected, the First Lady invited the reporter to visit the White House for a *Life* magazine profile. White, in turn, became the first journalist to write about "Camelot," thus becoming one of the chief architects of the Kennedy myth.

Eleven years after *The Making of the President 1960*, eight years after the Gulf of Tonkin resolution, it was apparent to Thompson that standing on ceremony at the altar of some political deity was not going to advance the cause of either responsible journalism or social reform. His mandate in following the campaign trail would be radically different from White's. "I went in with the same attitude I take anywhere as a journalist: hammer and tongs—and God's mercy on anybody who gets in the way," he said. He held out little hope for anything the Democratic party had to offer, and he had no qualms about saying so in his articles. The party itself was in trouble, in Thompson's view, unless it was purged of the hacks and toadies, organized-labor money, and the "peace with honor" prevarications that echoed the Nixon administration's Vietnam policy. "The assholes who run politics in this country have become so mesmerized by the Madison Avenue school of campaigning that they actually believe, now, that all it takes to become a Congressman or a Senator—or even a President—is a nice set of teeth, a big wad of money, and a half-dozen Media Specialists."

Thompson was well aware that the press corps covering the '72 campaign included some of the savviest political journalists in the country, including David Broder and Haynes Johnson of the *Washington Post*, the *Los Angeles Times*'s Jules Witcover, and the *New York Times*'s R. W. "Johnny" Apple—men not likely to be cowed by a handler's clumsy political spin. If Washington neophyte Thompson wanted to cover this campaign properly, he would have to use all of his skill and cunning to do so. "Nineteen seventy-two was a hinge between two tendencies in political reporting," said Frank Mankiewicz, the son of screenwriter Herman Mankiewicz and a former director of the Peace Corps who ran

South Dakota senator George McGovern's campaign. "We went from straight and serious reporting to highly opinionated reporting. Nixon had a lot to do with that, of course. And so did Hunter."

At the outset, the 1972 election didn't look as if it would provide the same drama as the 1968 campaign, where Hunter had been harrassed by Chicago's finest. President Nixon was a popular incumbent, and an unimpressive crew of Democratic sloggers would have to jockey for position all the way to the convention, which would be held in Miami in August. Maine senator Edmund Muskie, who was Hubert Humphrey's running mate when the Minnesota senator came within a hairbreadth of defeating Nixon in 1968, was the de facto front-runner. Humphrey was also having another go, Eugene McCarthy was pondering a fourth-party run, and New York mayor John Lindsay, Alabama governor George Wallace, and George McGovern were also angling for a chance to defeat Nixon.

Thompson wasn't obligated to report on the minutiae of the campaign and so was freed up to roam and wander, a method that helped him get some of his best material. His first face-to-face with McGovern was a chance meeting in the bathroom of the Exeter Inn in New Hampshire, right after the McGovern campaign had received word that Iowa senator Harold Hughes, a long-time McGovern ally, would be endorsing Muskie. As the two men stood at urinals, Thompson began asking McGovern questions:

> "Say . . . ah . . . I hate to mention this," I said. "But what about this thing with Hughes?"
>
> He flinched and quickly zipped his pants up, shaking his head and mumbling something about "a deal for the vice-presidency." I could see that he didn't want to talk about it, but I wanted to get his reaction before he and [press secretary Dick] Dougherty could put a story together.
>
> "Why do you think he did it?" I said.
>
> He was washing his hands, staring down at the sink. "Well . . . ," he said finally. "I guess I shouldn't say this, Hunter, but I honestly don't know. I'm surprised; we're *all* surprised."

That was all Thompson would get for the time being; McGovern retreated to the dining room for dinner, while Thompson was shunted off to the bar by McGovern's operatives.

Many of the "straight" journalists weren't averse to a few drinks after hours—the two-martini lunch was still alive and well—but Thompson's prodigious appetite for alcohol and drugs was a little too derelict for many of them; it reeked of the hippie crash pad, not the briefing room. "Certainly there were people who disapproved of him," said Nicholas von Hoffman, who was covering the campaign for the *Washington Post,* "but I don't think it was professional disdain so much as personal. He was drinker and a doper, and he banged around a lot—made a lot of noise. I was very fond of him, but I didn't want to be too closely associated with the rule breaking and such."

David Broder met Thompson for the first time in the bar at the Pfister Hotel in Milwaukee during the Wisconsin campaign and found him "wild and captivating," though in subsequent meetings in other cities Broder wasn't sure which Thompson he would get—the perspicacious diviner of political agendas or the barely coherent tippler. "I would never underestimate Hunter's wild streak," said Broder. "He would sort of just disappear, miss the press plane, and then we'd find him later in the next city."

To those campaign staffers who became friendly with Thompson, the wild streak was overplayed, but Thompson knew better than to burn bridges with those who could get him close to the candidates. Thomas B. Morgan, who was taking a respite from writing to work as the press secretary for Democratic candidate John Lindsay, never saw Thompson take a drink over the course of many late-night discussions. "Hunter was always well-mannered on the campaign bus, on the stops," said Morgan. "He never once stood up and said, you know, 'I'm Hunter Thompson, and you're all a bunch of shit.' I found that I could count on him to get the story straight."

Politics was blood sport to Thompson (shades of Breslin and Mailer, who frequently used sports metaphors when writing about politics), and he reveled in the gamesmanship of the primaries: taking wagers on who would win, place, and show with Frank Mankiewicz and Morgan, sizing up the candidates like prizefighters—who was against the ropes, who was coming out with both fists flying? "When Big Ed [Muskie] arrived in Florida for The Blitz," Thompson later wrote,

> he looked and acted like a man who'd been cracked. Watching him in action, I remembered the nervous sense of impending doom in

the face of Floyd Patterson when he weighed in for his championship re-match with Sonny Liston in Las Vegas. Patterson was so obviously crippled, in his head, that I couldn't raise a bet on him—at *any* odds—among the hundred or so veteran sportswriters in the ringside seats on fight night. . . .

Floyd came out of his corner and turned to wax the first time Liston hit him. Then, with a minute still to go in the first round, Liston bashed him again and Patterson went down for the count. The fight was over before I touched my second beer.

Thompson had a strong distaste for Muskie. Despite early victories in Iowa and New Hampshire, McGovern's strong second-place showing in both states appeared to weaken Muskie's resolve. He seemed wimpy and ineffectual to Thompson, and now he was self-destructing before the writer's eyes. In New Hampshire, Muskie had appeared to weep openly while making a speech defending his wife's honor a day after the *Manchester Union Leader* had written an article describing her as emotionally unstable. A man given to fits of pique on the stump and saying the wrong thing at the wrong time, Muskie was a singularly uninspiring and bumbling campaigner. "When Ed tried to shade something, everyone knew he was doing it," said Muskie's campaign manager Burl Bernard. "He wasn't a very good actor." What, Thompson mused, could possibly account for his erratic behavior? Shortly after the Wisconsin primary in April, in which McGovern had emerged victorious and Muskie was scrambling for momentum, Thompson posited a potential theory:

> Not much has been written about The Ibogaine Effect as a serious factor in the Presidential Campaign, but toward the end of the Wisconsin primary race—about a week before the vote—word leaked out that some of Muskie's top advisors had called in a Brazilian doctor who was said to be treating the candidate with "some kind of strange drug" that nobody in the press corps had ever heard of. . . .
>
> I immediately recognized the Ibogaine Effect—from Muskie's tearful breakdown on the flatbed truck in New Hampshire, the delusions and altered thinking that characterized his campaign in Florida, and finally the condition of "total rage" that gripped him in Wisconsin.

Thompson was having a bit of fun at Muskie's expense by claiming that the Maine senator was perhaps ingesting a South American hallucinogen that was known to enhance sexual performance. "Even some of the reporters who'd been covering Muskie for three or four months took it seriously," Thompson said. "That's because they don't know anything about drugs." Former *Rolling Stone* managing editor John Burks thought that Thompson's stunt was irresponsible and reckless and that it may have lost the nomination for Muskie. "Reporters believed it enough that they asked Muskie about it at press conferences," said Burks. "Pretty soon he was losing primary after primary, and he was out of the game. In my opinion, Muskie was the only guy that could have beaten Nixon."

Thompson liked to think that his story might have tipped the campaign in favor of McGovern, whom Thompson respected as a principled politician, but in point of fact, the story didn't have any legs; it was just a blip in the long media cycle of the campaign, and it went away in due course. No serious journalist on the trail ever really believed it. If anything, Muskie's public breakdown in New Hampshire contributed more to his downfall than the Ibogaine rumor. "I don't think anything Hunter wrote had an appreciable effect on Muskie's campaign," said Burl Bernard. "But I did tell him at one point, 'Hunter, you're not covering the campaign, you're looking to destroy it.'" "That stuff about Muskie was preposterous," said Frank Mankiewicz. "Everyone knew it was preposterous. But he did catch the essence of Muskie—the man did seem narcotized most of the time."

It was pure advocacy journalism delivered with a feint that tilted toward the absurd, and those who played along got off easier than the ones who didn't. A few interview subjects, such as Mankiewicz, got into the spirit of things with the writer after a few primaries. "If Hunter asked a left-field question, I'd give him a cockamamie answer." Thompson had more respect for guys like Mankiewicz, who maintained a healthy respect for the process but still regarded it as a game, just another beloved American pastime that never amounted to anything but mediocrity and deceit at the highest levels of government.

As journalists who had engaged in bids for public office on fairly radical platforms, Thompson and Norman Mailer, who was covering the campaign for *Life*, had little tolerance for mainstream politics. But while Mailer's experience had convinced him to stick to his strengths, Thompson had not given up on proselytizing from within. He buttonholed Mankiewicz on a few occasions during the primary campaign and drilled him on the salient points of his Freak Power political philosophy, but Mankiewicz just shrugged it off—a sure sign, Thompson thought, of myopia on the McGovern side.

Thompson was fortunate that Mankiewicz felt so charitable toward some of his more spurious reporting, particularly one incident in New Hampshire in which Thompson claimed to have been cold-cocked by Mankiewicz in the driveway of the Wayfarer Hotel—a contract hit apparently set up by Crouse, who tipped off Mankiewicz in exchange for a White House job. "All that talk about me chasing him with a tire iron is patently false," said Mankiewicz, "but there's a spirit of passion in there that clicks."

Jules Witcover, who was covering the campaign for the *Los Angeles Times*, found fault with Thompson's shoot-from-the-hip-flask reporting, which he felt was willfully fallacious and unfair to its subjects. "Hunter was a total screwball, a whirling dervish on the trail," said Witcover. "I understood what he was after and I found it amusing, but he didn't read people that well. He dealt in exaggeration, and I don't think it really ever did Muskie or anyone else any real damage. He was an entertainer first and foremost."

Bob Semple, who was covering the Nixon campaign for the *New York Times*, wasn't entertained. Semple and Thompson had forged a casual relationship while covering Nixon in New Hampshire, driving frantically from speech to speech across black ice with the *Los Angeles Times*'s Don Irwin in tow, nipping from a bottle of Jack Daniel's to keep themselves warm. "I feared for my life in that car," said Semple. "I've never been closer to my maker." Semple even managed to obtain White House plane press credentials for Thompson after reassuring Nixon's assistant for domestic affairs, John Erlichman, that Thompson "wouldn't harm a flea." (Erlichman was convinced that Thompson was a homicidal maniac.) But Semple felt betrayed by Thompson's description of him in his story "Fear and Loathing: The Fat City Blues," which ran in *Rolling Stone*'s October 26 issue, particularly a passage in which Thompson expressed revulsion at the sycophancy of Nixon beat reporters such as Semple, who whimpered around "kissing [White House press secretary] Ron Ziegler's ass."

"I understood that Hunter was looking for deeper truths, and that his reporting was part fiction, but it really pissed me off," said Semple. "I had gone out of my way to help him. I just didn't know what he had in mind."

Thompson was just trying to keep himself entertained, staving off the mind-numbing tedium of twenty-three primaries in five months, the boilerplate stump speeches, the glad-handing rituals, the horrid food in dingy motel rooms. With a mandate to file a story every two weeks, Thompson fulminated out loud in his stories about buckling under the weight of his burden.

"I am growing extremely weary of writing about politics," he wrote in "Fear and Loathing in California: Traditional Politics with a Vengeance" for *Rolling Stone*'s July 6, 1972, issue. "My brain has become a steam-vat; my body is turning to wax and bad flab; impotence looms; my finger-nails are growing at a fantastic rate of speed—they are turning into claws; my standard-size clippers will no longer cut the growth, so now I carry a set of huge toenail clippers and sneak off every night around dusk, regardless of where I am . . . to chop off another quarter of an inch or so off all ten fingers."

Every story that Thompson filed was an painful and protracted ritual of false starts and piecemeal construction. Thompson would agonize over a lead and toss it in the trash, only to have his wife, Sandy, iron out the wrinkles by hand and send it over. Thompson had to transmit every page though the telefax, which he nicknamed the "Mojo Wire"—an ante-diluvian creaker that transmitted one page every three minutes onto thermal paper at the receiving end. Invariably, the copy would be fired off at an ungodly hour of the morning, and it was Charles Perry's job to stand by and receive it as it moved though the phone lines.

"I had to wait for the call, which could come at any time," said Perry. The stories, which often ran to eight thousand words and more, came in sections, which Perry would then have to reconstruct according to Thompson's alphabetical system of inserts. "We'd shuffle it all around and arrange a story one way or another," said Perry. "Hunter could drive editors to tears," said David Felton. "He would be up on speed and write for three days in a row, producing a paragraph an hour, and Charles Perry would have to stay up for three days and retrieve it, and we'd have to fix it. And if he didn't like what you did, he would scream and yell at you."

In his stories Thompson laid waste to all of the Democratic contenders. Ed Muskie "talked like a farmer with terminal cancer trying to borrow money on next year's crop"; Humphrey was "a shallow, contemptible and hopelessly dishonest old hack," an unprincipled panderer who didn't seem aware that "his gibberish is not taken seriously by anyone except Labor Leaders and middle-class blacks." Only George McGovern gave Thompson hope, however faint, that a decent candidate might emerge from such a mediocre field, but even Thompson conceded that the South Dakota senator was perhaps too timid and too earnest to be taken seriously as a national contender. "Crowds turn him *off,* instead of on," Thompson wrote in his dispatch from the New Hampshire primary. "He lacks that sense of drama—that instinct for timing and orchestration that is the real secret of success in American politics."

Norman Mailer had a less charitable view of McGovern. Mailer shared Thompson's opinion of McGovern as a decent and principled politician, but virtue was not enough for him to support the ticket. McGovern's emergence was emblematic, for Mailer, of the Democratic party's transformation from a vibrant and sometimes chaotic alembic of ideas into a quiescent repository of uninspiring cant. In fact, McGovern was just as beige as Nixon; he projected "that same void of charisma which can prove more powerful than charisma itself."

Everywhere he turned at the Miami Democratic convention, Mailer saw the dissipated remnants of the youth movement that had galvanized the left in the sixties, coddled suburban kids lulled into a "complacent innocence altogether near to arrogance." The passions of the 1968 Democratic convention in Chicago, in which the clash of ideologies played out in a bloody street fight between Mayor Daley's cops and antiwar protesters, had died out. Television had asserted its control over the tenor and timbre of the event, leaving the dissenting protestors entirely out of frame, but also inducing an acquiescence to proper decorum. If TV didn't want a circus, then it wouldn't get one. The new, professional class of delegates made sure of it.

At McGovern headquarters at the Doral Hotel, Mailer mingled with the candidate's supporters, "Phi Beta Kappas with clean faces and horn-rimmed glasses, their presence to offer clear statement of a physiology which had little taste for liquor and much taste for good marks," as well as "suburban youth with long hair and the sense of boredom of waiting another evening for some tribal left wind to touch the hair of their nostrils." Mailer felt a twinge of nostalgia for the back-room horse trading of previous conventions; an utterly benign convention left little for Mailer to decode. Even Nixon disappointed him. The president's old, simmering misanthropy had been ground down to digestible gruel. He was now the perfect TV president, "a bland drone of oscillating ideological dots" preaching a policy of middle-class entitlement to "the wad," those Zenith supplicants out there in America's living rooms who tacitly approved a policy that spent almost twice as much on the Vietnam War as it did on welfare.

If Mailer was disheartened by the lack of intrigue in Miami, he wasn't as quick to dismiss the other major candidates as Thompson, who ranked them a notch above low-rent carnival barkers. In Thompson's view, the Democratic convention was nothing more than a procession of "shameless dingbats who saw no harm in cadging some free exposure on national TV by nominating each other for vice-president." So much convention time was devoted to chest-thumping rhetoric and jostling over the choice for the vice-presidential nominee on nomination night that McGovern didn't give his acceptance speech until three-thirty in the morning, by which time most of the TV audience had gone to sleep. As for the delegates, they were zonked out on booze and liquid THC administered by a "smiling freak" who "was giving free hits to anybody who still had the strength to stick their tongues out."

Mailer's reporting from the two conventions, which would be published in his book *St. George and the Godfather,* was more generous and nuanced than Thompson's, more willing to concede that a vestige of decency could be excavated if one looked hard enough. It was a waste of his time to write about subjects that weren't worthy of his consideration, that didn't have some latent complexity to be unearthed, and Mailer had complete confidence in his ability to tease out the superego from the id simply from standing on the sidelines with his notebook.

Unlike Thompson, who believed in absolute numbers and what they revealed, statistics weren't as important to Mailer as were the methods used to attain and broker power. The selection of a running mate, for example, was more or less a search for the perfect brand name: "Recognize that a man named Proctor running for President would look for Gamble to go along." Billboard euphony, the pleasing sound of the two names when combined, was more important than political compatibility, and thus McGovern, after being rejected by the likes of Boston mayor Kevin White, Ted Kennedy, and Florida governor Ruben Askew ("a perfect name! Govern and Ask-You"), settled on Missouri senator Thomas Eagleton, whose name "had connotations of the American Eagle, a stern virtue, a modest plus." But Eagleton would prove to be McGovern's undoing when it was revealed that he had been hospitalized for nervous exhaustion and had received electroshock therapy on two separate occasions.

Here was intrigue, at last, but Mailer was careful not to arrive at any easy conclusions about Eagleton, who had agreed to an interview with Mailer on the afternoon of his resignation. He accepted the fact that Eagleton had perhaps not given his past any serious thought when his name was being mentioned as a vice-presidential nominee, having whipped "a miserable recollection from shell to shell" so many times that he'd ceased to worry about it. He was a fallen character that might have stepped from the pages of an F. Scott Fitzgerald novel. Mailer maintained that Eagleton's sharp patrician features gave him a passing resemblance to F. Scott Fitzgerald (was Eagleton, like Jay Gatsby, a man who had learned to suppress his mysterious past?), but when Eagleton responded by telling him that *The Great Gatsby* was one of his favorite books, Mailer could sense the disingenuous pandering of the professional vote beggar, and the disappointing realization that politicians were "no more magnificent" than himself.

Thompson had dismissed Eagleton as a hack from the outset and chided McGovern for sharing the ticket with such an uninspired old-school pol. Eagleton's replacement, Sargent Shriver, the former head of the Peace Corps and a Kennedy in-law, was only a marginal improvement, a safe bet that inspired no one. McGovern's MO was being shanghaied by the entrenched party operatives; the liberal firebrand of the primaries who had fended off a last-minute parliamentary challenge by an anti-McGovern contingent on the floor of the convention in July had given way to the party pragmatist, working his inexorable way toward the old minority-and-union alliances that might prop him up high enough to level the playing field with Nixon come November. What had begun as a rekindling of the old Eugene McCarthy spirit of insurrection had curdled into business as usual. McGovern's vacillation regarding Eagleton's fate, his indecisiveness in the face of the campaign's first real crisis, was a red flag for Thompson, a indication of the McGovern staff's disorganization and incompetence. Nixon was many things, but he wasn't dumb: his gift for political maneuvering and strategy was Napoleonic. Things looked awfully grim indeed.

The action, or lack thereof, swirling around the Republican convention the week of August 18 was an apt metaphor for the enervated energy level of the election in general. In Flamingo Park (near the Fontaine-bleau Hotel, which served as an informal headquarters for the press), Thompson witnessed a clutch of demonstrators pathetically trying to summon up a head of steam. "With the exception of the Vietnam Veterans Against the War, the demonstrators in Miami were a useless mob of ignorant, chicken-shit ego-junkies whose only accomplishment was to embarrass the whole tradition of public protest," Thompson wrote in "Nixon Bites the Bomb," which ran in *Rolling Stone*'s September 28 issue. "They were hopelessly disorganized, they had no real purpose in being there, and about half of them were so wasted on grass, wine, and downers that they couldn't say for sure whether they were raising hell in Miami or San Diego."

Thompson found the Nixon supporters to be far more effective demonstrators and recruiters. Just prior to the formal nominating roll call, *Rolling Stone*'s intrepid reporter, who was en route to the free press bar, was waylaid by a throng of Nixon Youth wranglers. Seizing an opportunity to get close to the belly of the beast, Thompson merged with the mob and found himself in a holding room where preparations were being made for a demonstration. Thompson regarded ready-made placards with slogans such as FOUR MORE YEARS and NO COMPROMISE laid out on a table, and chose one to carry out on the convention floor: GARBAGE MEN DESERVE EQUAL TIME.

The ruse worked like a charm, until one of the demonstrators spotted the *Village Voice*'s Ron Rosenbaum running toward Thompson in an attempt to avoid being kicked out of the ready room.

> I looked up and shuddered, knowing my cover was blown. Within seconds, they were screaming at me, too. "You crazy bastard," I shouted at Rosenbaum. "You *fingered* me! Look what you've done!"

"No press!" they were shouting. "OUT! Both of you!"

I stood up quickly and put my back to the wall, still cursing Rosenbaum. "That's right!" I yelled. "Get that bastard out of here! No press allowed!"

"Well, I didn't point him out, and I don't think he would say that I did so," said Rosenbaum. "That part was made up for fun, but we were never at odds about this. That story was just consistent with that unique genre of Hunterism, between fact and fiction."

Thompson convinced the Nixon loyalists that he was merely a failed politician who had unsuccessfully run for sheriff in Colorado, and now he wanted to see what it was like to be on the inside of a winning campaign. Then someone noticed his McGovern button, which was affixed to his press badge. Using his finely honed instinct for wriggling out of awkward situations, Thompson avoided expulsion and walked right onto the floor of the convention with a few thousand Nixon Youth, where he wore a red, white, and blue plastic hat and carried his GARBAGE MEN DEMAND EQUAL TIME placard for the delectation of whatever television viewers might have been tuned in at that moment. But when the throng began chanting "Four more years," Thompson doffed his plastic hat and bailed.

The eventual reelection of Nixon by a record-breaking landslide (he won more than 60 percent of the national vote) confirmed what Thompson and Mailer had suspected all along—that Nixon appealed to the worst instincts of "The Wad," and that McGovern was perhaps too virtuous to fight in the trenches with such a seasoned and unscrupulous battler. "This may be the year," Thompson wrote in his article "Fear and Loathing: The Fat City Blues," "when we finally come face to face with ourselves; finally just lay back and say it—that we are really just a nation of 220 million used car salesmen with all the money we need to buy guns, and no qualms at all about killing anybody else in the world who tries to make us uncomfortable."

If many among the mainstream press corps were chagrined by Thompson's advocacy journalism, they soon realized that his aggressively subjective reporting was closer to the truth than the hard facts in the family newspapers and the mass circulation newsweeklies, which didn't really elucidate anything at all. "He hated that war in Vietnam with a passion," said George McGovern. "And he hated the hypocrisy of the establishment. Basically, I think he wanted to see this country live up to its ideals. And he wanted us to do better."

Watergate was still a whisper when Nixon was reelected. When the break-in at the Democratic party's national headquarters at the Watergate Hotel had occurred on June 17, the *New York Times* buried the story on page 50. On October 10, the *Washington Post* ran a story by Bob Woodward and Carl Bernstein that revealed a "massive campaign of political spying and sabotage on behalf of President Nixon's re-election and directed by officials of the White House and the Committee for the Re-election of the President." Still, many newspapers chose to ignore the story or else downplayed their coverage; Vice President Spiro Agnew's relentless campaign against the *Post,* a paper that he characterized as a liberal elitist organ with a political agenda, did much to silence or cow many press outlets into submission.

But Thompson knew better than to lap up the spin Agnew was spoon-feeding the press corps. He had an innate and absolute distrust of Nixon, whom he regarded as evil to the rotten core of his soul. Well before the *Washington Post* broke the story of the Nixon team's complicity in Watergate, Thompson wrote a story for *Rolling Stone* in which he wondered aloud at the mass delusion of a populace that would vote for a man as constitutionally dishonest as Nixon. "'Ominous' is not quite the right word for a situation where one of the most consistently unpopular politicians in American history suddenly skyrockets to Folk Hero status while his closest advisors are being caught almost daily in nazi-style gigs that would have embarrassed Martin Bormann."

If the sixties didn't really begin until Kennedy was assassinated in 1963, then they ended in 1972, when the left's last offensive against Nixon sputtered and fizzled out. It would take a final, epic act of hubris on Nixon's part for him to be removed from the White House for good, but if Watergate was sweet vindication for Thompson, it was a sobering cautionary tale for Mailer. "Richard Nixon is one of the great American villains, but that is *not* because he tried to cover up a scandal," Mailer wrote in 1976. "Rather he is a villain by way of the twenty-five years he did his best to murder the English language with a margarine of pieties—he is a villain because he had a negative charisma." While it was true that Nixon "was awful—with a force larger than himself," he was also a a litmus test for liberal forbearance. "The liberals failed. If Richard Nixon had been standing alone on the street and a thousand nonviolent liberals had been standing around him with flails, they would have beaten each other to death in their rush to get at him." Nixon's fumbling perfidy had inflamed both the left and the right and had distorted the political discourse beyond recognition: "He had scorched reason a little further out of existence."

13

VULGARIAN AT THE GATE

The ideological breakdowns of the sixties were a bitter disappointment to Thompson, Mailer, and all of those journalists who truly believed that they just might bear witness to a great American political awakening. But Nixon was reelected, the New Left splintered and faded, and Haight-Ashbury became a seedy countercultural Disneyland. There was a new revolution afoot, but it was directed inward, toward the cultivation of one's own personality, mental health, and physical well-being. It was the era of encounter sessions, EST, group therapy. Tom Wolfe called it the third great American awakening, a natural evolution arising from the drug experimentation and communal living of the previous decade. The Me Decade, for short. "Whatever the Third Great Awakening amounts to," Wolfe wrote in his 1976 *New York* story "The Me Decade and the Third Great Awakening," "for better or worse, will have to do with this unprecedented post–World War II American luxury: the luxury enjoyed by so many millions of middling folk, of dwelling upon the self."

This was good news for Clay Felker and *New York*. The magazine, which had positioned itself as an essential how-to manual for well-heeled urban survivalists, only benefited from a cultural movement toward self-fulfillment, as such a trend tended to involve *material* self-fulfillment as well.

New York had undergone a number of transformations in the five years since Felker had established it as a stand-alone publication, the most significant of which was a move toward service features. Felker ran stories that rated the best of everything New York had to offer: doctors, pastrami, Chinatown grocery stores, Tiffany lamps, whatever. The magazine provided card-carrying members of the Me Decade with tips for the best yoga classes and African-dance lessons. In converting *New York* into a lifestyle magazine, Felker created an editorial template that would be re-created in regional periodicals all over the country; by 1976, over seventy imitators had sprouted up nationwide.

Many of the writers who had established *New York*'s reputation had defected or found more remunerative homes. Gloria Steinem, whose career as a serious political writer had blossomed at *New York*, was moving toward a determined commitment to fight for women's reproductive rights and political representation, having campaigned on behalf of the women's caucus at the 1972 Democratic convention. Steinem was frustrated by Felker's lack of interest in the women's liberation movement. It was a curious blind spot for Felker, who did more to advance the cause of female journalists of his time than any other male editor. When Steinem first broached the idea of writing about the struggle for women's rights, Felker suggested that the magazine do a cover story about the need for more domestic help now that both spouses in many families were working.

New York eventually did cover women's issues, but Steinem felt that the magazine equivocated—Steinem wrote pro-equality pieces, while Julie Baumgold and Gail Sheehy argued the opposing view. One such article's headline read, "Waking Up from Women's Liberation—Has It Been All It's Cracked Up to Be?"

And yet when Steinem was struggling mightily to launch a women's magazine in 1971, Felker came to her aid. After trying for months to raise funds for the start-up with little success, Steinem approached Felker for help. His solution was to run a 30-page excerpt of the proposed magazine in the year-end double issue of *New York*, then publish a 130-page preview of the magazine to test the waters. New York would keep all of the advertising revenue from both the insert and the preview and half the newsstand profits for the market-testing issue. Beyond that, *New York* would have no continuing interest in the venture. Thus *Ms.* was born, and Steinem was on her way to becoming the face of women's lib.

Tom Wolfe's output for *New York* had slowed to a trickle. In 1972 he embarked on the most ambitious writing project of his career thus far—a history of the U.S. space program, from John Glenn to the Apollo missions. *The Right Stuff,* whose eventual historical scope Wolfe truncated considerably, took seven years to complete, but *Rolling Stone,* not *New York,* would publish three excerpts in 1973. The rest of his major magazine pieces of the seventies, with the exception of "The Me Decade," would run in *Esquire* and *Rolling Stone.*

It wasn't all bodegas and bialys at *New York,* however. The magazine was still capable of producing trenchant pieces on the machinations of power in City Hall and the boardrooms of Wall Street, and its best writers could sense cultural currents long before the national press caught up. Contributing writer Richard Goldstein's January 8, 1973, article on the Continental Baths and its star attraction, Bette Midler, alerted the magazine's readers to a thriving gay subculture in their midst, and Susana Duncan's piece on anorexia nervosa a few weeks later was one of the earliest mainstream features on the eating disorder. But *New York* was no longer reinventing regional magazine journalism the way it had in the early days. Investigative journalism was being supplanted by a move toward "Top Ten" service features and softer lifestyle stories. Banal covers such as "200 Things You Can Buy for $1" and "The Sound of the Cornball Invasion," a story on country music in the city whose cover featured Tony Randall with a corncob in his ear, were the rule rather than the exception. It was working, however: *New York* pulled in $9.7 million worth of advertising in 1973.

In the early seventies, a time when the overall magazine market was soft due to a national recession, Felker and his staff relied on a time-honored lure for newsstand sales: suddenly the cover was being graced by a procession of female models, even when the subject matter didn't warrant it. A story on graffiti, for example, featured a comely woman being scrawled upon with spray paint. In February 1973 the magazine devoted an entire issue to couples and draped a red XXL bathrobe over a naked man and woman for the cover.

Jimmy Breslin wanted no part of *New York*'s move toward service and lifestyle features and the uptown elitism of which, in Breslin's opinion, Clay Felker was so enamored. "Felker was never much of an editor in my view," he said. "He was good at taking ideas from other people, but not much else." There was a halfhearted attempt by Breslin at an editorial mutiny, in which the writer, with the help of publisher George Hirsch, who felt Felker was too extravagant with his own expense account, tried to right the course back to investigative journalism by doing an end run around Felker and wresting control of the magazine through the board of directors. It backfired miserably when the board fired Hirsch in the winter of 1971, leaving Breslin in the lurch. Breslin resigned shortly thereafter.

"Breslin doesn't like me, but there's a good reason for it," said Felker. "He wanted to change the direction of the magazine, and I didn't do it. He really wanted *New York* to be more of a political magazine. He wanted to know why we were doing stories about life in Manhattan and ignoring what was happening in East Brooklyn. But I felt that advertisers were buying a responsive audience and I could provide it for them."

Without Breslin's moral conscience and Wolfe's keen satirical eye, *New York*'s New Journalism was now being adulterated in the service of sensationalism. In the skillful hands of regulars such as Gail Sheehy or Julie Baumgold, New Journalism was a powerful tool, but it had to be wielded carefully. Given the freewheeling artistic license Felker permitted, the temptation to embellish the facts could be tempting. The first rule of New Journalism as laid down by Tom Wolfe, who published his anthology *The New Journalism* in 1973, was that whenever the style roamed freely, the facts had to be unassailable. Otherwise, the technique collapses, and its legitimacy along with it. When Hunter Thompson wrote that Ed Muskie was an Ibogaine addict, the claim was so outlandish that it entered the realm of metaphor—a Swiftian stab at character elucidation. When Sheehy conflated characters and senior editor Aaron Latham wrote about events he didn't witness firsthand, however, it created a credibility crisis for the magazine and called into question the whole enterprise of New Journalism.

Sheehy's most ambitious undertaking for *New York* to date was a sprawling, multipart examination of prostitution in New York—not only Times Square and Hell's Kitchen, but the glittering precincts of wealth along the Upper East Side and the $500-a-night suites in the Waldorf-Astoria. For six months Sheehy melded into the seedy milieu of streetwalkers and their pimps, slowly gaining the confidence of the various sex workers she encountered, and walking the Lexington Avenue beat during the peak hours for business—6:00 P.M. to 4:00 A.M. Occasionally she would be accompanied by her brother-in-law, Bernie Sheehy, who posed as a john or a peep show operator, thus providing an entry point for Sheehy to talk to her subjects. Over time, Sheehy gained the trust of a handful of prostitutes; she even had the great good fortune of being able to stash her tape recorder under a few fleabag hotel beds in order to record the seismic activity that transpired there. She interviewed cops and assistant DAs as well, and followed prostitution lawyers from criminal court to their favorite watering holes.

"Redpants and Sugarman," the first of five installments in the series, took up the entire feature well of the July 26, 1971, issue, and it was more sexually graphic and existentially bleak than anything *New York* had attempted before. Even Walter Pincus, a stockholder in *New York*'s holding company Aeneid Equities, questioned the use of so much explicit detail, and wondered whether the magazine was compromising its standards by publishing borderline smut. The story focused on Redpants, a black prostitute whom Sheehy encountered, and her initiation into the business of organized sex. Sheehy chronicles Redpants's passage from aspiring fashion model to her infamy as a star among the stable of girls controlled by her pimp, Sugarman, a "voluptuous figure of a man, radiantly clothed," who kept his charges in an apartment building in the Murray Hill district of Manhattan.

By utilizing her gift for mise-en-scène and shaping a gripping narrative from reams of source material, Sheehy elevated hustling from TV movie cliché. Less a cautionary tale than a look at how New York's working girls mortgaged their futures by tapping into the thriving, quick-return economies of sex and petty theft, "Redpants and Sugarman" spared no detail. Sheehy was privy to everything, as in this scene at the Lindy Hotel, where Redpants is about to turn a trick with a john:

"That's $7.75, pal." The john fills out a registration card. Halfway up the staircase the couple is stopped by a shout from the tattooed man.

"Hey, you're man and wife, right?" Redpants giggles.

"Right."

Speaking as a professor to a new student, he points to the registration card. "Well, you gotta put it down, sweetheart." Of course, his protection.

Nothing in the front room but a glass night lamp on a table and set flat out under the windows like a cheap plastic placemat, the bed. Above it rattle curtains of plastic brocade. Fluorescence intrudes; across the street is a block of windows framing eccentric postal workers at their night labors. Fixing on those windows, she bites down on the plastic brocade curtains and gives him fifteen minutes for 30 dollars.

The national press picked up on the series; *Newsweek* called Sheehy "the hooker's Boswell" and praised her vividly detailed reporting. Tom Wolfe wrote Sheehy an admiring letter, noting that the story "gives you such a rich emotional experience, from inside the skull, as it were, but also more to think about than all the bales of prostitution stories in the past."

But for some close readers of the series, particularly the "Redpants and Sugarman" installment, Sheehy's vivid details were a red flag indicating that something was amiss—there were too many undocumented statistics, anonymous sources, and interior monologues. Sheehy dissembled at first, claiming that "the original Redpants made an appointment to see me, but the other girls said they'd cut her up if she talked." The editors had neglected to publish a disclaimer explaining that the character of Redpants in the story was in fact a composite of many different prostitutes Sheehy had encountered in her research.

"Nobody had the good sense to realize what the hell we were doing," said former senior editor Shelly Zalaznick. "I knew the full meaning of the French word *chagrin*—I had a feeling of hopeless stupidity about the whole thing." Zalaznick allowed that a simple disclosure would have obviated the need to defend Sheehy's reporting after the fact, but he admits that the piece "was so seductive, you were swept into it and it suspended any disbelief of any kind. Everyone read it in manuscript, and it should have occurred to somebody to check it all out." Former senior editor Jack Nessel, who edited the piece, has a more pragmatic explanation for the lapse: "There was really no such thing as composite characters in *New York* in those days, Adam Smith notwithstanding, which is why no one thought of it."

Jack Nessel thinks Sheehy's eagerness to please Felker played a significant role. "I think Clay was in love with Gail from the start of their professional relationship, and she was extremely willing to be molded by him," he said. "Clay wasn't a writer—he needed people to be his writing implements, to set down his ideas on paper—and Gail fit the bill. They played into each other's needs. If ambition could be incarnated, it would look like Gail. I've never seen any man or woman as ambitious as her." (Felker and Sheehy were married in 1984.)

For traditional journalists who disparaged New Journalism and regarded its biggest stars with skepticism and a twinge of jealousy, Sheehy's gaffe was the beginning of the end of New Journalism. "New Journalism is rising," the *Wall Street Journal* wrote, "but its believability is declining." It was hard to dispute that, in the absence of a published disclosure or some explanation of Sheehy's methods, "Redpants and Sugarman" was New Journalism run amok.

Sheehy wasn't the only *New York* writer whose methods were called into question during the post-Breslin era. Two profiles by Aaron Latham were criticized by their subjects for massaging facts and not using proper editorial discretion. Latham, a former *Esquire* editor, had been assigned to write a profile of Gay Talese. Harold Hayes's favorite writer had already written two best-sellers—*The Kingdom and the Power,* a history of the *New York Times,* and *Honor Thy Father,* the first insider account of the inner workings of the Mafia, which had sold over 2.2 million copies in paperback. Talese's reputation as the most meticulous and aggressively immersive journalist in America had only been burnished by the two books, and now he was researching his most ambitious project; a history of American sexual mores, for which he had been paid $1.9 million by Doubleday as part of a two-book deal.

A key component of Talese's research involved working as the night manager in two different massage parlors in Manhattan, the Middle Earth and the Fifth Season; Latham, in true New Journalism fashion, decided to accompany Talese on his rounds in the summer of 1973. The piece, "An Evening in the Nude with Gay Talese," shocked readers who regarded Talese as a prim and proper gent, a writer who was rarely photographed without a suit and tie. Here was Talese in various stages of undress, engaging in erotically charged situations with sex workers:

> Amy reached out and took hold of Gay's penis as calmly as if it had been a pool cue. She was ready to play a new game.
>
> "I'm going to tear it off," she said.
>
> "I love it, I love it," he said. "Do it. I have dreams about it. I have fantasies about it."

Amy continued to tug gently at Gay as if his appendage were the knob of some reluctant bureau drawer.

Gay kidded, "Next time I work there you can chain me and then whip me."

Amy said, "I'd hit you with a chair."

Gay said, "I love chairs, especially Chippendale."

Talese felt that Latham's article, while factually accurate, lacked the dignity and compassion that he brought to the subject of professional sex, but Latham was merely abiding by *New York*'s new code of sensationalism, in which New Journalism was callously exploited. It was what Hunter Thompson had carped about in *Hell's Angels,* the "supercharged hokum" of the mainstream press resorting to certain "disparities in emphasis and context" in order to pump up the noise of a story.

Latham's profile of Sally Quinn, which ran a week after the Talese story, provoked even more outrage from its subject. Quinn, at the time a rising thirty-two-year-old star for the *Washington Post*'s Style section, had recently been hired to host CBS's morning show in order to create a credible competitor for NBC's ratings powerhouse *Today,* which was hosted by Barbara Walters. The article, which was the cover story for the July 16, 1973, issue, made a big deal of Quinn's sex appeal and implied that the *Washington Post* writer was perhaps exploiting her female attributes to advance her career. Which wasn't necessarily actionable on Quinn's part: Latham, after all, was entitled to speculate about her motives.

But one passage, in which Quinn allegedly conducted a "Gallup Poll" of penis sizes in Washington, was overheard by Clay Felker at a dinner party hosted by Walter Pincus and his wife, Arin. However, it had supposedly been Washington hostess Barbara Hower, not Quinn, who had sized up the sexual assets of one particular man, not "all the men in Washington." Quinn was a guest at the party, but she claimed that the quotes about sex that Latham attributed to her weren't accurate. "I've never read anything like this, even about a movie star," an irate Quinn told the *New York Times.* "And this is not supposedly *Screen* magazine. That's what shocks me."

This was all good business for the magazine, which managed to sustain its readership and healthy ad revenue even in the midst of New York City's fiscal crisis in 1975. That made it an attractive property for a young

Australian newspaper magnate who had set his sights on establishing a significant media beachhead in the most important city in the world.

At the age of forty-five, Rupert Murdoch had built a $100 million empire that stretched from San Antonio to Sydney, largely on the strength of lurid headlines and pinup cheesecake in his tabloid publications. He owned eleven magazines and eighty-four newspapers, the majority of them tabloids, including the *New York Post,* a paper that he had acquired by sweet-talking its seventy-three-year-old owner, Dorothy Schiff, into selling it to him for $32.5 million in November 1976.

The *New York Post* acquisition would turn out to be one of Murdoch's shrewdest moves, and he owed it all to Felker, who had introduced Murdoch to Schiff. As is often the case with ambitious social climbers, the two moved in the same social circles, and inevitably found themselves at the same dinner parties, their embossed placecards conveniently aligned on the same side of the table. Felker and Murdoch had first met in 1973 and had struck up a casual relationship in which the finer points of the publishing business were often discussed and argued. Felker envied Murdoch's uncanny business acumen, his genius for buying properties at fire-sale prices and growing his empire. Murdoch, for his part, longed for some of the cultural cachet that Felker had accrued with *New York.* But as anyone in the publishing business understood, it was awfully hard to reconcile both impulses into one enterprise, and both men's opposing tendencies would soon converge in ways that neither could have anticipated.

Like Felker, Murdoch had been born into the business. His father, Sir Keith Murdoch, was a famous World War I correspondent who had become one of the most famous practitioners of popular journalism in Australia. Sir Keith eventually became managing director of the Herald and Weekly Times, the largest newspaper group in Australia, but significant ownership in the company's properties always remained just out of his grasp, his efforts at a greater stake blocked by the consortium of bankers and industrialists who maintained an iron grip on majority control. When Sir Keith died, he bequeathed the *Adelaide News* and the *Sunday Mail,* the Herald and Weekly Times' two lowest-circulation papers, to his son and his four daughters.

Rupert Murdoch came to the newspaper business well prepared and eager to flex his muscle. His academic CV was impeccable: a secondary education at Geelong Grammar, one of Australia's best boarding schools, and then on to Worcester College at Oxford. But his education in the newspaper business had been hands-on from a very young age. "I was brought up in a publishing home, in a newspaper man's home," said Murdoch in 1989, "and I was excited by that, I suppose. I saw that life at close range, and after the age of ten or twelve never really considered any other."

Murdoch was studying at Oxford when his father died in 1953, and he wasted no time taking over the daily operations of both papers. He began as an obsessive micromanager, writing stories, designing the layout, and dashing off compelling headlines for the *Adelaide News,* but editorial stewardship was not what interested him. The goal was not to wind up like his father, who had grown embittered and frustrated by his lack of ownership in the company he helped to build. Two struggling papers would not provide Murdoch with the power and control he craved.

So he dragged both papers through the tabloid muck and emerged with two winners. Murdoch then merged the *Sunday Mail* with its most formidable competitor, the *Advertiser,* and purchased Perth's *Sunday Times* with the profits. In what would become standard operating procedure for him, Murdoch fired practically the entire staff of the *Sunday Times* and remade the sleepy regional paper into a splashy editorial amusement park ride.

From there, Murdoch's company, News Corporation Limited, grew exponentially. In 1965 he gambled on *The Australian,* the country's first national paper, whose sober-minded coverage of politics and finance veered sharply from Murdoch's usual tarted-up recipe for solvency. It took fifteen years for *The Australian* to turn a profit, but more important, it established thirty-four-year-old Murdoch as a serious newspaper publisher, Australia's answer to the *Washington Post*'s Katharine Graham.

In 1968, Murdoch acquired England's largest-circulation Sunday tabloid, the *News of the World,* in a fierce bidding war with publishing magnate Robert Maxwell. Nine months later, he beat Maxwell to the punch again by snatching up daily tabloid *The Sun,* then ratcheting up the paper's prurience. Murdoch published the first nude girlie shots ever to appear in a London paper and ran excerpts from middlebrow erotica such as Jacqueline Susann's *The Love Machine* and J's *The Sensuous Woman*. In less than a year, *The Sun*'s circulation jumped from eight hundred thousand to two million, and it would eventually become the most successful newspaper in Murdoch's vast media empire.

Despite the countless business triumphs, Murdoch still longed for the kind of prestige that he could accrue in the States through the acquisition of a quality title. Inch by inch, he began to acquire the stock that would give him majority control of Felker's magazine.

Felker was a revered and beloved editor, maybe the greatest magazine runner the city had ever seen, but he wanted to build an empire, perhaps even carry his ambitions beyond *New York* into national magazines. In 1974, despite a parlous economy, *New York* had $4 million in the bank and no debt. It was time, Felker thought, for the company to plow that money into another property. After getting Chemical Bank to agree to a $1 million loan, Felker made an offer to buy the *Village Voice*. If the *Voice*'s owners accepted, Felker could colonize the newsweekly business in the city and control the two most trusted cultural guides above and below Fourteenth Street. The *Voice*, which had made its reputation as a muckraker of the radical left, had always maintained a fierce independence from the kind of advertiser-friendly service stories that had become *New York*'s stock in trade, but Felker insisted that editorial autonomy would be maintained. "They're passionate about some things, we're passionate about others," he told *Time*. "They can pound away week after week on a single issue in a way that we can't."

New York's board of directors flatly rejected Felker's proposal. The magazine was in the black—why would Felker now want to saddle it with debt? But so desperate was Felker to control the *Voice* that he agreed to a merger with the *Voice*'s two largest shareholders, Carter Burden and Bartle Bull, even though it meant giving up a controlling interest in the magazine that he had spent ten years cultivating and nurturing until it had become an essential component of the city's civic life. When the deal was consummated in June 1974, Bull and Burden received six hundred thousand shares of New York Co. stock worth $800,000 and a 34 percent stake in the two weeklies, while Felker's equity position had shrunk to 10 percent. Burden was now the largest shareholder, with 24 percent.

"We didn't foresee the consequences of that decision, how weak it would leave us in terms of control," said Milton Glaser. "I guess we were blinded by what could have been. It could have been wonderful if there had been some sense of common purpose."

Instead of eliciting mutual comity between the two titles, the merger merely bred contempt. Many *Voice* writers were irate, fearful that their integrity would be compromised by a turn toward glib magazine feature journalism. *Voice* assistant editor Jack Newfield began writing mock headlines for potential *Voice–New York* stories, such as "The Favorite Recipes of the Ten Worst Bisexual Judges in New York."

The *Voice* staff's misgivings were valid, but the verdict was still out as to whether Felker would make any substantive changes. Felker's loss of control, on the other hand, was absolute. In order to compensate, Felker proposed that the board give him a 50 percent salary bump. It was, he reasoned, proper recompense for an editor and publisher who was now overseeing two weeklies and juggling a byzantine production schedule. Board member Alan Patricof balked; *New York* wasn't making enough money to justify the raise, and now that Felker had taken on the *Voice*, he was inevitably going to burn through more money. But the other board members overruled Patricof, albeit with great reluctance, and Felker got his wish.

It didn't quite work out as well for the *Voice* staff. Shortly after taking over as editor in chief, Felker engaged in a wholesale overhaul of the paper that amounted to a makeover in *New York*'s image. Milton Glaser was recruited to create a splashy redesign, while Felker fired writers and accepted the resignations of some others. Ron Rosenbaum announced his departure by dramatically tearing up his paycheck over Felker's desk.

The way Rosenbaum and other disgruntled writers saw it, Felker was pulling a Murdoch-style mutiny, jettisoning the epic investigative pieces that were the paper's specialty in favor of catty personality profiles, pithy and pointed jabs at local politicians, and stories that touched on matters of sex, violence, and celebrity. By year's end, Felker had pumped over $2 million into the *Voice*, but the net results were dispiriting. First-quarter earnings for 1975 were $46,000, as opposed to $255,000 the year before, and now *New York*'s losses were mounting, too: $151,000 as against $97,000 during the first quarter of 1974. Patricof and fellow board members Bob Towbin and Thomas Kempner were losing patience with Felker's profligacy, but they no longer had to answer to him now that the merger had created a power vacuum in which Burden and Bull were controlling partners. So Patricof tried to orchestrate an end run.

Carter Burden was not a man well suited to the calculated maneuvers of corporate power brokering. A scion of the Vanderbilt fortune who was reared in the embalmed, old-money culture of Beverly Hills, Burden was a prominent bleeding-heart dilettante in the city, throwing high-profile fund-raisers in his River House compound, which featured indoor tennis courts and a private heated pool—parties that were ripe targets for "Radical Chic" ridicule. In the fall of 1969 Burden, who had worked on Robert Kennedy's presidential campaign, announced his candidacy for City Council from the Fourth District, and won with more than 80 percent of the vote.

Felker didn't hesitate to send up Burden's political ambitions with a little deflating mockery. Julie Baumgold's cover story on Burden and his wife, Amanda, for the January 19, 1970, issue of New York stopped short of ridicule, but Baumgold's Wolfeian touch was unmistakably patronizing, from the way Burden's campaign buttons had given his wife "pinpricks on all her Ungaro's" to the way Baumgold described Carter, a rich man's son who was now the civic steward of East Harlem, as a "second-year Columbia Law student from peach stucco Beverly Hills" who had now become a foe of "lead-based paint and landlords."

Burden's inner-city Camelot didn't last long. In 1974 he divorced his wife, who had carried on an affair with Ted Kennedy, and the bottom fell out of his political career. That year, Burden had the worst attendance record on the City Council. "Burden was such a pipsqueak in my view," said former New York senior editor Byron Dobell.

Patricof recognized in Burden a man of means who longed to become a man of substance, and the acquisition of the Voice with his old Harvard classmate Bartle Bull was the first lurching move toward that reinvention. "Carter Burden was a very nice man who was looking for a place in life," said Milton Glaser. "He had decent instincts, but he did not have a forceful personality. He and Clay had a visceral dislike for each other." The New York merger was going to solidify his standing in the world's media capital, but with a fractious board of directors and a fiercely autonomous editor in chief with whom he had already tangled, the path toward ratifying his status as a publishing magnate was strewn with thorns.

Patricof, who had made his fortune running a private investment firm that had struck it rich in railroads, animal feed, and meat distribution, was intent on maximizing short-term profits in order to keep *New York*'s stock price at a comfortably profitable level for shareholders, but Felker's determination to expand the reach of his power beyond *New York* complicated matters. Ever since Patricof had attempted to dilute Felker's power by requesting that he sell a percentage of his stock to Jimmy Breslin in 1971, the two had been at loggerheads over just about every aspect of the magazine's operational budget; now the situation was becoming untenable.

In April 1976 Felker extended his reach to the West Coast by establishing *New West* as a California analogue to *New York*, but he had overspent on his upstart costs by nearly a million dollars. Much of that money, Patricof felt, had been spent frivolously on exorbitant expense accounts by the *New West* executive staff, who were tooling around L.A. in leased Alfa Romeos. Felker was convinced it was money well spent, goodwill that would curry favor with advertisers in virgin territory, but Patricof complained about the cost overruns and aired his grievances to Burden.

His back to the wall, Felker attempted a palace coup of his own, convincing Burden that the removal of Patricof and founding board member and Felker critic Bob Towbin from the board would be in the company's best interests. But without the leverage of controlling stock, Felker's overture meant little to the board, and Patricof and Towbin remained.

Back and forth it went like an Ealing farce, with Patricof and Felker trying to manipulate Burden behind each other's backs. Glaser was adamantly opposed to giving Burden, whom he regarded as weak and ineffectual, any more power than he already had, but the publishing business wasn't that abstruse; perhaps Felker and chief financial officer Ken Fadner could teach him the basics, reward him with a token editorial position, and win an ally in the process. But a crash tutorial had borne out Glaser's misgivings: Burden could barely wrap his mind around the most fundamental concepts, but that didn't stop him from submitting an attendance bill to the company for a total of $8,725.

Sidestepping Burden, Patricof held clandestine meetings with all of the board members, trying to convince them that Felker's irresponsible spending would lead the company to ruin. No one budged until the fall of 1976, when Patricof took his grievances public and began actively searching for a buyer for the company in order to definitively wipe the ledger clean.

While Patricof was recruiting a buyer, Felker was trying to convince Burden to sell him his stock, but Burden, who didn't know whether to fish or cut bait, refused to respond. The word on Wall Street was less ambivalent—if someone approached Burden with the right price, he might be willing to sell. Powerhouse investment firm White, Weld and Co. had the perfect candidate: Rupert Murdoch, who had just purchased the *New York Post* and was looking for more properties to increase his stateside market share.

Murdoch had been apprised of the internecine battles between Felker and the board by his investment banker, Stanley Shuman, and it pleased him: a board divided against itself cannot stand. If he could get verbal agreements with Towbin, Kempner, and Patricof to buy their stock, he could then approach Burden with a price and gain control. Felker would be out of the picture without having had any say in the matter.

New York's editor in chief knew none of this on November 29, the day before Shuman called Patricof, when Felker and Murdoch sat down to discuss the fate of *New York*. "What you ought to do," Murdoch told him, "is borrow a lot of money in order to own something like 51 percent, then work your tail off for two or three years, scrimp and save and pay off the thing, you'll own 100 percent and then you don't have to take any crap from anybody."

Two weeks later, Murdoch summoned Felker to his office on Third Avenue to discuss purchasing the company for $6 a share, with the proviso that Felker could retain ownership of *New West*—that is, if he agreed to buy it from Murdoch for a million dollars. Two days later, Felker called Murdoch to inform him that there was no deal.

"*New York* had a different meaning to Clay than it did to me," said Milton Glaser, who had continued to run Push Pin Studios while working on *New York*. "It was his child and the center of his life. To me, it wasn't, even though I loved the magazine. I just felt very sorry for Clay."

Felker was under siege. Murdoch was closing in on a hostile takeover, and Felker didn't have the financial resources to counter it. The company had only one other resource at its disposal, a right-of-first-refusal clause in the shareholder's agreement that would give Felker fifteen days to match any third-party offer made for Burden's stock. But he had to move fast: *New York*'s stock was trading heavily, which raised suspicions that Murdoch might already be maneuvering for control.

Felker sought council from his friend Felix Rohatyn, a mergers-and-acquisition specialist who had made a fortune for his firm, Lazard Frères. Rohatyn suggested that perhaps *Washington Post* owner Katharine Graham might be interested in helping out. Rohatyn, Felker, and Graham worked up an offer of $7 a share for Burden's stock, which Burden's lawyer, Peter Tufo, agreed to in principle. It seemed like a perfect fit: Graham would put up the capital and the company would be folded into the *Washington Post*, with Felker retaining complete editorial control.

But what Felker failed to understand was that Burden was not in it for the money, and a high bid couldn't salve his desire to become a media mogul. Murdoch instinctively understood that a few careful ego strokes would make Burden submissive to him, and so he offered him a job and a salary in the to-be-revamped *New York* magazine after Murdoch took over. "Clay could have been a bit more diplomatic with Burden, but he had no patience," said former contributing writer Ken Auletta. "But that was one of his more endearing qualities—his inability to suffer any bullshit. I think Clay's biggest mistake was inviting people on the board that would become his enemies."

Burden had already negotiated a deal with Murdoch to sell out to him for $8.25 a share while Felker, Graham, and Rohatyn sat on their hands in Graham's *Newsweek* office on New Year's Eve, waiting for Burden, who was vacationing in Sun Valley, Idaho, to ratify the verbal agreement they had hammered out the day before. Burden was skiing, Tufo told them, and couldn't be reached. But there was no snow on the ground in Idaho, and Burden hadn't purchased any lift tickets. Instead, he was waiting for Murdoch to arrive on his Gulfstream and hand Burden a check for $3.5 million to receive outright control of *New York, New West,* and the *Village Voice*.

On New Year's Day, Felker called his attorney, Reginald Duff, and told him to play his last remaining hand, the right-of-first-refusal clause that Burden had violated by going with Murdoch prior to fielding

Felker's offer. Judge Thomas P. Griesa agreed that Burden had not followed the terms of the clause and granted a temporary restraining order, enjoining the sale of the stock.

While Murdoch's money sat in an escrow account, Felker scrambled mightily for his company, marshaling every resource he could find, including the *New York* staff, who had sat on the sidelines while Murdoch and Felker jousted for their beloved magazine. The battle was joined; Felker's earnest and pious loyalists versus the crass media colonizers, a battle that would play itself out in the press and on the local TV news, no less. *New York* magazine, which had sustained itself in lean times with stories that foregrounded scandal, was now the subject of tabloid headlines.

A few *New York* contributors took the initiative to function as de facto mediators between the staff and the board of directors. Political writers Ken Auletta and Richard Reeves, who were practiced in the art of speaking truth to power, met with Patricof, Bob Towbin, and Thomas Kempner, who assured Auletta and Reeves that they had the best interests of the magazine at heart and that they would be happy to meet with the staff during the next board meeting to try to clean up this mess. To Byron Dobell, the board's overtures at reconciliation were just strategic maneuvers, and perhaps a way to assuage their guilt over going behind Felker's back. If they retained Auletta and Reeves in an editorial capacity after Murdoch took over, then *New York* might not lose its editorial continuity or integrity.

"I was tremendously loyal to Clay, and the board was the enemy," said Dobell. "I just felt Auletta and Reeves shouldn't dicker around with these people, as if they might stay on afterwards. It was terribly naive on their part." Dobell's skepticism was borne out on January 2, when Patricof and Kempner signed their stock over to Murdoch. Towbin followed soon after, and Murdoch had it all sewn up, at least until Judge Greisa's final ruling on the temporary restraining order. "The investment bankers on my board sold me out," said Felker, "and Murdoch was a prick."

About the only salutary thing that emerged from the takeover, according to Felker, was the tremendous display of solidarity that his staff demonstrated in the wake of the sale. "The troops really rallied when Murdoch made his move," he said. "It was very heartening to me."

On the morning after Murdoch held a cocktail party in his Fifth

Avenue apartment to celebrate his victory, 125 full-time staffers and free-lancers gathered at *New York*'s office on Second Avenue. With Felker and Glaser tied up in meetings with lawyers, Byron Dobell read a prepared statement from their beleaguered leader. "Despite recent developments," it read in part, "I intend to fight as hard as I can to keep what we have all built from being damaged." It was meant to be a battle cry, but it had the desperate ring of an SOS.

The nonunionized staff planned a work stoppage if Murdoch shang-haied the magazine from Felker. The indignation was rising to a hysterical pitch; it was all beginning to take on the tenor of a moral crusade. "Clay has been very good to me," Dobell told the reporters who had amassed in the office's dining room for a press conference. "I think of him as my brother—and sometimes he may be wrong—but I've always felt I needed Clay. That's why the passion is so enormous. I want to save my brother." Ken Auletta put a finer point on it: "We protest being treated like lumps of meat or widgets—being bartered and traded around."

But *New York*'s crew had no legal recourse, not a single bargaining chip, except their sweat equity. Felker was trying to appeal to the empathy of the board, but no one knew better than Murdoch that financial self-interest always trumped good intentions. "When push came to shove, the investors were interested in getting their money out," said Glaser. "They behaved as one would expect them to behave. Clay thought he could make them see the importance of his journalistic crusade—that they would stay on board for the sake of the editorial product—but why in the world would anyone think that was gonna happen?"

Despite Tom Kempner's assurances that the writers would have a significant role in the board meeting that would formalize the stock sale that night, *New York*'s minions were confined to a holding room adjacent to the boardroom in labor negotiator Ted Kheel's office. As staff members sipped from the half-gallon bottle of Chivas Regal that Kheel had provided, Auletta, Reeves, and writer Steven Brill decamped to the men's room, only to find Murdoch sitting on the sink, briefing Towbin and Stanley Shuman on strategy. They all regarded each other nervously, then Murdoch and his crew ducked out uneasily without a word exchanged between them. Pious indignation would no longer suffice; the script was being written by Murdoch now.

Felker and Glaser entered the boardroom at a little past seven o'clock to face their antagonists. Alan Patricof wasted little time in shifting the balance of power to Murdoch, proposing that Joan Glynn and James Q. Wilson, two Felker loyalists, be removed from the board, effective immediately. No sooner did Glynn and Wilson leave than Patricof conducted a roll-call vote for the removal of Kheel as company counsel. Towbin, Patricof, Tufo, Kempner, Bull, and Burden all raised their hands. Kheel was out. Felker and Glaser were poleaxed but did their level best to keep themselves in check.

Now the coup de grâce was at hand, and Patricof was on a roll: "I now propose that we put two new members on the board." Enter Murdoch and Shuman, who without ceremony seated themselves in the chairs vacated by Glynn and Wilson. The proxies were passed around the table, and the meeting was adjourned. The shareholders would now convene in private.

After a short interval, Patricof entered the writers' room and told Glaser that the board would now hear the grievances of the *New York* representatives. Brill, Dobell, Felker, Reeves, Auletta, and Glaser entered the boardroom and proceeded to lob verbal buckshot at their tormenters. It was the only weapon they had left.

Dobell berated the board for dining out on Felker's genius for years and then repaying him with a devastating betrayal. Towbin vociferously defended his behavior, telling Felker that he had called up Felix Rohatyn to get permission to sell his stock. "Bob," Felker barked, "you're a liar." Ken Auletta wanted Towbin to explain why he had told Auletta he would be interested in doing business with the *Washington Post* and that he wouldn't budge until he had met with the writers when in fact he had already initiated a deal with Murdoch. Towbin had no good answer for that.

But it was Carter Burden who bore the brunt of Felker and Dobell's ire. "Carter was presumably a man of civic virtue," said Dobell. "I thought he should be particularly ashamed, because *New York* magazine was a boon for the city, and by selling to Murdoch, he wasn't acting in the best interests of the city." At one point, Felker rose from his chair to address Burden, who all along had hoped that whoever owned the magazine would give him a proper title at the top of the masthead. "He [Murdoch] knows what you are," he said. "An incompetent dilettante. No one is going to give you what you want—a tin hat marked 'publisher.'"

None of this seemed to faze Murdoch in the least. Even after Felker had browbeaten nearly everyone in the room, Murdoch calmly turned to him and said, "Clay, I think you're an editorial genius. I want you to stay and run the magazine."

"I, like you," Felker responded, "am a publisher."

Felker still had an ace in the hole, or so he thought: the right-of-first-refusal clause that Burden had abrogated. But Peter Tufo had spotted a loophole in the agreement. If the company showed an aggregate loss over four consecutive quarters, Felker's right to purchase Burden's shares would have expired on December 31, 1976. *New West*'s losses had seen to that. Game, set, and match, Murdoch.

The staff made good on their vow to walk out en masse when Murdoch took over, but Felker wanted to make sure that *New York*'s new owner at least protected the jobs of some of the senior members of the staff, and Murdoch complied, offering two-year guaranteed contracts for ten staffers as well as the top editors of *New York, New West,* and the *Voice.* In exchange, Murdoch's lawyers released Felker from a non-compete clause in his contract that would have prevented him from working for or starting up any other publication in New York or Los Angeles, or any other national title. Murdoch also agreed to pay his $70,000 legal bill and gave him a year to pay off $250,000 in company debt.

After the contracts were drafted and all the papers were signed, Felker and Glaser made their way back to the office on Second Avenue, but the staff had gathered at a restaurant across the street, a few of them holding out the faint hope that Felker had pulled off a miracle. Instead, the scene took on the pallor of an Irish wake. In a cracking voice, Felker told his troops that "Rupert Murdoch's ideas about friendship, about publishing and about people are very different than mine. He should know that he is breaking up a family, and he does so at his peril."

No one was left to put out that week's issue of *New York.* Byron Dobell, who was offered Felker's job, resigned instead, while Ken Auletta demanded that his name be removed from *New York*'s masthead effective immediately. All of the other top editors and Glaser followed Auletta's lead. It was left to Murdoch and a few News Ltd. directors to finish production. Murdoch edited some movie listings, while men in three-piece suits who had never before seen a galley page pasted up layouts and line-edited stories.

When the smoke cleared, Felker made $750,000 on the sale; Burden came away with $4 million. James Brady, a News Ltd. vice president, took over as editor in chief of *New York*. Murdoch promptly fired *Village Voice* editor Marianne Partridge, then recanted over the vehement protestations of the paper's staff.

When Felker walked out after the final staff meeting onto Second Avenue, a phalanx of reporters was waiting for him. He tried to elbow his way through the scrum, but the TV cameras had him in their crosshairs. "I haven't been thinking about what I'm going to do next," Felker said. "I'm a journalist and that's what my life is."

Someone asked, "What kind of day was today for you?"

"A terrible day. It's also the best day of my life."

"Why is it the best day?"

"Because of the support and the love these people have shown me."

And then Clay Felker, who had cowed politicians and made society matrons blush, openly wept.

EPILOGUE

AFTER THE BALL

After Rupert Murdoch's palace coup, Clay Felker brushed himself off and started over again.

Ironically, he ventured back to *Esquire*, the magazine that had unceremoniously shoved him aside fifteen years earlier. But so much had changed since then. Harold Hayes, who had turned *Esquire* into the greatest American general-interest magazine of the 1960s, had left in 1973 after a dispute with the chairman of the board, John Smart. The magazine's management had decided, without Hayes's consent, that *Esquire* would use market testing in attempt to shore up its sagging bottom line, and perhaps even replace George Lois's covers with more obvious designs of their own choosing. Management wanted a harder sell, with multiple cover lines instead of those single, pithy cover lines that Lois and the editors had perfected over the years. In short, they were looking for a sexier, more appealing package that would sacrifice panache for ham-handed commercialism. Hayes wasn't having it, and on April 5, he turned in his letter of resignation to the board. (Hayes died of a brain tumor in 1989.)

Without Hayes's steady hand, the vitality seemed to drain out of *Esquire*. The magazine lost focus and market share, losing roughly $5 million from 1975 to 1977. In August 1977 Felker acquired the magazine with an investment from Vere Harmsworth, Viscount Rothemere, chairman of the British publishing giant Associated Newspapers, and recruited his old partner Milton Glaser to work by his side.

But Felker's editorial instincts, once so sure and sharp during his *New*

York tenure, abandoned him. A fatal decision to increase the magazine's frequency from monthly to biweekly left the magazine drowning in more red ink, and in May 1979 the majority interest of *Esquire* was sold to two thirty-something Tennesseans named Christopher Whittle and Phillip Moffitt.

From there, Felker had a cup of coffee or two at various publications (the *Daily News, Manhattan Inc., Adweek, U.S. News & World Report*), tried his hand at an alternative newsweekly called the *East Side Express* that he sold in 1984, and even worked as a producer at Twentieth Century Fox for a brief time in the early 1980s. But the Felker era was, for all intents and purposes, a past-tense phenomenon.

The same year that Felker lost *New York* to Murdoch, Jann Wenner moved *Rolling Stone* from San Francisco to New York, thus irrevocably altering what Hunter Thompson called "a hub of great journalism. My attitude at the time was, if it ain't broke, don't fix it. But Jann took his life so far in another direction that he destroyed the shining monument to himself that he had built."

From 1967 to 1977, *Rolling Stone* featured movie stars on seventeen covers. From 1977 to 1979, it had twenty-two such cover stories. Thompson continued to contribute to the magazine, but none of his subsequent work, which varied wildly in quality, could match the greatness or the impact of the first two *Fear and Loathing* sagas (one exception being "The Banshee Screams for Buffalo Meat," Thompson's encomium for his friend Oscar Zeta Acosta, who vanished mysteriously in Mazatlán, Mexico, in June 1974).

Nineteen seventy-seven was also the year that George Lucas's *Star Wars* was released, an event that landed the film's cast on the cover of *Rolling Stone* in August. A covenant, it seemed, had been struck between Hollywood and Madison Avenue, and magazines would now become press organs for movie stars. Stories shrank, and so did ideas. Puff pieces were no longer discouraged by scrupulous editors; they were career builders for magazine writers now, and big draws for advertisers.

It just got ugly in the 1970s for New Journalism, a process that was hastened by the decline of general-interest magazines. So what happened? Television, mostly, which siphoned away readers and ad dollars, turned celebrity culture into a growth industry and ensured the end of big tent magazines such as *Life,* the *Saturday Evening Post,* and *Collier's*—magazines that had published Mailer, Didion, Hersey, and many others.

Esquire, New York, and *Rolling Stone* were no longer must-reads for an engaged readership that couldn't wait for the next issue to arrive in their mailboxes, eager to find out what Wolfe, Talese, Thompson, and the rest had in store for them. As the seventies drew to a close, so too did the last golden era of American journalism.

But there was also a sense of psychic exhaustion, that the great stories had all been told and there was nothing left to write about. The last American troops pulled out of Saigon in 1975; mainstream culture had thoroughly colonized the counterculture, and women's lib just wasn't sexy enough for male journalists to cover with the same rigor and passion that they reserved for wars.

New Journalism as Wolfe envisioned it—as the great literary movement of the postwar era—died a long time ago, but its influence is everywhere. Once a rear-guard rebellion, its tenets are so accepted now that they've become virtually invisible. The art of narrative storytelling is alive and well; it's just more diffuse now, spread out across books, magazines, newspapers, and the Web.

There are great immersive reporters such as Ted Conover, who posed as a corrections officer in Sing Sing prison and wrote an award-winning book about it called *Newjack.* Jon Krakauer accompanied a mountaineering expedition to Mount Everest on assignment from *Outside* magazine and produced a narrative nonfiction classic, *Into Thin Air.* Barbara Ehrenreich posed as a domestic laborer and told the hard-luck stories of her fellow workers in *Nickel and Dimed: On (Not) Getting By in America.*

Other best-selling books such as *The Orchid Thief, Random Family, Moneyball, American Ground*—riveting stories buttressed by meticulous reporting, full-bodied character development, and flat-out great writing—are the children of *Dispatches, The Electric Kool-Aid Acid Test,* and *Armies of the Night.* The director of New York University's magazine journalism program, Robert S. Boynton, interviewed the authors of these and other recent nonfiction classics for a 2005 book called *The New New Journalism.*

With the exception of Jimmy Breslin, who continued to write a weekly column until retiring from newspaper work in November 2004, New Journalism's greatest practitioners moved on to other pursuits. Tom Wolfe virtually gave up journalism to devote himself to novels such as *The Bonfire of the Vanities* and *I Am Charlotte Simmons.* Michael Herr has published only three smallish titles in the years since *Dispatches.* Since publishing *Thy Neighbor's Wife,* his 1980 book about sexual mores in

America, Gay Talese has written only one other book (*Unto the Sons,* a multigenerational saga of his own family) and has spent ten years working on the next one. A collection of his magazine pieces called *The Gay Talese Reader* was published in 2003. It is essential reading. John Sack continued to traverse the globe for stories about the Chinese Mafia, the Holocaust, and the My Lai massacre until his death from cancer in 2004. Joan Didion remains a giant of journalism and continues to produce stunning work.

Norman Mailer also retreated from print journalism but didn't give up the practice entirely. *The Executioner's Song,* his epic about Utah killer Gary Gilmore, was the end result of hundreds of hours of interviews conducted by the writer and his partner, Lawrence Schiller. *The Executioner's Song* won Mailer his second Pulitzer prize in 1980.

As the years wore on, Hunter S. Thompson continued to fitfully produce good work, particularly during his brief run in the mid-1980s as a columnist for the *San Francisco Examiner,* when he inveighed against the evils of Reagan-era villains such as George H. W. Bush, Oliver Stone, Jim Bakker, Ed Meese, and the Gipper himself. By the late 1990s, Thompson's output had slowed considerably. He was no longer writing consistently for any print publications; instead there was a sports column for ESPN.com that was really a wide-open forum for whatever was on Thompson's mind come deadline's eve. Despite some occasionally hilarious and insightful pieces, it seemed an odd place for Thompson to land. Some claim that he was too strung out on drugs to produce another significant book; others claimed he was just letting his legacy speak for itself and leaving the present to younger people.

Thompson loved to talk about his salad days, but there was a wistful, almost rueful catch in his voice when the past was discussed. Two years before fatally shooting himself on February 20, 2005, he summed it all up thusly:

> The sixties were a distinct time, a trip. I looked around and I saw a lot of intimidating voices out there, but I never had to think about pleasing them. I had editors who let me write what I wanted to write, and I worked hard at it. It was no free ride, but it was a very exciting, intoxicating time for me. But it took me a while to realize that it's not gonna come back. Not in my lifetime, not in anyone else's.

Notes

INTRODUCTION

Page 1   "Look . . . we're coming out once a week": Tom Wolfe, *Hooking Up* (New York: Farrar, Straus and Giroux, 2000), 250.

Page 1   "Zonggggggggggg!": Lillian Ross, "Red Mittens!" *The New Yorker,* March 16, 1965.

Page 2   "If we tell someone": *Hooking Up,* 251.

Page 3   He reeled off a letter: Ibid., 253.

Page 3   "They have a compulsion in the *New Yorker* offices": Ibid., 256.

Page 4   "*The New Yorker* comes out once a week": Ibid., 278.

Page 5   Excerpts from Dwight Macdonald's counterattack on "Tiny Mummies" are from "Parajournalism, or Tom Wolfe & His Magic Writing Machine," *New York Review of Books,* August 26, 1965; and "Parajournalism II: Wolfe and *The New Yorker,*" *New York Review of Books,* February 3, 1966.

1. RADICAL LIT: SOME ROOTS OF A REVOLUTION

Page 10   "In New York in the early 1960s": Tom Wolfe and E. W. Johnson, eds., *The New Journalism* (New York: Harper & Row, 1973), 47.

Page 10   Roots of print journalism: Franklin Luther Mott, *American Journalism: A History, 1690–1960* (New York: Macmillan, 1962); George Boyce, James Curran, and Pauline Wingate, *Newspaper History from the Seventeenth Century to the Present Day* (London: Constable, 1978).

Page 11   "There is likewise . . . great advantage": Jonathan Swift, *A Modest Proposal,* 1729.

Page 12   "We thought we almost saw the dingy little back office": Charles Dickens, *Sketches by Boz,* excerpted from *The Oxford Illustrated Dickens* (Oxford: Oxford University Press, 1957).

Page 12   Background of Joseph Pulitzer: James McGrath Morris, *The Rose Man of Sing Sing* (New York: Fordham University Press, 2003); Kenneth T. Jackson, ed., *The Encyclopedia of New York City* (New Haven: Yale University Press, 1995), 964.

Page 14   "I went down into the under-world of London": Jack London, *The People of the Abyss,* Gutenberg Project e-book 1688 (1999; transcribed from the Thomas Nelson and Sons edition), available at www.gutenberg.org/etext/1688, 1.

Page 15   Biographical background of George Orwell: Bernard Crick, *George Orwell: A Life* (Harmondsworth: Penguin Books, 1980).

Page 16   "There was . . . an atmosphere of muddle": George Orwell, *Down and Out in Paris and London* (London: Secker & Warburg, 1986).

Page 17   In the introduction to the French edition of the book: Crick, *George Orwell*, 187.

Page 18   "The five-gallon can": A. J. Liebling, "The Foamy Fields," *The New Yorker Book of War Pieces* (New York: Schocken Books, 1988), 147.

Page 19   "I guess I'd been thinking from the beginning": Jonathan Dee, "Writers at Work: John Hersey," *Paris Review*, Summer–Fall 1986.

Page 20   "The journalist is always the mediator": Sybil Steinberg, ed., *Writing for Your Life: 92 Contemporary Authors Talk About the Art of Writing and the Job of Publishing* (Wainscott, N.Y.: Pushcart Press, 1992), 255.

Page 21   when Kennedy ran for the House of Representatives: Ben Yagoda, *About Town: The New Yorker and the World It Made* (New York: Scribner, 2000), 184.

Page 21   Background on the origins of the writing of *Hiroshima*: Ibid., 183–93.

Page 23   "At exactly fifteen minutes past eight": John Hersey, "A Reporter at Large: Hiroshima," *The New Yorker*, November 1, 1946.

Page 24   "Mrs. Nakamoto": Ibid.

Page 25   "I don't believe": Lillian Ross, *Reporting Back: Notes on Journalism* (Washington, D.C.: Counterpoint, 2002), 34.

Page 25   "Bogart nodded": Lillian Ross, "Come In, Lassie!" *The New Yorker*, February 21, 1948.

Page 25   "'Come In, Lassie!' taught me how to watch and wait": Lillian Ross, Ibid., 34.

Page 27   "About our old piece—the hell with them!": James R. Mellow, *Hemingway: A Life Without Consequences* (Boston: Houghton Mifflin, 1992), 574.

Page 27   "As I spent time with the characters": Lillian Ross, *Here but Not Here* (Washington, D.C.: Counterpoint, 1998), 90.

Page 27   "Huston as a person is almost too interesting": Ibid., 90–91.

Page 28   "I'm on the first floor": Lillian Ross, *Picture: 50th Anniversary Edition* (New York: Da Capo Press, 2002), 23.

Page 30   Ross's anecdote about Nicholas Schenck: *Here but Not Here*, 101–2.

Page 31   "It was as strange to me": Jane Howard, "How the 'Smart Rascal' Brought It Off," *Life*, January 7, 1966.

Page 31   "People who don't understand the literary process": Ibid.

Page 32   "It wasn't a question of my *liking*": Ibid.

Page 32   Using John Hersey's *Hiroshima* as a model: Yagoda, *About Town*: 347.

Page 33   "My theory": Howard, "'Smart Rascal.'"

Page 33   "During this visit Dewey paused at an upstairs window": Truman Capote, *In Cold Blood* (New York: Random House, 1965), 153.

Page 33   The *New Yorker* fact checker found Capote to be the most accurate writer: Yagoda, *About Town*, 347.

2. THE GREAT AMERICAN MAGAZINE

Page 35   "the publishing equivalent of a lemonade stand": Robert J. Bliwise, "The Master of New York," *Duke Magazine*, September–October 1996.

Page 36   One day Carl came home: Ibid.

Page 38   Background on Arnold Gingrich, the founding of *Esquire*, and the internecine battle between Hayes, Ginzburg, and Felker is taken from Arnold Gingrich, *Nothing but People: The Early Days at* Esquire (New York:

Crown, 1971) and Carol Polsgrove, *It Wasn't Pretty, Folks, But Didn't We Have Fun?* Esquire *in the Sixties* (New York: W. W. Norton, 1995), as well as interviews with Clay Felker and Ralph Ginzburg.

Page 41   "I floundered around for four or five years": From a speech given to Wake Forest students by Harold Hayes, Wake Forest University Archives, Winston-Salem, N.C. (henceforth WFA).

Page 41   "His persistent refusal to accept an ordinary approach": Harold Hayes, "Making a Modern Magazine," WFA.

Page 43   "Arnold's removal from the heat of everyday activity"; "They wore the same kind of clothes": Harold Hayes, "Building a Magazine's Personality," from an unpublished memoir, WFA.

Page 43   "our drinking editor": Gingrich, *Nothing but People,* 207.

Page 44   "a test of lung power": Ibid., 205.

Page 46   "I spent the whole afternoon reading these things": Bliwise, "The Master of New York."

Page 48   "Early in his act": Thomas B. Morgan, "What Makes Sammy Jr. Run?" *Esquire,* October 1959.

Page 49   "Well, Dave, baby": Ibid.

Page 49   "It takes a terribly long time": Ibid.

Page 50   "I had a hard time writing about Brigitte": Thomas B. Morgan, *Self-Creations: 13 Impersonalities* (New York: Holt, Rinehart and Winston, 1965), 98.

Page 50   "Brigitte swung around the car again and again": Thomas B. Morgan, "Brigitte Bardot: Problem Child," *Look,* August 16, 1960.

Page 51   "TIME: *Afternoon*": Thomas B. Morgan, "David Susskind: Television's Newest Spectacular," *Esquire,* August 1960.

Page 53   "I really think the watershed book was *Advertisements*": Hilary Mills, *Mailer: A Biography* (New York: Empire Books, 1982), 194.

Page 54   "He had the deep orange-brown suntan"; "Eisenhower's eight years": Norman Mailer, "Superman Comes to the Supermart," *Esquire,* November 1960.

Page 55   "enormously personalized journalism": Mills, *Mailer,* 195.

Page 57   "a more active control of all our materials": Hayes memo to Gingrich, WFA.

Page 58   Details of the Felker-Sahl confrontation can be found in Polsgrove, *It Wasn't Pretty.*

Page 59   "the rakish fashion of the Continental boulevardier": Gay Talese, *Unto the Sons* (New York: Alfred A. Knopf, 1992), 6.

Page 60   three hundred columns: Barbara Lounsberry, "Portrait of a (Non-Fiction) Artist," available at www.gaytalese.com.

Page 60   "I learned [from my mother]": Gay Talese, "Origins of a Nonfiction Writer," in Gay Talese and Barbara Lounsberry, *Writing Creative Nonfiction: The Literature of Reality* (New York: HarperCollins, 1996), 2.

Page 61   "Sports is about people who lose": Lounsberry, "Portrait of a (Nonfiction) Writer."

Page 62   As the men talked: Gay Talese, "Portrait of a Young Prize Fighter," *New York Times,* October 12, 1958.

Page 62   "I am currently trying to gather": Talese letter to Harold Hayes, February 24, 1960, WFA.

Page 62   "New York is a city of things unnoticed": Gay Talese, "New York," *Esquire,* July 1960.

Page 63   a piece that *Village Voice* writer: Hentoff letter to Hayes, September 18, 1961, from WFA.

Page 64   "it seemed he might be involved": Talese, "The Soft Psyche of Joshua Logan," *Esquire*, April 1963.

Page 64   when Talese read back the story to Logan: Polsgrove, *It Wasn't Pretty*, 60–61.

Page 65   "I had become almost an interior figure": Talese and Lounsberry, *Writing Creative Nonfiction*, 106.

Page 65   "It is not a bad feeling with you're knocked out": Gay Talese, "The Loser," *Esquire*, March 1964.

Page 66   *"And so then you know"*: Ibid.

3. KING JAMES AND THE MAN IN THE ICE CREAM SUIT

Page 67   The *Herald Tribune*'s lineage: Richard Kluger, *The Paper: The Life and Death of the* New York Herald Tribune (New York, Alfred A. Knopf, 1986).

Page 67   The history of the *New York Herald Tribune* is recounted in extraordinary detail by Richard Kluger in his book *The Paper: The Life and Death of the* New York Herald Tribune. All of the historical background is taken from this book.

Page 72   "I get there and I can't find her": Jimmy Breslin, *The World of Jimmy Breslin* (New York: Viking, 1967), 19–20. Introduction to "The Reds."

Page 73   "keep all storms in my life offshore": Jimmy Breslin, *I Want to Thank My Brain for Remembering Me* (Boston: Little, Brown, 1996), 24.

Page 73   "Without Throneberry": Jimmy Breslin, "The Mets," *The World of Jimmy Breslin*, 17–18.

Page 74   "I never thought about how to do a column": Jimmy Breslin, *The World of Jimmy Breslin*, introduction, xv.

Page 75   "It's news reporting": Jack Newfield, "An Interview with Jimmy Breslin," *Tikkun*, February 23, 2005.

Page 75   "were a little poorer than some": Jimmy Breslin, *The World of Jimmy Breslin*, 31.

Page 75   "Marvin the Torch never could keep his hands": Ibid., "Marvin The Torch," 34.

Page 76   "Yes, sir?": Ibid., "Jerry the Booster," 42.

Page 77   "into a shape like a bowling ball": Tom Wolfe and E. W. Johnson, eds., *The New Journalism* (New York: Harper & Row, 1973); Tom Wolfe, "The New Journalism," 13.

Page 78   The *New York Times*'s metropolitan editor A. M. Rosenthal: *Jimmy Breslin: The Art of Climbing Tenement Stairs*, radio documentary produced by Jon Kalish for KCRW.

Page 78   One day in March 1964: David W. Dunlap, "If These Walls Could Publish . . . ," *New York Times*, August 25, 2004.

Page 80   The call bothered Malcolm Perry: Jimmy Breslin, "A Death in Emergency Room One," *The World of Jimmy Breslin*, 169.

Page 81   "A guy's weight": "Keep Me Going," *Newsweek*, May 6, 1963. Unsigned.

Page 81   When Pollard got to the row of yellow: Jimmy Breslin, "It's an Honor," *The World of Jimmy Breslin*, 177–80.

Page 83   "different spectators have suggested": Toby Thompson, "The Evolution of Dandy Tom," *Vanity Fair*, October 1987.

Page 84   "Jack London of all people was my model": Elaine Dundy, "Tom
            Wolfe . . . But Exactly, Yes!" *Vogue,* April 15, 1966.
Page 86   "This must be the place!": Wolfe and Johnson, eds., *The New Journalism;*
            Tom Wolfe, "The New Journalism," 4.
Page 86   "electrical conduits," "industrial sludge," "big pie factory": Ibid.
Page 86   "I still get a terrific kick": Joe David Bellamy, "Sitting Up with Tom
            Wolfe," *Writer's Digest,* November 9, 1974.
Page 87   "Tom Sawyer": Dundy, "Tom Wolfe . . . But Exactly, Yes!"
Page 87   "mean, low-down cold streak": Tom Wolfe, "Miserable Weather to
            Continue; Ships, Aircraft, Shores Battered," *New York Herald Tribune,*
            December 8, 1962.
Page 87   "with eyes that looked like poached eggs": Tom Wolfe, "He Elevates
            Fraternities," *New York Herald Tribune,* December 2, 1962.
Page 88   "A willowy co-ed": Tom Wolfe, "600 at NYU Stage Lusty Rent Strike,"
            New York Herald Tribune, April 13, 1962.
Page 89   "usual non-fiction narrator": Wolfe and Johnson, eds., Tom Wolfe, "The
            New Journalism," *The New Journalism,* 17.
Page 90   "Is that Joan Morse": Wolfe, "The Saturday Route," *The Kandy-Kolored
            Tangerine-Flake Streamline Baby* (New York: Farrar, Straus and Giroux,
            1965), 223.
Page 91   "When I reached New York in the sixties": Wolfe and Johnson, eds., Tom
            Wolfe, "The New Journalism," *The New Journalism,* 30.
Page 91   "When great fame": Tom Wolfe, *The Pump House Gang* (New York: Farrar,
            Straus and Giroux, 1968; Bantam edition, 1978), 8.
Page 92   "Here you are, boy, put your name right there": Tom Wolfe, "The
            Marvelous Mouth," *Esquire,* October 1963.
Page 93   "It's the automobile that's the most important story": Emile Capouya,
            "True Facts and Artifacts," *Saturday Review,* July 31, 1965.
Page 94   "I don't mind observing"; "Plato's *Republic* for teenagers"; "They're like
            Easter Islanders"; "shaped not like rectangles": Thomas K. Wolfe, "There
            Goes (VAROOM! VAROOM!) that Kandy-Kolored (THPHHHHHH!)
            Tangerine-Flake Streamline Baby (RAHGHHHH!) Around the Bend
            (BRUMMMMMMMMMM . . .)," *Esquire,* November 1963.

4. TOM WOLFE ON ACID
Page 100   "he appeared in a white-on-white": Elaine Dundy, "Tom Wolfe . . . But
            Exactly, Yes!" *Vogue,* April 15, 1966.
Page 101   "wild and ironic": Tom Wolfe, *The Electric Kool-Aid Acid Test* (New York:
            Farrar, Straus and Giroux, 1968), 4.
Page 102   "Once an athlete so valued": Ibid., 5.
Page 104   "thick wrists and forearms": Ibid., 7.
Page 105   "Despite the skepticism I brought here": Ibid., 27.
Page 105   "only in poor old Formica": Ibid., 31.
Page 106   "Their faces were painted in Art Nouveau swirls": Ibid., 391.
Page 107   "The first part": Tom Wolfe, "The Author's Story," *New York Times Book
            Review,* August 18, 1968.
Page 107   "So far nobody in or out of the medical profession": Wolfe, "Super-Hud
            Plays the Game of POWER," *New York World-Journal Tribune,* February 5,
            1967.

Page 110   "I owe the *National Observer* in Washington": Letter from Thompson to Wolfe, in Hunter S. Thompson, *The Proud Highway: Saga of a Desperate Southern Gentleman: The Fear and Loathing Letters, Volume 1* (New York: Villard, 1997), 524.

Page 111   "several hours of eating": Hunter S. Thompson, *Hell's Angels: A Strange and Terrible Saga* (New York: Modern Library, 1999), 220.

Page 112   Certain vibrations of the bus: Wolfe, *The Electric Kool-Aid Acid Test,* 110.

Page 113   *A very Christmas card:* Ibid., 55.

Page 113   *Miles, Miles, Miles:* Ibid., 47.

Page 114   [S]ome blonde from out of town: Ibid., 176.

Page 114   "Certain passages—such as the Hell's Angels gangbang": From an interview sent to the author from Paul Krassner, used with Krassner's permission.

Page 114   "The ceiling is moving": Wolfe, *The Electric Kool-Aid Acid Test,* 40.

Page 115   Wolfe would revert to a "controlled trance"; "I felt like my heart": Toby Thompson, "The Evolution of Dandy Tom," *Vanity Fair,* October 1987.

5. THE CENTER CANNOT HOLD

Page 116   Biographical background on Joan Didion is taken from Joan Didion, *Where I Was From* (New York: Random House, 2003) and Michiko Kakutani, "Joan Didion: Staking Out California," *New York Times,* June 10, 1979.

Page 117   "I wrote stories from the time I was a little girl": Linda Kuehl, "The Art of Fiction No. 71: Joan Didion," *Paris Review,* Fall–Winter 1978.

Page 118   "Nothing was irrevocable . . . the shining and perishable dream itself": Joan Didion, "Goodbye to All That," *Slouching Towards Bethlehem* (New York: Farrar, Straus and Giroux, 1990), 229–30.

Page 118   "the way the rivers crested": Didion, *Where I Was From,* 157.

Page 119   "paralyzed by the conviction that the world": Kakutani, "Joan Didion: Staking Out California."

Page 120   "Most of my sentences drift off, don't end": Kuehl, "The Art of Fiction."

Page 120   "So they had come . . . to see Arthwell": Joan Didion, "How Can I Tell Them There's Nothing Left?" *Saturday Evening Post,* May 7, 1966.

Page 121   "adolescents drifted from city to torn city": Didion, "Slouching Towards Bethlehem," *Slouching Towards Bethlehem,* 84.

Page 121   "Debbie is buffing her fingernails": Ibid., 92.

Page 122   "wearing a reefer coat": Ibid., 127.

Page 122   "Every day I would go into [Allene Talmey]'s office": Kuehl, "The Art of Fiction."

Page 123   "Hathaway removed the cigar from his mouth": Joan Didion, "John Wayne: A Love Song," *Slouching Towards Bethlehem,* 34–35.

Page 123   "Joan Didion is one of the least celebrated and most talented writers": Dan Wakefield, "Places, People and Personalities," *New York Times Book Review,* July 21, 1968.

6. MADRAS OUTLAW

Page 124   "Wolfe's problem": Hunter S. Thompson, "Jacket Copy for *Fear & Loathing in Las Vegas: A Savage Journey to the Heart of the American Dream,*" *The Great Shark Hunt: Strange Tales from a Strange Time* (New York: Rolling Stone Press/Summit Books, 1979), 108.

Page 125   "I've always felt like a Southerner": E. Jean Carroll, *Hunter: The Strange and Savage Life of Hunter S. Thompson* (New York: Dutton, 1993), 25.

Page 125   "I had a keen appetite for adventure": Hunter S. Thompson, *Kingdom of Fear: Loathsome Secrets of a Star-Crossed Child in the Final Days of the American Century* (New York: Simon & Schuster, 2003), 10.

Page 126   "Turn back the pages of history": Hunter S. Thompson, *The Proud Highway: Saga of a Desperate Southern Gentleman, 1955–1967 (The Fear and Loathing Letters, Volume 1)* (New York: Villard, 1997), 5.

Page 126   "In short, we both know": Ibid., 10.

Page 127   "no one is hanging over me": Ibid., 16.

Page 127   "The whole thing": Ibid., 39.

Page 127   "rebel and superior attitude": Ibid., 59.

Page 127   "If this path leads up": Ibid., 76.

Page 129   "Do you realize that sunlight": Ibid., 112.

Page 129   "Goddammit, Hills": Ibid., 168.

Page 129   "It was not so much the money": Ibid., 272.

Page 130   "I am going to write massive tomes from South America": Ibid., 312.

Page 130   "As it turned out": Hunter S. Thompson, "A Footloose American in a Smuggler's Den," *The Great Shark Hunt*, 347.

Page 131   "I tried driving a cab": Craig Vetter, "The *Playboy* Interview: Hunter S. Thompson," *Playboy*, November 1974.

Page 132   "To my mind": Thompson, *Proud Highway*, 489.

Page 133   "quietly hysterical for five hours": Ibid., 494.

Page 133   "The difference between the Hell's Angels": Hunter S. Thompson, "Motorcycle Gangs: Losers and Outsiders," *The Nation*, May 17, 1965.

Page 134   "The moral here": Thompson, *Proud Highway*, 529.

Page 135   "For reasons that were never made clear": Hunter S. Thompson, *Hell's Angels: A Strange and Terrible Saga* (New York: Modern Library, 1999), 47.

Page 136   "I overslept": Ibid., 106.

Page 136   "grouped around a gray pickup": Ibid., 107.

Page 137   "When I went on runs with them": Vetter, "The *Playboy* Interview."

Page 137   "like being caught in a bad surf": Thompson, *Hell's Angels*, 135.

Page 137   "I was so firmly identified": Ibid., 137.

Page 139   "was convinced that he'd died": Ibid., 226.

Page 140   "When I grabbed the guy": Vetter, "The *Playboy* Interview."

Page 141   "using the dome of the rearview mirror": Ibid.

Page 142   Review excerpts: Richard M. Elman, *The New Republic*, February 25, 1967; Leo Litwak, *New York Times*, January 29, 1967.

Page 143   "There is not much argument about basic facts": Thompson, *Hell's Angels*, 34.

Page 143   "Into first gear": Ibid., 262.

Page 144   "The best of the Angels": Thompson, *Proud Highway*, 618.

7. INTO THE ABYSS

Page 145   "The existential heroes": Hunter S. Thompson, *Hell's Angels: A Strange and Terrible Saga* (New York: Modern Library, 1999), 236.

Page 146   "We have to confront them": William Prochnau, *Once upon a Distant War: David Halberstam, Neil Sheehan, Peter Arnett—Young War Correspondents and Their Early Vietnam Battles* (New York: Vintage, 1996), 11.

Page 146   "You couldn't believe anybody": Ibid., 22.

Page 148   "Of course I'd read that [George Goodman story]": All John Sack quotes, as well as the back story of *M*, are taken from transcripts of a series of 1993 interviews conducted by Carol Polsgrove; the quotes are used with Polsgrove's permission.

Page 149   "This week's *Time*": Letter from John Sack to Harold Hayes, October 25, 1965, WFA.

Page 149   "combat with all of its wild inanities": Ibid.

Page 149   "Jesus Christ": Letter from Harold Hayes to Sack, October 28, 1965, WFA.

Page 150   "These would be the only expenses": Sack to Hayes, November 5, 1965, WFA.

Page 151   "stiff IBM cards": John Sack, *M* (London: Corgi/Avon, 1986), 24.

Page 152   "the purist for whose sensibilities": Ibid., 57.

Page 152   "Peoples, all of your khaki shirts": Ibid., 58.

Page 152   "the Vietnamese in the village": Ibid., 108.

Page 152   "to kill, wound, or capture": Ibid., 123.

Page 153   "In actual fact": Ibid., 166.

Page 153   "A cavalry sergeant": Ibid., 168.

Page 154   "Rotarians": Michael Herr, "Fort Dix: The New Army Game," *Holiday*, April 1966.

Page 154   "Send any and all pictures": Telegram from Hayes to Sack, June 16, 1966, WFA.

Page 156   "You don't understand your story": Polsgrove interview transcript.

Page 157   "One, two, three": Sack, *M*, 11.

Page 158   "[T]he Marines had fought": Richard Tregaskis, *Guadalcanal Diary* (New York: Popular Library, 1962), 78.

Page 159   "Burn, burn, burn": Sack, *M*, 134.

Page 160   "*Charlie tries to creep up on me*": Ibid., 183.

Page 160   *M* reviews: *Publishers Weekly*, unsigned; "Two Sides of Our Side," Neil Sheehan, *The New York Times*, May 14, 1967; Leonard Kriegal, *The Nation*, October 23, 1967.

8. HELL SUCKS

Page 162   "higher journalism," "the best kind of journalism," "extended vignettes": Carol Polsgrove, *It Wasn't Pretty, Folks, But Didn't We Have Fun? Esquire in the Sixties* (New York: W. W. Norton, 1995), 172.

Page 162   "I don't have a journalist's instincts": Eric James Schroeder, *Vietnam, We've All Been There: Interviews with American Writers* (Westport, Conn.: Praeger, 1992), 33.

Page 163   "Conventional journalism": Michael Herr, "The War Correspondent: A Reappraisal," *Esquire*, April 1970.

Page 163   "As an overwhelming, unavoidable fact": Polsgrove, *It Wasn't Pretty*, 172.

Page 163   "This lapse of four months": Cable from Herr to Hayes, November 15, 1967, WFA.

Page 163   "I was twenty-seven years old": Schroeder, *Vietnam*, 34.

Page 164   "Tet changed everything here": Letter from Herr to Hayes, February 5, 1968, WFA.

Page 164   "passed through so many decimated towns and cities": Ibid.

Page 165   "Where we have not been smug": Ibid.

Page 165   "There are two Vietnams": Letter from Herr to Hayes, May 4, 1968, WFA.

Page 165   "$3,000 a month digs": Ibid.

Page 166   "For all the talk": Schroeder, *Vietnam*, 38.

Page 166   "We know that for years now": Michael Herr, "Hell Sucks," *Esquire*, August 1968.

Page 166   "made this an entirely different war": Ibid.

Page 167   "It stayed cold for the next ten days": Michael Herr, *Dispatches* (New York: Vintage, 1991), 68.

Page 167   "The eyes are ice-blue": Herr, "Hell Sucks."

Page 167   "I think the [television] coverage": Schroeder, *Vietnam*, 38.

Page 168   "extraordinarily perceptive": Polsgrove, *It Wasn't Pretty*, 176.

Page 168   "He's fiction": Letter from Herr to Hayes, May 18, 1968, WFA.

Page 169   Shortly after "Hell Sucks" was published: Polsgrove, *It Wasn't Pretty*, 47.

Page 169   "If all the barbed wire": Michael Herr, *Dispatches* (New York: Vintage, 1991), 123.

Page 170   Herr witnessed some savage scenes: Ibid., 152.

Page 170   "My ties to New York were as slight": Ibid., 101.

Page 170   centrifugal instinct: Garry Wills, *Lead Time: A Journalist's Education* (Garden City, N.Y.: Doubleday, 1983), xi.

Page 171   "You jus' another dumb Grunt": Herr, "Khesanh," *Esquire*, September 1969.

Page 172   "I say to myself": Schroeder, *Vietnam*, 43.

Page 172   "Everything . . . happened": Ibid., 44.

Page 173   "massive collapse": Ibid., 35.

Page 173   "Sometimes I was crazy in a very public way": Ibid., 40.

Page 173   "I had trouble adjusting to the seventies": Thomas B. Morgan, "Reporters of the Lost War," *Esquire*, July 1984.

Page 173   "This is already a long time ago": Herr, "High on War," manuscript, Bentley Historical Library Archives, University of Michigan, Ann Arbor.

Page 174   "Quite simply": C. D. B. Bryan, "The Different War," *New York Times*, November 20, 1977.

Page 174   "because I didn't want to become": Morgan, "Reporters of the Lost War."

9. HISTORY AS A NOVEL, THE NOVEL AS HISTORY

Page 175   an ad signed by 149 draft-age men: Nancy Zaroulis and Gerald Sullivan, *Who Spoke Up? American Protest Against the War in Vietnam, 1963–1975* (Garden City, N.Y.: Doubleday, 1984), 20.

Page 175   On July 3, 1964 . . . a group of protesters: Ibid., 20.

Page 176   In 1967 the Bertrand Russell Peace Foundation: Dana Adams Schmidt, "Sartre, at the 'Tribunal,' Terms Rusk a 'Mediocre Functionary,'" *New York Times*, May 5, 1967.

Page 176   Background on Mailer, the VDC march, and the march on the Pentagon taken from Peter Manso, *Mailer: His Life and Times* (New York: Simon & Schuster, 1985) and Mary V. Dearborn, *Mailer* (Boston: Houghton Mifflin, 1999) as well as interviews with David Dellinger, Edward de Grazia, Bob Kotlowitz, and Midge Decter.

Page 177   "embattled aging enfant terrible": Willie Morris, *New York Days* (Boston: Little, Brown, 1993), 211.

Page 178   "Mailer has grown": Manso, *Mailer*, 454.

Page 178	"There had been all too many years": Norman Mailer, *The Armies of the Night: History as a Novel, The Novel as History* (New York: Plume, 1994), 8.
Page 178	"helps you to think better": Richard Copans and Stan Neumann, *Mailer on Mailer,* American Masters documentary (New York: Thirteen/WNET, Reciprocal Films, Films d'lci & France 2, 2000).
Page 179	"[L]isten, Lyndon Johnson": Norman Mailer, *The Time of Our Time* (New York: Modern Library, 1999), 551.
Page 179	"He knew that by telling everyone": Manso, *Mailer,* 408.
Page 180	"Three cheers, lads": Ibid.
Page 180	"A Communist bureaucrat": Mailer, *The Time of Our Time,* 553.
Page 180	"under the yoke": Ibid., 540.
Page 181	"hit the longest ball in American letters": Seymour Krim, "Norman Mailer, Get Out of My Head!" *New York,* April 21, 1969.
Page 181	"Moving from one activity to another": Paul Carroll, "The *Playboy* Interview: Norman Mailer," *Playboy,* January 1968.
Page 182	"transmute myself": Norman Mailer, *Pontifications* (Boston: Little, Brown, 1982), 176.
Page 183	"Mailer received such news": Mailer, *Armies,* 9.
Page 183	"Mitch, I'll be there": Ibid.
Page 184	"kind of up in the air": Manso, *Mailer,* 45.
Page 185	"I pissed on the floor": Mailer, *Armies,* 50.
Page 185	"He was forty-four years old": Ibid., 78.
Page 185	"an obscene war": Ibid., 79.
Page 186	"Picture then this mass": Ibid., 108.
Page 186	"large and empty": Ibid., 119.
Page 187	"You Jew bastard": Ibid., 143.
Page 187	"In jail": Ibid., 165.
Page 188	"He was being treated worse than anyone in jail": Manso, *Mailer,* 458.
Page 188	"there was a part of me": Manso, *Mailer,* 461.
Page 189	"in many ways a literary genius": Morris, *New York Days,* 211.
Page 189	"one that would strike to the taproots": Ibid., 214.
Page 190	"We just closed the deal": Ibid., 214–15.
Page 190	Given the ambitious scope: Manso, *Mailer,* 463.
Page 191	"written in a towering depression": Mailer, *Pontifications,* 152.
Page 191	"I remember thinking at the time": Norman Mailer, *The Spooky Art: Some Thoughts on Writing* (New York: Random House, 2003), 99.
Page 191	"On the one hand . . .": Mailer, *Pontifications,* 153.
Page 192	"true protagonist . . .": Ibid., 153.
Page 193	"The kind of editing": Manso, *Mailer,* 462.
Page 193	"It's marvelous": Morris, *New York Days,* 217.
Page 194	"What will my father think?": Ibid., 219.
Page 194	"Mailer was a snob": Mailer, *Armies,* 14.
Page 194	"Lowell looked most unhappy": Ibid., 40.
Page 195	"Lowell's talent was very large": Ibid., 45.
Page 195	"The hippies were there in great number": Ibid., 91.
Page 195	"If it feels bad, it *is* bad": Ibid., 25.
Page 195	"He had no sense": Ibid., 68.
Page 196	"twenty generations of buried hopes": Ibid., 34.
Page 196	"[T]he center of Christianity": Ibid., 188.

Page 196   "To have his name": Ibid., 206.

Page 197   "not unlike the rare": Ibid., 213.

Page 197   "Some promise of peace": Ibid., 214.

Page 197   "All these people": Morris, *New York Days*, 222.

Page 197   *Armies of the Night* reviews: Alan Trachtenberg, "Mailer on the Steps of the Pentagon," *The Nation*, May 27, 1968; Henry S. Resnik, "Hand on the Pulse of America," *Saturday Review*, May 4, 1968; Alfred Kazin, "The Trouble He's Seen," *New York Times*, May 5, 1968.

10. THE KING OF NEW YORK

Page 199   For Clay Felker: Peter Manso, *Mailer: His Life and Times* (New York: Simon & Schuster, 1985), 405.

Page 200   83 percent of female readers: "About *New York*," publishing statement by George A. Hirsch, April 1968. From George Hirsch, personal archive.

Page 200   "I saw the impact of the magazine": Stuart W. Little, "How to Start a Magazine," *Saturday Review*, June 14, 1969.

Page 200   "The Beatles of illustration": Seymour Chwast, *Push Pin Graphic: A Quarter Century of Innovative Design and Illustration* (San Francisco: Chronicle Books, 2004), 11.

Page 200   Background material for the founding of *New York* was drawn from the following sources: Gail Sheehy, "A Fistful of Dollars," *Rolling Stone*, June 14, 1977; Little, "How to Start a Magazine"; interviews with Clay Felker, Jimmy Breslin, George Hirsch, Shelly Zalaznick, Milton Glaser, Pete Hamill, Gloria Steinem, and Tom Wolfe.

Page 203   sixty thousand subscribers: George A. Hirsch, "A Report from the Publisher," from George Hirsch, private archive.

Page 203   "You get hooked on this city": "About *New York*," editorial statement by Clay Felker.

Page 203 $1,250 for a black-and-white page: Temporary rate sheet, 1969. From George Hirsch, personal archive.

Page 204   "The people here met that challenge": Ruth A. Bower, "*New York* Announces Spring Rate Increase," press release, 11/7/69. From George Hirsch, personal archive.

Page 205   "Women stood with tears streaming down their faces": Gloria Steinem and Lloyd Weaver, "The City on the Eve of Destruction," *New York*, April 22, 1968.

Page 206   "Man, he only some itty-bit": Ibid.

Page 206   "Ethel Kennedy knows life from bullets": Gail Sheehy, "Ethel Kennedy and the Arithmetic of Life and Death," *New York*, June 17, 1968.

Page 207   "Right at the start"; "Armed robbery isn't a grin": Jimmy Breslin, "'Bonnie and Clyde' Revisited," *New York*, July 8, 1968.

Page 208   The idea had germinated at an after-hours story meeting: Manso, *Mailer*, 498.

Page 209   why Mailer was on the top of the ticket: Jimmy Breslin, "I Run to Win," *New York*, May 5, 1969.

Page 209   "I wanted to make actions": Steven Marcus, "Norman Mailer," *Writers at Work: The Paris Review Interviews, 3rd Series* (New York: Penguin, 1979), 278.

Page 209   Background of the Mailer-Breslin campaign: Manso, *Mailer*; Peter Manso, ed., *Running Against the Machine: The Mailer-Breslin Campaign* (Garden City, N.Y.: Doubleday, 1969).

Page 210   "[T]he condition of the city of New York at this time": Breslin, "I Run to Win."

Page 211   "I'd piss on it": Jimmy Breslin, *I Want to Thank My Brain for Remembering Me* (Boston: Little, Brown, 1996), 121.

Page 211   "After Norman Mailer and I finished": Jimmy Breslin, "And Furthermore, I Promise," *New York,* June 16, 1969.

Page 213   "A wistful Republican malaise": Julie Baumgold, "Going Private: Life in the Clean Machine," *New York,* January 6, 1969.

Page 214   "We'll show you how": *New York* ad, 1969. From George Hirsch, personal archive.

Page 214   "Writing is like performing": *Uncommon Clay: Notes on a Brilliant Career,* program for the opening of the Felker Magazine Center at the University of California at Berkeley, 1994.

Page 215   "Women . . . tend to have a more personal point of view": "Making It," *Newsweek,* July 27, 1970. Unsigned.

Page 215   Upper-level trains carry: Gail Sheehy, "The Tunnel Inspector and the Belle of the Bar Car," *New York,* April 29, 1968.

Page 217   With his tall, blond Establishment looks: Adam Smith, "Notes on the Great Buying Panic," *New York,* May 6, 1968.

Page 218   The magazine's circulation was 145,000: Confidential memo from George Hirsch to *New York* staff. From George Hirsch, personal archive.

Page 220   "The party was held": Tom Wolfe, prefatory note to "Radical Chic," *New York,* June 8, 1970.

Page 221   "There they were": Charlotte Curtis, "Black Panther Party Is Debated at the Bernsteins'," *New York Times,* January 15, 1970.

Page 221   a *Times* editorial: *New York Times,* January 16, 1970.

Page 222   "He could see himself, Leonard Bernstein" and all subsequent quotes: Tom Wolfe, "Radical Chic: That Party at Lenny's," *New York,* June 8, 1970.

Page 224   "As an American and as a Jew": Meryle Secrest, *Leonard Bernstein: A Life* (London: Bloomsbury, 1995), 323.

11. SAVAGE JOURNEYS

Page 225   "I suppose it's only fair": Hunter S. Thompson, *The Great Shark Hunt: Strange Tales from a Strange Time* (New York: Rolling Stone Press/Summit Books, 1979), 191–92.

Page 226   "You don't understand!": Thompson, *The Great Shark Hunt,* 79.

Page 226   "He is a handsome middle-class French boy": "The Temptation of Jean-Claude Killy," Ibid., 95.

Page 228   "Here is the Killy piece": Letter from Thompson to Hinckle, in Hunter S. Thompson, *Fear and Loathing in America: The Brutal Odyssey of an Outlaw Journalist: The Gonzo Letters, Volume II, 1968–1976* (New York: Simon & Schuster, 2000), 222.

Page 229   "a conspiracy of anemic masturbators": Ibid., 223.

Page 233   "socio-philosophical flashbacks": Ibid., 296.

Page 233   "In a narrow Southern society": "The Kentucky Derby Is Decadent and Depraved," Thompson, *The Great Shark Hunt,* 31.

Page 233   "Not much energy in these faces": Ibid., 34.

Page 233   "I'm ready for *anything,* by God!": Ibid., 25.

Page 234   "What riot?": Ibid., 25.

Page 234   "It's a shitty article": Letter from Thompson to Bill Cardoso, in
            Thompson, *Fear and Loathing in America*, 295.

Page 235   "Dear Hunter": Tom Wolfe to Thompson, in Thompson, *Fear and
            Loathing in America*, 335.

Page 235   "with the perhaps fading exception": Thompson to Wolfe, in Thompson,
            Fear and Loathing in America, 338.

Page 236   "writing copy for [Ford Motor Company] pamphlets": Thompson to Jim
            Silberman, in Thompson, *Fear and Loathing in America*, 261.

Page 236   "I wish I could explain the delay": Thompson to Jim Silberman, in
            Thompson, *Fear and Loating in America*, 258.

Page 237   "a very contemporary novel": Letter from Hunter Thompson to Jim
            Silberman, January 13, 1970, Ibid., 267.

Page 237   "semi-fictional": Letter from Hunter Thompson to Jim Silberman,
            January 13, 1970, Ibid., 268.

Page 237   Biographical material for Jann Wenner taken from Robert Sam Anson,
            Gone Crazy and Back Again: The Rise and Fall of the Rolling Stone
            Generation (Garden City, N.Y.: Doubleday, 1981).

Page 242   "I think psychedelic drugs": Ilan Stavans, *Bandido: The Death and
            Resurrection of Oscar "Zeta" Acosta* (Evanston, Ill.: Northwestern
            University Press, 2003), 47.

Page 244   "I recognized in Oscar": Yvette C. Doss, "The Lost Legend of the Real
            Dr. Gonzo," *Los Angeles Times*, June 5, 1998.

Page 247   "Your call was the key to a massive freak-out": Thompson to Tom
            Vanderschmidt, in Thompson, *Fear and Loathing in America*, 376.

Page 248   "Kerouac taught me": Douglas Brinkley, "The Art of Journalism I:
            Hunter S. Thompson," *Paris Review*, Fall 2000, 55.

Page 248   One morning: Lucian K. Truscott IV: "Fear and Earning," *New York
            Times*, February 25, 2005.

Page 249   "We were somewhere around Barstow": Hunter S. Thompson, *Fear and
            Loathing in Las Vegas* (New York: Modern Library, 1996), 3.

Page 249   "a classic affirmation": Ibid., 18.

Page 249   "cluster of grey rectangles": Ibid., 22.

Page 249   "burned out and long gone": Ibid., 23.

Page 250   "Their sound system": Ibid., 138.

Page 250   "All those pathetically eager acid freaks": Ibid., 178.

Page 251   "What I was trying to get at": Thompson to Tom Wolfe, April 20, 1971,
            Fear and Loathing in America, 375.

Page 251   "I think the thing to do is for you": Thompson to Wenner, in
            Thompson, *Fear and Loathing in America*, 392.

Page 252   "I've been mistaken for American Indian": Stavans, *Bandido*, 103.

12. FUN WITH DICK AND GEORGE

Page 254   "In twenty-eight papers": Hunter S. Thompson, *Fear and Loathing on the
            Campaign Trail '72* (San Francisco: Straight Arrow Books, 1973), 92.

Page 255   "It was as if the changing": Theodore H. White, *The Making of the President
            1960* (New York: Atheneum, 1961), 65.

Page 256   "I went in with the same attitude": Craig Vetter, "The *Playboy* Interview:
            Hunter S. Thompson," *Playboy*, November 1974.

Page 257   "Say ... ah ... I hate to mention this": Ibid., 73.

Page 258   "When Big Ed [Muskie] arrived": Ibid., 122–23.

Page 259   "Not much has been written about": Ibid., 151.

Page 260   "Even some of the reporters": Vetter, "The *Playboy* Interview."

Page 261   "kissing [White House press secretary] Ron Zeigler's ass": Thompson, *Fear and Loathing on the Campaign Trail '72*, 403–4.

Page 262   "I am growing extremely weary": Ibid., 219.

Page 263   "a shallow, contemptible": Ibid., 209.

Page 263   "that same void of charisma": Norman Mailer, *St. George and the Godfather* (New York: Arbor House, 1983), 23.

Page 263   "complacent innocence": Ibid., 33.

Page 263   "Phi Beta Kappas": Ibid., 66.

Page 264   "a bland drone": Ibid., 177.

Page 264   "shameless dingbats": Thompson, *Fear and Loathing on the Campaign Trail '72*, 319.

Page 264   "smiling freak ... was giving": Ibid., 319.

Page 264   "Recognize that a man": Mailer, *St. George and the Godfather*, 75.

Page 265   "had connotations of ": Ibid., 76.

Page 266   "With the exception of the Vietnam"; "They were hopelessly disorganized": Thompson, *Fear and Loathing on the Campaign Trail '72*, 382.

Page 266   "I looked up and shuddered": Ibid., 355.

Page 267   "This may be the year": Ibid., 413–14.

Page 268   "massive campaign": Timothy Crouse, *The Boys on the Bus* (New York: Ballantine, 1973), 306.

Page 268   "'Ominous' is not quite the right word": Thompson, *Fear and Loathing on the Campaign Trail '72*, 417–18.

Page 268   "Richard Nixon is one ...": Mailer, "A Conversation Between Norman Mailer and John Ehrlichmann," *Chic*, December 1976.

13. VULGARIAN AT THE GATE

Page 270   Background of the takeover of *New York* by Rupert Murdoch: Sheehy, "A Fistful of Dollars"; David Gelman (with Betsy Carter, Ann Ray Martin, Nancy Stadtman, Tony Clifton, Nicholas Proffitt, and Ronald Kaye), "Press Lord Captures Gotham," *Newsweek*, January 17, 1977; interviews with Clay Felker, Milton Glaser, Shelly Zalaznick, Pete Hamill, Ken Auletta, Jack Nessel, and Byron Dobell.

Page 270   "Whatever the Third Great Awakening": Tom Wolfe, "The Me Decade and the Third Great Awakening," *Mauve Gloves and Madmen, Clutter and Vine* (New York: Bantam, 1977), 144.

Page 271   over seventy imitators: Gail Sheehy, "A Fistful of Dollars," *Rolling Stone*, July 14, 1977.

Page 271   Felker came to her aid: Carolyn G. Heilbrun, *The Education of a Woman: The Life of Gloria Steinem* (New York: Dial Press, 1995), 217–19.

Page 273   Occasionally she would be accompanied: "The Hooker's Boswell," *Newsweek*, December 4, 1972.

Page 274   "voluptuous figure of a man": Gail Sheehy, "Wide Open City, Part II: Redpants and Sugarman," *New York*, July 26, 1971.

Page 274   "That's $7.75, pal": Ibid.

Page 275 "gives you such a rich": Gail Sheehy, *Hustling: Prostitution in Our Wide-Open Society* (New York: Dell, 1973), 31.
Page 275 "the original Redpants made an appointment": "The Hooker's Boswell."
Page 276 "New Journalism is rising": Ibid.
Page 276 "Amy reached out and took hold": Aaron Latham, "An Evening in the Nude with Gay Talese," *New York*, July 9, 1973.
Page 277 But one passage: Aaron Latham, "Waking Up with Sally Quinn," *New York*, July 1, 1973.
Page 277 "I've never read anything like this": Mary Breasted, "Two Interviews and Their Aftermath," *New York Times*, July 23, 1973.
Page 278 Biographical background of Rupert Murdoch: Gelman et al., "Press Lord Captures Gotham"; Jerome Tuccille, *Rupert Murdoch* (New York: Donald J. Fine, 1989).
Page 279 "I was brought up in a publishing home": Tuccille, *Rupert Murdoch*, 11.
Page 280 "They're passionate about some things": "The Odd Couple," *Time*, June 17, 1974.
Page 280 six hundred thousand shares: Ibid.
Page 281 "The Favorite Recipes": Ibid.
Page 281 First-quarter earnings for 1975: "The Voice of Felker," *Newsweek*, June 23, 1975.
Page 282 "pinpricks on all her Ungaro's": Julie Baumgold, "Carterandamanda: Learning the *New York* Lesson," *New York*, January 19, 1970.
Page 283 tooling around L.A. in leased Alfa Romeos: Gelman et al., "Press Lord Captures Gotham."
Page 283 an attendance bill: Sheehy, "A Fistful of Dollars."
Page 284 "What you ought to do": Ibid.
Page 287 "Despite recent developments": Ibid.
Page 287 "Clay has been very good to me": Ibid.
Page 288 "Bob," Felker barked: Ibid.
Page 288 "He [Murdoch] knows what you are": Ibid.
Page 289 "Clay, I think you're an editorial genius": Ibid.
Page 290 "I haven't been thinking about": Ibid.

EPILOGUE: AFTER THE BALL
Page 291 losing roughly $5 million: N. R. Kleinfield, "Owners Still Gamble on *Esquire*," *New York Times*, April 9, 1981.

Bibliography

Acosta, Oscar Zeta. *The Autobiography of a Brown Buffalo* (New York: Vintage, 1989).

Anson, Robert Sam. *Gone Crazy and Back Again: The Rise and Fall of the* Rolling Stone *Generation* (Garden City, N.Y.: Doubleday, 1981).

Barger, Ralph "Sonny." *Hell's Angel: The Life and Times of Sonny Barger and the Hell's Angels Motorcycle Club* (New York: William Morrow, 2000).

Baron, Herman. *Author Index to* Esquire, *1933–1973* (Metuchen, N.J.: Scarecrow Press, 1976).

Bates, Milton J., Lawrence Lichty, Paul L. Miles, Ronald H. Spector, and Marilyn Young, advisors. *Reporting Vietnam, Part One: American Journalism 1959–1969* and *Part Two: American Journalism 1969–1975* (New York: Library of America, 1998).

Bellows, Jim. *The Last Editor* (Kansas City, Mo.: Andrews McMeel, 2002).

Bernstein, Walter, et. al., contributors. The New Yorker *Book of War Pieces* (New York: Schocken Books, 1988), p. 147.

Boyce, George, James Curran, and Pauline Wingate. *Newspaper History from the Seventeenth Century to the Present Day* (London: Constable, 1978).

Boynton, Robert S. *The New New Journalism: Conversations with America's Best Nonfiction Writers on Their Craft* (New York: Vintage, 2005).

Breslin, Jimmy. *The World of Jimmy Breslin* (New York: Viking, 1967).

———. *The World According to Breslin* (New York: Ticknor and Fields, 1984).

———. *I Want to Thank My Brain for Remembering Me* (Boston: Little, Brown, 1996).

Capote, Truman. *In Cold Blood* (New York: Random House, 1965).

Carroll, E. Jean. *Hunter: The Strange and Savage Life of Hunter S. Thompson* (New York: Dutton, 1993).

Chwast, Seymour. *Push Pin Graphic: A Quarter Century of Innovative Design and Illustration* (San Francisco: Chronicle Books, 2004).

Clarke, Gerald. *Capote: A Biography* (New York: Simon & Schuster, 1988).

Crick, Bernard. *George Orwell: A Life* (London: Penguin Books, 1980).

Crouse, Timothy. *The Boys on the Bus* (New York: Ballantine Books, 1973).

Dearborn, Mary V. *Mailer* (Boston: Houghton Mifflin, 1999).

Dickens, Charles. *Sketches by Boz,* excerpted from *The Oxford Illustrated Dickens* (Oxford: Oxford University Press, 1957).

Didion, Joan. *Slouching Towards Bethlehem* (New York: Farrar, Straus and Giroux, 1990).

———. *Where I Was From* (New York: Random House, 2003).

Dundy, Elaine. *Life Itself* (London: Virago, 2001).

Gingrich, Arnold. *Nothing but People: The Early Days at* Esquire, *a Personal History, 1928–1958* (New York: Crown, 1971).

Hamilton, Ian. *Robert Lowell: A Biography* (New York: Random House, 1982).

Heilbrun, Carolyn G. *The Education of a Woman: The Life of Gloria Steinem* (New York: Dial Press, 1995).

Herr, Michael. *Dispatches* (New York: Vintage, 1991).

Jackson, Kenneth T., ed. *The Encyclopedia of New York City* (New Haven, Conn.: Yale University Press, 1995), p. 964.

Kerouac, Jack. *On the Road* (New York: Penguin, 1991).

Kerrane, Kevin, and Ben Yagoda, eds. *The Art of Fact: A Historical Anthology of Literary Journalism* (New York: Touchstone, 1997).

Kluger, Richard. *The Paper: The Life and Death of the* New York Herald Tribune (New York: Alfred A. Knopf, 1986).

London, Jack. *The People of the Abyss* (e-book #1688, transcribed from the Thomas Nelson and Sons edition, 2005), p. 1.

Mailer, Norman. *Pontifications* (Boston: Little, Brown, 1982).

——. *St. George and the Godfather* (New York: Arbor House, 1983).

——. *The Armies of the Night: History as a Novel, the Novel as History* (New York: Plume, 1995).

——. *The Time of Our Time* (New York: Modern Library, 1999).

——. *The Spooky Art: Some Thoughts on Writing* (New York: Random House, 2003).

Manso, Peter. *Mailer: His Life and Times* (New York: Simon & Schuster, 1985).

——, ed. *Running Against the Machine, A Grass Roots Race for the New York Mayoralty* (Garden City, N.Y.: Doubleday, 1969).

Mellow, James R. *Hemingway: A Life Without Consequences* (Boston: Houghton Mifflin, 1992).

Mills, Hilary. *Mailer: A Biography* (New York: Empire Books, 1982).

Morgan, Thomas B. *Self-Creations: 13 Impersonalities* (New York: Holt, Rinehart and Winston, 1965).

Morris, James McGrath. *The Rose Man of Sing Sing: A True Tale of Life, Murder, and Redemption in the Age of Yellow Journalism* (New York: Fordham University Press, 2003).

Morris, Willie. *New York Days* (Boston: Little, Brown, 1993).

Mott, Franklin Luther. *American Journalism: A History, 1690–1960* (New York: Macmillan, 1962).

Orwell, George. *Down and Out in Paris and London* (London: Secker & Warburg, 1986).

Perry, Paul. *Fear and Loathing: The Strange and Terrible Saga of Hunter S. Thompson* (New York: Thunder's Mouth Press, 1992).

Plimpton, George, ed. *Writers at Work: The Paris Review Interviews, Third Series* (New York: Penguin Books, 1979).

Polsgrove, Carol. *It Wasn't Pretty, Folks, But Didn't We Have Fun?* Esquire *in the Sixties* (New York: W.W. Norton, 1995).

Prochnau, William. *Once Upon a Distant War: David Halberstam, Neil Sheehan, Peter Arnett—Young War Correspondents and Their Early Vietnam Battles* (New York: Vintage, 1996).

Ross, Lillian. *Here But Not Here: A Love Story* (Washington, D.C.: Counterpoint, 1998).

——. *Picture: 50th Anniversary Edition* (New York: Da Capo Press, 2002).

——. *Reporting Back: Notes on Journalism* (Washington, D.C.: Counterpoint, 2002).

Sack, John. *M* (London: Corgi/Avon, 1986)

Schroeder, Eric James. *Vietnam, We've All Been There: Interviews with American Writers* (Westport, Conn.: Praeger, 1992).

Secrest, Meryle. *Leonard Bernstein: A Life* (London: Bloomsbury, 1995).

Sheehy, Gail. *Hustling: Prostitution in Our Wide-Open Society* (New York: Dell, 1973).

Stavans, Ilan. *Bandido: The Death and Resurrection of Oscar "Zeta" Acosta* (Evanston, Ill.: Northwestern University Press, 2003)

Steinberg, Sybil, ed. *Writing for Your Life: 92 Contemporary Authors Talk About the Art of Writing and the Job of Publishing* (Wainscott, N.Y.: Pushcart Press, 1992).

Swift, Jonathan. *A Modest Proposal* (London, 1729).

Talese, Gay. *Unto the Sons* (New York: Alfred A. Knopf, 1992).

——, and Barbara Lounsberry. *Writing Creative Nonfiction: The Literature of Reality* (New York: HarperCollins, 1996).

Thompson, Hunter S. *Fear and Loathing: On the Campaign Trail '72* (San Francisco: Straight Arrow Books, 1973).

——. *The Great Shark Hunt: Strange Tales from a Strange Time* (New York: Rolling Stone Press/Summit Books 1979).

——. *Fear and Loathing in Las Vegas: A Savage Journey to the Heart of the American Dream* (New York: Warner Books, 1982).

——. *The Proud Highway: Saga of a Desperate Southern Gentleman, 1955–1967 (The Fear and Loathing Letters, Volume 1)* (New York: Villard, 1997).

——. *Hell's Angels: A Strange and Terrible Saga* (New York: Modern Library, 1999).

——. *Fear and Loathing in America: The Brutal Odyssey of an Outlaw Journalist (The Gonzo Letters, Volume II, 1968–1976)* (New York: Simon & Schuster, 2000).

——. *Kingdom of Fear: Loathsome Secrets of a Star-Crossed Child in the Final Days of the American Century* (New York: Simon & Schuster, 2003).

Tregaskis, Richard. *Guadalcanal Diary* (New York: Popular Library, 1962).

Tuccille, Jerome. *Rupert Murdoch* (New York: Donald J. Fine, 1989).

White, Theodore H. *The Making of the President, 1960* (New York: Atheneum, 1961).

Wills, Garry. *Lead Time: A Journalist's Education* (Garden City, N.Y.: Doubleday, 1983).

Wolfe, Tom. *The Kandy-Kolored Tangerine-Flake Streamline Baby* (New York: Farrar, Straus and Giroux, 1965).

——. *The Pump House Gang* (New York: Farrar, Straus and Giroux, 1965).

——. *The Electric Kool-Aid Acid Test* (New York: Farrar, Straus and Giroux, 1968).

——. *Mauve Gloves & Madmen, Clutter & Vine* (New York: Bantam Books, 1977).

——. *Hooking Up* (New York: Farrar, Straus and Giroux, 2000).

Wolfe, Tom, and E. W. Johnson, eds. *The New Journalism* (New York: Harper & Row, 1973).

Yagoda, Ben. *About Town:* The New Yorker *and the World It Made* (New York: Scribner, 2000).

Zamiatin, Eugene. *We* (New York, Dutton, 1952).

Zaroulis, Nancy, and Gerald Sullivan. *Who Spoke Up? American Protest Against the War in Vietnam, 1963–1975* (Garden City, N.Y.: Doubleday, 1984).

TV AND RADIO DOCUMENTARIES

Copans, Richard, and Stan Neumann. *Mailer on Mailer,* an American Masters documentary (New York: Thirteen/WNET, Reciprocal Films, Films d'Ici, and France 2, 2000).

Kalish, John, producer. *Jimmy Breslin: The Art of Climbing Tenement Stairs* (Santa Monica: KCRW, 2004).

Pollak, Amanda and Steven Ives, producers. Ives, Steven, director. Ferrari, Michelle, writer. *Reporting America at War* (Washington, D.C.: Insignia Films and WETA, 2003).

ARCHIVES

Harold Hayes Collection, Rare Book and Manuscripts Department, Z. Smith Reynolds Library, Wake Forest University, Winston-Salem, North Carolina.

Esquire and Arnold Gingrich Collections, Michigan Historical Collections, Bentley Historical Library, University of Michigan, Ann Arbor.

INTERVIEWS

Marco Acosta
Ken Auletta
Ken Babbs
Ralph "Sonny" Barger
Julie Baumgold
Jim Bellows
John Berendt
Burl Bernard
Patricia Bosworth
Stewart Brand
Jimmy Breslin
David Broder
Brock Brower
Bill Brown
Art Buchwald
David Burgin
John Burks
Midge Decter
Ed de Grazia
David Dellinger
Byron Dobell
Elaine Dundy
Clay Felker
David Felton
Tom Ferrell
Timothy Ferris

Marshall Fishwick
"Mouldy" Marvin Gilbert
Ralph Ginzburg
Milton Glaser
George Goodman
Pete Hamill
Christopher Lehmann-
    Haupt
George Hirsch
Clifford Hope
David Horowitz
William Kennedy
Robert Kotlowitz
Michael Kramer
Paul Krassner
Zane Kesey
George Lois
Frank Mankiewicz
Martin Mayer
Charles McAtee
Ed McClanahan
Larry McMurtry
Thomas B. Morgan
Lynn Nesbit
Jack Nessel
Charles Perry

George Plimpton
Bert Prelutsky
Alan Rich
Hugh Romney
Lillian Ross (via email)
Ron Rosenbuam
Mort Sahl
Lawrence Schiller
Robert Semple
Robert Sherrill
Jim Silberman
Ralph Steadman
Gloria Steinem
Gay Talese
Hunter S. Thompson
Nicholas von Hoffman
Dan Wakefield
Richard Wald
George Walker
Bernard Weinraub
Jann Wenner
Les Whitten
Jules Witcover
Tom Wolfe
Sheldon Zalaznick

Acknowledgments

Thanks to the following people for tracking down recalcitrant, elusive, or otherwise indifferent interview subjects: Doug Brinkley, Fritz Clapp, Jim Bellows, and Anita Thompson. Thanks to Carol Polsgrove for the John Sack interview. Sharon Snow at the Harold Hayes archive was a model of decency and patience. Thanks to George Hirsch for all of the wonderful *New York* magazine effluvia he sent my way. Roger Director is a stand-up guy for passing along that amazing commemorative program from the Felker Magazine Center, a piece of gold that fell into my lap.

My crack researcher Kathrin Shorr endured a lot of grunt work with no gripes, and I want to thank her for all of the sweat equity. In New York, Andy Gensler tracked down some key documents that I couldn't obtain otherwise, short of spending a lot of money on airfare.

My agent, David McCormick, sold this sucker just like he said he would, and for that I'm eternally grateful. My first editor, Doug Pepper, bought the book, and my second editor, Chris Jackson, nurtured it along with empathy and keen insight.

Thanks as always to my friend Tom Hackett for his counsel, his razor-sharp editorial instincts, and his unwavering friendship. Thanks to the family-in-law for the kudos and the scotch-a-roos: Lori, Timmy, Jean, Louis, Lisa, David, Marshall, Rae, Uriah, and Madison.

Ilene, thanks for the phone calls and the encouraging words. Mom and Dad, I couldn't have done it without your support. Sam and Ally, you're the light in my life. Love you all.

My wife, Lynn, is as rock solid a support system as any husband could ever wish to have. You're the greatest.

Finally, thanks to Tom Wolfe, whose work inspired me to write this book in the first place.

Index